£30

THE NEWSPAPER PRESS
in the
FRENCH REVOLUTION

HUGH GOUGH

ROUTLEDGE

First published in 1988 by
Routledge
11 New Fetter Lane, London EC4P 4EE

© 1988 Hugh Gough

Printed and bound in Great Britain by Mackays of Chatham Ltd, Kent

British Library Cataloguing in Publication Data

Gough, H.
    The newspaper press in the French Revolution.
    1. French newspapers — History — 18th century
    I. Title
    074   PN5176

ISBN 0-415-00369-5

Contents

Abbreviations

The following abbreviations are used in the chapter end-notes:

A.D.   *Archives Départementales*

A.M.   *Archives Municipales*

A.N.   *Archives Nationales* (Paris)

B.H.V.P. *Bibliothèque Historique de la Ville de Paris*

B.M.   *Bibliothèque Municipale* (various locations)

B.N.   *Bibliothèque Nationale*

Preface

The idea for this book emerged from a study that I carried out several years ago of the history of the Jacobin club newspaper, the *Journal de la montagne*, and the career of its editor, Jean-Charles Laveaux. It seemed apparent then that there were two major gaps in the press history of the revolution, the first of which was the lack of any adequate study in English. That particular lacuna has been partially filled since then by the appearance of several publications analysing different aspects of the Parisian press, most notably of the radical press during the period 1789–91, and of the right-wing press both before and after the fall of the monarchy in August 1792. I remain indebted to these studies, and have used many of their findings in this work, but their appearance has left untouched the lack of a general press history to provide a context into which to fit the detail.

Such general press histories exist in French, but here the second major gap emerges, that of an adequate integration of the provincial press. The great majority of French press histories concentrate on journalism in the capital, at the expense of its provincial counterpart. For the latter, the reader has to use instead a number of provincial monographs, usually in regional historical journals, which are usually of very high quality, but only cover small areas and are necessarily divorced from their national context. Yet the national context is important, for although Parisian newspapers were certainly more numerous than provincial ones, and were both influential and close to the source of major events, the local press played an important role in providing the provincial population with at least some of the news from which opinion was formed, and in acting as the organ for local pressure groups. Analysis of the provincial press is nevertheless made difficult by the lack of any central government statistics for it between 1789 and the Consulate, which was the inevitable result of the collapse of censorship. Historians need records, and the sad paradox is that authoritarian regimes are most efficient at compiling them.

Research is not made easier by the state of surviving holdings, for they are scattered between Parisian and provincial libraries, and between the Archives Nationales, departmental and municipal archives. There is no central catalogue, the série 'T' in the Archives Nationales which embraces the press only operates from 1800, and the collections that do exist are fragmentary. Complete runs are usually available for the major Parisian newspapers, but they are rare for the lesser ones. This is even more so in the case of the provincial press, where in many cases there are no copies left at all of titles which other evidence indicates most certainly existed, and which have gone the way of all ephemera by the way of flame or food. I am currently working with Gilles Feyel, of the Institut Français de Presse, on the compilation of a national catalogue, listing the surviving holdings on a departmental basis, which should make them more accessible in future. In the meanwhile the research for this book has provided much of the information for such a catalogue, and unearthed several titles whose existence was either unknown or long forgotten.

No book can provide the last word on any subject, least of all a subject as voluminous as the one under study. The reading of all the newspapers produced in the revolution, even if they had survived, would take a lifetime, and that in itself would only provide a fraction of the research material needed. It is therefore important that I make clear the precise aims of the present work. Its main concentration lies in the growth of the press in the decade of the revolution, and the relationship of that growth with political events. Within that brief I have tried above all to give the provincial press equal weight with its Parisian counterpart, and to examine both the political influences on its development and the political form that it took. Thus, the introduction gives a broad picture of its development down to 1789, the first chapter covers the impact of the collapse of censorship in 1789, and the following four chapters its development down to Napoleon's seizure of power in late 1799. The final two chapters then examine the business end of the spectrum: how newspapers were financed and produced, how they were marketed and sold, who bought and read them, and why their growth was so rapid.

My concern throughout has been with the material and political circumstances of the press, rather than with its ideological content. The latter is an important subject in itself, but embraces the entire political spectrum of the revolution, and would have required a much longer book than this. It is not an easy task, particularly in the case of the provincial press where political arguments must often be read within their particular local context, and one which cannot easily be compressed into succinct analyses or convenient formulae because most newspapers during the revolution were intensely personal, one-man affairs, with strongly individual characters. For similar reasons I have shied away from lengthy quotations, and from providing pen portraits of individual papers, for neither could do justice, within the limits of this book, to the complexity of their subject. The limitation in subject matter is therefore a deliberate decision, taken in order to provide an overall view of the press as a whole. This overall view is nevertheless the first in the English language, and the first in any language to give the provincial press the weight that it deserves.

The research for and writing of this work has taken several years, and left me in debt to many people. My interest in French history, like that of many Oxford students, was first awakened by Richard Cobb, who infected me with a love of France, its history and culture, that has remained with me ever since. The late Albert Soboul was generous with advice and hospitality on several occasions, as were Pierre Albert, Gilles Feyel and Professor Michel Vovelle. I am also grateful to the Master and fellows of Corpus Christi College, Cambridge, for awarding me a Senior Research Scholarship in the summer of 1985, which allowed me to write the first draft in the idyllic pastoral surroundings of Leckhampton. My visits to France have always been made into a pleasure by the kind co-operation of the staff of the Bibliothèque Nationale in Paris, and by the staff of provincial archives and libraries throughout France, always generous in the time and help that they gave to a migratory — and frequently unannounced — researcher. My wife, Mary, and children, Paul and Brian, have put up with the same migratory habits with great kindness and good humour, and to them I am especially grateful. My oldest debt of all is in the dedication. However, all the views that I have expressed, and omissions or errors that I may have made, are my responsibility alone.

Hugh Gough

For my Mother and my late Father

with thanks for everything

Introduction:
Towards the Revolution

The history of the newspaper press can be traced back to the civilisa-
tions of ancient China, Egypt and Rome; but in its modern and
familiar form it dates essentially from the early years of the seventeenth century, when Gutenberg's invention of the printing press
was already almost two centuries old. Since the mid-fifteenth century the printing press had been used for a variety of purposes. First
deployed on the reproduction of classical and sacred texts, it had
adapted itself to a propaganda role during the Reformation and
Counter-reformation, and widened its scope to include scientific,
literary and travel interests as the sixteenth century progressed.
Much of it was in the form of books, but there were pamphlets and
broadsheets too, including, from the early years of the sixteenth
century, *occasionnels*, or small format brochures, containing news
of recent political events, battles and major crises. Others were
canards, published in the same format but catering more for the kind
of sensationalist interest represented by the modern tabloid press,
with accounts of miracles, monsters and floods, as well as of other
exceptional 'events' such as comets, catastrophes and plague.[1] Yet
none of these were regular and sequential publications in the style
of a modern newspaper; they merely came out in response to specific
events, whether political or religious, astronomical or
meteorological.

Almanacs and calendars, on the other hand, dating in printed
form from the late fifteenth century, were the earliest form of
periodical publication, but their rhythm was usually annual and
their content, like that of the *occasionnels*, non-political, concerned
with prophesies and predictions, mapping out the calendar of
festivals, religious days and seasons. In France, from 1611 onwards,
an annual publication, the *Mercure français*, provided a résumé of

1

the year's major political events, and reproduced the contents of major brochures. Richelieu acknowledged its importance by confiding its editing to Father Joseph between 1624 and 1638.[2]

The transition from occasional pamphlets to a fully fledged newspaper press required a number of varied factors to come together. One was the political interest caused, on a European level, by the religious wars of the latter half of the sixteenth century and, from 1618 onwards, by the Thirty Years War. Another was the increasing importance of urban life, and the growth of major administrative, trading and financial centres in which news of commerce, diplomacy and military events was needed by a sizeable, compact and increasingly literate population. Improved road and communications systems also played a part, as did the development of postal services, dating back to the late fifteenth century in France, to 1516 in the Holy Roman Empire and 1625 in England, which accelerated the interchange of news, providing the basis of a convenient delivery service that newspapers could later use. The encouragement to education, and to literacy rates, provided by the Protestant Reformation and the Tridentine decrees of the Catholic Reformation helped too, resulting initially in the emergence of a network of correspondents and intelligence agents who exchanged manuscript news sheets and items of information, then printed newspapers, beginning with Antwerp (1605), Cologne (1610), Frankfurt am Main (1615) and Berlin (1617).[3]

Worthwhile news material, improved communications, and a growing market were the essential preconditions for the existence and survival of newspapers and, from their early beginnings in the Empire, they rapidly spread to the United Provinces, Spain and Denmark, reaching France in 1631. In May of that year a protégé of Richelieu, Théophraste Renaudot, was given permission to publish and distribute 'news, newspapers and accounts of everything that has happened, and is happening, both inside and outside the kingdom'. The result was the *Gazette*, a small four-page weekly newspaper which began publication at the end of the month, with political news from around the courts of Europe.[4] To modern eyes a rather drab pamphlet, with brief summaries of diplomatic dispatches and international news, it was nevertheless destined to last for almost two centuries. From the outset, moreover, it was closely associated with a *Bureau d'adresses* which Renaudot had founded two years earlier, and which was a charitable institution established to tackle the roots of urban poverty by providing an information exchange for those seeking work or workers and for traders with goods to sell.

Renaudot's monopoly of the publication of political news was challenged on several occasions before his death, most notably during the mid-century Fronde, when a flood of pamphlets and newspapers appeared. Yet none proved lasting and, with the re-establishment of royal authority, the *Gazette* consolidated its position as the century progressed. It was continued first by Théophraste's sons, Isaac and Eusèbe, then on their death by his grandson, the abbé Eusèbe Renaudot, who edited it into the early years of the eighteenth century. Secure in their monopoly of political news, they allowed provincial booksellers, from the 1660s onwards, to reprint local editions, first in Toulouse, then in Grenoble and elsewhere, a practice which continued until the 1760s.[5] In addition, during the early years of Louis XIV's reign it was joined by two other major titles, which catered for different readership interests and also enjoyed monopoly status over the subject matter that they covered: the *Journal des savants*, a weekly paper created in 1665 by Denis de Sallo to cover news from the rapidly expanding world of science, mathematics, history, the fine arts and theology; and a monthly, *Mercure galant*, launched in 1672 by a dramatist, Donneau de Vizé, and covering court news, literary reviews, anecdotes and society gossip.[6]

These three titles formed the cornerstones of the French press until the revolution of 1789, and their origins are closely linked to the consolidation of royal authority over printing and publication in all its forms. This dates back to the reign of Henry II, with the Edict of Fontainebleau in 1547, and proliferated during the Wars of Religion in the latter half of the century. However, Louis XIV, in his concern to regulate dissent and orchestrate royal authority, extended its scope, refining the mechanics of censorship and progressively exerting control over the printing and publishing trades.[7] Controls on the newspaper press were similar to those applying to all other publications and worked in two ways. In the first place, the privilege granted to any newspaper was revocable at will, subject to the payment of a sizeable annual fee, and specified the news areas that the newspaper could cover. As the big three newspapers — the *Gazette*, *Mercure* and *Journal des savants* — owned privileges which covered the major sectors of news, this meant that all the others allowed on to the market had to pay an additional annual fee to the title whose news area they intended to share. Secondly, as with books and pamphlets, all text had to be approved prior to publication by government-appointed censors, who could demand excisions, exclusions or alterations. Books and pamphlets frequently avoided this problem by publishing abroad, or adopting a fictitious foreign imprint, and then circulating through the underground distribution system, a practice which became commonplace during the eighteenth century. Yet newspapers were unable to practise the same evasion because they sold by subscription and depended on the facility of postal circulation, with the result that censorship control was much more effective. Apart from the anomalous cases of Britain and Ireland, such control was common throughout much of continental Europe during the eighteenth century, but nowhere else was it so successfully and consistently applied.[8]

Strict though they were, government controls did not entirely stultify the development of the press in the century before 1789, for the eighteenth century in particular saw a number of developments which enhanced its appeal. Literacy rates, for example, though badly affected by the troubles of the mid-seventeenth century, rose steadily from the end of the century onwards: in the 1680s some 21 per cent of the adult population could sign their names at marriage, yet a century later the proportion had risen to 37 per cent.[9] Moreover, the latter figure applied to a population that had grown by some six million during the hundred years, with the result that the number of literate people had probably increased by more than 100 per cent. Economic growth from the 1720s onwards also helped, creating prosperity for the landed and merchant classes and, in its wake, an increased demand for diplomatic and commercial news. Furthermore, the Enlightenment, although it flowed primarily through the channels of book, salon and pamphlet, and although several of its leading figures had a poor opinion of the value of newspapers, increased public interest in intellectual issues. Annual book production alone more than trebled in the 50 years between the 1720s and the 1770s. Political factors also played their part. France's poor performance in the War of the Austrian Succession and the Seven Years War focused attention on governmental problems, as did the unpopular Austrian alliance after 1756, the issues of Jansenism and taxation, and the crisis caused by Louis XV's conflict with the Parlements in the dying years of his reign. French intervention in the American War of Independence, along with disturbances nearer home in Geneva, the United Provinces and Belgium were additional factors, and in the late 1770s the Duc de Choiseul noted the impact that this had had on the growth of the political press: 'These days political newspapers outsell others by a ratio of ten to one.'

The result was that during the century successive ministries assented to the appearance of new titles, all of which had to submit to censorship in the normal way and make an annual pay-ment to the privilege holder. The literary press was strongest, with titles such as the Jesuit-inspired *Mémoires de Trévoux* from 1701 onwards, the *Journal de Verdun* from 1704, the *Spectateur français* — modelled on the English *Spectator* — in 1721, or the celebrated anti-*philosophe Année littéraire* in 1754, edited by Elie Fréron and carried on after his death by his widow.[11] In addition on 1 January 1777, Paris saw its first daily newspaper — some 80 years after England — the *Journal de Paris*. Launched by Pierre-Antoine de La Place, its privilege allowed it to cover a wide range of non-political news, ranging from literary reviews to fashion, from weather to the more noted criminal trials. It had its problems with the censor, and was suspended for several weeks in the summer of 1785 after publishing a poem that satirised the princess Christina of Saxony. Yet it was a rapid commercial success, and from December 1778 it was joined by an advertising newspaper, the *Journal général de France*, which concentrated on commercial news and information.[12]

As a result of this, by the early 1780s, some 27 journals were being published in Paris, with 14 foreign papers also being allowed to circulate freely. By 1789, the respective figures were 37 and 29. The existence of the foreign press was important, and merits explanation. Foreign newspapers, and in particular the Dutch press, had always been able to avoid border controls, either through smuggling, or through being printed clandestinely in Paris under a fictitious foreign imprint. Ideally the government would have preferred to stamp out the penetration, but in practice this proved impossible, and it opted instead to allow certain of them to circulate legally, while putting pressure on their owners to moderate their contents. As a result Parisians and provincials could subscribe to titles such as the *Gazette de Leyde*, the *Courrier du Bas-Rhin* or the *Gazette d'Amsterdam*, which had a European circulation and reputation, as well as the *Courrier d'Avignon*, published from the Papal enclave of the comtat Venaissin within France. They were all expensive, however, for foreign-based titles circulated through the normal letter post, while the indigenous product benefited from a special tariff negotiated with the postal authorities. The foreign press consequently cost three to four times its Paris equivalent — a factor which encouraged printers in Avignon, for example, to reprint them locally and organise their own distribution within France, at a fraction of the cost.

In 1750, however, the postal farmers contracted with a Parisian bookseller, David, to distribute them on a national basis at normal concessionary rates, and in 1759 he teamed up with a protégé of the Duc de Choiseul, Palissot, to exploit the market for them more effectively.[13] As a result he was able to increase sales considerably over the following decades, and new titles sprang up to benefit from the arrangement. One was the *Journal encyclopédique* in Liège and Bouillon which, from 1756 onwards, under the editorial control of Pierre Rousseau, propagated *philosophe* ideas with sufficient commercial success to finance its own publishing house. Another was the *Annales politiques* of Simon-Nicolas-Henri Linguet which, edited in London in 1777, then from Brussels in following years, defended the diametrically opposed point of view. In 1785 the future Girondin minister, Pierre Lebrun-Tondu, launched the *Journal général de l'Europe* in Liège, which defended Physiocrat ideas, the reforms of Joseph II and the Brabant revolution. When the latter collapsed in 1790, he took the newspaper to Paris and published it there.[14]

If the foreign press had gained a solid foothold by the 1780s, another area of growth was the commercial press. The *Journal général*, launched in 1778, was essentially a modification of a journal called the *Petites affiches*, a newspaper that had first appeared in 1752 and catered principally for advertisements, the privilege of which belonged to the *Gazette*. There were two versions of the *Petites affiches*, one for Paris and the other for the provinces, and the latter provided the impetus for the development of provincial *Affiches*, which, under a variety of names, extended the growth of journalism to the provinces. Provincial journalism had pushed out its first roots in the latter half of the seventeenth century, when a number of provincial printers had obtained permission to produce local reprints of the *Gazette*; but these had mostly died out by the middle of the century, and it was the *Affiches* that replaced them. The first, in Strasbourg, started in 1731, but the *Affiches de Lyon* launched in 1748 proved to be the start of really rapid growth, and by 1789, some 42 towns throughout the kingdom had a newspaper based on the same model.[15]

Owned by provincial printers, booksellers or local dignitaries, on a privilege granted from the Chancellor's office, subject to paying an annual fee to the *Gazette* for infringing on its monopoly of newspaper advertisements, and censored prior to publication, they were for the most part weekly papers made up of four pages in

6

quarto. At first sight their content appears closely restricted to property sales, investment news, legal announcements, financial affairs, commodity prices and the like; yet the pill was sugared with book reviews, poems and puzzles, short items of political news extracted from the Parisian press, and a range of general interest articles. Many of the latter provided information on regional events and local history, thereby fostering a sense of provincial identity and local patriotism. Others covered recent discoveries and inventions, reflecting an increasing utilitarian interest towards science and material knowledge. Furthermore, running through them all was a preoccupation with social responsibility, secular charity and *bienfaisance* that was so characteristic a feature of the latter half of the century. In this way they popularised Enlightenment ideas and, in the words of one historian, ' . . . were able, in less than ten years, to transform Enlightenment into social practice and, without ever formulating opinions, contributed to the creation of public opinion".[16]

Despite this growth of journalism at both national and provincial level, the government's powers of censorship had come under increasing attack, from the middle of the eighteenth century onwards, from Enlightenment-based demands for freedom of intellectual expression. Book censorship was more relaxed during the 1750s, when Malesherbes became director of the book trade and used his influence to smooth the way for the publication of the Encyclopedie; and the underground pamphlet trade in *libelles* became particularly prominent from the early 1770s, with Louis XV's attack on the power of the Parlements. Many *libelles* aimed at political targets through the use of personal and sexual innuendo and, printed abroad, were sold clandestinely in France by *colporteurs* and booksellers who were willing to take the risk. London was one centre for such publications, Amsterdam, Bouillon and Neuchâtel others and, if the reports of Lenoir, lieutenant de police for Paris in the 1770s are to be believed, some ministers even kept presses on their own premises in order to wage pamphlet warfare against each other.[17]

The growth of the *libelle* trade and of the foreign press had a serious impact on domestic newspapers. By the middle of the century the circulation of the *Gazette*, the government's own official newspaper, had slumped below 2,000, and its readership was dwarfed by the many thousands of subscribers who preferred to read its foreign rivals. Worse still, its very financial survival was threatened by the practice of burdening its revenues with the payment of pensions to courtiers, crown servants and men of letters — an obligation imposed on its privilege holders by the Crown as a painless way of paying for its own patronage. In 1761 its privilege was therefore suppressed by letters patent and reissued under the authority of the Ministry of Foreign Affairs, which now took it over directly in an attempt to revive its flagging fortunes. It was renamed the *Gazette de France*, two new and experienced editors were appointed — the abbé Arnaud and Jean-Baptiste Suard — and ministerial offices charged with drawing up reports for its columns so that its supply of political news would be authoritative and up to date.[18] Circulation stubbornly refused to rise, however, and in 1768, Arnaud and Suard took over the paper on lease instead, paying the Ministry 16,000 *livres* per annum until, in 1771 it was taken from them again and restored to ministerial control.

This did not solve the paper's problems, however, and before the end of the decade the government edged towards a different solution. This centred on an up-and-coming publisher, Charles-Joseph Panckoucke, who had begun his career in Lille during the 1760s, but moved to Paris later in the decade, and had rapidly risen to prominence in the publishing world through an adroit mixture of political deference and commercial acumen.[19] While in Lille he had already launched an *Annonces et avis divers pour les Pays-Bas français* in January 1761, which had lasted for less than two years. In 1772, however, he returned to journalism when he was granted the privilege for a *Journal historique et politique*, later known as the *Journal de Genève*, in the hope that it would blot out the influence of Pierre Rousseau's *Journal encyclopédique*. It was a start, and over the next two years Panckoucke bought up several smaller titles and fused them with the *Journal de Genève* in order to bolster its circulation.

Then, in the autumn of 1774, Panckoucke launched a second major paper, the *Journal de politique et de littérature*, better known as the *Journal de Bruxelles*. The takeovers also continued, and by 1778, Panckoucke's ability was evident enough for the government to pin its hopes of recovering control of political news on him, by granting him a 25-year lease on the monopoly of political news, hitherto attached to the *Gazette de France*, in the hope that his newspapers would take over the role that should have been that of the *Gazette*. In the same year he was given a 26-year lease on the *Mercure*, whose fortunes had sunk to an all-time low, again as a result of foreign competition, and immediately broadened its appeal by adding the *Journal de Bruxelles* to it as a political supplement, as well as absorbing no less than seven smaller papers into it over the succeeding ten years. Eight years later, at the end of 1786, he was also given a 25-year lease on the *Gazette de France*, thus bringing together both his monopoly of political news and the official government political newspaper.[20]

Panckoucke was a pragmatist. He accepted the restraints of government censorship, but worked within them with a combination of astute commercial acumen and genuine commitment to the progress of the Enlightenment. He was also a business man, providing his newspapers with a sound financial base through careful promotion, the buying up of rivals, skilful marketing and the recruitment of first-rate editorial staff. The latter included well known literary figures such as La Harpe, Suard, Linguet and Condorcet, and the Swiss-born Mallet du Pan, who was probably the most able journalist of the pre-revolutionary decades, recruited as political editor of the *Mercure*.[21] However, he had only mixed success. The *Mercure*, for example, saw its production almost triple from two to six and a half thousand within four months of his takeover in 1778, and it reached 20,000 in 1784. Much of this interest was generated by the American war, however, and sales dropped back to 11,000 over the next four years. As for the *Gazette*, Panckoucke's takeover in late 1786 appears to have had very little effect on sales, which remained depressingly low after a slight uplift, again caused by the American war. Nevertheless, on the eve of the revolution, sales of his four major titles — the *Journal de Genève*, the *Journal de Bruxelles*, the *Mercure* and the *Gazette de France* — totalled 24,000 per week. He had the theoretical monopoly within the country for political news — all other newspapers covering politics having to pay him an annual fee for infringing on it — and dominated the newspaper market in a way that no one had done since Renaudot.[22]

Panckoucke's rise, although it took place within the old mould of government control, also coincided with a gradual change in the public perception of journalism. Since the 1740s the prestige of writers had grown steadily in France, largely as a result of the spread of the Enlightenment.[23] This had little immediate impact on writers' financial situation, except for the fortunate and outstanding few, partly because the restricted size of the literate market kept print runs down to a few hundred — or at best little over a thousand — and also partly because, until the revolution, there were no copyright laws to protect authors from the all-too-frequent counterfeiting of their works by domestic or foreign publishing houses.[24] If someone like Diderot was able to make a comfortable living from the sizeable salary he was paid for editing the *Encyclopédie*, he was the exception rather than the rule, and the great majority of writers continued to survive, as they had done since the sixteenth century, in a variety of ways. Patronage continued to be the most important support, as writers worked to secure for themselves royal or private pensions, official sinecures, or posts as private tutors in aristocratic households and foreign courts. Alternatively many found work as compilers of grammars and dictionaries, or collaborators on encyclopedias, profiting from the century's growing interest in the secular world. Frequently, however, this involved the descent into Grub Street, where a living had to be patched together from translating, ghost writing or the writing of pamphlets, close to the murky world of clandestine publishing. The early careers of many future journalists of the revolution, men such as Brissot or Carra, were hacked out in this way, and behind them lay dozens more, ready to turn their pen to the writing of *libelles* and broadsides in return for money, in the hope that more legitimate chances of advancement would follow.[25]

In the increasing competition for survival, journalism provided an attractive career in terms of both prestige and money. Earlier in the century its status had been low, regarded as the refuge of second-class minds, who were prepared to compromise with the dictates of censorship, and forge a dubious reputation for themselves by indulging in polemical literary criticism. Voltaire, while well aware of the power of the press, had few kind words to say for the literary journalists of his day — least of all for Fréron who criticised him remorselessly in his *Année littéraire* — yet shortly before his death he contributed to Panckoucke's *Mercure*. Diderot and Rousseau shared his initial antipathy, again towards the literary press. As for the political press, the usual charge made against it was its triviality and the inevitably ephemeral quality which resulted from the fact that it had to report events before adequate time had elapsed for reflection and assessment. Yet as the century wore on, a growing interest in public affairs, coupled as it was among the intellectual elite with admiration for the British and American political systems, generated respect for the role of political journalism in the creation of a sense of public awareness. The journalist's role was increasingly seen as that of providing readers with an account of events, which would be inevitably limited by a lack of the perspective that only time could bring, as well as by the difficulties of obtaining adequate information; yet nevertheless be committed to impartiality and to the need to place events into their political and historical context.

This development was reflected in the calibre of writer that the higher financial rewards of journalism attracted. Elie Fréron for example, was reputed to get 20,000 *livres* per year from the *Année littéraire* during its halcyon days of the 1760s, a sum similar to that claimed for Suard from a combination of salary and profits on the *Journal de Paris* after 1785. Panckoucke, whose role in recruiting and rewarding first-rate writers was second to none, paid Linguet 10,000 *livres* per annum for working on the *Journal de Bruxelles* between 1773 and 1776, and La Harpe a salary of 6,000 *livres* in 1776 — well above the average annual income of many provincial nobles — for editing the literary section of the *Mercure*. Mallet du Pan was paid some 7,200 *livres* in 1783 for editing the political section of the *Mercure*, with commission for extra sales and feature articles on top.[27] Neither was this pure philanthropy, for Panckoucke was able to pay these salaries because of the substantial money that he made from his newspapers. In 1788, for example, he made a profit of 163,605 *livres* from his four major titles, even after paying the 66,328 *livres* that he had to pay to the government.[28]

Journalism was becoming both respectable and profitable, carried upwards by the twin forces of commercialism and political interest, and the position of the newspaper press on the eve of the revolution was therefore delicately balanced. On the one hand, its role as a source of information and analysis was becoming increasingly accepted, while on the other the reality of government control and prior censorship remained unmoved. The revolution was to bolster the former and shatter the latter, tipping the balance in favour of press freedom, and creating a new and more challenging concept of the journalist's political role.

Notes

1. J.-P. Seguin, *L'Information en France de Louis XII à Henri II* (Geneva, 1961); J.-P. Seguin, *L'Information en France avant le périodique. 517 canards imprimés entre 1529 et 1631* (Paris, 1965); C. Bellanger (ed.) *Histoire générale de la presse française. Tome I. Des origines à 1814* (Paris, 1969), Chapter I, parts i–iv. For an example of such a canard, see Natalie Zemon Davies, *The return of Martin Guerre* (Harvard, 1983). Chapter 11.
2. Bellanger, *Histoire générale*, I, 78–9.
3. Anthony Smith, *The newspaper. An international history* (London, 1979), Chapter 2, *passim*. For the importance of *nouvellistes*, see Robert S. Tate Jr, *Petit de Bachaumont and the memoires secrets. Studies on Voltaire and the eighteenth century* (Banbury, 1973), pp. 129–35; Eugène Hatin, *Histoire politique et littéraire de la presse en France*, 8 vols (Paris, 1859–61), i, pp. 3–60.
4. For the beginnings of the *Gazette*: R. Chartier, *Histoire de l'édition*

française. Tome I. Le Livre conquérant. Du moyen âge au milieu du XVIIe siècle (Paris, 1982), pp. 411–25.

5. Gilles Feyel, *La 'Gazette' en province à travers ses réimpressions, 1631–1752* (Amsterdam and Maarssen, 1982), Chapter 1.

6. Bellanger, *Histoire générale*, I, 199–219.

7. Claude Lannette-Claverie, 'La librairie française en 1700', *Revue Française de l'Histoire du Livre*, 3 (1972), pp. 3–31; H.-J. Martin, *Livres, pouvoirs et société à Paris au XVIIe siècle (1598–1701)*, 2 vols (Paris and Geneva, 1969), ii, pp. 678–98; for the lasting effects of this in the eighteenth century, see R. Chartier, 'L'Imprimerie en France à la fin de l'ancien régime: l'État Général des Imprimeurs de 1777', *Revue Française de l'Histoire du Livre*, 3 (1973), pp. 253–79.

8. G. Weill, *Le journal. Origines, évolution et rôle de la presse périodique* (Paris, 1934), pp. 87ff; Smith, *The newspaper*, Chapter 3; G. Cranfield, *The development of the provincial newspaper* (Oxford, 1962), pp. 1–11; Robert Munter, *The history of the Irish newspaper, 1685–1760* (Cambridge, 1967), pp. 189–190.

9. F. Furet and J. Ozouf, *Lire et écrire. L'alphabétisation des Français de Calvin à Jules Ferry* (Paris, 1977), Chapter 1.

10. Suzanne Tucoo-Chala, *Charles-Joseph Panckoucke et la libraire française 1736–1798* (Paris-Pau, 1978), pp. 191–3; Ferdinand Brunot, *Histoire de la langue française des origines à 1900*, vi (Paris, 1966), 1er partie, i, pp. 41–2. For the growth in public opinion, see Keith Michael Baker, 'On the problems of the ideological origins of the French Revolution' in Dominick La Capra and Steven L. Kaplan (eds), *Modern European intellectual history. Reappraisals and new perspectives* (Ithaca and London, 1982); Keith Michael Baker, 'French political thought on the accession of Louis XVI', *Journal of Modern History*, 1 (1978), pp. 279–303; Dale Van Kley, *The Damiens affair and the unravelling of the ancien régime, 1750–1770* (Princeton, 1983).

11. Jean Sgard, 'La multiplication des périodiques' in H.J. Martin and R. Chartier (eds), *Histoire de l'édition française. vol. II. Le livre conquérant* (Paris, 1984), p. 200.

12. Bellanger, *Histoire générale*, I, pp. 240–250.

13. Eugène Hatin, *Les Gazettes de Hollande et la presse clandestine aux XVIIe et XVIIIe siècles* (Paris, 1865), pp. 36–49; Rene Moulinas, 'Du rôle de la poste royale comme moyen de contrôle financier sur la diffusion des Gazettes en France aux XVIIIe siècle' in *Modèles et moyens de la reflexion politique au XVIIIe siècle. Colloque à Lille, 1973*, vol. 1 (Paris, 1977), pp. 383–95.

14. R. Birn, ' "Le Journal Encyclopédique" et l'ancien régime' in *Colloque Voltaire* (Geneva, 1963), I, pp. 219–240; J. Cruppi, *Un avocat journaliste au XVIIIe siècle: Linguet* (Paris, 1895). See also G. Charlier and R. Mortier, *Une suite de l'Encyclopédie. Le Journal Encyclopédique (1756–1793)* (Brussels, 1952); Bernadette Vanderschueren, 'Les premières années du "Journal général de l'Europe" ', *La vie wallonne*, XXXIV (1960), pp. 245–87.

15. Gilles Feyel, 'La presse provinciale au XVIIIe siècle: géographie d'un réseau', *Revue Historique*, CCLXXII (1984), pp. 353–62; D. Mornet, *Les origines intellectuelles de la révolution française, 1715–1789* (Paris, 1933), pp. 349–51; F. L'Huillier, 'Remarques sur les journaux strasbourgeois de la première moitié du XVIIIe siècle (1715–1760)', *Revue d'Alsace*, 1936, pp. 129–41; M. Gasc, 'La naissance de la presse périodique locale à Lyon.

Les Affiches de Lyon, annonces et avis divers' in *Études sur la presse au XVIIIe siècle*, no. 3, (Lyon, 1978), pp. 61–80.

16. J. Sgard, 'La presse provinciale et les lumières' in *La presse provinciale au XVIIIe siècle* (Paris, 1983), p. 64. Not all provincial newspapers were weeklies: the *Journal de Bordeaux*, launched in 1784, was daily; the *Journal* (launched in 1781) was thrice weekly; others, in Lille, Valenciennes and Rouen, were twice weekly: see Feyel, 'La presse provinciale', pp. 370–3.

17. B.M. Orléans, Lenoir papers, Ms 1422, pièce 250; for an evaluation of Lenoir's memoirs, see Robert Darnton, 'The memoirs of Lenoir, lieutenant de police of Paris, 1774–1785', *English Historical Review*, LXXXV (1970), pp. 532–59. For *libelles* earlier in the eighteenth century, see Kenneth E. Carpenter, *Books and society in history* (New York–London, 1983); for the broad lines of its scope in the 1770s, see 'Trade in the Taboo: the life of a clandestine book dealer in pre-revolutionary France' in Paul Korshin (ed.), *The widening circle. Essays on the circulation of literature in eighteenth century Europe* (Pennsylvania, 1976), pp. 11–83; 'The world of the underground bookseller' in E. Hinrichs (ed.), *Vom Ancien Régime zur franzosischen Revolution: Forschungen und Perspektiven* (Gottingen, 1978), pp. 439–78; J. Bénétruy, *L'Atelier de Mirabeau* (Paris, 1961), Chapters 2–7, *passim*.; and Mallet du Pan, *Memoires et correspondance*, I (Paris, 1851), pp. 131–2. For the attitude of Malesherbes, see P. Grosclaude, *Malesherbes. Témoin et interprète de son temps* (Paris, 1961); and for the survival of the pornograpic genre into the revolution, *Le tailleur patriote, ou les habits de Jean-Foutres*, 8 nos (Paris, 1790).

18. Denise Aimé Azam, 'Le ministère des affaires étrangères et la presse à la fin de l'ancien régime, *Cahiers de la Presse*, no. 3 (1938), pp. 428–30.

19. On this important personality in the publishing world of late eighteenth-century France, see Tucoo-Chala, *Panckoucke, passim*; for his activity in journalism in Lille, L. Trenard, 'La presse périodique en Flandre au XVIIIe siècle, *Dix-Huitième Siècle*, i (1969), pp. 99–105.

20. Tucoo-Chala, *Panckoucke*, pp. 191–251; Aimé Azam, 'Le ministère des affaires, pp. 431–8.

21. Frances Acomb, *Mallet du Pan (1749–1800). A career in political journalism* (Durham, NC, 1973), Chapters 4–5.

22. Tucoo-Chala, *Panckoucke*, pp. 240–51.

23. J. Lough, *Writer and public in France from the Middle Ages to the present day* (Oxford, 1978), pp. 199–214, 242–4; John Moore, *A view of society and manners in France, Switzerland, and Germany: with anecdotes relating to some eminent characters*, 2 vols (London, 1779), pp. 26–7; Eric Walter, 'Les auteurs et le champ littéraire', in Martin and Chartier, *Histoire de l'édition*, II, p. 390ff. For similar developments in Germany, see Jean Mondot, 'Rôle et fonctions du journaliste et de la presse chez W.L. Wekhrlin' in Pierre Grappin (ed.), *L'Allemagne des lumières. Périodiques, correspondances, témoignages* (Paris, 1982), pp. 322–3: 'The growth in personal income enabled people to buy power, and that power gave freedom to journalists to criticise authority.'

24. Walter, 'Les auteurs et champ littéraire', pp. 395–6.

25. Robert Darnton, 'The high Enlightenment and the low life of literature in pre-revolutionary France', *Past and Present*, 51 (1971), pp. 81–115; Robert Darnton 'The Grub Street style of revolution: J.-P. Brissot, police spy', *Journal of Modern History*, Sept. 1968, pp. 301–27.

26. See, for example, Diderot's *Encyclopédie*, vol. vii, p. 534: 'A good gazetteer must have up to date news which is accurate and impartial, and be simple and correct in his style; as a result, good gazetteers are very rare. For a detailed analysis of Enlightenment views, see J. Lough, *The philosophes and post-revolutionary France* (Oxford, 1982), pp. 231–40; and Gary Bruce Rogers, *Diderot and the eighteenth century French press* (Banbury, 1973), pp. 7–12.

27. Suzanne Tucoo-Chala, 'Presse et vérité sous l'ancien régime', *Revue du Nord*, vol. lxvi, no. 261–2 (1984), pp. 713–21. See also the new prospectus for the *Gazette de France* at the time of its re-launch in 1761, quoted in L. Trenard, 'Histoire et presse au XVIII^c siècle, *Bulletin de la Sociéte de l'Académie du Bas-Rhin*, 1967–8, p. 9.

28. Lough, *Writer and Public*, pp. 210–14; Acomb, *Mallet du Pan*, pp. 155–6.

1

The Emergence of a Free Press

An anonymous satirical pamphlet, published sometime during the winter of 1788-9, conjured up for its readers the picture of a smoke-filled garret in the centre of Paris, formerly used by Jansenist *convulsionnaires*, fortune tellers and followers of Mesmer, but now occupied by political pamphleteers who were using it as a propaganda centre in the months before the meeting of the Estates General. Liberal aristocrats, *abbés* and commoners met there in shared clandestinity to plot the contents of their next brochures, confident of their chances of capturing the market:

> People everywhere are talking about the Estates General, and our pens are busy satisfying their demand. We have toppled the English novel, travel books translated from English, and German poetry, and are now almost at the stage where people are bored with the theatre. Booksellers cannot keep up with our output, and neither can our readers. We alone are producing enough to keep all the printers busy too.

However, their dreams were rudely interrupted by the arrival of a group of irate booksellers who announced that a glut of brochures had flooded the market and swamped consumer demand. As a panic solution several pamphlets were quickly bound together and put on sale at bargain prices, but it was too late: the party was over, bankruptcy loomed, and the garret was quickly deserted to await the devotees of the next fringe sect.[1]

This satire was probably aimed at the activities of the *société des trente*, or one of the other clubs or political groups that sprang up in the capital during the autumn of 1788. Yet it also reflects the wider role played by pamphlet warfare in the vacuum left by the collapse of royal authority in the winter of 1788–9. Pamphlet output began to increase early in 1787, with the meeting of the first Assembly of Notables, and production had accelerated during the crisis of the summer of 1788, amidst the controversy that followed the Lamoignon decrees.[2] Published in defiance of censorship, they were technically illegal, as had been many hundreds of *libelles* during the course of the eighteenth century. However, from 5 July 1788 they were effectively freed from the restraints of censorship by a decree from Brienne, Louis XVI's chief minister, which called for opinions to be submitted to the Crown on the procedures to be followed in the convoking of the Estates General. This was widely interpreted as an open invitation to air political views freely. Mallet du Pan, editor of the *Mercure*, was just one of many to complain of the ' . . . violent, bizarre, anarchic' works which appeared daily, preaching utopian reforms and overnight solutions to the country's problems. The booksellers of the *rue Saint-Jacques* complained that their legitimate trade was being drained away by illicit operators in the Palais Royal who, under the protection of the Duke of Orléans, had long been able to ignore censorship, while complaints of evasion also came from Bordeaux.[3]

Certainly there was no lack of entrepreneurs, both in Paris and the provinces, willing to take the risks involved in what could be a highly lucrative activity, and a number of clandestine presses sprang up which lured workers away from their law-abiding employers, at wages well above the legal rates. Mirabeau's future publisher, Le Jay in the *rue d'Argenteuil*, was raided at the end of January 1789 by police in search of a clandestine press, and a week earlier his son had been arrested at the Passy customs barrier, in possession of a bundle of clandestine works by the great man himself. The director of the book trade, de Maissemy, replying to complaints from Toulouse in late May, registered his own despair at the collapse of legality, commenting: 'You are quite right to complain of such abuses, and I share your concern; but things have reached such a pitch that it is now almost impossible to prevent the circulation of these pamphlets.'[4]

As pamphlet censorship collapsed during the winter of 1788–9, many of the pamphlets that appeared concerned themselves with the general question of press freedom, with several of them also raising the specific issue of newspaper censorship. In December Mirabeau published a translation of Milton's *Areopogitica* of 1644, prefacing it with a long introduction in which he chided supporters of censorship as ' . . . cultivated conservatives . . . who are really dangerous because they fail to work from basic principles and to examine social problems in the round'. He defended press freedom as a natural right, inherited from the state of nature, and also invoked the utilitarian argument of its value to political life, pointing to its beneficial effects in the United States and in Britain, in instances such as the Wilkes case. The brochure ended with a ringing call to the Estates General to make the abolition of prior censorship 'the first of your laws'.[5] Given his heavy involvement in the *libelles* of the pre-revolution, Mirabeau was a predictable protagonist, but there were many other leading writers who argued a similar case too, including Condorcet, Target and the *abbé* Sieyès. So also did Malesherbes, the tolerant and humane director of the book trade under Louis XV who, in a *Mémoire sur la liberté de la presse*, circulated privately in the early months of 1789, argued that freedom of publication was necessary in order for deputies to be fully informed of their constituents' needs and wishes. Yet comparing France with England, he noted the greater latitude permitted to French judges in their interpretation of the law; and, fearing that they would use that latitude to interpret press legislation in a restrictive fashion, he suggested instead a dual system for France, whereby authors could either submit to prior censorship and be exempt from subsequent prosecution for libel or sedition, or publish freely and take the legal consequences.

Other pamphlets, by lesser-known authors, also took up the familiar eighteenth-century themes of natural rights and social utility, echoing Mirabeau's and Malesherbes' references to the Anglo-Saxon precedents, and calling for their extension to France.[6] The only serious dissenting voice came from a royal censor, Thiébault, who in a lengthy pamphlet defended the right of the state to use censorship in defence of public order, and — while willing to see some relaxation in the censorship of books — was particularly adamant on the need to keep close controls on the newspaper press, arguing the need to protect foolish publishers and journalists from the consequences of their own optimism:

> It should be noted that ill educated people, who need money and have no other means of supporting themselves, will quickly turn their hands to these unfortunate enterprises; and that the inevitable failure of most of them will result in huge losses for those who provided the finance, for others who were unwise enough to take part, and especially for the regrettably large number of their subscribers.[7]

Reservations over the consequences of press freedom were more frequently aired in certain of the *cahiers de doléances*, drawn up during the elections of the spring of 1789. The great majority of primary *cahiers*, drawn up at parish or guild level, were concerned with local issues and pressing economic needs; most made no mention of relatively esoteric question of press freedom at all, while those few that did often copied their wording from one of the many model *cahiers* in circulation, or consented to the wording of a local notable or priest. The question was raised, however, in over 80 per cent of the general *cahiers*, drawn up at *bailliage* or *sénéchaussée* level. Those of the clergy were mostly hostile towards any further liberalisation. Certainly some, such as the clergy of Bouzonville, in Lorraine, advocated press freedom as 'utterly indispensable', with the proviso that provision be made for slander or sedition to be punished, and the clergy of Autun, Le Mans, Montpellier and Aix — while wanting religion to be utterly forbidden territory — supported the idea of free debate in secular affairs. The *cahier* of the clergy of Provins, on the other hand, condemned ' . . . press chaos, which spawns hundreds of scandalous publications every day, full of libertine ideas, a spirit of scepticism, and sacrilege against the Christian faith, modesty, throne and altar.' In Clermont-Ferrand and the Boulonnais, the clergy even wanted more repressive legislation rather than less, arguing ' . . . that it should be made illegal for just anybody to have his ideas appear in print, when they are often just the product of a wild imagination and more liable to cause trouble than to enlighten people'. Several clerical *cahiers* notably denounced the censorship chaos that had reigned over the previous nine months.[38]

Amongst the *cahiers* of the nobility, on the other hand, the mood was generally more favourable. Certainly a minority sided with most of the clergy in wanting the retention of existing prior censorship arrangements. Some specifically called for even stricter measures against the authors of seditious works, one even suggesting the appointment of clerical censors to cover works on religion. Yet the majority welcomed the trend towards greater freedom and claimed, like the nobility of the Boulonnais, that had press liberty existed prior to 1789, ' . . . the nation would have been better informed of its real interests'.[9] This attitude was even more prevalent in the *cahiers* of the Third Estate. 'Freedom of the press for all publications', demanded the *cahier* in Bordeaux; while from Saint-Léger in the Beaujolais came the argument, to be used many times over the next few years, that it was ' . . . the only way to enlighten the government, to control ministers, to establish a barrier to abuse of the law and to make citizens of all social ranks accountable to the public'. Many *cahiers* echoed this unconditional support, but the majority acknowledged the need for some kind of control too, particularly in the areas of sedition and libel. The Third Estate of Ploermel, for example, wanted printers to hold a register of their authors so that if the occasion arose, they could be identified for prosecution. Rhodez wanted the register to be an official one, while in Senlis and Soissons the presence of witnesses to signatures in such a register was suggested. This concern to be able to identify the authors and printers of seditious publications was one which was to run through successive legislative reforms throughout the revolution, along with the stipulation that trials should be held before a jury, but apart from this, most *cahiers* were at this stage prepared to leave the details to future legislators and confine themselves to a statement of general principle. The small walled town of Chateau-du-Loir in the Maine asked: 'Let the Estates General work on the drafting of a law which will establish legitimate press freedom,' while la Suze stated simply: 'Let press freedom be both acknowledged and defined by law so that its only limitation be merely minimal legislation to prevent the abuse of libel.'[10]

Yet whatever the views of the electorate, the Crown for its part had no intention of making any hasty concessions. The *Résultat du conseil* of 27 December 1788 contained a vague promise of a more liberal approach, but the official line was that nothing could be changed until the Estates General itself had examined the matter. Several requests for permission to launch new titles were made during the early months of 1789, by an assorted collection of curates, vicar generals, *abbés*, army captains, merchants, unemployed apothecaries' sons — and even by one old man who wanted to devote the proceeds to the encouragement of breast-feeding mothers from the poorer classes. All were intended specifically to cover the proceedings of the Estates General, but all were met with a stone wall of refusal, on the grounds that a privilege for such a newspaper had already been granted — although the archives have no record of it — and that it was for the Estates General to decide how best to handle the publicity of its own debates. It was probably no great loss to journalism, as all the applicants appear to have been slightly odd, and none more so than a certain Du Morier, son of a *bailli* from Anjou, who saw such a newspaper as his lifeline from poverty and fantasised that he would be able to use it to influence deputies towards the adoption of Crown policies. Only one of the applicants

19

actually worked as a journalist subsequently, and then only for a matter of weeks before injury forced him to retire.[11]

The first cracks in the wall, however, appeared not in Paris, where police controls were probably effective enough to stamp out an illegal periodical, but in Britanny. There, Rennes saw two newspapers in December and January, which may well have had the tacit collusion of Necker, anxious to break the obdurate resistance of the Breton nobility to increased representation for the province's Third Estate deputation to the Estates General. The first of them, the *Sentinelle du peuple*, appeared between 10 November and 25 December 1788, lasting for just five editions, and was published first in Rennes itself, and then from the nearby *château* of Maurepas. Its author, Louis-Francois Volney, came originally from Craon in the Mayenne and was a well established *philosophe* and pamphleteer, active in the Paris salons of Mme Suard, Holbach, and Helvétius, known to Jefferson, Mirabeau and Sieyès, and a member of the *société des amis des Noirs*. It was in Paris that he had met Necker who, possibly on the prompting of the Intendant of Brittany, Bertrand de Moleville, appears to have engaged him to write the *Sentinelle*. Volney used it to endorse warmly Necker's policies. He attacked the province's Estates for extravagance, voiced support for the principle of fiscal equality, and called for equality of access to public office, as well as doubled representation for the Third Estate in the Estates General.[12] Indeed, he went further, supporting the campaign for voting by head, and through his use of simple and direct language, clearly aimed his appeal at the emerging political consciousness of the middle and lower ranks of the Third Estate. Quite why he ceased publication in late December is not clear, for he subsequently published a number of pamphlets and was elected to the Estates General for the Third Estate of Angers.

Nevertheless, the *Sentinelle* was swiftly replaced in late December by the *Hérault de la nation*, a thrice-weekly newspaper edited by Michel Mangourit, who claimed — probably fictitiously — to be acting as the mouthpiece of an anonymous patriotic club. The claim was probably fictitious, although it was used by many journalists over the next ten years to give their work an added air of authority, but Mangourit shared Volney's political stance, arguing that all men shared the same right to legal equality, and that it was the function of reason, of 'humanity' and of 'philosophy' to destroy the prejudices which denied that right.[13] Ministerial protection, again from Necker, appears to have allowed Mangourit to survive until late June of 1789, although copies were seized in Paris in early February and orders for confiscation given as late as 27 May. Two other attempts to launch an unauthorised newspaper, this time on the opposite side of the country in Besançon, and without ministerial protection, were less successful. The first, the anonymous *Journal de Besançon*, appeared in mid-January, and appears to have been an attempt to revive the city's long-defunct *Affiches*: but it never progressed beyond the prospectus stage. Then, on 26 January the first edition of a *Feuille hebdomadaire* appeared which nailed its colours to the mast of the Third Estate, by deriding seigneurial rights and social privilege, and supporting the city's parish priests against their ecclesiastical superiors. However, its first edition also appears to have been its last, and when it was later revived in the following July, it again proved stillborn.[14]

Despite these early provincial beginnings it was in Paris that the decisive breakthrough came. On 16 March Jacques-Pierre Brissot de Warville, pamphleteer, journalist and anti-slavery campaigner, who had recently returned from America, published, under cover of anonymity, a six-page prospectus for a *Patriote français* which he claimed would appear twice weekly. He had deliberately not sought government permission for the newspaper and the prospectus was a direct challenge to royal authority, citing as it did the precedents of America and Britain to show that newspapers were an essential part of political life.[15] It drew no immediate response from the government, so on 1 April he issued another, this time stating that the paper would appear four times weekly from 20 April, and naming both himself as its editor and Buisson, a Parisian bookseller, as its distributor. This time the government responded swiftly, and the Director of the Book Trade summoned Buisson to account for himself. Probably following a pre-arranged plan, he denied all knowledge of the affair, complained that his name had been cited without his consent, and undertook to observe the law. Nevertheless, the government took no risks and, on 15 April, the *chambre syndicale* in Paris, and inspectors of the book trade throughout the kingdom, were ordered to confiscate any copies of the prospectus that came to their attention.[16]

Brissot fell silent, and there the matter rested for almost three weeks. On 6 May, however, the day after the formal opening of the Estates General, he published his first number. By this time two other journals had already appeared: one was an anonymous *Corréspondance nationale*, which appeared on 4 and 7 May, and the other an *Etats-Généraux*, published by Mirabeau, on 5 and 6 May.[17] The government once again responded swiftly, reiterating its prohibition on unauthorised journals on 6 May, and banning Mirabeau's *Etats-Généraux* by name on the following day. Brissot promptly withdrew again, publishing a pamphlet defence of press freedom while he bided his time, but Mirabeau used his position as a deputy in the Estates General to defy the ban. On 8 May, probably due to the intervention of his friend Target, the electoral assembly of the Third Estate of Paris denounced the government's action, and on 10 May Mirabeau resumed publication under the new title of *Lettres du comte de Mirabeau à ses commettants*. Claiming that he was merely doing his duty as a deputy by communicating with his constituents in the most convenient manner available, he defied the government to stop him and threw down the gauntlet to the Ministry on the question of principle, taunting Necker in particular:

> Twenty million voices are crying out for press freedom: nation and King are unanimous in their wish for help and ideas. But then we are presented with a ministerial veto, after being misled by a treacherous and deceptive policy of tolerance.[18]

The government drew back from open conflict, reluctant to take on so powerful a personality, and at such a sensitive time. Yet on 19 May, in a clear attempt to reassert some kind of control, it authorised the existing privileged journals in Paris — the *Journal de Paris*, the *Mercure* and the *Gazette de France* — to carry reports on the Estates General, provided the text had been cleared with the censor beforehand. Because provincial papers had always been allowed to reprint political reports from the authorised Paris press, this also applied to them and was clearly intended as a tactical concession, designed to prevent the further growth of an unofficial press.[19] This is evident from the orders sent on the following day, 20 May, to the inspector of the book trade in Dijon reiterating that any unauthorised journals were still to be confiscated. Moreover, on 21 May there was a direct attempt to call Mirabeau's bluff, when orders were given for the confiscation of the third number of his *Lettres à ses commettants*. An inspector and *commissaire de police* went to the premises of Le Jay, his publisher, on the *rue d'Echelle*, to implement the order. However, word of the raid had already leaked out and the two men were greeted by a doorkeeper who claimed that Le Jay had been away on business for three months, his wife was in Versailles, and the principal *commis* had just left, taking the keys of the shop with him. It seemed an unlikely story, but the inspector decided to push the matter no further, and a raid that same day on the premises of another bookseller, Cussac, in the Palais Royal, produced a mere six copies, the rest having been sold during the morning. Six other booksellers avoided raids by closing up shop, while three hapless women *colporteurs* who were arrested claimed to have sold all their copies that morning.[20] Nevertheless, the government pressed on, sending orders to Bordeaux on 27 May for the confiscation of a *Bulletin des États-Généraux* that had begun publication there, repeating that the King had expressly forbidden any journal unless authorised by the deputies themselves — 'especially as Parisian papers are already publishing everything that needs to be said'. A letter to Rennes on the same day also banned a printed version of correspondance sent home from Versailles by the province's clerical and Third Estate deputies from Versailles, and made it clear that even deputies' newspapers were not exempt from the ban. Mirabeau's arguments had clearly not been conceded and the fate of press freedom, as late as the end of May, still hung in the balance.[21]

Yet in reality the cause was already lost, for the rot had already spread too far. Press freedom was caught up in the slide towards wider political freedom, for, as the inspector of the book trade in Dijon noted in a letter of mid-May, in response to the orders from Paris banning the *Patriote français* and the *États-Généraux*: ' . . . it will be all the more difficult to call a halt to this abuse because press freedom is one of the principal demands being made by deputies to the Estates General'. On 20 and 22 May those very deputies rejected the suggestion that they should publish their own journal and, on 23 May, turned down a request from Panckoucke that he be authorised to publish one as a supplement to the *Mercure, Journal de Genève* and *Gazette*.[22] This effectively gave the green light to the unauthorised press, and open defiance of censorship rapidly grew: in early June, Le Hodey de Saultchevreuil launched a *Journal des États-Généraux*, which was to last until October 1791, and a *Petite poste de l'Assemblée Nationale* quickly followed. On 19 June, Bertrand Barère, deputy for Tarbes, started his *Point du jour*, which was to provide full and accurate accounts of Assembly debates until October 1791, to be followed on 20 June by the *Nouvelles de Versailles* and, a week later, by the *Courrier français*, edited by one of the more successful press barons of the decade, Poncelin de la Roche Tilhac.

July's events, which saw the fall of the Bastille and the consolidation of the Assembly's position, quelled any remaining fears over the permanency of the revolution, and resulted in a surge of over 20 new titles in both Paris and Versailles, many of which broadened their horizons beyond the debates of the Assembly, to include both provincial and foreign news: Gorsas' *Courrier de Versailles* on the 5th, Maret's *Bulletin de l'Assemblée Nationale* on the 7th, Prudhomme's *Révolutions de Paris* on the 18th, and Brissot's *Patriote français* — at the third attempt — on the 28th. July also saw Mirabeau change the title of his *Lettres à ses commettants* to the *Courrier de Provence* and, according to one of his Genevan ghost writers, ' . . . subscribers came in such crowds, though the price was very high, that we already imagined ourselves rolling in wealth'.[23] Several of these early titles had started off in hesitant fashion, appearing initially in the form of brochures rather than as regular newspapers, but by the end of the month most felt secure enough to move over from sale by number to sale by subscription, a move which consolidated their financial base and also helped guard against the problem of forgery and counterfeiting of titles. Barère began with subscription rates on 18 July. Le Hodey's *Journal des États-Généraux*, which was originally hawked around the gardens of the Palais-Royal by *colporteurs*, announced its term eight days later, and the *Courrier national* and *Courrier français* followed suit by the end of the month.

August saw another 16 titles come on to the market, including Millin and Noël's *Chronique de Paris*, Louise Kéralio's *Journal d'état et du citoyen* and the *Journal des débats et des décrets*, which was to provide detailed accounts of Assembly debates until 1797. September saw a slight drop, with only ten new titles, but this was probably because of temporary controls imposed by the Municipality during August, reinforced after the disturbances at the end of the month; even then, the ten included Marat's *Ami du peuple*, which began life for its first few numbers as the *Publiciste*. During the following month of October newcomers included the *Annales patriotiques et littéraires*, set up by the bookseller Buisson, after he had lost the distribution contract for the *Patriote français*, and soon dominated by one of its contributors, Jean-Louis Carra. In November Pierre-Jean Audoin's *Journal universel* began its five-year existence as a mouthpiece of the democratic left, and on the 28th, Camille Desmoulins converted himself from pamphleteer to journalist with the *Révolutions de France et de Brabant*. From the very outset he adopted the familiar and enthusiastic tone towards his readers that was to become a hallmark of his style, lacing his accounts of Assembly debates with frequent comment, providing news of the activity in 'the incomparable Cordeliers District', and relating the details of conversations that he had in *cabinets littéraires* or the contents of readers' letters.[24] Panckoucke too, disappointed in his effort six months previously to become the official journalist of the Third Estate, launched the prestigious *Moniteur*, one of only two newspapers in the whole year to be published in the large folio format, which provided serious readers with a wide range of political news.

Almost all of these 1789 creations were patriotic or pro-revolutionary, for the right-wing press was slow to get off the ground, reflecting the time lag that was needed before coherent opposition to the revolution could emerge. The first right-wing paper to appear was the *Journal politique national* which, although owned and nominally edited by a well-known opponent of the *philosophes*, Sabatier de Castres, was mostly written by Antoine Rivarol, a literary star of the *ancien régime*. Appearing first on 12 July, then thrice weekly, it deliberately tried to break away from the pattern of instant news reporting to become a journal of analysis and reflection: 'Other journalists offer their readers fresh news, along with weak and stale analysis; we shall strive to do the opposite, as it is the only area left open to us.' Rivarol went on to aim his thoughts 'at the small number of thinking people' and to claim that his paper was 'more a novelty than just a collection of news'.[25] One of the novelties indeed was that it was the first newspaper to voice a consistent and reasoned opposition to the revolution, and it ran into immediate opposition as a result, changing printer several times during its initial weeks and causing Sabatier and Rivarol to move out of Paris for their own safety. In mid-October the *Année littéraire*, hitherto a predominantly literary paper, opened out into political comment because of the inroads made into its sales by the political press, publishing a number of articles from the *abbé* Royou, critical of the flow of events since the previous July.[26] Later in the month the *Actes des Apôtres* joined the fray in its own individual and unorthodox fashion. In mid-December the *Journal général de la cour et de la ville*, which had already been on the market for three months, underwent an editorial coup which saw it decisively move away from the patriotic left towards the counter-revolutionary right. Meanwhile, Mallet du Pan, writing in Panckoucke's *Mercure*, had cautiously begun to align himself with the *monarchien* cause of moderate constitutional monarchy since September in a way that would mark him out as one of the more formidable critics of the National Assembly over the next two years.[27]

By the end of 1789 Paris had seen over 130 new political newspapers come on to the market, to replace or rival the six that can be described as political, which had been in circulation at the beginning of the year. It was a substantial change by any standards, and although over two-thirds of these new titles were to prove short-lived, lasting for less than two months, some 31 of them were to prove solid enough to remain in production for over a year, and in some cases substantially longer. The *Patriote français* and *Chronique de Paris*, for example, were to last until the fall of the Girondins in the summer of 1793, the *Révolutions de Paris* until the following spring, and the *Annales patriotiques* until 1797. Moreover, with this increase in numbers went an increase in frequency. In January the only daily paper in the capital had been the non-political *Journal de Paris*; by the end of 1789 there were over 20 political dailies, with at least as many tri-weeklies and bi-weeklies as well. Political life had not merely been opened up to public view, but its tempo had also been increased, making the daily event the preoccupation of the hour. It was the newspaper which, to a far greater degree than the pamphlet or the book, was uniquely equipped to handle this new tempo.

The politicisation of the Parisian press also had inevitable repercussions on the provincial press, and posed dilemmas for owners and editors which were by no means easy to resolve. Most provincial *Affiches* were fragile and small-scale enterprises, dependent on government permission for their very existence, and relying on subscriptions and advertisements from their local social elite for financial survival. Their staple diet of commercial news, advertisements, literary pieces and political articles taken from the authorised Parisian press, had proven to be a reasonable formula for modest commercial survival under different circumstances, and the inclusion of full-blown political news now ran the risk of offending the political susceptibilities of subscribers and advertisers, as well as involving the problems of either compressing the existing commercial news or adding extra pages. The first might drive business readers away, while the second involved extra work — and almost all provincial journalists were part-time — as well as extra costs for both publisher and subscriber alike. It is also important to remember the local context of eighteenth-century provincial life, and the close relationship that existed between a journalist and his social milieu. A journalist was in many senses a client of his local social elites, for their patronage and protection had often helped him gain the privilege to publish in the first place, their advertisements provided much of his copy, their subscriptions most of his revenue, and their occasional literary and poetical contributions with useful small articles with which to entertain readers and fill up space. To break too radically from them was to risk both patronage and friendship, both of which would remain useful long after the immediate political excitement had passed away. Who could be certain in the autumn of 1789 about how long the revolution would last, and whether the powers of the local censor would not return, with dire consequences for those who had broken ranks? Who could be sure that there was even room in the market for a political provincial press, given the fact that the Parisian newspapers, operating the hub of events, enjoyed such enormous advantages?[28]

In practice the reaction of provincial journalists and newspaper owners varied according to individual temperament and the potential of the local market. Many ignored political events entirely, or at best gave them the kind of bland coverage that would have been acceptable under the *ancien régime*, reprinting summaries of Assembly debates from the older established Parisian press. The *Affiches de Senlis*, which was to cease publication entirely in 1790, never stretched beyond the occasional patriotic song or brief report of legislative debates. Likewise the *Affiches pour la généralité de Moulins* gave only brief reports on legal and political changes, with almost no political comment.[29] The *Annonces de Picardie* avoided politics altogether, as did the *Affiches de Sens* and the *Affiches d'Auxerre* (probably, in the latter case, because its owner printed political news in other titles that he launched), while the innocent reader, scanning the *Journal de Troyes et de la Champagne méridionale* throughout 1789, could be forgiven for remaining ignorant of the fact that there had been a revolution at all.[30] In Le Mans also, Charles Monnoyer's *Affiches du Maine*, throughout 1789 and 1790, carried the same blend of official announcements and decrees, commodity prices, cures for epilepsy, breast cancer, gallstones and chest ailments as before, with only a short column outlining the main legislation of the Assembly, devoid of political comment. The same holds true of the *Affiches de Montargis*.[31]

Many others did, however, take up the political challenge, first reprinting the officially censored news that appeared in the *Mercure* or the *Journal de Paris*, then moving on to extend their sources to the new unauthorised political press, and adding their own correspondence and comment. Some, like the *Affiches de Toulouse*, the *Journal de Normandie* or the *Affiches de Périgueux*, did so within their existing format, with no extra pages or weekly issues and little more than a slight title change to welcome the new era. The *Affiches de Périgueux*, for example, changed title on 23 September to the *Journal de Périgord*, having carried brief reports on the Assembly and small items of local news since July.[32] The *Affiches de Toulouse* for its part carried its first news on the Estates General on 10 June, with a report taking up just one-third of a column and noting that 'little of interest' had happened. During the next six months its reports remained brief, and often lagged far behind the events that they covered — the creation of the National Assembly on 17 June, for example, went unmentioned, the fall of the Bastille was reported a full fortnight after it happened, the Declaration of the Rights of Man was omitted entirely, and the October days were revealed to readers only at the end of November. However, in December came a title change to *Journal universel at affiches de Toulouse*, and from January 1790 onwards, its editor, Broulhiet, provided an extra weekly edition and launched himself fully into political journalism — a career that was to involve him in court cases, imprisonment and flight over the next ten years.[33]

Other *Affiches* went further much faster, adding a political supplement well before the end of the year. One of the first was the *Affiches d'Angers*, owned by the town's leading printer, Charles-Pierre Mame, which began publishing an extra weekly edition on 22 June to cope with Assembly news. Mame told his readers:

> An ordinary sized newspaper, even with an extensive supplement, could only publish news a long time after the various bulletins, gazettes and periodicals from Paris. Moreover, the sheer length of reports on the Estates General would also squeeze out the very advertisements that *Affiches* owe their existence to.

He therefore published an extra weeky edition on Tuesdays; but even then the news outstripped available column space and, after experimenting with a smaller typeface which gave rise to complaints from readers that it hurt their eyes, Mame changed from octavo to quarto format, using longer lines. By the end of the year he had also updated his title, to *Journal national de la province d'Anjou*.[34] On 3 July Couret de Villeneuve, brother-in-law of the Parisian publisher Panckoucke, and owner of the *Journal général de l'Orléanais*, announced his intention of launching a weekly supplement, using 'reliable Parisian newspapers' to publish news of Assembly debates.

Despite difficulties in attracting the 250 subscribers that he needed to make the project break even, the first number came out by the end of the month. By then its sources ranged far beyond the official Parisian press and by the end of the year Couret, had increased his production to three times per week, employing a part-time editor, Taboureau de Montigny, to provide political analysis and comment.

On 4 July the *Courrier d'Avignon*, until then a weekly, also added a supplement to cover events in Versailles, providing a third weekly number at the end of August and completing its transition to a daily paper by the end of the year. It also then experimented with a new title, *Journal politique d'Avignon*. ' . . . because the paper will become a genuine daily, appearing some six times per week, and publishing the latest news every day',[35] Ferreol de Beaugeard, in Marseilles, was not far behind. Criticised by some of his subscribers during June and July for including political news at the expense of commercial, he solved his space problems by launching a weekly supplement on 4 August for the *Journal de Provence*, acknowledging that he had little option but to follow the example of his other provincial colleagues.[36] Six days later, Giroud followed suit in the *Affiches de Dauphiné*, having first tried to stretch his weekly edition from four pages to six, and then on 10 August opting for a weekly supplement instead. From 23 November onwards a third weekly edition was added, with publication days carefully chosen to fit in with the arrival of the latest postal news from Paris and the departure of the mail coach to subscribers in the surrounding areas. All this involved extra work, and the editor, Giroud *fils*, who had complained of the non-payment of subscriptions earlier in the year, increased his rates and warned readers to pay promptly: 'I would ask subscribers to send in the extra money promptly, or it will be deducted from the total of their ordinary subscription and the dispatch of the main paper halted when the money has been used up.'[37] In Lille the *Feuille de Flandres* provided an extra weekly edition from 25 August, also increasing subscription rates by some 25 per cent, but offering subscribers a generous coverage of Assembly news in compensation. Other newspapers, in Limoges, Metz and Lyons, were ready to do so by the end of the year.[38]

Yet political supplements did not always work. In Poitiers the editor and owner of the *Affiches de Poitou*, Michel-Vincent Chévrier, began including news of the National Assembly from mid-June onwards, taken from the government authorised accounts in the *Journal de Paris*, but usually a month or so behind events. Part of his problem was space and at first he tried experimenting with a smaller typeface in order to crowd more copy in. Then in mid-August he resorted to a weekly political supplement, charging 6 *livres* per year, but this folded up within three months when too few subscribers proved willing to take the extra cost, and National Assembly reports returned to the main body of the paper.[39] Adrien-Joseph Havé, editor of the *Affiches de Rheims*, resorted to a weekly supplement earlier, telling his readers on 15 June that he would be publishing one to cover political news, at a monthly price of 1 *livre* 15 *sols*; but although the first number appeared on 20 July with the news of the fall of the Bastille — and what better lead story could any journalist want? — it collapsed before the end of the summer through lack of subscribers.[40] Similarly, the *Journal de Nismes*, which had already given detailed coverage of election results during April, announced on 28 May that it would be publishing an extra weekly supplement at the cost of 6 *livres* per annum if sufficient interest were shown; but it obviously was not, for not until the beginning of 1790 did its editor, Boyer-Brun, who was by now an outspoken advocate of counter-revolution, step up production.[41]

Adaptation by existing *Affiches* to the new political environment was matched by a gradual growth of new titles, albeit at a less spectacular rate than in Paris. An embryonic form of this was the reprinting of Parisian newspapers by local printers, a practice carried out on the *Gazette* under the *ancien régime*, with or without the permission of the owner. In Grenoble, Dunkirk and Bordeaux, Barère's *Point du jour* was reprinted for short periods over the summer months, while Bordeaux also saw the *Journal général de la France* reprinted as the *Courrier de Paris à Bordeaux* for three months in the early autumn. Grenoble saw Poncelin's *Courrier français* reprinted during June and August by Cuchet, a prominent local printer, of the local *Affiches*, as well as reprints of the *Patriote français* and an amalgam of Parisian papers put together by a bookseller Falcon under the title of *Bulletin patriotique*.[42] These reprints were usually short-lived, providing provincial readers with news from Paris at a time of particular crisis, when copies of the original ran short. However, in Nancy, for example, a reprint of Maret's Parisian-based *Bulletin de l'Assemblée Nationale*, which was later absorbed into Panckoucke's *Moniteur* because of its reputation for accuracy, was brought out by a local printer, Haener, from 12 September 1789 onwards. It lasted until the following July and, according to Haener, brought its readers the benefits of Maret's reporting a day earlier than they would otherwise have had it, and at half the price.[43]

In Villeneuve-lès-Avignon a local printer-bookseller, Jean-Albert Joly, began reprinting Mirabeau's *États-Généraux* in mid-May, slowly broadening his net to encompass several other Parisian papers as well. By mid-July he was also including correspondents' letters, and changed his title to *Loisirs d'un patriote français* in early July, and then to *Veillées d'un français* in mid-August. By September the *Veillées* was a daily paper, and in December, Joly finally adopted the title of *Courrier de Villeneuve-les-Avignon*, setting himself up as a rival to the older and more prestigious *Courrier d'Avignon*. He covered news from provincial France and Europe, as well as Paris, claiming to have correspondents in several capital cities: ' . . . impartiality will always be our first duty, and the way in which we have organised our delivery service, along with our correspondence network, make us confident of being able to provide readers with news as promptly as possible'.[44]

Other new titles emerged from published versions of the letters sent home to their constituents by deputies from Versailles, correspondence which was frequently read aloud in the local town square, or at public meetings and Sunday gatherings. The best known example of this, the *Journal des débats*, began in late August 1789 as the printed version of letters sent home to their electoral committees in Clermont and Rioms by the Auvergnat deputies François Gaultier de Biazat, Jacques Antoine Huguet and Jean-Baptiste Grenier. After several had been printed locally, they took the initiative of having them printed themselves in Versailles, then Paris, as an autonomous newspaper. Yet they had already been preceded in many provincial towns, by other similar ventures which were to prove equally long-lasting.[45] In Rennes two printers, Audran and Vatar, had printed the correspondence of the town's Third Estate and clerical deputies from early May onwards in the form of a newspaper, the *États-Généraux. Corréspondance de Bretagne*. Then, at the end of June they went their separate ways, with Vatar at first strictly confining himself to the correspondence, but Audran supplementing it with information from the Parisian press such as the *Point du jour*, the *Journal de Paris*, Gorsas' *Courrier* and the *Patriote français*. He continued publication until the autumn of 1790, while Vatar, who later followed his lead in broadening his sources, was to remain in business until the beginning of the Directory.[46]

In another Breton town, Nantes, the correspondence sent home by two deputies, Legendre and Moyot, became the *États-Généraux. Journal de la corréspondance de Nantes* from 24 June onwards, published three times per week under the editorial control of the secretary of the municipal correspondence committee, Le Febvre de la Chauvière, and distributed throughout the principal towns of the *sénéchaussée*, until its demise in November 1790.[47] Brest saw a similar venture, the *Bulletin de la corréspondance de la députation du Tiers-État*, published by the printer Romain-Nicolas Malassis from 12 May 1789 until February 1791, while in Angers the *Corréspondance de MM. les députés de la commune d'Anjou avec leurs commettants* was the work of two substitute deputies, Pilastre and Leclerc, who accompanied the Angevin deputies to Versailles and filled in their spare hours by setting themselves up as part-time journalists.. Their letters, sent to the *bureau de correspondance* in Angers, provided the essential core of the newspaper, but from October of 1789 a supplement was published to cover local news also.[48]

Further south, the *Journal national* in Montauban owed its origins to a similar initiative. Started in July 1789 by a printer, Vincent Teulières, probably to prop up his ailing printing business, which had already been affected by fall-off in business from his traditional municipal and clerical clients, its basis was a weekly manuscript sent from Versailles to the town's correspondence committee by the deputy Poncet-Delpech, which Teulières supplemented with short snippets of local news thrown in for good measure. The mixture soon proved incompatible, as Teulières sided increasingly with counter-revolution during the winter of 1789–90, forcing Poncet-Delpech to withdraw his contributions in the following spring. However, the *Journal national* continued to appear until the autumn of 1791 and, like the *Journal de Nismes* in Nîmes, did a great deal to encourage the rise of Catholic counter-revolution in a town where sectarian feelings ran deep.[49] In Agen, on the other hand, events were more harmonious, for the correspondence bureau for all three orders, created during the elections of the previous spring to maintain contact with the deputies in Versailles, published its correspondence from 19 November onwards as the *Journal patriotique de l'Agenais* and, when the *bureau* finally disbanded in the following May, handed the enterprise on to its printer, Raymond Noubel, who kept it going on his own account until the end of February 1792.[50]

The transformation of many *Affiches*, the reprinting of Parisian titles and the growth of correspondence bulletins into fully fledged newspapers, all brought about a rapid transformation and politicisation of the provincial press — as did the emergence of other new titles, launched by printers or journalists anxious to exploit the new market. In August 1789 Auxerre saw the launch of the *Courrier provincial*, which provided a summary of news from Paris and Versailles.

On 1 September the printer widow Machuel, in Rouen, launched a daily paper, the *Nonciateur ou nouvelles du jour*, which covered the same range of news, while on the same day in Lyons a local lawyer, Champagneux, a close friend of the Rolands, launched the *Courrier de Lyon* to defend the cause of the revolution in the distinctly tepid atmosphere of Lyons, ' . . . strengthened by the example of Parisian journalists who had shaken ministerial censorship'. November saw the launch of the *Extrait des papiers publics* in Limoges, the *Journal politique hebdomadaire* in Metz, and the *Nouvelliste national* in Toulouse, while December produced the *Vedette des Alpes* in Grenoble and the *Courrier politique et littéraire* in Strasbourg.[51] Slower off the mark than its Parisian counterpart, the provincial press was nevertheless on the move.

The government's initial attitude towards this moved slowly from hesitancy to fatalism. At first it felt bound to observe legal formalities until new legislation, promised in article XI of the Declaration of Rights, had been enacted. Indeed, there were many journalists who were cautious enough still to ask for permission to establish a new newspaper, prudently hedging their bets on an uncertain political future. The feminist activist, Olympe de Gouges, later to be responsible for the murder of the journalist Suleau on 10 August 1792, had two requests for a privilege to publish turned down in May and June of 1789.[52] In mid-August *abbé* Ouvrière wrote in from Marseilles with a similar request and, receiving no reply, went on to publish two editions of a *Spectateur provençal en divers discours* from Avignon, outside direct French jurisdiction. Still wanting to publish from Marseilles, however, he then put in a second request to the *directeur de la librairie* later in the year, but received no reply. Officials could not make up their minds whether it was sufficient for Ouvrière to put his name at the end of each copy, or whether he should add the printer's as well, and whether the granting of a permission to him would offend the Marseilles municipality, which might want to exercise some censorship controls of its own. In mid-August a manuscript journalist in Bordeaux, Dutrey, had been given a privilege to publish his newsletter which had been in existence for several years — 'as the cost of manuscript copies is too great and absorbs all his profit' — on condition that he submit the text to a local censor, an already archaic idea, but there is no indication that he did.[53] Neither did the printer Corail de Ste Foy in Toulouse, when granted permission to publish his *Nouvelliste national* on the same conditions.

The government's censorship machinery was being progressively bypassed, and although occasionally a new journalist might send in specimen copies out of habit or courtesy — or simply to hedge his bets — it was essentially an empty gesture. Neither could the owners of the old privileged newspapers rely on government protection against new interlopers. When Boyer-Brun wrote in to the *directeur* in mid-August to complain that an unauthorised daily rival to his *Journal de Nismes* had been appearing for over a month, with the apparent approval of the town's *comité permanent*, he was advised to remain silent until the 'times of trouble' were over.[54] In September, when the royal commissioner for Strasbourg, Frédéric de Dietrich, asked for advice 'dans des termes positifs' on the precise limits of press liberty, as printers and booksellers in the city were pressing for the same freedom as their Parisian counterparts, he was left without a reply, for no such positive advice existed.[55] On 22 October the *inspecteur de la libraire* in Rouen complained of the proliferation of press abuses in the city that he was powerless to stop, while the *abbé* Genty, who wrote in from Orléans in mid-November to complain that the owner of the *Journal général de l'orléanais*, Couret de Villeneuve, was no longer submitting the text to him for censorship prior to publication, was advised to tolerate Couret's behaviour and try to win him back to the old ways by an appeal to friendship and loyalty.[56] In November the inspector of the book trade in Toulouse complained that matters there were out of control and that a local printer, Seurès, had even had the audacity to publish the prospectus for a literary journal that would cut across the terms of a privilege granted earlier in the year to himself for just such a paper. The response from Paris was, however, terse and unsympathetic: 'It is true that this is all very unfortunate for M. de Villeneuve. But what can we suggest, other than that he tries to pit his talents against those of M. Seurès?'[57]

The old regime was dead, and its system of press control had vanished. Prior censorship was obsolete, privileges meaningless and newspaper monopolies a thing of the past. In the summer of 1790 the owner of the *Journal de Champagne* in Rheims threatened to sue Louis Bablot, who had launched a new *Observateur du département de la Marne*, for publishing advertisements which, as owner of the *Journal*, he claimed as his own monopoly. However, he was unable even to bring the case to court. In May 1790 the legatees of a certain Madame Fauconnier successfully sued the owners of the *Journal de Paris* for refusing to continue to pay the 4,000 *livres rente* due to her under an agreement of 1782, when her *Journal des deuils de la cour* had merged with it. However, the ruling was overturned by the *tribunal de deuxième arrondissement de Paris* on 22 July 1791, on the grounds that privileges had effectively terminated as from the beginning of 1790. Indeed, even before then Panckoucke had ceased paying the Ministry of Foreign Affairs for the privilege on his *Mercure*, as well as the pensions and censor allocated to it. The *Journal encyclopédique* and the *Journal des modes* followed suit, pointing out. that such payments imposed an unfair burden on them, at a time when the newly established press had no such obligation.[58]

Another closely related monopoly, that of printers, had also effectively collapsed. On 12 November 1789 the *chambre syndicale* of the Parisian printers petitioned the Minister of the Interior for the suppression of all new printing houses that had sprung up over the previous summer; but the reply that they received was negative:

> The opinion of the Minister is that this request is perfectly in accordance with existing law, but he regrets that this is not the time to order the law to be strictly applied, as new legislation is about to be discussed. He also doubts that any means exists of enforcing the suppression being asked for, and believes that in this, as in other more essential matters, the best thing is to wait.[59]

Early in 1790 they returned with a request for numbers to be at least limited, but by this time the new printers had formed their own pressure group and vigorously resisted the demand, accusing the old-established printshops of self-interest and hypocrisy. A climate of fear and caution certainly remained, for the radical printer Momoro defended his failure to put his name and address at the foot of his publications as late as March 1791 on the grounds that he feared retaliation from established printers, while many provincial printers were hesitant to exploit their new-found freedom, even as late as the summer of 1790, because of uncertainty over their legal status.[60] Their fears were groundless, however, and their caution soon thrown to the winds.

The end of the old regime opened up a new era for the political press, and also for journalism: for what emerged in 1789 was not merely just a set of new titles, but a new subject matter as well. The press of the *ancien régime*, prevented from handling domestic news in anything other than the most anodine of ways, had instead developed its traditions and skills of verification and analysis on foreign news, sifting fact from fiction, and integrating its account of events into an analytical background framework. As a tradition, it was perpetuated into the revolution and adapted to the hitherto forbidden domain of domestic politics by the many newspapers which sprang up to report on the debates of the National Assembly and the wider political changes in the country as a whole. Most continued to pay lip service to the ideals of accuracy, factual reporting and informed responsible comment which, despite its handicaps, the *ancien régime* press had struggled to fashion.[61] Yet a new role for the press had also emerged, that of the campaigning journalist — not the detached observer of events, but a participant in them, using his newspaper not as an analytical mirror held up to the face of reality, but as a weapon in political campaigns. Mirabeau was the first to achieve this, with the successful and defiant launch of his *États-Généraux* (later *Courrier de Provence*) in May of 1789, but by the end of the year a host of others had overtaken him in their definition of the role, most notably on the radical left where Marat, Loustallot and Desmoulins had already made their mark. Brissot had outlined its parameters in his first prospectus for the *Patriote français* in March, when he had written:[62]

> We have to look for an alternative to pamphlets for the continuous education of Frenchmen, in a form that will be both cheap and interesting. This alternative is a political newspaper or gazette; it is the only way of educating a large nation, unaccustomed to freedom or to reading, yet looking to free itself from ignorance and slavery.

It was Desmoulins who captured the mood best, however, in the second number of his *Révolutions de France et de Brabant*:[63]

> Here I am a journalist, and it is a rather fine role. No longer is it a wretched and mercenary profession, enslaved by the government. Today in France it is the journalist who holds the tablets, the album of the censor, and who inspects the senate, the consuls and the dictator himself.

The journalist was now a participant in the political process. He had finally entered Aladdin's cave.

Notes

1. *Les politiques du galetas* (Paris, undated).
2. Ralph W. Greenlaw, 'Pamphlet literature in France during the period of the aristocratic revolt (1787–1788)', *Journal of Modern History*, 1957,

pp. 352–3. See also *Pour et contre sur la liberté de la presse, ou Dialogue entre une auteur et un censeur, sur l'objet le plus important dont puissent s'occuper les états-généraux; avec une digression sur la noblesse. Par un homme du Tiers-état* (Paris, 1789): 'An immense quantity of brochures has been pouring out for the last six months! Just a catalogue of them would make up a large volume. What reader would be brave enough to wade through all this drivel?' A catalogue of several hundred brochures, drawn up by François Furet, can be found in the *Salle des Inventaires* in the Archives Nationales.

3. Mallet du Pan, *Mémoires et correspondance*, I (Paris, 1851), pp. 130, 153; *Remerciement des librairies de la rue Saint-Jacques* (Paris, 1789), B.N. 8°Lb³⁹ 6788; A.N. V¹ 551, letter of 14 March 1789. For the decree of 5 July, see *Recueil général des anciennes lois françaises, depuis l'an 420 jusqu'à la révolution de 1789. Par MM. Jourdan, Isambert, Dacrusy. Du 1 janvier 1785 au 5 mai 1789* (Paris, 1827), pp. 601–4.

4. A.N. V¹ 551, 28 May 1789. See also A. Söderjhelm, *Le régime de la presse pendant la révolution française*, 2 vols (Helsingfors and Paris, 1900–1), I, pp. 41–2; Marcel Vogne, *La presse périodique en Franche-Comté des origines à 1870*, 3 vols (Besançon, 1977–8), I, pp. 34–5; Michel Lheritier, *La révolution à Bordeaux dans l'histoire de la révolution française. La fin de l'ancien régime et la préparation des États-Généraux, 1787–1789* (Paris, 1942), pp. 49, 97–8.

5. *Sur la liberté de la presse, imité de l'Anglois de Milton. Par le comte de Mirabeau. A Londres 1788* (Paris, undated), pp. 63–4.

6. Pierre Grosclaude, *Malesherbes, témoin et interprète de son temps* (Paris, 1961), pp. 665–83; Söderjhelm, *Le régime de la presse*, I, pp. 44–7. For other pamphlets, see *abbé* Pétiot, *Liberté de la presse. Mars 1789* (Paris, undated); *Pour et contre sur la liberté de la presse* . . . , B.N. 8° LB³⁹ 7275; *De la liberté de la presse par M.S. ***. A Paris. Dans le temps de la convocation des États-Généraux de 1789* (Paris, 1789), B.N. 8° LB³⁹ 6787.

7. *Mémoire sur la liberté de la presse. Suivi de quelques autres mémoires concernant la librairie* (Paris, undated), B.N. 8° Lb³⁹ 6786, pp. 108–9.

8. C. Bellanger, *Histoire générale de la presse française. Tome I. Des origines à 1814* (Paris, 1969), p. 419; *Archives parlementaires de 1787 à 1860*. 1ᵉʳ série, 94 vols (Paris, 1867–1985), II, p. 759; for a useful collection of *cahiers*, see *Archives parlementaires*, vols I–VI; for an analysis, Albert Desjardins, *Les cahiers des états-généraux en 1789 et la législation criminelle* (Paris, 1883), Chapter vi.

9. Soderjhelm, *Le régime de la presse*, I, pp. 61–71; Vogne, *La presse périodique*, I, p. 33. See also the favourable attitude of the nobility of Lyons in L. Trenard, *Lyon de l'encyclopédie au préromantisme*, 2 vols (Lyon, 1958), I, p. 139.

10. Ibid. (Trenard). See also Daniel Ligou, *Cahiers de doléances du tiers-état du pays et jugerie de Rivière-Verdun pour les états-généraux de 1789* (Gap, 1961), p. 18; M.-T. Blanc-Rouquette, *La presse et l'information à Toulouse, des origines à 1789* (Toulouse, 1969), pp. 205–6; Paul Bois, *Cahiers de doléances du tiers-état de la sénéchaussée de Château-du-Loir pour les états-généraux de 1789* (Paris, 1960), pp. 22, 54–5.

11. A.N. V¹ 549 and 551. For Le Scène-Desmaison, who had applied for a privilege on several occasions previously, without success, and was refused permission on 3.April 1789 for a *Journal de toutes les Académies* on the grounds that it would infringe on the monopoly of the *Journal des Savants*: see his *Feuille politique* (B.N. 8° Lc² 158), xxii, p. 6.

12. Jean Gaultier, *Un grand témoin de la révolution et de l'empire. Volney* (Paris, 1959), pp. 71-7.

13. *Le Héraut de la nation sous les auspices de la patrie*, i, pp. 1-2; see also R.R. Palmer, 'A revolutionary republican: M.A.B. Mangourit', *William and Mary Quarterly*, vol. ix (1952), pp. 483-96.

14. Vogne, *La presse périodique*, I, pp. 55-6; there was also a brief *Bulletin hebdomadaire* in Rioms during the winter of 1788-9, featuring both local and international news, the work of a friend of the future *conventionnel* Gilbert Romme, Amable Faucon. It appears to have ceased by the summer of 1789; see A. Galante Garonne, *Gilbert Romme: histoire d'un révolutionnaire 1750-1795* (Paris, 1971), pp. 150-1.

15. *Le Patriote français ou journal libre, impartial et national, par une société de citoyens*, undated; M. Tourneux, *Bibliographie de l'histoire de Paris pendant la révolution française*, 5 vols (Paris, 1900-13), II, pp. 500-1.

16. Pierre Laborie, *Étude sur le Patriote français. Journal libre, impartial et national par une société de citoyens et dirigé par J.-P. Brissot* (Diplôme d'Études Supérieures, Toulouse), 1960, p. 3. For Buisson's disclaimer, see A.N. V^1 551, letter of 13 April, in which he cites from a letter written to him by Brissot, dated that same day, which bears all the signs of a pre-arranged agreement:

> Please find enclosed the prospectus of a journal, on which I have given your name as receiving subscriptions, and which I intend to have distributed soon. I do not think that it will cause you any difficulty as, by putting my own name to it, I have made myself responsible for anything that appears in it.

A letter from Maissemy, Director of the Book Trade, to Barentin, Keeper of the Seals, dated 15 April, also reflects government intransigence:

> It is without doubt the ultimate in audacity, encouraged by our failure to be more severe until now. It is obvious from the prospectus that it would be a highly dangerous paper, and your lordship will remember that he has persistently refused consent for any journal of this kind . . . (ibid).

17. Tourneux, *Bibliographie*, II, p. 502.

18. A.N. V^1 551, *Arrêt du Conseil* of 7 May 1789; Jean-Sylvain Bailly, *Mémoires d'un témoin de la révolution* (Slatkine Reprints: Geneva, 1975), I, pp. 38-41; *Première lettre du comte de Mirabeau à ses commettants*, p. 1. It is interesting to note that Necker's protégé, Mangourit, responded to Mirabeau's attack in his *Le Héraut de la nation*, no. 42, pp. 657-61.

19. A.N. V^1 551, letter of 19 May. The *Journal de Paris* and *Mercure* immediately started political reports, the former employing Dominique-Joseph Garat, who rapidly proved to be a master of the craft: see below, Chapter 2.

20. Ibid., and A.N. V^1 553.

21. A.N. V^1 551, letter of 27 May to M. Martignac in Rennes:

> The head of the judiciary asks you to use all the means in your power,

and in that of the officers of the *chambre syndicale*, to prevent the circulation of these kinds of publications, and especially the periodicals, the King having decided that only the Parisian press will be allowed to publish information on the Estates General, unless the representatives themselves wish to supervise and be responsible for another. You will realise that it is most essential to ensure that this decision is respected, and to stop any transgression of it.

For the papers concerned, see below, pp. 31-2.

22. A.N. V^1 551, letter of Cortot, 14 May 1789; Eugene Hatin, *Histoire politique et littéraire de la presse en France*, IV (Paris, 1859-61), p. 132; P. Raphael, 'Panckoucke et son programme de journal officiel en 1789', *La révolution française*, vol. lxiv (1913), pp. 216-19.

23. *The great Frenchman and the little Genevese. Translated from Etienne Dumont's Souvenirs sur Mirabeau by Lady Seymour* (London, 1904), pp. 69-70.

24. *Révolutions de France et de Brabant*, i, p. 5 and 36; ii, p. 89.

25. *Journal politique national*, 1e abonnement, no. 7; 2e abonnement, no. 7.

26. A.N. V^1.549, pièce 2.

27. W.J. Murray, *The right wing press in the French Revolution* (London, 1986), pp. 12-22; Frances Acomb, *Mallet du Pan (1749-1800). A career in political journalism* (Durham, NC, 1973), p. 207ff.; see also A. Chuquet, 'Les journaux de Paris en 1789', *Feuilles d'Histoire du XVIIe au XXe siècle*, I (1909), pp. 217-27. The *Journal général de la cour et de la ville* was founded by a future marshall of France, Brune, who in 1789 was a young law student, hopeful of a literary career. He appears to have purchased a small press and launched the paper, enlisting the help of a somewhat disreputable pamphleteer, Jacques Louis Gautier de Syonnet. In December the two men quarrelled and, from 16th of the month the paper passed into Gautier's hands: see Hatin, *Histoire politique*, VIII, pp. 78-90; and Leopold Monrayssé, 'Le Journal général de la cour et de la ville et le polémique antirévolutionnaire (16 septembre 1789-10 août 1792)', *La Révolution française*, 61 (1911), pp. 392-4.

28. For a sensitive analysis of the reactions of one provincial journalist, see René Gérard, *Un journal de province sous la révolution. Le 'journal de Marseille' de Ferréol Beaugeard, 1781-1797* (Paris, 1964), pp. 82-4.

29. De Maricourt, 'Le journalisme à Senlis à la fin du XVIIIe siècle, *Comité Archéologique de Senlis. Comptes-rendus et Mémoires*, 1862-3, pp. 56-8; M.L.J. Alary, 'Histoire politique littéraire de la presse périodique dans le Bourbonnais et dans le département de l'Allier 1782 à 1864', *Bulletin de la Société d'Émulation du Département de l'Allier (Sciences, Arts et Belles-Lettres)*, IX (1864), pp. 69-85.

30. Nadine Grain, 'Les Affiches de Picardie (1787-1793)', *Revue du Nord*, liv (1972), pp. 19-23; H. Ribière, *Essai sur l'histoire de l'imprimerie dans le département de l'Yonne, et spécialement Auxerre, suivi du catalogue des livres, brochures et pièces imprimés dans cette ville, de 1580 à 1857* (Auxerre, 1858), pp. 90-1.

31. See copies of the *Affiches du Maine* in B.N. 8° Lc^9 94bis; Monnoyer remained neutral throughout the decade, leaving it to his son to try political

journalism (see below, p. 171). For Montargis, see H. Stein, *La presse locale à Montargis au XVIIIe siècle* (Orléans, 1887).

32. A. Dubuc, 'Le Journal de Normandie avant et durant les États-Généraux, *Actes du 89ᵉ Congrès national des sociétés savantes* (Lyons, 1964), I, p. 403; Anatole de Roumejoux, *Bibliographie générale du Périgord*, 2 vols (Slatkine reprint: Geneva, 1971), I, pp. 3–5.

33. Diane Escamez, *La presse périodique à Toulouse de 1789 à 1794* (Mémoire de maîtrise: Toulouse, 1969), pp. 5–6, 47–8. Broulhiet had a past history of trading in forbidden books: see A.N. V^1 551.

34. *Affiches d'Angers*, 26 (23 June 1789), p. 109; 63 (31 Oct. 1789), p. 263. For the *Affiches* prior to 1789, see F. Lebrun, 'Une source d'histoire sociale: la presse provinciale à la fin de l'ancien régime. Les 'Affiches d'Angers' (1773–1789)', *Le Mouvement Social*, XL (1962), pp. 56–73; details on Mame, a central figure in Angers press history during the decade, can be found in *abbé* Emile Pasquier and Victor Dauphin, *Imprimeurs et libraires d'Anjou* (Angers, 1932), pp. 178–180; and Céléstin Port, *Dictionnaire historique, géographique et biographique de Maine-et-Loire*, 3 vols (Paris, 1876), II, p. 582.

35. *Journal général de l'Orléanais*, xxvii (3 July 1789), p. 131; xxix (17 July 1789), p. 129; xxx (24 July 1789), p. 133; li (18 December 1789), p. 221; *Courrier d'Avignon*, 1 Jan. 1790, p. 1; Musée Calvet, Fonds Chobaut, Ms. 5989, pièce 283.

36. Gérard, *Un journal de province*, pp. 74–80.

37. *Affiches de Dauphiné*, 10 and 13 August, and 23 November 1789; Giroud was an enthusiastic supporter of Mounier and the monarchien party, and was finally closed down by the Municipality in the summer of 1792: see Vital Chomel, *Histoire de Grenoble* (Toulouse, 1976), p. 226; and below, Chapter 3.

38. Xavier Maeght, *La presse dans le département du Nord sous la révolution française* (Thèse de troisième cycle: Lille, 1971), pp. 246–9.,

39. *Affiches de Poitou*, 11 June 1789, p. 96; 18 June, p. 101; 13 August, p. 129; 19 Nov., p. 185; see also René Perlat, *Le journalisme poitevin. Coup d'oeil historique* (Poitiers, 1898), pp. 16–19.

40. Georges Clause, 'Le premier journal champenois, le 'Journal de Rheims' de Havé au cours de la révolution française', *Mémoires de la Société d'Agriculture, Commerce, Sciences et Arts de la Marne*, 1973, p. 191–3.

41. *Journal de Nismes*, 28 May 1789, p. 179; 17 Dec., pp. 427–8.

42. B.M. Grenoble, 013802 and Jd 752; Colomb de Batines and Olivier Jules, *Mélanges biographiques et bibliographiques relatifs à l'histoire du Dauphiné* (Valence-Paris, 1837), I, pp. 56–8; H. Rousset, *La presse à Grenoble. Histoire et physionomie, 1700–1900* (Grenoble, 1900), pp. 5–6.

43. *Bulletin de l'Assemblée Nationale*, 12 September 1789:

This journal is much sought after in Paris, and should be as popular in the provinces. It has the advantage of being a postal delivery ahead of all other papers, including the *Journal de Paris* and *Patriote français*, and of reporting the same events as them a day or two in advance.

For Haener, see Albert Troux, *La vie politique dans le département de la Meurthe, d'août 1792 à octobre 1795* (Nancy, 1936), I, p. 394.

44. *Courrier de Villeneuve-lès-Avignon*, 9 Dec. 1789, p. 21; copies of all the paper's various titles are in Musée Calvet, 8° 2243-4 and 26.624; see also E. Requien, *Bibliographie des journaux publiés à Avignon, et dans le département de la Vaucluse* (Avignon, 1837), pp. 13–16. For postal and subscription arrangements, see *Courrier de Villeneuve-les-Avignon*, xxiv (6 Sept. 1789) and xxxviii (15 Sept. 1789) The practice of reprinting Parisian papers did not die out easily; as late as January 1791 the *Journal de Paris* was still being reprinted in Nantes, blended with articles taken from other papers, as the *Courrier de la veille de Paris à Nantes:* Réné Kerviler, *Essai d'une bibliographie des publications périodiques de la Bretagne. 4ᵉ fasc., Loire-Inférieure* (Paris, 1898), p. 21.

45. See *Le Livre du centenaire du journal des débats, 1787-1799* (Paris, 1889), pp. 1-6; and Ulysse Rouchon, *Un fondateur du Journal des débats, Jean-Baptiste Grenier* (Paris, 1925), pp. 27-30. Copies of editions printed locally in July and August are in A.D. Puy-de-Dôme, L6389. For the wider background, see G. Lefebvre, *The coming of the French Revolution* (New York, 1947), pp. 73-4.

46. G. Rouanet, 'La corréspondance de Bretagne', *Annales révolutionnaires*, X (1918), pp. 542-9; see also P.M. Juret, *La presse à Rennes* (Typewritten ms., 1964), p. 8.

47. Copy consulted in B.N. 8° Lc² 4006 see also Réné Kerviler, *Loire-Inférieure*, p. 15.

48. *A Messieurs des communes de la province d'Anjou,* (undated); see also Benjamin Bois, *La vie scolaire et les créations intellectuelles en Anjou pendant la révolution (1789-1799)* (Paris, 1929), pp. 165-6; E. Quéruau-Lamerie, 'Notice sur les journaux d'Angers pendant la révolution', *Revue d'Anjou*, n.s., xxiv (1892), pp. 146-8. The first edition of the *Corréspondance* appeared on 9 June 1789 and it lasted until 1793. One of its editors, J.-B, Leclerc, was no stranger to publication, having published two pamphlets in 1789 in an effort to get elected (see Port, *Dictionnaire historique*, II, p. 474). For Brest, see Y. Le Gallo, *Bibliographie de la presse française . 29, Finistère* (Paris, 1973), p. 10.

49. Jean-Joseph Lebon, *La presse montalbanaise des origines au début du dix-neuvième siècle* (Mémoire de maîtrise: Toulouse, 1972), pp. 91-2 and 108-9: 'Teulière's newspaper speaks for the wealthy and very conservative sections of society, which are profoundly catholic; in other words, the nobility, clergy and bourgeoisie.' See also Daniel Ligou, *La première année de la révolution vue par un témoin (1789-1790). Les 'bulletins' de Poncet-Delpech député du Quercy aux États-Généraux de 1789* (Paris, 1961), p. 7.

50. Jules Andrieu, *Histoire de l'imprimerie en Agenais depuis l'origine jusqu'a nos jours* (Paris-Agen, 1886), pp. 100-3; Robert Marquant, *Aux origines de la presse agenaise: le 'Journal patriotique de l'Agenais' 1789-1792* (Agen, undated; tirage à part de la Revue de l'Agenais, 1945-7), pp. 7-11. For two further examples, in Grenoble and Troyes, see *Journal des États-généraux, tenu par la députation du Dauphiné*, 6 nos (B.M. Grenoble, 013785); and Henri Diné, 'Le journal des états-généraux de Camusat de Belcombe, député du Tiers de la ville de Troyes (6 mai-8 août 1789)', *A.h.r.f.*, 37 (1965), p. 257-69.

51. H. Ribière, *Essai sur l'histoire de l'imprimerie dans le département de l'Yonne* (Auxerre, 1858), pp. 90-1; B.M. Rouen, Norm M904; Trenard,

Lyon de l'encyclopédie, II, pp. 252–3; B.N., N.A.F. 6241, Papiers Roland, iv; Auguste Du Boys, 'Calendriers, annuaires, journaux. Revues et recueils périodiques du Limousin', *Annuaire de la Haute-Vienne*, 1854, p. 313; Paul Ducourtieux, 'Contribution à l'histoire des périodiques limousins', *Le Bibliophile Limousin*, 1 (Jan. 1905), pp. 1–3; A. Ronsin, *Les périodiques lorrains antérieurs à 1800* (Nancy, 1964), pp. 71–2; B.N. 8° Lc^{11} 989(33); B.M. Grenoble Jd33; B.N. and U. Strasbourg, M109.389.

52. A.N. V^1 552, letter of 12 June 1789.

53. A.N. V^1 553, letters of 21 August and undated, 1789; and 17 Sept. and 12 Nov. 1789. See also E. Labadie, *La presse à Bordeaux pendant la révolution* (Bordeaux, 1910), p. 24.

54. A.N. V^1 552, letter of 14 August 1789. See also the response of administrators to a letter from a M. Alveruhe in Montpellier, sending in on 11 November a letter announcing his intention of starting a *Mémorial politique et littéraire*: ' . . . nothing to be done . . . It is difficult to recommend any decision on this, as M. Alveruhe is not really asking for one' (ibid.). Or, on the next day, comments written in the margin of a prospectus of a *Courrier bordelais* sent in from Bordeaux by Bernadau: 'The note does not ask for any permission; all it seems to contain is the wish to offer the author's respects to his lordship, and to ask for his good wishes and protection.' (ibid.).

55. A.N. V^1 553, letter of 9 September 1789.

56. Ibid., letter of 17 November 1789. The first provincial paper to ignore the censor appears to have been the *Journal de Saintes*, whose censor went to Versailles as a locally elected member of the Second Estate in April and, when the *lieutenant général de police* in Saintes was appointed substitute, its owner and editor, Bourignon, refused to accept him because of previous conflicts (ibid., letter of 13 June 1789). Elsewhere *Affiches* dropped their censors in October (Toulouse and Angers) or December (Metz).

57. A.N. V^1 552, letter of 12 December 1789.

58. G. Clause, 'Le journalisme à Chalons-sur-Marne en 1790 et 1791', *Mémoires de la Société d'Agriculture, Commerce, Sciences et Arts du Département de la Marne*, 89 (1974), p. 309; A. Douarche, *Les tribunaux civils de Paris*, 2 vols (Paris, 1905), I, p. 94. A.N. V^1 553, letter of 9 September 1789; V^1 552, undated letters (Sept. 1789).

59. A.N. V^1 553, ms. note of 12 November 1789.

60. A. Tuetey, *Répertoire générale des sources manuscrites de l'histoire de Paris pendant la révolution française*, 11 vols (Paris, 1890–1914), II, p. 379; *Requête des nouveaux imprimeurs et librairies: contre les ennemis de la liberté, et les injustes persécutions qu'ils éprouvent journellement; à la Nation* (Paris, undated), B.N. 8° Lb^{39} 8224. Charles Nusse, *Histoire de la presse*, IV, 1789–1815 (B.N. N.A.F. 23114) p. 27. On the hesitations of provincial printers, see P. Vaillandet, 'Les débuts de la société des amis de la liberté de la presse', *A.h.r.f.*, VI (1926), pp. 83–4; and *Mémoire pour Jean-Georges Treuttel, citoyen français à Strasbourg, concernant une imprimerie à établir dans sa maison pour l'exécution de ses deux gazettes* (Strasbourg, 1790), B.N. Q 1551.

61. See Pierre Retat, 'Les journaux de 1789: quelques perspectives

d'ensemble' (unpublished ms.) pp. 10-13; and Suzanne Tucoo-Chala, 'Presse et vérité sous l'ancien régime', *Revue du Nord*, vol. lxvi, no. 261-2 (1984), pp. 713-21.

62. *Le patriote français, prospectus*, 16 March 1789.
63. *Révolutions de France et de Brabant*, ii, pp. 46-7.

2

The Paradise of Freedom:
Paris and the Provinces, 1790–1791

Between the summer of 1789 and the completion of the constitution in September 1791, the French press enjoyed a period of
unprecedented political freedom. Combined with low publishing
costs and intense political interest, this resulted in a rapid growth
in the number of newspapers on the market. In Paris alone over
300 new titles were published during 1790, and almost as many
again during the first nine months of 1791. In the provinces the
total probably reached 200 over the same 21-month period. Many
were short-lived, collapsing sometimes after their prospectus or,
more often, after the first few numbers; yet a significant number
survived for months or years, to find a secure foothold in the market.
The result, as one pamphleteer lamented in 1790, was a bewildering
choice of titles, but much greater freedom of choice and style.[1]

In both Paris and provincial France there were daily newspapers;
many others that published twice, three or four times weekly; and
several weekly, fortnightly and monthly reviews. Some provided
hard news, some specialised in analysis, several were little more
than successive political pamphlets which carried on the pre-
revolutionary traditions of Grub Street, while many attempted to
provide the balance of information, comment and diversion which
is the hallmark of the present-day press. Serious journals vied with
a raucous popular press, and the views of the radical left rivalled
those of the counter-revolutionary right. Neither were minority
groups neglected, for the illiterate, patois speakers, public func-
tionaries, merchants, women, National Guards, peasants, priests,
paupers and pariahs were all targeted by different editors, anxious
to find a clientele. Yet if all tastes were covered, the core of the
press in these years was concerned with the central political issues
of the day: with the drafting of the constitution, the powers of the

King and his ministers, the administrative reorganisation of the kingdom, the religious reforms of the civil constitution of the clergy, the rivalry of competing political groups and ideologies, and the problems of food and social stability. It is the development of this political press, in both Paris and the provinces, that this chapter is concerned to trace.

The principle of press freedom, snatched from the wreckage of the *ancien régime* over the summer of 1789, was enshrined in article 11 of the Declaration of the Rights of Man in late August, an article which, like so many of the Declaration's other articles, stated the general principle, while leaving its detailed application to subsequent legislation. 'Free expression of thought and opinions' were therefore asserted to be 'one of the most precious rights of man'; as a consequence, all citizens were to be able to 'speak, write and publish freely'. However, this right, in the words of the Declaration, was to be 'subject to the penalties for the abuse of this freedom provided for by the law'.[2] This last phrase proved to be the stumbling block, for previous press regulations had collapsed during the preceding months, and the problem of drafting a new definition of 'abuses' was to bedevil the National Assembly for the next two years. The question was raised frequently by deputies, usually as the result of a particularly provocative article or press campaign, but on only three occasions did discussion come close to legislation.

The first was in late January 1790 when, in response to mounting concern at the growth of political *libelles*, the *abbé* Sièyes brought forward a detailed set of proposals from the *comité de constitution*; but the initial welcome that they received rapidly faded during the course of debate and they were quietly shelved and forgotten. In the following July and August the right-wing deputy, Malouet, briefly succeeded in persuading his colleagues to vote through a decree designed to curb the excesses of the radical press, but after second thoughts it was quickly withdrawn. A year later, on 18 July 1791, in the aftermath of the massacre at the Champ de Mars, emergency decrees were swiftly voted through, restricting both the radical and counter-revolutionary press. However, although they led to the arrest of a number of journalists, and drove others such as Marat and Desmoulins into temporary hiding, they too proved short-lived and were withdrawn by an amnesty in mid-September.[3]

On all three occasions it is quite clear that, although a majority of deputies clearly wanted legislation to punish seditious or libellous articles — as indeed the majority of *cahiers de doléances* favouring press freedom had requested — they were unable to agree on how to define such articles in law, without running the danger of stifling legitimate political criticism. The whole issue was not made easier by the fact that until 1797, no distinction was made between newspaper legislation and pamphlet or book legislation: all three were lumped together as printed works, and hence regarded as part and parcel of the same principle of freedom of expression. Thus, although many deputies wanted more control exerted over *libelles*, fewer wanted that legislation to affect newspapers and fewer still to affect printed books: the memory of the *ancien régime* was too close for that. Moreover, there was a distinct reluctance on the part of most deputies to entrust the surviving *ancien régime* courts — which stayed in place until the autumn of 1790 — with enforcement of a press law which, however carefully worded, they might interpret in a manner suited to their own politically conservative views. There was consequently much talk and little action. With few exceptions, right-wing deputies and pamphleteers were adamant on the need for legislation, primarily to protect the central institutions of the state, and in particular the monarchy and its ministers, from corrosive criticism, but also to prevent the erosion of religion and public morality. Without such protection, order would disintegrate into anarchy, with no one willing to risk reputation and life by taking on ministerial positions. As Malouet argued in a denunciation of Marat during the summer of 1791:

> What stability is there in a government when patriotic writers, friends of the people, are the ones who condemn the head of state to ridicule and scorn, who defame those who respect him, who denounce as infamous and consign to public vengeance any legislator who does not fall in with majority opinion . . . who constantly summon people to arms; or who call for five or six hundred executions?

It was an argument which placed a premium on social order and stability, and which could cite in its support the opinion expressed in the great majority of *cahiers de doléances* favourable to press liberty, almost all of which had favoured some kind of residual controls.

Left-wing opinion, on the other hand, most forcefully articulated by Robespierre and Pétion, but backed up by the Cordeliers club and many radical journalists, opposed the need for any law at all. It argued that any legislation to protect the state from sedition or its agents from libel would be used by the courts to stifle legitimate political criticism and make a nonsense of open political debate. Times were exceptional: national reconstruction was impossible without free speech, and enlightened public opinion was the ultimate safeguard — as Pétion argued:[5]

> One of the greatest benefits of press freedom is the constant surveillance of government officials, opening up their conduct of affairs to public scrutiny, exposing their intrigues and warning society of the danger; it acts like a watchful sentry, guarding the state day and night.

Moreover, adapting the physiocrats' views of the economy to the world of ideas, they argued that criticisms would always find their own level: if they were true, they served the public interest; if not, they discredited their author and exonerated their target. In Robespierre's idyllically optimistic words: 'Can you not see that by the ordinary course of events errors are always banished and truth emerges triumphant? Leave good and bad opinions an equal freedom, for only the former are destined to survive.' Neither did he concede the need for a press law to cover libellous attacks on individuals, for libel was covered by the civil law anyway, whether spoken or written.[6]

Between these two diametrically opposed positions most deputies swayed one way or the other, depending on the prevailing political atmosphere and the specific instance of press abuse under discussion. It was only in late August 1791, when the final details of the constitution were being hammered out, in the atmosphere of political reaction following on the massacre of the Champ de Mars, that legislation was finally passed. In two brief articles, passed on 22 and 23 August, it defined a range of press 'offences' covering all published material, including incitement to commit illegal acts, the encouragement of resistance to lawful authority, the discrediting of public officials, and libel. It also stipulated that all cases be tried before a jury, in the relevant civil or criminal departmental court. In theory this was a significant advance from the practices of the *ancien régime*, safeguarding the principle of the right to publish without prior permission or censorship, and introducing jury trial, in which juries, unlike their contemporary English counterparts, would be called upon to decide both whether a statement was libellous, and whether the accused was guilty of publishing it. However, in practice, press freedom had already gone too far for its provisions to be easily accepted. Bitterly contested by the left during the course of debate, it was to be widely ignored and rarely used.[7]

The lack of adequate legislation before August 1791 did not mean that the press was totally free from controls. In the first place, until the summer of 1790, the *ancien-régime* courts and police authorities did remain in existence, ready and willing to prosecute, when asked to do so by the appropriate authorities, where they believed that articles posed a threat to public order. In Paris this meant the *Châtelet*, the police authority and royal court responsible for the enforcement of the civil and criminal law. In early October 1789, at the request of the Paris Commune it went into action against Marat. Since mid-September, in several issues of his *Ami du peuple*, Marat had denounced officials of the Commune, as well as its *comité des subsistances*, accusing them of malpractice and dishonesty. On 7 October the Commune's patience finally snapped, and it denounced that day's edition to the *procureur du roi*. The *Châtelet* duly impounded Marat's presses and ordered his arrest, but Marat went into hiding in Versailles, before returning to Paris in early November and finding refuge in the radical stronghold of the Cordeliers district. When an attempt was made to arrest him there on 22 January 1790, the district's National Guard obstructed the *Châtelet* officers, giving him time to escape and flee to England, where he stayed for the next four months. Marat, not for the last time, had evaded the law.[8]

During the spring and summer of 1790 two right-wing papers, the *Journal général de la cour et de la ville* and the *Gazette de Paris*, were both convicted and fined for libel in civil cases — the *Journal général* for insulting the inhabitants of Caen, and the *Gazette de Paris* for criticising army regiments in Brest and Britanny. It was on the left-wing press, however, that the heaviest blows fell. In January 1790 Desmoulins, Prudhomme and Gorsas were convicted of libelling Charles-Henri Sansom, the public executioner of Paris, whom they had accused of hosting counter-revolutionary meetings, and were ordered to retract publicly. Over the next six months three further civil cases were brought against Desmoulins, for articles in the *Révolutions de France et de Brabant*, all of which went against him and resulted in verdicts which offered the invidious choice between a public retraction or a crushing fine. Then, in June 1790, the supposed editor of the *Orateur du peuple*, Martel, was arrested on the *Châtelet*'s authority, for publishing an article, entitled 'Horribles manoeuvres du comité autrichien des Tuileries', which questioned the loyalty of the King to the constitution. The police interrogations were long drawn out, attracting widespread public attention, and the case against Martel finally collapsed when it emerged that he had merely been acting as a front man for the paper's real editor, Fréron. It nevertheless aroused considerable concern amongst radical journalists over their future freedom of action, for it appeared that the *Châtelet* was hounding the radical press, largely on its own authority, to suppress political criticism of either the King or the royalist right.[9]

The zeal shown by the *Châtelet* was much rarer in the provinces, and only the *chambre des vacations* of the Parlement of Toulouse matched it. In January 1790, it ordered the arrest and trial of the editor of the *Journal universel et affiches de Toulouse*, Broulhiet, for reprinting several polemical articles critical of the nobility and clergy, from Desmoulins' *Révolutions de France et de Brabant*. Broulhiet's two lines of defence — namely, that the Declaration of Rights guaranteed press freedom, and that the offending articles had gone unpunished in Paris, where the *Révolutions de France et de Brabant* was published — cut no ice with the Toulouse magistrates, who clearly regarded themselves as the last bastion of public order. He was found guilty and fined 1,000 *livres*, to be paid to charity, and it was 18 months before the Assembly got round to overturning the verdict and returning his money.[10] Elsewhere, the only case that came to trial was in Lyons where, in May 1791, several copies of the radical *Journal de Lyon* were seized on the orders of the Department and denounced to the criminal court of the Rhône-et-Loire for alleged incitement to civil war and subversion of the constitution. The court prudently ducked the issue and, deciding that the charges amounted to reason, referred the matter to the National Assembly. The *Journal de Lyon* was allowed to continue, and the Assembly buried the affair beneath the paperwork of the *comité de constitution*.[11]

By the summer of 1790 many radical journalists nevertheless feared that the newly won prize of press freedom was being eroded by the courts, and in particular by the *Châtelet*, which, in apparent defiance of article 11 of the Declaration of Rights, was enforcing the law of libel and *ancien-régime* concepts of public order against them. Desmoulins, initially an ardent opponent of any press law, temporarily abandoned his opposition in June 1790 and called for the legislation provided for in article 11 to be brought in, so that journalists would at least know what they could and could not publish, and be free from arbitrary harassment:

At least during the *ancien régime* I knew that I could not speak my thoughts without being buried alive in the dungeons of the Bastille; but today the practice of misleading patriotic journalists and encouraging them to speak their thoughts freely, only in order to prosecute and imprison them, is rather like the behaviour of the crocodile, which imitates the human voice and childrens' whimpers in order to attract passers by into its trap.[12]

Loustallot, political editor of the *Révolutions de Paris*, echoed his fears and argued that the partiality of the *Châtelet* might force Parisian journalists to seek refuge in the provinces. The two men therefore organised a *société des amis de la liberté de la presse*, to co-ordinate a campaign of mutual defence. This gathered support from a number of journalists and radicals both in Paris and the provinces, and held its first meeting in the Cordeliers Club, under the chairmanship of Danton, in mid-July 1790, pledged to campaigning against the restrictive attitude of the courts and to present a 'mathematical' defence of press freedom to the National Assembly. However, the replacement of the *Châtelet* and introduction of the new court system in the autumn of 1790 took the heat out of the issue and the club petered out in the following October.[13] No more criminal prosecutions were initiated against the press before the Champ de Mars massacre in the following July, with the exception of Lyons, and the only private prosecution, taken out against Marat in January 1791, ended in ignominious failure.[14]

Yet the courts were not the only restraint on the press, for the Paris Municipality also played a role, attempting periodically to supervise the sale and distribution of newspapers within its own jurisdiction, in the interests of public order. In late July 1789, for example, it ordered all newspapers to carry the name of their printer and to have a circulation permit, issued by its own provisional police committee. This aroused a storm of protest from the radical press, which denounced it as back-door censorship, but appears to have been only intended as a means of ensuring that the identity of the publisher was available, in the case of prosecution for sedition or libel. In the event it lasted only until the end of September because the Municipality appears to have feared that permission to circulate might be interpreted as an endorsement of a paper's contents. Some attempt was also made to restrict the activity of street sellers — or *colporteurs* — whose numbers had risen rapidly over the summer months. On 20 July 1789 they were forbidden to call out the contents of brochures and newspapers, and this ban was reiterated on 1 September. On 20 December, after repeated complaints about their activity from a number of District authorities, a detailed regulation reduced their number to 300, providing for the issue of badges. and permits to legal operators, but this appears to have been largely ineffective over the next two years.[15] Colportage was frequently a part-time job, done by women and children to make ends meet, and they were unimpressed by the threat of prosecution. Moreover, it was a measure contested by many radical journalists, who argued that sale by the number brought newspapers within the reach of those unable to afford the more expensive — and more widespread — alternative of three-monthly or six-monthly subscriptions.[16]

Where legislation or administrative action was ineffective, intimidation often worked, although it tended to be used most frequently against the right-wing press. As early as September 1789 Mounier, leader of the *monarchiens*, complained that printers were loath to handle his pamphlets, during the bitter debates on the royal veto and upper house, because of threats of reprisals. Similar considerations forced Sabatier de Castres to move his *Journal politique et national* out of Paris and Versailles in the autumn, as distributors were afraid to handle it.[17] Mallet du Pan received threatening visitations in September 1789 for criticising Brissot in the *Mercure*, and another in November 1790, from self-styled representatives of patriotic societies from the Palais Royal, anxious that he should abandon criticism of the work of the Assembly and conform instead to the 'democratic' views of the majority. This he refused to do, losing little sleep over the incident, but his daughter suffered from insomnia for weeks.[18] Perhaps her thoughts were on the treatment already meted out to the counter-revolutionary press, for the bookseller Gattey, who specialised in counter-revolutionary material, had seen his premises in the Palais Royal raided on 21 May 1790 by a crowd which fumigated the shop with sugar and vinegar, then confiscated some 12,000 copies of the *Actes des Apôtres* and burnt them, along with counter-revolutionary pamphlets and books, in the gardens outside. The offices of the *Gazette de Paris* suffered a similar fate on the following day and only the intervention of the National Guard prevented further damage; its editor, Du Rozoi, had to suspend publication for a week. Sporadic acts of vandalism recurred later in 1790 and well into 1791, while in the climate of fear that followed the King's flight in late June 1791. Mallet du Pan prudently absented himself from the *Mercure* for several weeks and du Rozoi again ceased publication for two days.[19]

Occasional violence erupted in the provinces too. In Dijon, for example, the first number of the right-wing *Ami des bons citoyens* was publicly burnt by a group of local patriots outside its subscription office, when it appeared in December 1790, persuading it to close down. In Arras the owner of the *Journal général* left town early in 1791 after threats on her life, continuing publication elsewhere for the next 18 months.[20] In Limoges threats persuaded the *abbé* Lambertie, editor and owner of the *Feuille hebdomadaire*, to cease publication at the end of 1790, and abandon his defence of *monarchien* policies, while in Montauban, where sectarian animosity gave a biting edge to political divisions, the owner and editor of the *Journal national*, Vincent Teulières, had his bookshop ransacked in the middle of June 1791 by a crowd which burnt piles of his newspapers on the *place Trimond* outside. For his own safety, he moved to nearby Cahors, leaving behind his printshop manager, Jean Sagnes, to act as nominal editor; but the municipality moved in and closed down the paper and printshop in late September, on the flagrantly illegal pretext that Sagnes had no printer's *brevet* and was therefore not qualified to run the press.[21]

Incidents such as this, although overwhelmingly aimed against the right-wing press, were nevertheless the exception rather than the rule, and the political atmosphere for much of the Constituent Assembly remained free enough to encourage an extremely diverse press to develop. The numbers and variety of that press make only an impressionistic picture of it possible. First off the mark in Paris were a number of informational newspapers, many of them launched in the summer of 1789, which concentrated on reporting political news, and especially Assembly debates. Most of them were dailies, and because of the speed at which they worked, the consequent complexities of printing and delivery arrangements, and the size of their editorial and managerial staff, were large-scale businesses. The oldest established was an *ancien-régime* remnant, the *Journal de Paris*, the country's first daily paper dating from 1777, which successfully made the transition from the *ancien régime* to the revolution, by employing Dominique-Joseph Garat from late May 1789 onwards to edit its accounts of Assembly debates. Garat, a writer and journalist from the Panckoucke stable, stayed until the end of October 1791, by which time the newspaper had increased its daily sales to over 12,000; but although his own sympathies lay on the side of the revolution, the overall tone of the paper was by then slowly drifting towards the right. Under the editorial influence of Andre Chénier and Regnault Saint-Jean-d'Angély, it was subsequently to grow increasingly sympathetic to the *Feuillant* cause, and in the summer of 1792, after the dethronement of Louis XVI, was forced to suspend publication.[22]

Of those which started up during the summer and autumn of 1789, Barère's *Point du jour* dated from late June, and largely written by the deputy of Tarbes, was to last as a daily newspaper until the end of the Assembly. Even more durable was the *Courrier français* edited by Poncelin de la Roche Tilhac, another daily which, under a bewildering variety of titles, was to last until the autumn of 1797. The *Journal des débats*, edited by the three Auvergnat deputies, dated from late August, Panckoucke launched the *Moniteur* in late November and the *Gazette universelle*, edited by Pascal Boyer, who had already gained experience abroad on the *Courrier de l'Europe* and the *Gazette de Leyde*, and by Cerisier, reserve deputy for Bourg-en-Bresse at the National Assembly, first appeared on 1 December. In addition to its coverage of Assembly debates, it provided readers with Paris and court news, as well as foreign events taken from the Dutch, Italian, English, German and Spanish papers. It also claimed to draw on correspondents from 'the principal European cities', including Hamburg, Vienna, The Hague, London, Rome and Madrid.

Others started up in the more settled days of 1790 and the first half of 1791. In March of 1790, for example, a former bookseller from Lyons, J.-B. Duplain, who had already published a highly successful *Lettres au comte de B****, launched a *Courrier extraordinaire* which specialised in the reporting of Assembly debates and Jacobin club news, and provided express delivery to major provincial towns through a network of private coaches.[23] Another approach was that of the *Réviseur*, launched on 1 May 1790, which, in addition to a daily paper containing Assembly decrees, offered subscribers free access to its own reading room, where a range of newspapers was available. A year later four leading deputies of the National Assembly, Adrien Duport, the Lameth brothers and Barnave, concerned to stem the growth of political radicalism, joined together to found the *Logographe*, in order to get their views to a wider audience. In the detailed instructions that he drew up for the newspaper's editors, Barnave stressed that it was to be a paper for '. . . serious minds . . . men who want a genuine education . . .'. It would therefore abstain from polemics or satire and offer its readers instead the most detailed account yet of Assembly debates, provided by a *société logographique* that used an advanced note-taking technique, and a full account of diplomatic developments abroad.[24]

Several evening newspapers also concentrated on Assembly debates, often providing up-to-date coverage by publishing a first edition at around noon, which covered the morning's debates and was dispatched to provincial readers in the afternoon mail, then a second edition in the early evening which, in some cases, was on the streets within an hour or so of the conclusion of the day's session. One of the first was the *Postillon* launched by Mme Fontrouge and her father, Jean Calais, on 4 February 1790, and published from the *rue d'Argenteuil* and the *rue Basse-du-Rempart-de-la-Madeleine*, strategically close to the *salle du manège*. It was rivalled by a plethora of plagiarists over the following months, which latched on to its title and tried to share the popularity generated by its cheapness and speed. Calais took many to court and forced them to close down or change title, but they appear to have had little effect on his substantial sales figures. Another successful evening paper came six months later, the *Journal du soir*, launched by the Chaigneau brothers, from the *rue de Chartres*, which prided itself on being available within one and a half hours of the close of session. It owed much of its success to the willingness of the Chaigneaus to accept large value *assignat* notes in payment for subscriptions, giving as change the money taken in by colporteurs from street sales. At a time when no small *assignat* denominations were available, this proved an attractive bait for many. Like the *Postillon*, however, it had its work cut out, fighting off a host of plagiarists who tried to muscle in on its sales by copying both title and format.[25]

Few of these newspapers concentrated exclusively on Assembly debates: most supplemented them with reports from Paris and the provinces, news from abroad and — in some cases — cultural and commercial information too. Thus, the *Moniteur*, for example, in addition to its detailed reports on the National Assembly, carried daily columns on court events, news from Paris, the provinces, Europe and the colonies; accounts of the activities of various ministers; and a wide range of legal news, theatrical reviews and financial reports. Nevertheless, for most papers the key to success lay in the skill with which they covered Assembly debates. Almost all of them used notetakers to provide their basic material, and an editor-in-chief to write up the final copy for publication. His ability to put shape on to material was crucial to success. Several papers therefore used a deputy as editor-in-chief, because of his access to inside knowledge.[26] Gaultier de Biauzat, for example, deputy for the Auvergne, wrote the reports for the *Journal des débats*, and Barère provided the copy for his own *Point du jour*; Dinocheau, deputy from Blois, edited the *Courrier de Madon*, and Regnauld Saint-Jean-d'Angély the *Journal de Versailles*. Yet this was far from being an invariable rule. The reputation of the *Moniteur*, for example, was built on the talents of a young lawyer from Dijon, Hugues-Bernard Maret, who had come up to Paris in 1788 and attended the early sessions of the Estates General, working with a friend, Etienne Méjan, to write up a manuscript version of proceedings which achieved great success when read out in *salons*. From September onwards it appeared in published form as a *Bulletin*, and came to the attention of Panckoucke, anxious to provide the best possible Assembly coverage in the *Moniteur*. As a result, the *Bulletin* was incorporated into the *Moniteur* from February 1790 onwards, until Maret abandoned Assembly reporting some 18 months later to pursue a career that took him into politics, and a ministerial position under the Napoleonic Empire.[27]

Maret's success stemmed partly from his own swift style of note-taking, and partly from his ability to seize on a phrase, a pose, or some physical characteristic of the speaker, to give shape to debates. He was also one of the first reporters to provide readers with the names of each speaker, in heavier typeface, so that the visual monotony of the page was broken up as well. Another with similar talent was Garat in the *Journal de Paris*, who in his own words

> . . . prepared readers to witness a kind of dramatic scene, rather than a meeting of legislators. I gave a brief description of speakers before putting them into action, conveying all their opinions — although not always using their own expressions. I made words from their shouts, and opinions out of their frenzied gestures . . .[28]

This was a technique imitated by others, hoping, as the editor of the *Bulletin national* put it in early July 1789, that a reader would be able to imagine himself in the *salle du manège* itself, '. . . will follow the progress of opinions, discuss them himself and believe himself to be actually participating'. Nevertheless, there were others who turned their backs on this kind of approach and saw their role more as impartial reporters, providing the raw material from which readers could form their political views with no interpretative gloss. Gaultier promised the readers of the *Journal des débats* '. . . absolute impartiality, and scrupulous accuracy in all factual reports', while Le Hodey de Saultchevreuil provided the same to readers of his *Journal des États-Généraux*, and Mallet du Pan likewise to readers of the *Mercure*.[29]

If the informational press captured a sizeable market, the most spectacular growth came from the political press which was more concerned to argue a case and mount campaigns. On the left of the spectrum lay a range of titles which stretched from radical to. moderate, and included some of the best known and most influential titles of the whole decade. Amongst the radicals were a number of weeklies, such as Desmoulins' *Révolutions de France et de Brabant* and Prudhomme's *Révolutions de Paris*. Others, such as the *Mercure national* and *Père Duchesne*, appeared two or three times per week, and there were also several dailies, such as Marat's *Ami du peuple*, Fréron's *Orateur du peuple*, or Audouin's *Journal universel*. Their style and structures varied greatly. Prudhomme, for example, ran the *Révolutions de Paris* as a sophisticated and successful business enterprise, employing a large team of radical journalists — including, until his premature death in September 1790, one of the most celebrated of the whole decade, Elysée Loustalot — but imposing complete anonymity on them all, and exerting his own strong editorial control. The newspaper contained a great deal of news, including items from the provinces and abroad, as well as theatre and book reviews. Yet its main thrust, at least initially, came from Loustalot's leading articles, which campaigned on current democratic issues.[30]

The *Révolutions de France et de Brabant*, on the other hand, was essentially a one-man show, for Desmoulins wrote it single-handed until the summer of 1790, when he took on Stanislas Fréron to share the load. Desmoulins always carried much less news than the *Révolutions de Paris*, and some subscribers complained that he was too inclined to conduct his own political crusades at the expense of overall balance — but this was probably also one of the paper's main attractions, enlivened by Camille's own powerful literary style.[31] Marat's *Ami du peuple* was also a one-man operation, again with occasional help from Fréron, but its vitriolic style, combining denunciations of plots and treachery with libellous attacks on prominent political figures, put it into a different category, much closer to Fréron's own polemical *Orateur du peuple*, launched amidst controversy in early June 1790. Audouin, in the *Journal universel*, adopted a less polemical style, concentrating more on news and accounts of Assembly debates, while Hébert, in the *Père Duchesne*, once he had found a settled format and outlook at the beginning of 1791, was quite distinct from the others in his use of the mythical fairground figure, Père Duchesne. Foul-mouthed and familiar, he declaimed directly to his readers in a vernacular style which had an instant appeal to *sans-culotte* readers and was well suited to reading aloud for the illiterate.[32]

At a more elevated level stood the *Cercle social*, which later changed title to the *Bouche de fer*, and was the organ of the quasi-masonic club, the *Cercle social*. It was edited by Nicolas Bonneville, and featured regular articles from the future bishop of the Calvados, Claude Fauchet. Nominally devoted to printing letters found in the club's letter-box — the *Bouche de fer* — it served in practice as a mouthpiece for the club's propaganda, with detailed accounts of democratic activity around Paris.[33] The radical Cordeliers club also produced two papers, the *Observateur du club des Cordeliers*, which appeared in March-April 1791, and the *Journal du club des Cordeliers*, which was published during the following June and July. The *Observateur* was mainly concerned with attacking Lafayette and the Parisian National Guard in the aftermath of the Vincennes affair, while the *Journal* voiced the club's demands for a republic in the weeks following the flight to Varennes, combating 'une foule d'écrivains soudoyés et sans pudeur' who were opposed to the agitation mounted by political clubs.[34] One of the *Journal*'s editors, Raymond Senties, was also linked with several other radical papers which were sold cheaply by *colporteurs*, and read out in cafés, workshops or at street corners, helping to spread radical ideas. He printed the *Remontrances bougrement patriotiques du véritable Père Duchene* in November 1790, and a *Soirées du Père Duchêne* in the following months, in which his own transition from moderate to extreme politics can be traced. Another to exploit the same genre was the *abbé* Jumel, who later migrated to the Corrèze to become a leading light — and happily married man — in the Jacobin club there.[35]

Varied though these newspapers were, they shared some common features, the most important of which was their political stance: for despite differences of emphasis, all were critical of the moderate nature of many of the Assembly's reforms, and voiced support for the ideas of direct democracy that had taken root in several Parisian districts. On central issues, such as the question of the royal veto, the *marc d'argent* qualification for deputies' eligibility, the franchise, or the political reorganisation of the Paris Districts, they campaigned against the Assembly's decisions. Similarly, on incidents such as the Nancy massacre or cases of press censorship, they condemned its failure to support the democratic cause. They were also markedly anticlerical from an early stage, increasingly so from the early months of 1791 when the divisions over the civil constitution of the clergy became apparent, and also shared common personal targets, growing progressively sceptical of the credentials of Necker, then of Bailly, Mirabeau, Lafayette and the triumvirate of Duport, Barnave and Lameth. By the summer of 1791 several of them, most notably Brissot and Robert, were openly republican, and Robert was to be a powerful force behind the Cordelier club's activity after the flight to Varennes.[36] Almost all of them were close colleagues, but although their political views often coincided on major issues, they rarely co-ordinated their campaigns in advance, despite the claims of right-wing pamphlets. Rather, their unity was one of attitude and basic ideology, forged by the nature of events in 1790 and 1791, and shaped by the impact of personalities and the growth of popular radicalism.

A second common factor was political involvement, for Robert, Desmoulins, Prudhomme, Marat, Hébert and Audouin were all members of the Jacobin and Cordeliers clubs, and particularly prominent at the latter. Club activity and journalism were complementary activities, both components of the political education of the nation, encouraging debate on major issues and the *surveillance* of politicians. As a result many of them were to progress rapidly into national politics, gaining election to the Legislative Assembly in September 1791, or to the National Convention in the following year. Linked to this was a third common factor, that of geographical concentration on the left bank of the Seine, in the heart of the Cordeliers district. This was where the historical centre of the Parisian printing industry lay, and although the collapse of government controls in the summer of 1789 led to increasing numbers of new printing houses opening up on the *île de la Cité* and the opposite side of the Seine, the bulk of it remained there. Yet it was also an area which, as early as the summer of 1789, stood out as a centre of political radicalism. The Cordeliers district assembly was a thorn in the side of the Paris Municipality during the winter of 1789-90, and when the district was partially transformed into the *section du Théâtre français*, in the municipal reform of the summer of 1790, the Assembly reconstituted itself into the Cordeliers club, which charged a low entrance fee and attracted a more popular and artisanal audience than its Jacobin counterpart across the river. It was from here that most of the radical press operated and drew its ideological roots.

Marat was welcomed there in November 1789 while avoiding the *Châtelet* arrest warrant, and protected from arrest in the following January; and in February 1791, he was even offered money by the club, to keep his *Ami du peuple* going. He lived in the *rue des Cordeliers*, and his printer for much of this time, Ann-Félicité Colomb, operated from the *rue de l'ancienne comédie* and the *place Dauphine*, near the Pont Neuf. The *Orateur du peuple* shared the same base: distributed from the *rue de la Bucherie* and printed originally in the nearby *rue de Bièvre*, which linked the *quai de la Tournille* to the *boulevard Saint-Germain*, it briefly passed north of the river, after its tenth issue, to a newly established printer in the *rue des Prouvaires*, before returning to the left bank, with Mlle Colomb, and ending up with the printer Provost on the *rue Mazarine*. In the meanwhile, Fréron, its editor, had moved into the district with his brother-in-law, La Poype, to a third floor appartment at no. 1, *place du Théatre français*, where they would not have been amused to find a plaster bust of Lafayette as part of the furniture.[37] Prudhomme lived close by, at no. 19 *rue Jacob*, then from December 1789 moved to the *rue des Marais*, where he set up his presses and provided a furnished room for Loustalot, who lived, worked and died there. One of his journalists, Manuel, lived on the *rue Serpente*, while the Cordeliers club printer, Momoro, had his presses on the *rue de la Harpe*. The *Journal universel* was printed first on the *cité*, in the *rue Notre Dame*, then from the *rue du Fouare*, with its distribution office on the *rue de Petit-Bourbon*, near Saint-Sulpice. Camille Desmoulins also lived in the *rue Serpente*, then moved to the *rue du Théâtre français* in the spring of 1790 where he lived in the same house as Danton and praised the atmosphere of the quarter repeatedly in the columns of the *Révolutions de France et de Brabant*. François Robert and Louise Keralio lived on the north of the river, in the *rue Gramont*, but the offices of their *Mercure* were on the *place Henri IV* and both of them were heavily involved in the Cordelier club. All of them must have met each other regularly, in the Cordeliers club, on the street, at private meetings or in printers' premises, giving their existence an almost incenstuous air.

Rather like the radical press, the moderate patriot press also included a number of titles which had made their debut in the latter half of 1789: the *Patriote français* in July, the *Chronique de Paris* in late August, and the *Annales patriotiques* in early October. The spring of 1790 saw more, notably with the launch of the *Feuille villageoise*, which was specifically aimed at a rural audience through the intermediary of their priests and notables, while later in the year came the first of a steady flow of Jacobin club newspapers, reporting on the correspondence and debates of the Paris Jacobin club: Choderlos de Laclos' *Journal des amis de la constitution* in late October, the *Journal des clubs, ou sociétés patriotiques* at the end of November, and the *Journal des débats de la société des amis de constitution* in the following March.

Over the summer of 1790 too, the *société de 1789*, which had broken away from the Jacobin club in protest against its growing radicalism, published its own newspaper under Condorcet's editorial control.[38] One common link between these titles and the radical press lay in their editors' political activity, although it usually took place in the Jacobin rather than the Cordelier club. In addition, many of them, like Brissot and Condorcet, used both their papers and the club as springboards to a political career, and were later elected to the Legislative Assembly and National Convention.

They also shared a great deal with the radical press ideologically, most notably a common hostility to the nobility, marked anticlericalism and suspicion of the influence of the court. Brissot in particular used the *Patriote français* to voice his sympathy with direct democracy, calling for the Declaration of the Rights of Man and the constitution to be put to a referendum. He disliked the system of indirect elections adopted by the Assembly, along with the division of citizens into active and passive, accusing it of creating an 'aristocratie des propriétaires'. The theme of moral regeneration also runs throughout much of his writing, a theme which he shared with Marat, Carra, Loustallot and many other pre-revolutionary pamphleteers. The *Chronique de Paris*, on the other hand, was more moderate, as was the *Feuille villageoise*, which consistently attacked Marat and Robespierre and also kept a careful distance from Jacobin club politics.[39]

There were other ways in which several of them differed from the radical press. None of them, for example, used the gutter vocabulary of Hébert, or the polemic of Marat and Fréron. Brissot even felt compelled to lecture Desmoulins in the spring of 1791, during an argument over the respective roles of political clubs and the press, on the serious obligations of maturity and accuracy that fell upon the shoulders of a 'popular journalist':

> The functions of a popular journalist which you have taken on yourself oblige you to study and research the principles of freedom, to know the history of modern republics, and study the ways in which wily aristocracies undermine all great principles.[40]

They also offered a more complete spread of news. The *Chronique de Paris*, for example, modelled itself on the London *Morning Chronicle*, and was launched by its founders, A.-L. Millin and J.-F. Noel, as a rival to the similarly styled *Journal de Paris*. As a result it only began to print reports of Assembly debates from its eighth number onwards, after repeated requests from readers, but always retained an extensive literary and arts section, a letters column, a section which acted as a kind of marriage bureau through the publication of letters from lonely hearts — 'as long as they are short and contain only the bare essentials' — and also advertising and theatre supplements.[41] Similarly, the *Patriote français* usually gave over its first page or two to a carefully written analysis of Assembly debates, usually written by Brissot himself, and followed this with a regular section on Paris, which covered everyday events as well as the political, provincial and foreign news, and occasional literary and theatrical reviews, financial reports and editorials.

Editorial organisation reflected this wider news coverage, for most of the moderate press employed editorial teams, in the same way as the informational press, closer to the model of the *Révolutions de Paris* than to the *Ami du peuple* or *Père Duchesne*. The *Chronique de Paris*, for example, had a large editorial panel, which included well known political personalities, such as Pierre Manuel, Anacharsis Clootz and Rabaut Saint-Etienne. So also did the *Annales politiques et littéraires*, for although Carra emerged as its dominant contributor, it was nominally directed by Louis-Sebastien Mercier and employed at least six other editorial assistants, including the future Jacobin general, Doppet.[42] On the *Patriote français*, Brissot had a dozen or so collaborators, many of them recruited through his friendship with the Rolands: Lanthenas, who wrote on financial affairs and Jacobin club debates, Bosc d'Antic, Bancal des Issarts who wrote on diplomatic affairs, Bois Guyon, the *abbé* Gregoire and, not least, Jean-Marie Girey-Dupré who was to take over editorial control in the autumn of 1791 after Brissot's election to the Legislative Assembly.[43]

Whatever their differences, the radical, moderate and informational press all, in their different ways, supported the revolution. On the opposite side of the political fence, however, lay a sizeable right-wing press which, until the fall of the monarchy in August 1792, had a larger influence than mere circulation figures might suggest, because of its vivacity and literary style.[44] It was slow to get off the ground, for only the *Actes des Apôtres* and the *Journal politique et national* were clearly opposed to the revolution before the end of 1789. Yet it picked up strength in the early months of 1790, when the *Gazette de Paris* and the *Journal général de la cour et de la ville* changed sides, and by the summer of 1790 over 20 right-wing satirical papers appeared, the most durable of which was the *Chronique du manège*.

All of them drew deeply on the character assassination and erudite wit that had characterised both salon conversation and the underground *libelles* of the *ancien régime*.[45] In June, to reflect its change of emphasis from literature to politics, the *Année littéraire* also changed title to the *Ami du Roi*, under the editorial control of Galart de Montjoye. However, disappointing sales of the initial numbers soon led to quarrels between him and the paper's former owner, Mme Royou, so that she and her brother broke away to launch their own *Ami du Roi* instead. The two of them remained in existence until the summer of 1792, campaigning for similar objectives — namely, the rejection of the Assembly's social and political reforms and a return to the royal programme as outlined in the *séance royale* of 23 June 1789.[46]

Further reforms in the summer of 1790, such as the abolition of nobility and the civil constitution of the clergy, soon encouraged more titles to appear. The common defence of nobility and church, for example, was a feature of the bi-weekly *Royaliste, l'ami de l'humanité*, launched in September, and of the *Journal de Louis XVI et son peuple* and *Journal de la noblesse*, which both began rolling off the presses before the end of the year. In January 1791 the *Journal général de la France* acquired a new editor in the shape of Boyer-Brun who had been editor of the *Journal de Nismes* until just six months previously, and who now injected into the newspaper much of the anti-Protestant sectarianism that he had practised there. Meanwhile Marat received his right-wing counterpart in the form of the *Journal de M. Suleau* in March and, just as the acerbic wit of the *Actes des Apôtres* was beginning to flag, another satirical paper, the *Rocambole des journaux*, took over its role.[47] The winter of 1790–1 also saw a number of newspapers launched which specifically attacked radical politicians: the *Feuille du jour*, for example, was launched in December 1790 by Pierre-Germain Parisau and concentrated its attention on the activities of the Paris Jacobin club, while the spring months saw a flurry of *monarchien Père Duchesnes* which tried to rival the radical polemic of Hébert and harness his style to counter-revolution. The *Correspondance des mécontents*, for example, attacked the revolution for 'degrading' both nobility and clergy, and also for destroying the livelihood of the poor by removing their benefactors and employers:

> The worker who is unemployed, the artisan who has to divide his time between enforced idleness in his shop and the pleasure of aping soldiers, have no feelings of loyalty towards you. Do

you not think that there are now millions like them who regret
the passing of the *ancien régime*, and even its abuses?

Its conclusion was that the lawyers had won out, dominating the
new bureaucracy and monopolising office: 'Seven to eight thousand
people are happy. Just think of the fate of the rest.'[48]
During the summer months this broadened into a wider attack
on radical republicanism: on 3 June, for example, the *Babillard* was
launched, and six days later Théveneau de Morande launched the
Argus patriote with the help of court money, training his sights largely
on Brissot, whose secrets he knew embarrassingly well from their
common involvement in the pre-revolutionary publishing world of
London. Neither newspaper achieved much success, and they both
quickly closed down, but the radical republicanism that they had
set out to attack reached its peak in the events that led up to the
massacre of the Champ de Mars, and this event in itself helped
to push over several centrist papers towards the right, in common
fear of democracy — papers such as the *Gazette universelle* or the *Spectateur*, which from now on aligned themselves with the Feuillant
cause.[49]
The right-wing press was no more coherent in format or ideology
than its radical counterpart. There were dailies, such as the *Gazette
de Paris* and the *Feuille du jour*, alongside weeklies such as the *Journal
général*. The *Actes des Apôtres* even had no set appearance date, just
guaranteeing its subscribers 13 copies per subscription period,
without specifying what that period was. Several of them were one-
man newspapers, such as the *Gazette de Paris*, which Du Rozoi wrote
largely single-handed, or Montjoie's *Ami du Roi*; while others, such
as the *Mercure* or the *Journal général*, were the work of an editorial
team. The most unusual team of all worked on the *Actes des Apôtres*,
which, although owned and directed by Jean-Gabriel Peltier, was
written by a loose band of 'apostles' — over 80 of them all told
— who met periodically to write each issue in one of the expensive
restaurants of the Palais-Royal, usually sketching out their articles
on the paper table-cloth, which was then left behind for delivery
to the printer. There was also great variety in content, for although
most of them prominently featured National Assembly debates, if
only as a convenient peg on which to hang their own political views,
or in order to highlight the contributions of orators from the right,
a significant minority ignored them either partially or altogether.
The *Actes des Apôtres* in particular had almost no concrete news,
focusing instead on anecdotes, anagrams, personality attacks and

salon wit. The *Journal général* was similar, lampooning and savaging the reputation of politicians from the centre right to the radical left: Mirabeau for his ugliness and venality, Orléans for his venality, Lafayette for his size — playing on the pun between his name. 'Mottié' and the word 'moitié' — Talleyrand for his lack of religious belief, and Gobel for his alleged sexual misdemeanours. Indeed, the tendency was for such attacks to increase, for both the *Journal général* and Du Rozoi's *Gazette de Paris* reduced their coverage of Assembly debates during the course of 1790, while the *Petit Gautier* quickly ignored them, as being beneath contempt.[50]

There was also a great variation in ideology, reflecting the diversity within the counter-revolution itself. From the constitutional monarchy of Mallet du Pan or Parisau, to the reactionary outlook of Du Rozoi and the rabid sectarianism of Boyer-Brun there yawned an almost unbridgeable chasm. The *Petit Gautier* and the *Rocambole*, for example, wanted the fiscal privileges of the nobility to return, using the traditional argument that they were the compensation for military service and the ban on entry into retail trade or manual labour. Du Rozoi even demanded that the nobility be purged of *anoblis*, and enoblement through venal office terminated. Suleau and Fontenai, on the other hand, were more concerned with defending the virtues of the thrifty provincial nobility, whom they compared favourably with their decadent court counterparts, and Royou was emphatically in favour of enobling talented commoners and retaining the abolition of fiscal and social privilege. *Monarchiens*, such as Rivarol, Mallet du Pan, or Bergasse and Clermont-Tonnerre in the *Actes des Apôtres*, were in favour of a constitutional monarchy with a bi-cameral legislature, but Du Rozoi intransigently rejected it, as did the *Journal général* and the *Rocambole*, as a betrayal of national tradition.[51]

Yet behind these differences of opinion there stood a broad philosophical opposition to the revolution. Certainly, there was a lunatic fringe which portrayed the whole revolution as a cosmic masonic plot, a Huguenot takeover, or a manifestation of divine revenge for a century of impiety. Yet most right-wing journalists based their opposition more consistently on a deep distrust of rationalism, and of the tendency for revolutionary reform to treat French society as a kind of *tabula rasa*, studiously ignoring the important role to be played by tradition and history.[52] Occasionally they proved surprisingly adept at using revolutionary ideology as a stick with which to beat the revolution, using the Rousseauist idea of popular sovereignty to criticise the restriction of the suffrage to the propertied classes, pointing to the tolerance of certain private corporations, such as the Jacobin clubs, at a time when others — such as nobility or the Parlements — had been swept away. Some also pointed out how the widely trumpeted concept of the balance of powers had been subtly distorted by the way in which meagre powers had been left to the King. There was no lack of life, therefore, in the right-wing press, and although it was consistently outsold by the patriot and radical press, and was later to be almost wiped out with the dethronement of the King in the summer of 1792, it had articulated much of the basic ideology that was to fuel the right for the rest of the decade.[53]

These same years also saw rapid growth in the provincial press, although numbers are difficult to come by because of the lack of any national catalogue and wide gaps in the many surviving collections. Growth was most in evidence in the larger towns, where the intensity of political life, the infrastructure of the printing trade and the existence of a sizeable literate market all combined to create favourable conditions. Lyons, for example, second city in the kingdom, with a population in excess of 100,000, had just two newspapers at the beginning of 1789, the *Affiches de Lyon* and the *Journal de Lyon*. The latter, edited by Mathon de la Cour, became deeply conservative during the second half of 1789, but by October 1791 had been joined by a further 14 political newspapers, which spanned the full range of the political spectrum. Sharing its readers on the right wing was the *Surveillant*, launched in August 1791. The moderate left had Champagneux's *Courrier de Lyon* until its demise in the spring of 1791, while the *Journal de la société populaire* and the *Moniteur du département de Rhône-et-Loire* were .nore radical. The first of these, which appeared thrice weekly between January and April 1791, was launched to publicise the activities of the *Club central*, which co-ordinated the activities of the popular clubs that had sprung up in the city since the previous autumn. The *Moniteur*, on the other hand, was an independent newspaper which, in its early stages, was dominated by the personality of its editors, Prudhomme and the *abbé* Laussel. Laussel in particular brought to the paper an aggressive style of denunciation, aimed particularly against the conservative departmental administration, which rapidly ruffled feathers. The Department prosecuted him for libel in the summer of 1790, but the departmental court ducked the issue by deciding that the charges amounted to treason, and forwarding the case to Paris. There it died a quiet death in the offices of the Ministry of Justice. Further charges brought against the paper in the following

November met a similar fate, and it was able to survive into the spring of 1793.[54]

Bordeaux, which had just one newspaper before 1789, the *Journal de Guienne*, saw another 16 appear within the next two years. The *Journal de Guienne* changed its title to *Journal patriotique et de commerce* and, from the summer of 1789 onwards, carried political news. To its left, however, the *Journal de Bordeaux*, launched in the spring of 1790 by two printers, the Labottière brothers, supported liberal reform, until the flight to Varennes in the summer of 1791. By the end of the year it had switched to support the Feuillant cause and dismissed its editor, Bruno-Gabriel Marandon, who promptly launched the *Chronique de Bordeaux* as a more liberal rival to it, forging links with the city's *société des amis*.[55] Both Rouen and Marseilles, though not far behind Lyons and Bordeaux in population, were less prolific, producing only three new titles each during the period of the Constituent Assembly. In Rouen the *Journal de Normandie* survived from the *ancien régime* and quickly opened its columns to political news and comment; but it was rivalled by the *Concilliateur*, which, launched in September 1789, provided basic political information — mainly National Assembly debates — without analysis or editorials; by the *Abeille politique*, launched in January 1790, which was *monarchien*; and by the *Chronique nationale*, which came out in July 1790 and, despite claiming to tread a middle path between demagoguery and aristocracy, and to offer its readers '. . . with impartiality, decency and truth, an analysis of what the future holds', was basically Feuillant.[56] Journalism in Marseilles was dominated by the presence of Ferreol de Beaugeard, whose *Journal de Marseilles*, dating back to 1781, increased its output to four times weekly and was able to beat off the more radical opposition of three short-lived papers in the spring and summer of 1790, produced by members of the city's Jacobin club in the *rue Thubaneau*.[57]

Many medium-sized towns also spawned a thriving press, and few more so than Avignon, which was split by bitter divisions over its status and the future of Papal sovereignty. It produced seven new newspapers before the autumn of 1791 to rival the long-established *Courrier d'Avignon* which, under the editorial control of Sabin Tournal, threw its weight behind the cause of radical democracy and union with France during the course of 1790. Four of the newcomers took the same course — the *Courrier de Villeneuve-les-Avignon*, the *Courrier du Pont-du-Gard*, the *Journal patriotique de la révolution d'Avignon* and the *Journal patriotique de France* — while three were resolutely opposed: the *Ami de tous* — which borrowed extensively from Parisian right-wing papers such as the *Rocambole* — and two papers published from Carpentras until its capture by Avignon forces in January 1791, the *Annales patriotiques* and the *Nouvelles annales*.[58] Strasbourg, situated strategically on the eastern frontier, and with a long history of cultural contacts with Germany, saw nine new titles, all but one published in German, and consequently, circulating chiefly within Alsace and the Holy Roman Empire. They all supported the revolution, despite the substantial changes wrought in the status of the province, the most prominent being the *Geschichte der Gegenwartigen Zeit*, edited by two Lutheran activists, Simon and Meyer, and the *Courrier politique et littéraire*, owned and edited by a local Lutheran printer, Jean-George Treuttel. As the sole paper published in the city in French, the *Courrier politique* circulated widely within the rest of France, as well as coming out in a German language edition for the Alsatian market.[59] Angers, a clerically dominated town with several sizeable printshops, saw some 18 new titles try to compete with the *Affiches d'Angers*, which dated back to 1773. Most of them concentrated on factual reporting of events in Paris and the provinces, but two of them — the *Journal du département de Maine-et-Loire* and the *Creuset* — were on the moderate left and closely linked to the city's *club de l'est*. In Nantes there were also four new titles, while Auxerre could also boast five to rival its long-established *Affiches d'Auxerre*.

Nevertheless, in medium-sized towns, given the limitations of the market, it was more common for just two or three newspapers to appear, often as rivals to the existing *Affiches*. This was the case in Grenoble, for example, where the *monarchien* views of the *Affiches de Dauphiné* were challenged from December 1789 onwards by the radical *Vedette patriotique*, launched by the city's future Jacobin club. In Orléans too, the *Journal général de l'orléanais*, owned and directed by Panckoucke's father-in-law , Martin Couret de Villeneuve, found itself in competition with the *Annales orléanaises*. In Caen the *Affiches de Basse-Normandie* was forced to share the market with the *Courrier des cinq jours*, while in Limoges the *abbé* Lambertie's conservative *Feuille hebdomadaire* clashed with the newly founded *Extrait des papiers publics*, which forged close links with the city's National Guard and Jacobin club. In Montauban the *Journal national*, launched by Vincent Teulières in late July 1789, and rapidly sympathetic to the counter-revolution, met competition from the *Nouvelles intéressantes*, owned by a fellow printer, Jean-Pierre Fontanel, in November 1790, which soon forged close links with the town's Jacobin club and probably enjoyed the support of the city's Protestant administrators.

Nancy too saw a *Bulletin de l'Assemblée nationale* competing with the *Journal du département de la Meurthe*, and Metz its *Affiches des évêchés* sharing the market with a *Journal politique hebdomadaire* and *Gazette nationale*.[60]

The most novel feature of the provincial press in these years, however, was its spread to small towns and remote areas which had never seen a local paper before. In some ways this was a natural extension of the growth that had been taking place in the provincial press over the previous 40 years, but it was now encouraged by the creation of new administrative divisions, which replaced provinces with departments, and elevated many small and sleepy provincial towns from stagnant backwaters into administrative capitals. Administration required documentation; documentation required printers — of which there was no shortage once the controls on their activity collapsed in 1789 — and printers required work. In addition, the growth was made qualitatively different by the politicisation of public life that the revolution brought about, greatly widening the scope of news and comment. As a result newspapers sprang up which attempted to foster a sense of local identity in newly created departments and provide both local and national political news. In Guéret, for example, administrative department of the rather patchwork department of the Creuse, the printing press made its first appearance in the spring of 1790, and this gave a local highway engineer, Du Planier de la Sablière, the idea of launching a newspaper, the *Journal politique, patriotique et littéraire du département de la Creuse*. A cultivated man, and a disciple of Rousseau, he combined political news and literary articles with more pragmatic needs, leading each number with advertisements and a short report on the proceedings of the National Assembly, then providing snippets of news from around the department, as well as poems and anagrams sent in by readers.[61]

Similarly, in Melun, the printer Tarbé published a *Journal de Seine-et-Marne* from May 1790 onwards, using reports from the first meeting of the electoral assembly of the department as his initial launch-pad, drawn up from notes supplied to him by several participants. From then on he usually led with news of the activities of the newly elected authorities at departmental, district and municipal level, then followed this with extracts from the Parisian press, advertisements, local news and small literary pieces, poetry, news of scientific discoveries and the like. His intention, as laid out in the prospectus, was to ' . . . establish correspondence links with all the towns and cantons in the department', and this concern with local issues increasingly dominated the paper as national news was increasingly squeezed out through lack of space, and from July 1790 onwards, a section was introduced covering news from neighbouring departments as well.[62]

The case of the *Journal pour le département de l'Orne* is somewhat different. Launched in March 1790 by the town's only printer, Malassis le jeune, it laid more emphasis on Parisian news from the outset, providing summaries of Assembly debates which often took up the whole paper, despite the use of microscopic print. As a result, Malassis had to resort to supplements to provide local news, although Assembly debates also frequently spilled over into them.[63] In the Deux-Sèvres, Louis Averti, a former professor in the Oratorian college in Niort who turned his hand to printing once the revolution broke out, edited and published the town's first ever newspaper, the *Journal des Deux-Sèvres*, in the summer of 1790, to provide coverage of local news.[64] Other departmental centres to follow suit included Blois, and Châlons-sur-Marne, where in August 1790 a local doctor, Louis Bablot, launched the *Observateur du département de la Marne*. The *Observateur* was a response to the interest generated by a newsheet, *le Caducée* that Bablot had published to cover the events of the departmental electoral assembly during May and June, and he deliberately ignored national news, seeing his mission as that of encouraging the inhabitants of small towns and villages throughout the Marne to take an interest in politics and local affairs — providing, as he put it, the 'source of the rural, civil, political and literary history of the department'. As an added attraction he also tried to build up a network of local correspondents to funnel news in to him, and published a regular *feuilleton* of commercial news, advertisements and official circulars, which rivalled the *Affiches* published nearby in the departmental capital of Reims.[65]

Several small towns, which found themselves district administrative centres after the reforms of 1790, now also had newspapers. In the Morbihan, Lorient had a *Feuille hebdomadaire*, launched in March of 1790; Beziers in the Herault a *Journal du département de l'Erault*, published from 3 May 1790 onwards by the local printer, Jean-Joseph Fuzier, who was an enthusiastic supporter of reform and founder member of the town's Jacobin club. Montélimar in the Drôme had its own *Courrier de Montélimar* at the end of March 1791, while nearby Vienne, in the department of the Isère, an *Affiches patriotiques du district de Vienne*, in the following July, printed — and probably edited — by Joseph Labbé. These, and many others, tried to throw down local roots by focusing on regional activities and interests. The *Citoyen surveillant* in Rioms, for example, launched in January 1791 by two local Jacobin activists, Gaspart-Antoine Beaulaton and Gabriel Chossier, announced its intention of providing its widely scattered readers in the department of the Puy-de-Dôme with all the local news, as well as exercising careful surveillance of the activities of local officials. Thus, in its early numbers, it provided readers with a supplement which summarised all the rural legislation of the revolution, and a brief history of the Auvergne, along with an analysis of its new administrative divisions and their workings. The *Feuille hebdomadaire* in Lorient had a similar focus. Its first number, in late March 1790, gave readers a review of the municipal elections of the previous month, and set the tone for following issues in its concentration on Lorient news, support for the revolution, and inclusion of readers' letters. Many of them were, however, bitterly critical of the bias of the editor, Pierre Dejordanis. 'Your paper is much criticised, Sir,' said one letter, 'for it contains much useless information drowned in a sea of platitudes'; or, as another correspondant complained: 'War is your game, Sir, and there are people who derive their only pleasure from the misfortunes of others. Journalists and Lawyers, for example, would die of hunger if everyone was always in agreement.'[66]

The spread of the provincial political press was by no means uniform, for there were several towns and departments which proved immune. Toulon and the department of the Var, somewhat surprisingly, had no newspaper throughout the whole decade; neither did the Lozere or the Haute-Saône. Several other departments, including the Aveyron, the Lot, the Ariège, the Saône-et-Loire and the Pyrénées Atlantiques, had to wait until later in the revolution. Yet departments such as these were in a minority, and this raises the question of why the growth of a political press was as extensive as it was. Straightforward ambition, whether political or commercial, was probably the largest single factor, and it was certainly the major motive in persuading the owners of the pre-revolutionary *Affiches* to switch their emphasis. Political ambition was evident in the case of Pipaud Desgranges, for example, who transformed the *Affiches de Périgueux* into the radical *Journal patriotique du département de la Dordogne* in 1791, and later became involved in federalism. Political commitment was probably also important with Jean-Baptiste Broulhiet in Toulouse, who made the *Journal universel* into a liberal newspaper, supported the early reforms of the National

Paris and the Provinces, 1790–1791

Assembly, had several clashes with the local administrative authorities of the Haute-Garonne, and survived imprisonment during the terror to become a powerful political influence in the city during the Directory. The same is true of Paris de l'Espinard in Lille, who similarly supported the early phase of the revolution, but later sided with the Girondin cause and spent the whole of the terror in prison in Paris. Nevertheless, commercialism also played a part, for both men made a great deal of money out of their journalism, enough to buy their own presses and set up wealthy printshops.[67] A similar mixture of motives probably operated in the case of Couret de Villeneuve in Orléans, although his early support for the revolution appears to have evaporated before that of Broulhiet or l'Espinard, and he retired into commercial safety more rapidly than them.[68]

In other cases, political or personal rivalry played a part. In Lyon, for example, Champagneux launched his *Courrier de Lyon* to counteract the conservatism of Mathon de la Cour's *Journal de Lyon* in the autumn of 1789. In Marseilles the *Annales patriotiques, Courrier de Marseille* and *Observateur marseillais* in the summer of 1790 were attempts, encouraged by the Jacobin club, to counteract the moderation of the *Journal de Marseille*. In Bordeaux the *Journal de Bordeaux* was a liberal alternative to the *Journal patriotique de commerce*, while in Caen the *Courrier des cinq jours*, launched by a local lawyer, Pierre-Michel Picquot in January of 1790, was a counterblast to the *monarchien Affiches de la Basse-Normandie*.[69]

Personal rivalry, on the other hand, is evident in Angers, with the case of Charles-Pierre Mame. Born in Avignon, Mame had settled in Angers while on his *tour de France* as an apprentice, bought up the business of an established printshop in 1781 and, with it, the privilege for the *Affiches d'Angers*. During the 1780s he had gone from strength to strength, as *imprimeur de la ville, imprimeur de l'éveque* and *imprimeur du Roi*, and was influential enough to be chosen to draw up the *cahier de doléances* of the corporation of printers for the city during the elections of 1789. Once the revolution began he opened up the *Affiches* to political news and increased its output to twice weekly. He also sided with the cause of moderate constitutional reform and was a founder member of the *société des amis* in the spring of 1790, printing much of its literature and for the first six months of 1791, its newspaper too. Yet his success left resentment in its wake, principally from another printer, Louis-Victor Pavie, who had outbid him to buy up a rival printshop in 1779, but then had his licence suspended in 1782

71

for handling illicit material and had subsequently seen his fortunes slide. In the spring of 1789 he had been quick to grasp the opportunity of publishing the correspondence sent home by the city's Third Estate representatives to the Estate General and, later in the year, added to it a supplement, the *Observateur provincial*, which covered provincial and foreign news. In the following May the electoral assembly of the Maine-et-Loire adopted him as its official printer and recommended that the newly elected departmental authority follow suit. However, old rivalries surfaced as Mame skilfully lobbied to have himself nominated as printer, stressing his greater resources and experience; and consequently, the department chose him instead of Pavie, despite the latter's bitter protests.

> M.Mame is printer to the King, the municipality, the bishops, the university, all the colleges in the town and surrounding areas, the presidial court and financial offices. He also prints the Affiches, which bring in a great deal of money. Now, in violation of all basic rights, he has been named printer to the department, and I am cruelly deprived of the post by manoeuvres which can only be described as unpleasant, and which are against all spirit of justice.

By the end of 1792 Pavie had also closed down his newspapers.[70]

Rivalry was also a factor in Orléans, where Couret de Villeneuve's speed in converting his *Journal général de l'orléanais* into the patriot cause aroused the anger of a rival printer, Jacob l'aîné. He already had a quarrel with Couret, for publishing a rival to his own almanac, the *Calendrier de Province*, earlier in the 1780s, and for several sharp practices in commercial deals at the time of his father's death:

> I would merely say that his conduct . . . at the time of my father's death, shows the kind of character that he now accuses me of having, since he has profited from an odious ban imposed on me, by stealing some of the business done by my press, including one extremely profitable one which he still holds and which we had held for sixty years.

He therefore launched the *Annales orléanaises* as a rival to Couret, boasting a wider news coverage, a dozen editorial assistants, and free advertising. Couret promptly responded by attacking Jacob as a rancid failure, a usurper and a plagiarist, and the rivalry continued until the end of 1791 when, probably for financial reasons, the *Annales orléanaises* had vanished from the scene.[71]

Political clubs also helped to spread the press, for they had a strong commitment to political propaganda which frequently led them to organise propaganda missions and distribute pamphlets and wall-posters. Newspapers were a natural extension of this. The *Vedette patriotique* in Grenoble was the first club paper, but it was soon followed by others: in Arras, for example, where the *société des amis* produced an *Ami de la constitution* in May 1790 to rival the conservative *Annonces, Affiches et nouvelles diverses pour la province d'Artois*; or in Angers, Versailles and Aurillac, where newspapers were launched in the first half of 1791. In other towns, financial and moral support was lent to journals owned and run by members: in Strasbourg to the *Courrier politique et littéraire*, in Caen to the *Courrier des cinq jours*, or in Perigueux to the *Journal patriotique du département de la Dordogne*. Nor were Jacobin clubs alone, for of the few right-wing clubs that formed in provincial France, those in Lyons and Dijon also sponsored their own papers.[72]

Despite its variety, the provincial press tended to be more narrowly concentrated within the political spectrum than its Parisian counterpart. As in Paris, some were devoted to the straightforward reporting of national political news: the *Nouvelliste national* in Toulouse or the *Nonciateur* in Rouen, for example, both of which were essentially scissors and paste jobs, based largely on the Parisian press. Others, such as the *Annales de la municipalité de Bordeaux*, concentrated on local government news or, like the *Journal des douanes nationales* in Lyons, the *Publicateur* in Nantes or the *Feuille maritime* in Brest, on commercial information for a restricted clientele.[73] Their political role in both cases was largely passive, reporting events and decisions as they happened, without comment and employing little or no editorial staff. The great majority, on the other hand, were actively political, as in Paris, and provided a creditable range of news along with comment.

Compared with their Parisian counterparts, relatively few backed the political extremes of right or left. There were right-wing newspapers in Rouen, Arras, Auxerre, Caen, Lyon, Limoges and Grenoble, which were largely *monarchien* in allegiance, faithful to the ideal of a strong constitutional monarchy, and virulently anti-Jacobin.[74] Open support for counter-revolution, on the other hand, surfaced only in the *Journal de Nismes* and the *Journal national* in Montauban — both cities where sectarian animosity sharpened feelings — and in the cases of short-lived titles such as the *Ami du Roi* in Dole, the *Quatre Evangélistes* in Toulouse, and two titles in Auxerre.[75] As for the radical left, it was also thin on the ground, with perhaps just two titles in Lyons, a short-lived *Patriote français cadet* in Troyes during the summer of 1790, the *Courrier d'Avignon* and *Courrier du Pont-du-Gard* in the future department of the Vaucluse, and the spasmodic *Cantaliste* in Aurillac.[76] The great majority of titles shunned both extremes — often ostentatiously so — and lay to the moderate left of the political spectrum. They would probably have endorsed the words of Chasles, writing in his *Corréspondant* in the spring of 1790, when he stated himself to be '. . . genuinely and cordially patriotic. I say patriotic and not madly radical. I have no time for any kind of fanaticism'.[77] Their political home lay somewhere between the cautious support for the revolution given someone like Ferreol de Beaugeard in his *Journal de Marseille*, and the more militant democratic sympathies of Paris de Lespinard in the *Gazette du département du Nord* or of Pipaud Desgranges in the Dordogne. In this way they therefore reflected the strength of moderate political opinion in the country at large, before religion and war tore the revolutionary consensus apart.

Yet there are certain issues and attitudes which stand out in their columns. One, evident from much of what has gone above, was a commitment to the local identity made possible by the division of the old provinces into new departments. This was evident in the concern to report on local events, to cover local administrations' activities, and to provide short histories of the area and its major events.[78] Another was a concern to provide readers with a balanced diet of political news, commercial information and literary articles, in order to maximise readership and interest. In this context, many tried to have regular articles on farming matters, including the relevant rural legislation passed by the National Assembly, in order to attract a peasant readership and bind them to the revolution. As the *Journal patriotique de Grenoble* put it:[79] 'The main object and the most useful purpose of our work is to bring home to the less well educated the great advantages that French citizens, and rural dwellers in particular, are going to gain from the new constitution.'

A third factor was the strong preoccupation with religious affairs from the winter of 1789–90 onwards, when the problems associated with the civil constitution began to bite, which was marked by a strong anticlericalism. The *Citoyen surveillant* in Rioms, for example, openly attacked the bishop of Clermont-Ferrand for his opposition to the civil constitution, accusing him of wanting to become a leader of counter-revolution, and praised the firm stand taken by the departmental administration against non-jurors.[80] The *Journal patriotique* in Dijon came out in favour of married priests and civil divorce by the summer of 1791, and welcomed the legislation against non-jurors in the following November in strongly male chauvinist terms:

> Fine women who need to be controlled, yet dislike being ordered around by their husbands because it is in their nature to want to be mistresses in their own homes, give themselves over to these bigots. They do not believe in paradise, because their pleasures lie elsewhere, but they believe in hell because they are stupid . . . yet men are tough, and since they have been threatened with hell so often, no longer fear it.[81]

The *Annonces de Chartes* and *Journal du département de l'Orne* were also anticlerical, while the *Correspondance générale* in Rheims specialised in tales of clerical misdemeanours and failings.[82]

Finally, most departmental journals claimed for themselves the role of *surveillants* of political opinion and local administrations. None argued this more cogently than Pipaud Desgranges in Périgueux when, in the spring of 1791, he countered a call from the departmental administration of the Dordogne for more effective press censorship. France, argued Desgranges, now had representative government which reserved to the electorate just two political functions: those of periodic election and of censure. The latter was the only guarantee of popular freedom between elections, and could be exercised through clubs or newspapers. Newspapers, however, exercised it most effectively, and journalists were therefore an essential part of the political machine:

> In this way writers have become political figures; they wield a respectable power, delegated to them by the people, . . . and which has no need of physical force . . . the kind of power that, if humanity had reached its final level of perfection, would be the only one used by those who govern, and the only one tolerated by the governed.[83]

The new provincial press therefore extended the role of the pre-revolutionary *Affiches*. Its political content injected a vital new element into provincial journalism and changed it from a pleasant cultural diversion into an important element in local affairs. Newspapers took sides in political disputes, they acted as a sounding board for the political views of their readers, they watched over and publicised the activities of their local administrations, and acted as a springboard for the political careers of many of their editors. René Vatar, Claude Basire, Jean-Joseph Lagarde and Pierre-Jacques-Michel Chales were among those who, through local journalism, made the first moves in what were to become national political careers. Many others followed, or built themselves a reputation that was useful in local politics instead. Nevertheless, journalism remained a cottage industry because of its low circulation figures, with part-time editors at best, and frequently no other editor than the owner or printer himself, backed up by a handful of voluntary helpers. Certainly none of them could boast the financial resources or managerial organisation of the larger Parisian newspapers such as the *Moniteur* or the *Révolutions de Paris*, none of them could appeal to the national market in the same way as they could, and only a very few were even successful in finding a readership outside their own town or its immediate area. In this sense at least, their continuity with the humble origins of the *ancien-régime Affiches* remained unbroken.

The small scale also explains one other feature of this early provincial press — namely, its extreme fragility. At the beginning of 1789 there were 44 provincial newspapers in the country, almost all of them the traditional style *Affiches*. Over the next two and three-quarter years, some 167 new titles came on to the market, of which 85 (or little over a half) lasted as long as three months, and 45 remained in production for as long as a year. The casualty rate was substantial, with little over a quarter of all new papers lasting for a significant length of time. The reasons for this are many. Several of the new papers that appeared were speculative: badly organised and inadequately thought out, they lacked the organisational backup to survive, and were doomed to an early end. Several appeared in towns and areas that had never nurtured a press before, and rapidly discovered — as Du Planier did in the Creuse, for example, or Dejordanis in Lorient — that a sufficient market was difficult to find, because of poverty, and because readers preferred to get their political news at source, from the Parisian press, which was quick to exploit the national market. Those who survived, and the few that thrived, tended to be based in medium-sized or large towns, where an adequate readership and hinterland existed. The problems of finding adequate readership are emphasised by the contrasting experience of the *ancien-régime Affiches*, for no less than 35 out of the 44 that were in existence at the end of 1788 were still publishing at the end of the Legislative Assembly, partly because of customer loyalty towards a title that they knew and trusted, and partly also because of the financial resources, slim though they were, that advertising continued to provide. For even those *Affiches* which turned to politics over the summer and autumn of 1789 always retained their extensive advertisements and announcement sections, the main attraction for much of their readership prior to 1789, and they continued to do so for many years afterwards. Advertising revenue, in itself, was not particularly significant; but the readership that both it and official news attracted formed a solid kernel of support that survived through the ups and downs of political fortunes. More so than in Paris, therefore, the provincial press was an amalgam of old and new. However, the events of the next two years were to put both to the test.

Notes

1. *Quand dormirons-nous?* (Paris, undated), p. 1.
2. For the debate surrounding article 11, see *Moniteur*, 23-6 August 1789, pp. 379-80; *Archives Parlementaires*, viii, 256-61; A. Söderjhelm, *Le régime de la presse pendant la révolution française*, I (Helsingfors and Paris, 1900-1), pp. 109-14; J. Egret, *La révolution des notables. Mounier et les monarchiens 1789* (Paris, 1950), p. 116.
3. *Moniteur*, 14 Jan. 1790, pp. 115-6; 22 and 23 Jan. 1790, p. 180, 183-5; 19 June 1790, pp. 662-3; 2 August 1790, pp. 281-2; 20 July 1791, p. 167; Söderjhelm, *Le régime de la presse*, I. pp. 118-43.
4. P.V. Malouet, *Dénonciation à l'Assemblée nationale de deux imprimés ayant pour titre, l'un: C'en est fait de nous; et l'autre: Révolutions de France et de Brabant. Par M. Malouet, député d'Auvergne* (Paris, 1789), pp. 13-14; for less elevated defences of the same position: *Pour et contre sur la liberté de la presse. Par un impartial* (Paris, undated); *Questions importants à résoudre* (undated); and *Dénonciation de plusieurs écrivains incendiaires* (Paris, undated).
5. *Discours sur la liberté de la presse; par J. Pétion* (Paris, 1791), pp. 9-10.
6. *Discours sur la liberté de la presse, prononce à la sociéte des amis de la constitution, le 11 mai 1791, par Maximilien Robespierre, député à l'Assemblée nationale, et membre de cette société* (Paris, undated); Felix Guynement de Kéralio, *De la liberté d'énoncer, d'écrire et d'imprimer sa pensée* (Paris, 1790).
7. *Moniteur*, 23 August 1791, pp. 461-3; Söderjhelm, *Le régime de la presse*, I, pp. 143-8.
8. A.N. BB30 162 d.3; S. Lacroix, *Actes de la Commune de Paris pendant la révolution*, 16 vols, (Paris, 1894-1914) II, pp. 164, 201, 204-6; III pp. 465, 471, 517, 523-5, 540-51; Söderjhelm, *Le régime de la presse*, I, pp. 160-76; G. Walter, *Marat* (Paris, 1933), Chapter iv, *passim*.
9. *Révolutions de France et de Brabant*, ix, p. 350; for full details of the Martel affair, see A.N. Y10508B; see also Lacroix, *Actes de la Commune*, VI, pp. 339, 350-6; Raoul Arnaud, *Journaliste, sans-culotte et thermidorien*.

fils de Fréron 1754–1802 (Paris, 1909), 2e partie, Chapter 2. For Desmoulins' problems, *Révolutions de France et de Brabant*, ix, pp. 387–407; xxxi, pp. 323–46; Soderjhelm, *Le régime de la presse*, I, pp. 215–7. For the right-wing press, Lacroix, *Actes de la Commune*, v. pp. 338–9; Madeleine Albert, *Le Gazette de Paris et du Rozoi* (D.E.S., Paris, 1959), pp. 180–1; A. Tuetey, *Répertoire général des sources manuscrites de l'histoire de Paris pendant la révolution française*, 11 vols (Paris, 1890–1914), I. nos. 1362–9.

10. E. Lamouzèle, 'Le premier procès de presse à Toulouse sous la Révolution', *Revue des Hautes-Pyrénées*, xvii (mars-avril 1922), pp. 41–53.

11. A.N. F18 Rhône 20, pièce 1; A. Vingtrinier, *Histoire des journaux de Lyon depuis leur origine jusqu'à nos jours* (Lyon, 1852), p. 25. For a similar case in Arras, over the *Journal général du département du Pas-de-Calais*, see A.N. Dxxixbis 29, d.296, pièce 5.

12. *Révolutions de France et de Brabant*, ix, p. 350.

13. *Révolutions de France et de Brabant*, xxxi, p. 329; *Révolutions de Paris*, lii, p. 237ff.; P. Vaillandet, 'Les débuts de la société des amis de la liberté de la presse', *A.h.r.f.*, 6 (1926) pp. 83–4. For the club's collapse, see *Journal général de la cour et de la ville*, iv, no. 13 (13 Oct. 1790); *Dénonciation d'un grand club de conspirateurs* (Paris, undated); *Grande dénonciation d'un nouveau club de conspirateurs, rue Jacob* (Paris, undated). For provincial support: *Observateur marseillais*, xxxiii (13 July 1790), pp. 130–1.

14. For details of this curious affair, see *Ami du peuple*, 315 (19 Dec. 1791), pp. 1–2; *Dénonciation des libelles intitulés l'Ami du peuple; et reflexions sur la liberté de la presse. Par Antoine Estienne* (Paris, 1791); Walter, *Marat*, pp. 188–99.

15. M. de Lescure, *Corréspondance inédite sur Louis XVI, Marie-Antoinette, la cour et la ville de 1777 à 1792* (Paris, 1866), II, p. 379. The *Révolutions de Paris*, xxiv (26 Dec. 1789) gives the figure of 1,500. Soderjhelm, *Le régime de la presse*, I, pp. 155–6; Lacroix, *Actes de la Commune*, I, pp. 421, 432–3, 443; E. Hatin, *Manuel théorique et pratique de la liberté de la presse* (Paris, 1868), I, p. 38ff.; Lacroix, *Actes de la Commune*, III, p. 179; E. Hatin, *Histoire politique et littéraire de la presse en France*, IV (Paris, 1858–61), p. 78; *Extrait des registres du District des Minimes de la Place Royale* (Paris, undated); A.N. Dxxixb 2, no. 12. For the continuation of problems with *colporteurs* into 1790 and 1791, see Tuetey, *Répertoire*, I, no. 1660; II, nos 619, 660, 723, 1062 etc.

16. *Lettres à Monsieur le comte de B****, vii (21 March 1790), p. 380. See also *Dénonciation de plusieurs écrivains incendiaires* (Paris, 1791).

17. G. Dupeux, *Le journal politique national* (D.E.S., Paris, 1940), p. 18; M. Tourneux, *Bibliographie de l'histoire de Paris pendant la révolution française*, II, (Paris, 1900–13), pp. 514–6; J. Mounier, *Exposé de ma conduite dans l'Assemblée nationale et motifs de mon retour en Dauphiné* (undated), pp. 35 and 52.

18. F. Acomb, *Mallet du Pan. A career in political journalism* (Durham, NC, 1973), pp. 214–15, 217–8, 225.

19. A. Laurens, *Les Actes des Apôtres. Journal contre-révolutionnaire 1789–1790* (D.E.S., Toulouse, 1963), pp. 149–53; M. Albert, *'La Gazette de Paris' et du Rozoi*, Diplôme des Études Supérieures (Paris, 1959), pp. 182–3.

20. L. Hugueney, *Les clubs dijonnais sous la révolution* (Dijon, 1905), p. 73; A.N. DXXIXbis 29, d.296 pièce 5; P. Bougard and G. Bellart, 'La presse arrageoise des origines à 1870', *Mémoires de l'Académie des Sciences,*

Lettres et Arts d'Arras, 5ᶜ série, iv (1960-5), pp. 67–71.

21. P. Ducourtieux, 'Contribution à l'histoire des périodiques limousins', *Le Bibliophile Limousin*, 19ᵉ année, 2ᵉ série, no. 3 (1904), pp. 131–2; J.-J. Lebon, *La presse montalbanaise, des origines au début du dix-neuvième siècle* (Mémoire de maîtrise: Toulouse, 1972), pp. 18–22, 112–13.

22. Ḥatin, *Histoire politique*, V, pp. 126–87.

23. A. Fribourg, 'Le club des jacobins en 1790. D'après de nouveaux documents', *La Révolution française*, LVIII (1910), pp. 80–2; P. Caron, 'Une organisation de journal en l'an II', *La Révolution française*, 85 (1932), pp. 80–2; A.N.F⁷ 4694 d.1.

24. A.N. AA⁴⁰ d. 1228; J. de Beylié, 'Contribution à l'histoire de la presse sous la révolution (le Logographe)', *Bulletin de la Société de Statistique des Sciences Naturelles et des Arts Industriels du Département de l'Isère*, 4ᵉ série, xi (1910), p. 47. For the method, see below, Chapter 6.

25. *Journal de la Ville (Modérateur)*, xxiv (24 October 1789). See also *La Revue des Journaux rédigés à Paris. Par J.P.L.A.P.I.E.D.L.I.* (Paris, 1797).

26. *Journal de la ville*, 1 January 1790: 'We felt that this kind of work was suitable only for a deputy. He alone can bear in mind the wide perspectives of the revolution.'

27. MM. Didot frères, *Nouvelle biographie générale*, 46 vols (Paris, 1857-66), 33, pp. 535–9.

28. Hatin, *Histoire politique*, V, p. 60.

29. *Bulletin de l'assemblée nationale, prospectus*, p. 2; Tourneux, *Bibliographie*, II, p. 505; Hatin, *Histoire politique*, V, 53. See also the *Journal des débats*, which promised its readers '. . . absolute impartiality and the most scrupulous accuracy in all our factual reports . . .' (*Livre du centenaire*, 3.) For similar aims in a provincial newspaper, see *Journal général de l'Orléanais. Avis concernant le Journal du département. Année 1791.*

30. G. Villacèque, *Les Révolutions de Paris, journal patriote 1789–1790*, Diplôme d'Études Supérieures (Toulouse, 1961), *passim*; Fr. Greppo, 'Un lyonnais imprimeur et journaliste: le journal les 'Révolutions de Paris', *Revue Lyonnaise*, 5ᵉ série, xix (1900), pp. 42–59.

31. Arnaud, *Journaliste*, pp. 137–40; Jean-Paul Bertaud, *Camille et Lucille Desmoulins. Un couple dans la tourmente* (Paris, 1986), Chapter 3, *passim*.

32. L. Jacob, *Hébert. Le Père Duchesne. Chef des sans-culottes* (Paris, 1960); F. Braesch, *Le Père Duchesne d'Hébert. Réimpression avec notes*, 7 fascs (Paris, 1922-38), I, p. 20ff.

33. Gary Kates, *The Cercle Social, the Girondins and the French Revolution* (Princeton, 1984), pp. 184–8.

34. Both have been reprinted by *Editions d'histoire sociale*. For Momoro, see Raymonde Monnier, 'L'évolution du personnel politique de la section de Marat et la rupture de germinal an II', *A.h.r.f.*, 263 (Jan.-March 1986), pp. 63–4.

35. Braesch, *Le Père Duchesne*, pp. 59–65.

36. J.R. Censer, *Prelude to power. The Parisian radical press 1789–1791* (Baltimore and London, 1976), Chapters 3-5, *passim*; see also Bertaud, *Camille*, p. 97ff.

37. A.N. Minuterie centrale, Étude Giard, xviii, p. 891. 3 Aug. 1790.

38. Melvin Allen Edelstein, *La Feuille villageoise. Communication et modernisation dans les régions rurales pendant la révolution* (Paris, 1977);

H. Gough, 'Les Jacobins et la presse: le Journal de la Montagne (juin 1793-brumaire an III' in A. Soboul (ed.), *Actes du colloque Girondins et Montagnards* (Paris, 1980), pp. 270–1.

39. P. Laborie, *Étude sur le Patriote français. Journal libre impartial et national par une société de citoyens et dirigé par J.-P. Brissot* (Diplôme d'Études Supérieures, Toulouse), 1960, p. 186ff.

40. *Patriote français*, 659 (quoted in L. Gallois, *Histoire des journaux et des journalistes de la révolution*, 2 vols (Paris, 1845), I, 232).

41. *Chronique de Paris. Avis au Public*, p. 2; ibid., XI, 3 Sept. 1789.

42. M. Kennedy, 'L'"Oracle des Jacobins des départements": Jean-Louis Carra et ses "Annales patriotiques" ' in A. Soboul (ed.), *Actes du Colloque Girondins et Montagnards* (Paris, 1980), pp. 249–50; Edelstein, *La Feuille villagevise*, pp. 21–5; Hatin, *Histoire politique*, V, pp. 224–38.

43. Laborie, *Étude sur le Patriote français*, p. 78ff.

44. For the right-wing press in general, see the excellent, but contrasting treatments of W.J. Murray, *The right wing press in the French Revolution* (London, 1986), Chapter 1, and J.-P. Bertaud, *Les Amis du Roi. Journaux et journalistes royalists en France de 1789 à 1792* (Paris, 1984), Chapter 1.

45. Madeleine Albert, *La Gazette de Paris et du Rozoi* (D.E.S., Paris, 1959), pp. 55–63; Monrayssé, 'Le Journal général de la cour et de la ville et la polémique anti-révolutionnaire, 16 Septembre 1789-10 août 1792', *La Révolution Française*, 61 (1911), pp. 397–8. M. Bouloiseau, 'Aux origines des légendes contre-révolutionnaires. Robespierre vu par les journaux satiriques (1789–1791)', *A.h.r.f*, XXX (1958), p. 152.

46. *L'Ami du Roi, prospectus*, no. lxxxvii (26 August 1790), supp., and xciii, 1 Sept. 1790, p. 381; J.P. Bertaud, *Étude des journaux: l'Ami du Roi de Royou, l'Ami du Roi de Montjoye, le Courrier extraordinaire de Duplain* (D.E.S., Paris, 1958-9), pp. 5–6.

47. P. Bouju, *Un journal contre-révolutionnaire en 1791–1792. La Rocambole des Journaux* (D.E.S., Paris, 1945).

48. *Correspondance des Mécontents*, ii (18 March 1791), pp. 4–5.

49. Murray, *The right wing press*, p. 128ff.

50. Laurens, *Les Actes des Apôtres*, pp. 67–73; Hélène Maspéro-Clerc, *Un journaliste contre-révolutionnaire. Jean-Gabriel Peltier (1760–1825)* (Paris, 1973), pp. 31–2. Albert, *La Gazette de Paris*, pp. 65–70; Murray, *The right wing press*, pp. 64–9.

51. Murray, *The right wing press*, Chapter 8, *passim*.

52. Bertaud, *Les Amis du Roi*, pp. 115–17.

53. Ibid., pp. 252–7.

54. M. Loche, 'Journaux imprimés à Lyon', *Bulletin de la Société Archéologique, Historique et Artistique. Le Vieux Papier*, fasc. 229 (December 1968), pp. 8–20. L. Trenard, *Lyon de l'Encyclopédie au prémontisme*, 2 vols (Lyon, 1958), pp. 255–7; Bill Edmonds, 'The rise and fall of popular democracy in Lyon, 1789–1795', *Bulletin of the John Rylands Library*, vol. 67, no. 1 (1984), 419ff.

55. E. Labadie, *La presse à Bordeaux pendant la révolution* (Bordeaux, 1910), pp. 47–93.

56. B.M. Rouen, Norm. M904; M718; 260(6), 2 October 1791, pp. 3–4.

57. M. Kennedy, Some journals of the Jacobin club of Marseilles',

French Historical Studies, 1972, pp. 607–9. For a complete collection of the most important, the *Observateur marseillais*, see B.N. 8° Lc¹¹ 635(95).

58. E. Requien, *Bibliographie des journaux publiés à Avignon, et dans le départe-ment de Vaucluse* (Avignon, 1837), pp. 11–21; copies in B.N. 8° Lc² 2245; Musée Calvet 4 3770 (5–6); 8° 26.626; 8°27.276; 8° 26.634.

59. Roland Marx, *Recherches sur la vie politique de l'Alsace prérévolution-naire et révolutionnaire* (Strasbourg, 1966), pp. 73–93; for the circulation of the *Courrier politique*, see *Adresse aux diverses sociétés des amis de la constitution établies dans le royaume,* (undated: A.D. Haute-Vienne, L830); and *Courrier,* 27 October 1791, p. 1042.

60. Lebon, *La presse montalbanaise*, pp. 108–21; A. Ronsin, *Les périod-iques lorrains antérieurs à 1800* (Nancy, 1964), pp. 68–72.

61. Jacques Levron, *La presse creusoise au XIXᵉ siècle* (Limoges, 1931), pp. 9–10.

62. *Journal de Seine-et-Marne, prospectus* and no. xxi (31 July 1790).

63. See copies in A.N. AD XXa 364, and R. Jouanne, 'La presse alençonnaise de la révolution au Second Empire', *Société Historique et Archéologique de l'Orne*, XLV (1926), pp. 353–7.

64. Henri Clouzot, *Notes pour servir à l'histoire de l'imprimerie à Niort et dans les Deux-Sèvres* (Niort, 1891), pp. 119–20; Anon, 'La tragique inaugura-tion du buste de Mirabeau à Niort (16 février 1792)', *Bulletin de la Société Historique et Scientifique des Deux-Sèvres*, vol. XII, nos 5 and 6 (undated), p. 255.

65. *Observateur du département de la Marne, prospectus*, vi–vii; Georges Clause, 'Le journalisme à Chalons-sur-Marne en 1790 et 1791', *Mémoires de la Société d'Agriculture, Commerce, Sciences et Arts du Département de la Marne*, 89 (1974), pp. 291–332. For a similar example in the Lot-et-Garonne, see Robert Marquant, *Aux origines de la presse agenaise: le Journal patriotique de l'Agenais' (1789–1792)* (Agen, undated), p. 10ff; Jules Andrieu, *Historie de l'imprimerie en Agenais depuis l'origine jusqu'à nos jours* (Paris-Agen, 1886), pp. 100–3.

66. *Feuille hebdomadaire*, 17 June 1790, p. 229; 1 July 1790, pp. 250–1; for the *Citoyen Surveillant*, see copies in A.D. Puy-de-Dôme L6389 and L6391; for Béziers, see Roland Andréani, 'Un chef-lieu d'arrondissement et ses journaux. Béziers de 1790 à 1858', *Bulletin de la Société Languedocienne de Géographie*, vol. 16, nos 3–4 (1982), pp. 501–3; Emile Bonnet, *L'imprimerie à Béziers au XVIIᵉ et au XVIIIᵉ siècle* (Béziers, 1898).

67. L. Lemaire 'Joseph Paris de Lépinard, journaliste à Lille. Son arrestation sous la Terreur', *Bulletin du Comité Flamand de France*, 2ᵉ fasc. (1921), pp. 299–330; X. Maeght, *La presse dans le département du Nord sous la révolution française*, Thèse de troisième cycle (Lille, 1971), pp. 122–31; A.N. F⁷ 4774(76), d.3. There is no biography of Broulhiet, but for useful information, see M.J. Lescure, *La presse périodique à Toulouse sous la révolu-tion*, Diplôme de maîtrise d'histoire (Toulouse, 1969–70).

68. H. Herluison, *Recherches sur les imprimeurs et libraires d'Orléans* (Orléans, 1868).

69. J. Gralle, 'Certains aspects du journalisme à Caen pendant la révolution', *Bulletin de la Société des Antiquaires de Normandie*, 56 (1961–2), pp. 807–10; see also *Courier des cinq jours*, 4 July 1790, pp. 15–16.

70. E. Quéruau-Lamerie, 'Notice sur les journaux d'Angers pendant la révolution, *Revue de l'Anjou*, n. sér., 24 (1892), pp. 136–48; *Observateur*

provincial, 3 sér., no. 19 (undated), p. 73. For Mame, see Emile Pasquier and Victor Dauphin, *Imprimeurs et libraires de l'Anjou* (Angers, 1932), pp. 179–82; Céléstin Port, *Dictionnaire historique, géographique et biographique de Maine-et-Loire*, 3 vols (Paris, 1876), II, p. 582; and, for his own self-assessment, A.N. F^7 3448B, letter of 10 *vendémiaire* VI.

71. For the rancour in Orléans, see *Annales orléanaises*, 15 Dec. 1789, pp. 1–2, and 18 March 1790, p. 375.

72. H. Gough, 'The provincial Jacobin club press during the French Revolution', *European History Quarterly*, 16 (1986), pp. 55–60.

73. *Annales de la municipalité de Bordeaux* (complete collection in B.M. Bordeaux, 18 mars 1790–27 mars 1791); see also B.M. Bordeaux, Fonds Bernadau, Ms. 713(xli), p. 210. Rene Kerviler, *Essai d'une bibliographie des publications périodiques de la Bretagne. 4e fasc. Loire-Inférieure* (Paris, 1898), p. 18.

74. Bougard and Bellart, 'La presse arrageoise', p. 68; A. Lecler, 'L'abbé Pierre-Montet Lambertie', *Bulletin de la Société Archéologique et Historique du Limousin*, LXIII (1913), pp. 283–5; Ducourtieux, 'Contribution à l'histoire', *Le Bibliophile Limousin*, 4 (1904), pp. 131–2; Trenard, *Lyon*, II, pp. 256–7.

75. B.M. Nîmes 33.640; Lebon, *La presse montalbanaise*, pp. 16–21, 108–15; M. Vogne, *La presse périodique en Franche-Comte des origines à 1870*, 3 vols (Besançon 1977–8), pp. 56–7; D. Escamez, *La presse périodique à Toulouse de 1789 à 1794* Mémoire de maîtrise (Toulouse, 1969), p. 13; H. Ribière, *Essai sur l'histoire de l'imprimerie dans le département de l'Yonne, et spécialement Auxerre, suivi du catalogue des livres, brochures et pièces imprimés dans cette ville, de 1580 à 1857* (Auxerre, 1858), pp. 90–3; Trenard, *Lyon*, II, p. 252.

76. *Journal de la société populaire des amis de la constitution, etablie à Lyon* (copies in B.N. 8° Lc^{11} 490 and B.M Lyon 356.015; see also the prospectus in A.D. Hérault L1083. Emile Socard, 'Le journalisme à Troyes', *Revue de Champagne et de Brie*, I (1876), p. 238. Copies of the *Courrier d'Avignon* and *Courrier du Pont-du-Gard* are in Musée Calvet 4.853(1--); see also François Rouvière, *Lundis révolutionnaires. Études sur l'histoire de la révolution dans le Gard* (Nîmes, 1891), p. 145ff. For copies of the *Cantaliste*, see A.D. Cantal, Fonds Delmas, D132.

77. *Le Corréspondant*, 38 (27 Dec. 1790).

78. *Nouvelles lunes du cousin Jacques*, xx (16 May 1791), p. 9: 'Newspapers are the barometer of public opinion, and when one is successful in a department, public opinion in that department can be judged by the principles of the newspaper that it favours.'

79. *Journal patriotique de Grenoble*, 4 March 1790.

80. *Citoyen surveillant*, 22 January; 3 February; 10 February 1791.

81. *Journal patriotique du département de la Côte-d'Or*, 13 December 1791, pp. 413–6.

82. G. Clause, 'Un journal de grande information au début de la révolution à Reims', *Mémoires de la Société d'Agriculture, Commerce, Sciences et Arts de la Marne*, 1977, pp. 279–81.

83. *Journal patriotique du département de la Dordogne*, 17 April 1791, pp. 7–8.

3

The Wheel of Fire: Censorship, War and Terror, 1792–1794

The outbreak of war between France and Austria on 20 April 1792 transformed peaceful domestic reform into an international crusade which rapidly backfired. The result was a steady slide towards terror and the revolutionary government of Year II, with press freedom as a major casualty. Firstly the royalist press was devastated by Louis XVI's overthrow on 10 August 1792, then the Girdondin press suffered a similar fate when the *journée* of 2 June removed the leading Girondin deputies from the National Convention, and throughout the following year dissidence in all its printed forms was hunted down by the new Jacobin orthodoxy. It was a brusque retreat from the idealism of 1791, from the freedom of expression so eloquently defended by Robespierre as late as the spring of 1791, and it destroyed many journalists, along with their newspapers. As their heads fell under the guillotine, a new official press emerged, sponsored by clubs, officials, ministers and generals, dedicated to the task of propaganda for the new democratic order.

Without ever returning to the mechanisms of privilege or of prior censorship, and without exercising a total control of editorial content, the revolutionary government of Year II was able to extend its control of the press through a mixture of intimidation, elimination, exhortation and subsidy. In the short term its methods worked, but they were bound to collapse when the terror came to an end in the autumn of 1794, and when they did, they left behind a vastly different landscape of political journalism. Many old faces had gone and many new ones emerged to replace them; but above all the reputation of the press as one of the palladia of political liberty had been severely dented. Those who defended its role pointed to the deaths of Brissot, Carra, Gorsas and many more, arguing that only when their voices had been stifled had the terror been possible. On the other side, those critical of the press's role argued that the freedom of the 1789–92 period had failed to prevent the terror, and could point to many dozens of journalists who, from conviction or necessity, had sung the praises of the guillotine and revolutionary government. Was a free press still a crucial component of political freedom, or were journalists dangerous time-servers, more concerned with profit and survival than with principle and freedom? It was a problem that the terror left behind for the Directory to debate.

In its initial stages the build-up to war during the winter months of 1791–2 acted as a stimulus to the press, encouraging editors to increase their coverage of international affairs and providing the opportunity for new titles to come on to the market, catering specifically for military and diplomatic news. In Paris, a *Courrier des frontières* appeared as early as January 1792, and two others with identical titles followed in February and March. A *Journal de la guerre, Postillon de la guerre, correspondance des nations, Journal du soir*, two more *Courrier des frontières* and a *Journal de la guerre et des frontières* joined them in April, while Robespierre launched his first newspaper, the *Défenseur de la Constitution*, in the same month, to publicise his scepticism over the whole war movement. Camille Desmoulins and Stanislas Fréron also returned briefly to the fray on 30 April, having abandoned the *Révolutions de France et de Brabant* and the *Orateur du peuple* at the time of the massacre of the Champ de Mars, with a short lived *Tribune des patriotes*, which closed down through lack of finance after only four numbers.[1] In the provinces, the *Courrier de Strasbourg* was launched in late December 1791 to provide news from the Rhine frontier to readers in both France and Germany, and during its first few months, it exuded optimism over the prospects of rapid victory and popular uprisings in the German Rhineland states. Brissot used several of its reports to back up his own campaign in the *Patriote français*, and the *Chronique de Paris* adopted it as a special supplement for its readers interested in diplomatic news.[2]

In Valenciennes the *Ami Jacques, Argus de département du Nord* was launched on 2 April by François Melletier, promising its readers 'one eye permanently on the watch for the activities and plans of aristocrats, and the other on the resolute, assured and glorious progress of patriots'. Its early numbers also enthused over the prospects of swift conquest, predicting total victory within three months, and in mid-June Melletier moved his newspaper to the headquarters of the *armée du Nord* with the consent of the local commanders, changing his title to *Argus du département et de l'armée du Nord*. When Dumouriez arrived there in late June, shortly after losing his ministerial post, the *Argus* rapidly became aligned to him, providing propaganda for the troops in the field at a depressing time, and disseminating controlled reports of news from the front for use by the Paris press. In its own way it acted as a primitive press agency for the army, reflecting Dumouriez's own political views until the early months of 1793.[3]

Elsewhere the changed political atmosphere was responsible for the appearance of new titles. A *Défenseur de la Vérité* and *Courrier patriotique* were launched in Le Mans during the course of February, both closely linked to the town's *société des amis de la constitution*.[4] In March a Protestant pastor, Koenig, started a *Journal d'Annonay ou le Babillard* in the Ardèche, particularly outspoken in its attacks on non-juror clergy, while a *Journal des départements méridionaux*, again with close Jacobin links, was launched in Marseilles. April saw the appearance of a short-lived *Journal du département de Loir-et-Cher* in Blois, and a *Journal du département du Tarn*, launched by the *société des amis* in Castres in order to tighten up links between the many clubs scattered around the department.[6] Laval followed in May, with the *Patriote du département de la Mayenne*, edited by Dominique Rabard, a constitutional priest and Jacobin activist, with the intention of encouraging 'amicable correspondence between all friends of the public good'.[7] A month later, on 10 June the club in Nancy produced the *Journal des frontières pour l'instruction des habitants des campagnes* to rally spirits for the ' . . . war to the death between reason and madness, freedom and oppression', while Tulle, chef-lieu of the Corrèze, saw the launch of its first-ever paper, the *Journal du département de la Corrèze*, which sported the topical epigraph 'Vivre libre ou mourir!'[8]

All of these newspapers, in their different ways, reflected the new political mood that was emerging in the spring of 1792. The *Journal du département de Loir-et-Cher*, for example, promised to ' . . . support with the strength of reason all elected deputies' and to 'avenge political clubs whose only enemies are the enemies of the people'. The *Patriote de la Mayenne*, for its part, wanted to ' . . repress the activity of trouble makers, whose tactics are the same in all departments'.[9] Yet once battle was joined on 20 April, it rapidly led to attacks on press freedom. The first signs of this arose in Paris, when on 3 May 1792, Dumouriez reported to the Legislative Assembly on the deteriorating situation at the front, attacking press criticism in particular, singling out Marat and Royou for attention and suggesting that they were secretely working together, from opposite ends of the political spectrum, to bring about defeat and anarchy. After a short and confused debate the Assembly ordered proceedings for treason to be taken against both; but Marat went into hiding. and continued publication from there, while Royou, plagued by ill-health, appears to have abandoned the *Ami du Roi* to his brother, and no action was taken.[10] However, the momentum of suspicion quickly passed to the provinces, where administrators felt freer to flout the law than their more closely supervised colleagues in Paris. On 7 May the postmaster in Tulle was severely chastised by the town's Jacobin club for handling right-wing papers, and offered profuse — if somewhat bewildered — apologies.[11] Two weeks later, on 20 May, the departmental administration of the *Côtes-du-Nord* appointed *commissaires* to inspect the post and confiscate 'aristocratic' brochures or journals, brushing aside the illegality of the measure with the assertion that 'The authors of these lies cannot claim the protection of press freedom, for its only purpose is to enlighten citizens, not to allow the printing of stories which are contradicted by all the official sources.'[12]

In mid-June it was the turn of the Hérault, at the opposite end of the country, when the municipal authorities of Clermont de l'Hérault marched *en bloc* to the local post office to inspect the newspapers passing through there, and confiscated 'several which profess the same principles'. Almost all of them were right-wing titles which appear to have been sent through the post, free, to would-be sympathisers.[13] Before the end of the month regular daily visits were also arranged by the Municipality in Bédarieux, defying both condemnation of its activity by the district authorities in Béziers, and complaints from six local merchants, who complained that, in addition to violating postal secrecy and press freedom, the measure cut them off from the valuable financial and commercial news needed for their trade.[14] Their appeals met with little sympathy, and on 22 July the departmental administration of the Hérault played its part, banning twelve papers, and then extending the list to 35 — all but two of which were right-wing — two days later. When the postal director of Montpellier refused to comply, agents were appointed to do the job for him because ' . . when the fatherland is in danger, it is absolutely essential to take all necessary precautions for the maintenance of order, and one of the most effective precautions is to stop the distribution of all anti-constitutional papers'.[15]

Other areas of the country also saw similar action during July.

In Grenoble, the Municipality banned Giroud's *Affiches de Dauphiné*, long a vexed source of *monarchien* views, once the decree declaring a national emergency was received from Paris, adding to the ban a long list of Parisian newspapers. On 30 July the departmental administration of the Bouches-du-Rhône ordered the Municipality of Marseilles also to set up a commission to open packets of newspapers and pamphlets arriving in the post, so that 'suspect' ones could be confiscated.[16] In Lyon, the Municipality acted on its own initiative, flouting the warnings of the Department by banning twelve counter-revolutionary journals by name ' . . and any others whose unconstitutional views are similar'. Similar action was taken in the Calvados, while in the Gers the Jacobin club in Auch consigned a local right-wing paper — the *Journal constitutionnel* — to the flames on 8 August, and the departmental administration banned the circulation of eleven Parisian titles a week later. In the Aude similar action was to follow at the end of the month.[17]

The insurrection of 10 August saw these initiatives transferred to Paris and taking a more violent turn. On the morning of the attack on the Tuileries, Suleau was arrested on the *terrasse des Feuillants*, on his way to fight in defence of the King. Recognised that evening by Théroigne de Méricourt, he was killed in a skirmish with his guards and his head paraded around the streets for all to see, on the end of a pikestaff.[18] Several of his fellow journalists, including Suard, Rivarol, Dupont de Nemours and the entire editorial staff of the *Petit Gautier*, actually fought at the Tuileries during the day, and were able to escape undetected in the subsequent confusion. However, none of the leading right-wing papers appeared on 11 August, and on the following day, the all-powerful provisional Paris Commune named seven of the most influential, and banned the postal authorities from handling them. On that day too, the 12 August, the offices of the *Journal de Paris* were ransacked and its presses broken, causing a hiatus in its production which lasted until October, when it returned under new management. The presses of the *Petit gautier* and of Duplain's *Courrier extraordinaire* were also destroyed, while those belonging to some other right-wing newspapers were confiscated by the Commune and distributed to radical journalists such as Gorsas or Marat.[19]

Over the following week several journalists wisely vanished from sight. Beffroy de Reigny, editor of the *Conservateur*, sheltered in the provinces until tempers cooled, while others such as Peltier and Montjoie, editors of the *Actes des Apôtres* and *Ami du Roi* respectively, went abroad to England and Switzerland. However eight were arrested. Du Rozoi was picked up on 12 August and sent for trial before a *tribunal extraordinaire* which had been expressly established to try 'crimes' relating to the *journée*, accused of corresponding with the emigrés, sending money to them and using his paper to provoke civil disorder. Tried and convicted on 25 August, he left behind him in the courtroom a note for the judge to read out, with the words 'A royalist like I should die on the feast day of Saint Louis.' He died the following morning at 9 a.m., under the guillotine, but his wish that his blood be transfused into the veins of an older man, to test his theory that it would lead to rejuvenation, was ignored.[20] Cazotte, an old man who had contributed several articles to the *Journal à deux liards*, survived the September massacres when his daughter threw her arms around his neck and defied the crowd to attack him; but, although released, he was re-arrested three weeks later, tried and executed. De Charnois, editor of the *Spectateur national*, was even less lucky, for he was murdered in the Abbaye during the prison massacres, but Duplain, owner of the express delivery *Courrier extraordinaire*, fought off his attackers in the *église des Carmes* with an iron bar until his brother was able to secure his release.[21] Although severe in Paris, retribution on the press was much lighter in the provinces, where there were no arrests or executions of journalists. On the other hand, several papers had closed down in the face of threats prior to 10 August, and several more closed down immediately afterwards in order to avoid trouble: the *Feuille de Strasbourg* in the Bas-Rhin, the *Echo des journaux* and *Courrier d'Avignon* in the Vaucluse, and the maverick *Journal constitutionnel du département du Gers* in Auch.

Yet the *journée* of 10 August never entirely eliminated the right-wing press, and neither did legislation passed later by the Convention, on 4 December 1792 and 29 March 1793, which made royalist journalists — and their printers — liable for the death penalty. Instead, several royalist journals re-emerged under new names, modifying their colours to those of moderate republicanism, and new ones were also launched which hid their true sympathies behind double meanings and ambiguity. The royalist *Journal général de politique*, for example, closed down forcibly on 10 August, returned in November as the *Bulletin national* with the same owner and editor, Bérard de Favas and Jean-Pierre Gallais respectively.[22] The *Gazette universelle*, also closed down in August for its Feuillant sympathies, reappeared as the *Nouvelles politiques et étrangères*, with the same owner, Pascal Boyer, helped now by a new shareholder and editor, Jean-Baptiste Suard, formerly of the *Journal de Paris*.[23] The *Petit gautier* bounced back in November as the *Feuille du matin*, still with Gautier de Syonnet at the helm, while the *Postillon de la guerre*, a paper which had been financed by court money during the spring and summer of 1792, reappeared on 20 August as the *Gazette générale de l'Europe*, with its owner and printer, Porte, doing little to conceal his royalist sympathies.[24] As for the totally new right-wing papers, many of them were the work of men who had never before worked as journalists. The *Quotidienne* and the *Révolution de 92* appeared at the beginning of the National Convention, on 20 September 1792, the latter later providing very full reports of the King's trial and surviving two suspensions in the summer of 1793.[25] In November came the *Journal français*, which concentrated its fire on the Paris Jacobin club, and the twice-weekly *Observateur à la Convention Nationale* and weekly *Semaines parisiennes*, both of which campaigned openly against the King's trial, the latter urging that prominent Jacobins be put into the dock instead. The *Abréviateur universel*, which proved agile enough to last for over five years, appeared in December, while in the following month a resourceful lawyer from Fécamp, François Robert, who had sharpened his editorial skills in Normandy, launched an evening paper, the *Observateur de l'Europe*, which was to claim 16,000 subscribers by the summer of 1793 for its scarcely concealed message of scorn for republican democracy.[26]

Yet although it survived, the right-wing press remained marginal in terms of political influence until the end of the terror, and political life was dominated instead by the struggle for power between Girondins and Montagnards. An early indication of the importance attached to the press in this struggle came on 28 August, when officials of the Jacobin-dominated provisional Paris Commune summoned Girey-Dupré before them to answer for criticisms that he had published of their activities in the *Patriote français*. He refused to appear, and when the Commune ordered his arrest two days later, he went into hiding so that they were only able to imprison his printer, Laporte. On 31 August the Assembly, prompted by Servan, intervened to declare their action illegal and Laporte was released, thus avoiding almost certain death in the prison massacres which started two days later — a fate which Girey-Dupré argued had been intended for himself.[27] The September massacres did, however, widen the rift between the two groups still further; and once the Convention met, Girondin deputies wasted little time in going on to the offensive and attacking Marat, who, as early as 25 September, was denounced for an article in his newly named *Journal de la république française* advocating, and not for the first time, the need for a dictatorship. Shortly afterwards a commission was set up to recommend methods of tightening up press legislation, but its report, presented by Lepelletier de Saint-Fargeau on 30 October, produced no agreement, and debate dragged on until the end of November before the issue was quietly dropped.[28] Not in the Jacobin club, however, where resentment against the Girondin press ran high throughout the autumn and winter. Brissot was struck off the membership list on 10 October and a prolonged effort was made to counteract the influence of Girondin newspapers, particularly in the provinces where, by common consent, they were highly influential.[29]

In late October the club decided to establish a weekly paper to present its own case, only to reverse the decision within days because several members expressed the fear that no editor could be trusted to reflect official views accurately. On 19 December, Deflers, who had for 18 months published the only officially authorised version of the club's correspondence, and a widely respected account of its debates, in his *Journal des débats de la société des amis de la constitution*, was expelled on suspicion of Girondin sympathies. Milscent-Creole, owner and editor of an evening paper, *le Créole patriote*, was asked to increase his coverage of club debates in compensation, but proved unable to do so, subsequently closing down completely at the end of February.[30] Tallien, who had published a highly successful *Ami des citoyens* with financial support from the club after the Champ de Mars massacre, was also asked to step into the breech by publishing a weekly paper covering debates and the King's trial — 'to combat the progress of the Girondin errors spread by Roland's, Brissot's and the Girondin faction . . . '; but he declined, pleading pressure of work elsewhere. Anxiety had reached such a pitch by now, however, that on 4 January a motion to expel all journalists from club meetings was only narrowly defeated, and instead a censorship committee was set up to examine their notes before they left meetings, with authority to exclude those guilty of consistent bias.[31]

Jacobin fears combined exaggeration with realism. The exaggeration centred around Roland's activity as Minister of the Interior between August 1792 and late January 1793, in subsidising the Girondin press. There was nothing new in this, for government patronage and subsidy were *ancien-régime* practices that had carried over into the revolution. From 1790 onwards Louis XVI had used money from the civil list to subsidise or set up newspapers favourable to the royalist cause, as became fully evident with the discovery

of the *armoire de fer* in late October.[32] During the first Girondin
Ministry in the spring of 1792, Dumouriez, as Minister of Foreign
Affairs, had used money allocated to the secret fund to reorganise
the *Gazette de France* — paying new editors and changing it from
a weekly to a daily paper — as a mouthpiece of government policy.
He may also have channelled money to Melletier's *Argus du département et de l'armée du Nord* in Valenciennes.[33] Roland too, while at
the Ministry of the Interior in the spring of 1792, channelled money
earmarked for the administration of Paris towards the setting up
of a wall paper, *la Sentinelle*, edited by his friend Jean-Baptiste
Louvet, to propagate Girondin policies in the streets of the capital.
It survived until 21 November 1792, when Louvet left to work on
the *Journal des débats*, developing in its latter stages into a weapon
of war in the Girondin-Montagnard struggle.[34]

However, in his second spell as minister Roland extended the
practice, with the help of a 100,000 livre grant voted to him by the
Legislative Assembly on 18 August

> . . . for the printing and distribution, both in the departments
> and in the armies, of anything capable of enlightening people
> on the criminal plots of the enemies of the state, and on the
> true causes of the evils which have for too long divided the
> country.

Roland set up a *bureau de l'esprit public* within the Ministry to
administer the fund, under the direction of a close friend,
Lanthenas, and the money went to writers and journalists sympathetic to the Girondin stance. One hundred subscriptions were
bought up for Gorsas' *Courrier*, and smaller amounts distributed
to the *Courrier de l'Égalité*, the *Trompette du Père Duchesne*, the *Feuille
villageoise*, the *Thermomètre du jour* and the *Fanal parisien*. The sums
involved were tiny, and certainly pale in comparison with the sums
disbursed by the Committee of Public Safety a year later; but the
secrecy of the operation and the evident political bias led to
exaggerated fears of the operation and bitter complaints from the
Jacobin club. As a result the 18 August decree was repealed on 21
January and the *bureau* wound up; but the resentments that it had
created ran deep, and were resurrected by Robespierre as late as
10 May 1793, during the course of a speech in the Convention on
the drafting of a new constitution.[35]

Yet if the fears of Roland's machinations were exaggerated, the
widespread assumption in Jacobin circles that the Girondin press

dominated the market was not. In terms of major newspapers the Mountain and Jacobin club had on its side Marat's *Journal de la République française*, Hébert's *Père Duchesne*, Robespierre's *Lettres à ses commettants*, and the *Journal des hommes libres*, which began publica-. tion in late November. Although we have no circulation figures for any of these papers for this period, there is little reason to doubt that they were relatively low. Two others, the *Premier journal de la Convention Nationale* and the *Créole patriote*, appear to have had no national impact either, while the lively *Journal de la savonette republicaine*, edited by a former colleague of Fréron, Labenette, and campaigning principally in favour of the King's execution and against Girondin influence — 'the infernal clique which had war declared' — appears to have had a mainly Parisian circulation.[36] In contrast the Girondins had the support of the *Annales patriotiques*, with its daily circulation of 12,000 and widespread readership amongst provincial clubs, and of Gorsas' *Courrier*, the *Patriote français*, the *Chronique de Paris*, and the *Révolutions de Paris*, which, with Prudhomme still at the helm, was carefully trimming its former radicalism. In addition there was the *Chronique du mois*, a monthly review which featured regular contributions from Brissot, Condorcet and another wilting radical, Nicolas de Bonneviulle; and the *Journal de Paris*, which, after its reappearance in October 1792, transferred its allegiance from monarchy to moderate republic. In December their influence was reinforced by the *Bulletin des amis de la vérité*, another of Bonneville's papers, which featured articles by Condorcet, Guadet, and Gensonné, and in the following month by the *Journal des amis*, edited by Bonneville's former collaborator in the Cercle Social, Claude Fauchet. Many of the crypto-royalist newspapers also supported Girondin policies — over the King's trial, for example — in common tactical opposition to Jacobinism.[37]

Amongst the provincial press the Jacobins were also on the defensive. Most provincial journalists, somewhat bewildered by the fragmentation of republican unity after the *journée* of 10 August, and appalled by the brutality of the September massacres or the violent rhetoric of Marat, hedged their bets by leaning towards the apparently moderate policies of the Gironde, sharing their anti-Parisian bias. The few Jacobin newspapers that existed appear to have either closed down, or else changed sides as the winter progressed, sometimes because of financial problems, and at other times in response to readers' pressure. The *Journal du département du Tarn*, produced by the Jacobin club in Castres since the spring, closed down in October through lack of support. A *Journal du département de l'Ardèche*, launched in the aftermath of 10 August, closed down in late November, while the *Journal du département de la Corrèze* followed suit in December, probably for financial reasons too. That same month saw the end of the *Correspondance générale* in Rheims, as its editor, Beaucourt, became preoccupied by his work as a departmental administrator; and of the *Courrier du Midi* in the Vaucluse, where Paul Capon transferred his readers to Sabin Tournal's *Courrier d'Avignon* for the same reason.[38] On 2 March the *Nouvelles intéressantes* closed down in Montauban, as its owner and printer, Fontanel, cut his financial losses and distanced himself from the Jacobin cause; while later in the same month the *Vedette* in Besançon, a paper which had begun publication in late 1791 and moved slowly from the centre to the radical left, was forced to suspend publication by anti-recruitment riots which almost led to the lynching of its editor.[39]

Worse was to come in early April, when the influential *Courrier de Strasbourg* lost its editor, Jean-Charles Laveaux, and passed back into the control of its more moderate owner, the printer, Jean-Georges Treuttel; while in May the *Journal des départements méridionaux*, organ of Marseilles' Jacobin club, went under as the revolt against Paris began in earnest.[40] Meanwhile, in the second city, the *Journal de Lyon*, once the most vociferous of the radical papers outside Paris, discreetly changed sides over the winter, probably in response to the provision of much-needed funds from the departmental administration of the Rhône-et-Loire.[41] To compensate for these losses, only three of the new provincial papers to come on to the market over the winter and spring of 1792–3 reveal any support for the Jacobin cause at all: the *Journal de la République française* launched by François Caron-Berquier in Amiens on 13 March 1793; the *Vérité au peuple* in the Ardèche, and the *Observateur montagnard* produced in Tulle by a former Parisian priest, J.C. Jumel. None of the three had more than a tiny local readership.[42]

This weakness fuelled Jacobin hostility to the Girondin press, and helped foster the belief that its journalists were part of a secret plot to pervert public opinion. Minor incidents reinforced this belief. On 27 January, for example, Nicolas Ladevèze, editor of the crypto-royalist *Journal français*, was arrested on the orders of the Committee of General Security for describing its members as 'men of blood'; but three days later he was released on the intervention of Buzot, a leading Girondin, who invoked the principle of press freedom. That freedom was obviously not open-ended, however, for after the food riots of 25–26 February Girondin deputies denounced Marat for encouraging them in his *Journal de la République*, and referred his case to the courts, where he was duly acquitted.[43] Yet the Girondins were not alone in having a narrow concept of free speech, as the incidents that took place on the evening of 9 March revealed. Durng the previous day news had filtered into Paris of Dumouriez's defeats in the United Provinces, and this had led to bitter criticism on the floor of the Convention against the prominent Girondin politicians closely identified with him. One montagnard deputy, Duhem, took the opportunity to denounce the Girondin press as ' . . . lying insects . . . the real obstacles to the progress of the revolution . . . inflammatory — or rather somniferous — papers . . . unworthy objects . . . ', and asked for all journalists to be expelled from Convention debates until the Committee of General Security had drawn up a full report on their activities. Nothing was put to the vote, but that same evening at the Jacobin club Bentabole fanned the flames by calling for the setting up of a revolutionary tribunal to deal with 'all brissotins and rolandists', and Desfieux advocated the arrest of the leading Girondin journalists.[44] Early the following evening, just before 8 p.m., armed gangs raided Gorsas' business premises on the *rue Ticquetonne*, smashing the presses, hacking up rolls of paper and starting a small fire. Gorsas himself escaped through the back door and over the garden wall, to raise the alarm at the meeting of his sectional assembly. Similar treatment was meted out an hour later to the presses of the *Chronique de Paris*, on the *rue Serpente*, while an attack on the presses of the *Journal français* only failed because word had got through in time for the equipment to be removed in advance. Prudhomme and Panckoucke felt threatened enough to organise an armed guard for their premises, while Lepage, printer for the *Patriote français*, prudently ended his three-year association with the paper, leaving Brissot to find a new printer.[45]

When news of these attacks reached the Convention, scant sympathy was shown for their victims by Montagnard deputies. Instead, there were suggestions that those involved had brought trouble upon themselves, and a law was passed forbidding deputies to work as journalists. This was intended as a blow against the Girondin press, and before it was repealed on 2 April, only Brissot and Condorcet complied with it, while Marat pointedly refused to do so.[46] Girondin attempts to strike back, by prosecuting Marat in mid-April and arresting Hébert in May, both backfired, and in the meanwhile, the tide of the Jacobin counter-offensive passed to the provinces. In the Vaucluse, representatives on mission, Boisset and Bayle banned the circulation of a number of Girondin papers on 22 April, and three weeks later, took similar action in the Bouches-du-Rhône against Gorsas' *Courrier*, the *Patriote français*, the *Quotidienne* ' . . . and all other maliciously hypocritical writings of a similar kind'. Similar action was taken by the departmental administration of the Indre-et-Loire, while Julien and Bourbotte, on mission in the Loiret, ordered the postal administration there not to handle a list of 20 newspapers

> . . . which are harmful to true political principles, character-
> ised by revolting partiality in the way that they report various
> opinions within the National Convention, liable to corrupt
> public opinion, [and] damaging to the spirit of equality which
> is the sole fundamental basis of public and individual liberty.

The Convention overruled this on 25 May, but to little effect.[47]

The *journée* of 2 June proved to be decisive in tipping the balance against the Girondin press. On the day of the insurrection itself several sections in Paris responded to a call from Hanriot, commander of the National Guard, for the arrest of 'anti-patriotic' journalists, and the *section des Piques* decided to confiscate their presses for the benefit of the poor, just as the provisional Commune, some ten months previously, had redistributed presses from royalist newspapers to the benefit of radical journalists. Two days later the Commune's *comité central révolutionnaire* ordered a detailed report to be drawn up on all journalists, so that action could be taken against any who were suspect.[48] It was probably never done, but meanwhile the *Patriote français* and the *Courrier* had already ceased publication on 1 June, as Girey-Dupré and Gorsas fled the capital, while Prudhomme was arrested and detained for 24 hours on 2 June in what appears to have been a clumsy attempt on the part of the *comité révolutionnaire* of his section, the *section de l'unité*, to close down the *Révolutions de Paris*. He was only released after the direct intervention of Hébert and Chaumette, much to the annoyance of the *comité révolutionnaire*, which accused him of causing more damage to the country by his publications than the combined Austrian and Prussian armies.[49] Fauchet's *Journal des amis* went out of business on 15 June, and although the *Chronique de Paris* limped on for another two months without many of its major contributors, it too succumbed on 25 August, handing on its subscribers to the *Feuille de salut public*. Throughout the summer the Municipal *comité de surveillance* kept a close eye on many other papers, confiscating copies in the post, cautioning editors and, on occasion, also arresting them.[50]

In the provinces, on the other hand, the initial effect of the coup, particularly in areas affected by the federalist revolt, was to provide a temporary boost to the anti-Jacobin press. In Lyon the *Journal de Lyon*, having already fallen under the control of the departmental authorities during the spring, went on to serve them faithfully during the rebellion; and the *comité général de surveillance* also published its own daily *Bulletin du département du Rhône-et-Loire* with news of the progress of the siege, starting on 8 August and ending shortly before final defeat, on 30 September. In Bordeaux too the *commission populaire de salut public* set up its own daily *Bulletin*, which was posted up daily on walls around the city to the sound of the trumpet between 9 June and 1 August; while in Marseille, Beaugeard's *Journal de Marseille* had already been adopted during May by the *comité général de sureté*, which co-ordinated sectional activity in the city. From 1 June, it carried a new rubric, 'Sections', in which Beaugeard openly campaigned for the revolt and against the Montagnard seizure of power in Paris.[51] Similar bulletins were published by administrations hostile to the *coup d'état* in Rennes, Caen, Besançon and Lens, while the counter-revolution in the Vendée produced its own *Bulletin du conseil supérieur* from Châtillon-sur-Sèvre during September and October.[52] None of these papers, however, survived the collapse of their respective revolts, and by the late autumn, the opposition press in the provinces, as in Paris, was coming to heel.

How close to heel it actually came remains somewhat unclear, as there has never been a detailed textual study of the lesser-known Parisian or provincial newspapers to reveal the degree to which ambiguities, double meanings and omissions allowed many right-wing and royalist titles to conceal their true ideological loyalties. Moreover, even within Jacobin and *sans-culotte* ranks it is also clear that, despite the increased role played by direct crowd action, sectional politics and Jacobin club discussions in formulating policy and putting pressure on government, the press continued to be used, during the terror as before, as a weapon in political campaigns. Between June and September 1793 the authority of the Convention and Committee of Public Safety was frequently challenged from the left, by radical *sans-culottes* in several of the sections of Paris, by activists within the Ministry of War led by François Vincent, and by agitators in both the Jacobin and Cordeliers clubs. All of them wanted increased economic controls, an intensification of the terror against former nobles, and more radical military measures to counteract the danger of defeat. Their criticisms were articulated in several newspapers, which, because of their circulation and popular appeal, were extremely effective in putting the government on the defensive. The *Journal de la montagne*, for example, joined with the *Père Duchesne* in attacking Custines, the noble commander of the *armée du Nord*, and bringing about his trial and execution.[53] At the same time, during July and August, the *Enragés* Jacques Roux and Théophile Leclerc profited from Marat's assassination by reviving two of the dead hero's titles, the *Publiciste* and the *Ami du peuple* respectively, to campaign for price controls, the death penalty for hoarders and the extension of their own versions of popular democracy. This in turn forced Robespierre to wheel out Marat's widow to disown them in public, and by September both were silenced.[54]

Their success nevertheless needled Hébert into radicalising his stance further in the *Père Duchesne*, and to demand during August the implementation of the constitution of 1793, reform of the executive branch of government, and swingeing economic controls to eliminate food shortage. His skill in catching the wind of popular demands was also partly responsible for the *journée* of 5 September, enabling him to gain a marked ascendancy in the Jacobin club during the late autumn. This became evident during the early stages of dechristianisation, when he forced the editor of the club's paper, the *Journal de la montagne* to resign over his opposition to atheism, and his allies in the War Office meanwhile ensured that thousands of copies of the *Père Duchesne* were distributed amongst the troops, where its earthy style proved popular.[55] Resistance to Hébert's influence, and to *sans-culotte* power, which was mounted by the so-called Indulgents in December, found its principal outlet in Camille Desmoulin's *Vieux Cordelier* which, for several numbers between December 1793 and March 1794, attacked both political extremists and the structures of the revolutionary government. Both it and the *Père Duchesne* vanished when the two factions were liquidated in the spring of 1794, and the press's role in political debate sank to a low ebb. Indeed, political debate itself vanished beyond the low-tide mark over the summer of 1794, except perhaps within the Committee of Public Safety, in which personal and policy rifts were beginning to appear. Carnot set up an army newspaper in early July 1794, as the crisis was coming to a head, to prepare military opinion for Robespierre's fall and ensure that the army did not intervene.[56]

Yet any influence that the press did have during the terror was progressively whittled away by legislation. Although article 7 of the Declaration of Rights prefacing the constitution of 1793 guaranteed freedom of expression, and article 122 of the constitution itself promised ' . . . complete freedom of the press', both provisions remained as theoretical as the constitution itself. Instead, emergency legislation went in precisely the opposite direction. On 29 March 1793 the Convention had already struck at the extremes of both left and right, ordering the death penalty for those found guilty of advocating either a return of the monarch or attacks on property. The law of suspects of 17 September widened the net still further to include all those who ' . . . through their writings have revealed themselves to be supporters of tyranny or federalism, and enemies of liberty'.[57] On 17 October further legislation made editors personally responsible for criticisms levelled against government committees or the Convention, while the notorious law of 22 *prairial* in the following summer enabled conviction to be made on suspicion rather than fact, without benefit of a defence lawyer.[58]

Louis XVI's head, solitary though it was, might well have smiled in its grave, for the *ancien régime*'s rationale for censorship — namely, the need for political stability and state security — was now being adopted by its former republican opponents. Robespierre, whose consistent and eloquent defence of press freedom stretched from the autumn of 1789 into the spring of 1793, changed tack once the Mountain had gained the levers of power. On 16 June he urged the Committee of Public Safety to punish ' . . . treacherous journalists who are the most dangerous enemies of liberty', and the same vein runs through entries made subsequently in his private diary. 'What obstacles exist to the people's education?', he asked himself; only to reply: 'Mercenary writers who lead it astray by impudent daily lies. What can be done about it? . . . Ban writers as the most dangerous enemies of the fatherland.' Or, in his plans for a report to the Convention on Danton's arrest:

> There is a trait of Danton which proves that he had an ungrateful and dark mind: he had loudly recommended the latest numbers of the *Vieux Cordelier*: he had dared, at the Jacobins, to support press freedom at a time when I proposed that those numbers be consigned to the flames![59]

It is perhaps too easy to juxtapose these statements with

Robespierre's earlier pleas for the tolerance of error, for political circumstances had radically changed and the entire future of the revolution was at stake; but their importance lies in the light that they throw on the way in which Jacobin attitudes towards the press had changed due to these circumstances during the terror. The Committee of Public Safety, for example, once Robespierre was a member, hounded Panckoucke for suspected nuances, omissions and typographical errors in the *Moniteur*. On 2 *frimaire* Thuau-Grandville was told that his report of Robespierre's speech in the Convention five days previously was too short and that the full text should be published in the next available number. A month later Panckoucke was rebuked sharply when one of his workers lost the text of a report from Barère that had been sent for printing: ' . . . we would warn you, citizen, that you must ensure that it is found again, for an error of this magnitude would be too serious for the committee of public safety not to follow it up with the utmost severity'. Seven days later there were loud protests when the almost Clootzian phrase 'one and universal republic' was attributed to Robespierre instead of 'one and indivisible republic'; while the failure in *messidor* to print a full list of the signatories to one of the Committee's decisions was denounced as implying a disturbing lack of unanimity in its ranks.[60]

Similar attitudes were echoed in the Convention. Chabot denounced journalists on 26 *vendémiaire* as 'scribblers', urging that government subsidies be withdrawn and that journalists be made personally responsible for their misdeeds. Amar too, announcing on behalf of the Committee of General Security the arrest of Rabaut Saint-Etienne, who had written for the *Moniteur* and *Chronique de Paris*, stressed the importance of nailing down ' . . . these scribblers [who are] in the pay of the enemies of the Republic, treacherous and ambitious men. *Sans-culotte* and Jacobin opinion took up the same refrain. On 18 August 1793 citizen Eynaud, from the *section des sans-culottes*, delivered a speech at the bar of the Convention on the very subject of press freedom, urging that it be subordinated to the greater good of the community as a whole, and that journalists be controlled through censorship for the duration of the war, with imprisonment for those foolish enough to criticise the republic.[61] A veteran of the Paris Jacobins, Ferrières-Sauveboeuf, argued that the only legitimate freedom that the press could enjoy was freedom to defend the revolutionary government, as any criticism of it could only serve to comfort supporters of the old-style tyranny.[62] The same selective view permeates a report drawn up for the *commission de l'instruction publique* in the summer of 1794 by two former journalists, Payan and Fourcade, and it was perhaps most succinctly stated by the *société populaire* of Angers in a *profession de foi politique* drawn up in the autumn of 1793, shortly after a purge of its ranks to weed out federalist sympathisers, in which the conditional carried more sting than the statement of principle:

> The freedom to express one's thought aloud or in writing is one of the most precious of man's rights, and can only be restricted in the case of a revolution carried out by the people or by its representatives.[63]

The new mood of political orthodoxy had two important consequences for the press: on the one hand, enforced closures, imprisonment and the execution of journalists and printers; on the other hand, increased official patronage and subsidy aimed at creating a compliant press to disseminate revolutionary propaganda. The former resulted in the elimination of many famous names. Brissot, for example, one of the 29 deputies banned from the Convention on 2 June, abandoned the *Patriote français* and avoided house arrest by leaving Paris and heading south, armed only with a bundle of clothes, two guidebooks and some *assignats*. However, he was recognised and arrested when he reached Moulins, sent back to the capital and guillotined on 31 October. His friend, and the effective editor of the *Patriote français* since the winter of 1791, Girey-Dupré, also escaped from Paris, heading to the centres of federalist resistance in the Eure and the Calvados, before going south to his native Bordeaux. There he was also recognised and sent back to Paris to be executed, two days before Brissot, at the age of 24.[64]

Gorsas sent the last edition of his *Courrier* to readers on 31 May, for the edition of 1 June was confiscated in the post early that morning, and his chief typesetter and compositor arrested. He wisely stayed away from the Convention on 2 June, and when news of his house arrest came through, he left the city to join friends organising resistance in Evreux. From there he went to Caen and, after the failure of the Normandy revolt, to Rennes, where he stayed for two months with his eldest daughter. Then, anxious to learn of the fate of his wife and children, he returned to Paris where, on 6 October, he was recognised while foolishly reading a newspaper in a public reading room. He was executed as an outlaw, without trial, on the following day.[65] Other journalists executed in these same months included Rabaut Saint-Étienne and Claude Fauchet, while Carra met the guillotine on 31 October, having been arrested two months previously and vainly tried to save his life by promising to abandon journalism for ever. Condorcet, suspended from the Convention on 2 June, had an arrest warrant issued against him on 8 July, but went into hiding immediately, staying with a friend on the *rue Servandoni* until the following spring. Then, fearing arrest, he went to the southern Paris suburb of Fontenay-les-Roses to seek refuge with Jean-Baptiste Suard, but was recognised and arrested in Clamart, committing suicide while in prison at Bourg-la-Reine.[66]

The fate of Girondin journalists was matched by that of many of their Jacobin rivals during the following spring and summer as the boundaries of political orthodoxy narrowed. Marat's murder at the hands of Charlotte Corday on 13 July 1793 had been an isolated event, but the factional struggle between *hébertistes* and *indulgents* during the winter of Year II led inexorably to the executions of Hébert, Philippeaux and Desmoulins, and several others followed over the summer. Among them was Duplain, editor of the *Courrier universel* and pioneer of express delivery systems, guillotined on 21 *messidor* for publishing an article on French war plans copied from the *Courrier du Bas-Rhin*.[67] Antoine Tournon, one-time partner of Prudhomme and editor of a number of democratic newspapers, followed on 22 *messidor* for writing for the *Mercure universel*, after a perfunctory appearance before the revolutionary tribunal:

> The president asked him if he had not worked on the *Mercure universel*: he replied yes: but I only did the article on the Convention, and without making any judgements; he wanted to continue speaking, but the president cut him short.[68]

Accompanying him to the guillotine was Pierre-Germain Parisau, a man with impeccable right-wing credentials, who received a similarly unsympathetic hearing:

> The president of the jury asked him if he was not a journalist, and which journal he had worked for. The accused replied, 'I worked for the *Feuille du Jour*, but it was a paper that supported the revolution and everything that I wrote was legal. The reason for my arrest is that I criticised Carra and Gorsas.' The president of the jury then said: 'Did you not write in your paper that trees of liberty were being planted in France, but

that they had not roots?' The accused replied, 'I cannot remember, but I do not think so.' The president: 'Ah! Ah! That is enough. Say no more.'[69]

Roch Marcandier, one-time secretary to Camille Desmoulins, also went to the guillotine on the following day, along with his wife, Marie Gouarnot,

> . . . as one of the main leaders of the federalist faction, having published a pamphlet called the *Véritable ami du peuple*, in which he said that the Convention was nothing more than a place of sedition, a group of anarchists, a monstrous assembly of men without character.[70]

Pascal Boyer followed in early *prairial* because of his 'aristocratic' paper — the *Nouvelles politiques* — and on the seventh of that month a former editor of a Jacobin club newspaper, Milscent-Créole, was also guillotined.[71] Louis Réné Quentin de Richebourg, chevalier de Champcenetz, co-author with Rivarol of a satirical *Petit dictionnaire des grands hommes de la révolution*, and one-time contributor to the *Actes des Apôtres*, was executed in *thermidor* for articles contributed to the *Journal de Paris* in which he apparently revealed himself to be one of the ' . . . emulators of Royou, Fontenay, Durosoy [sic]', and for articles in the *Actes des Apôtres* in which he ' . . . constantly attacked the revolution and sought to destroy popular sovereignty and liberty'.[72] Sharing his fate in the early days of that month were Roucher and André Chenier, for articles in the *Journal de Paris*, Boyer-Brun of the *Journal du peuple*, the printer and distribution manager of the *Gazette de Paris*, Girouard and Mme Feuchère, and the bookseller Gattey, renowned for stocking counter-revolutionary pamphlets and periodicals.[73]

Repression in the provinces was less severe, but it still took lives, especially in areas of federalism or counter-revolt. In Lyons the editor of the pro-federalist *Journal de Lyon*, Fain, was guillotined in October 1793 once the town was reconquered, as was Mathon de la Cour, editor of a previous right-wing *Journal de Lyon*, banned in 1792 for its counter-revolutionary views, who had gone on to act as president of the sections during the rebellion.[74] In Bordeaux three journalists were executed: Duvigneau and Marandon — former editors of the *Journal de Guyenne* and *Courier de la Gironde* respectively — more for their participation in the *commission populaire* during the revolt than for their journalism, while Jean-François

Cornu was executed because he had, in the *Journal de Bordeaux* from late 1791 onwards, ' . . . opposed all good citizens in supporting *feuillantisme*, whose aim was to re-establish the monarchy and dissolve the republic'.[75] From Périgueux and Limoges, Pipaud Desgranges and the *abbé* Lambertie, both of whom had abandoned journalism two years previously, were sent to Paris on charges of federalism and guillotined there in the autumn of 1794, while in Dijon the business manager of a short-lived right-wing paper of 1790, the *Ami des citoyens*, was executed for federalism.[76] Further east, in Strasbourg, Euloge Schneider, editor of the *Argus* and public prosecutor for the criminal court of the Bas-Rhin, was arrested in December 1793 and executed in Paris several months later.[77] Elsewhere journalists either took evasive action or escaped with spells of imprisonment. Ferreol de Beaugeard, closely involved in the federalist insurrection, fled Marseille after it was reconquered in late August and went into hiding, abandoning his *Journal de Marseille* for two years. Broulhiet, editor of the *Journal universel* in Toulouse, was imprisoned in late September for the duration of the terror, as were Nicolas Blouet, editor of the *Journal des départements de la Moselle* in Metz, Bruslon, printer of the *Journal partriotique de l'Indre-et-Loire*, and Paris de l'Espinard, editor of the *Gazette du département du Nord*.[78]

The terror was therefore hard on certain journalists, but the stick was accompanied by liberal supplies of carrot as the Committee of Public Safety and other government agencies sought to use the newspapers to direct and control public opinion through subsidies and the establishment of an official press. In this they were following the footsteps well worn by the monarchy and by the Girondin ministers before them, but they did it more extensively and with a great deal more money. On 16 April 1793 the Provisional Executive Council was allocated 6 million *livres* by the Convention and promptly used some of this to prop up the ailing *Gazette de France*, which was directly managed by the Ministry of Foreign Affairs but had been in financial trouble since Dumouriez had reorganised it and made it into a daily the year before. It also took out sizeable subscriptions to struggling independent newspapers, such as the *Logotachygraphe*, to keep them afloat.[79] However, the Committee of Public Safety intervened in force during the autumn when, using some of the 50 million *livres* voted to it by the Convention on 2 August, it took out 600 subscriptions to the *Moniteur*, the *Journal universel*, the *Antifédéraliste*, the *Père Duchesne* and the *Journal des hommes libres*, for distribution to local *sociétés populaires* and administrations.

The Ministry of the Interior, the *commission d'instruction publique* and the *commission des subsistances* all followed suit — the latter distributing 2,000 copies of each edition of the *Feuille du cultivateur* around the country in the spring of 1794.[80]

The meatiest pickings of all, however, came from the Ministry of War, which, during Bouchotte's tenure of office between the spring of 1793 and that of 1794, became a hotbed of *sans-culotte* radicalism. Already, in December 1792, one of Bouchotte's predecessors, Pache, had organised the distribution of the *Bulletin de la Convention Nationale* to the armies, to keep them in touch with political life, but Bouchotte went further, using 50,000 *livres* voted to him specifically in May 1793 ' . . . in order to provide for the despatch to the armies of newspapers capable of enlightening and motivating patriotism', and a further one million *livres* allocated in July, to buy up huge numbers of the radical press and distribute them to the troops at the front through the *commissaires de guerres*. The *Journal des hommes libres* began with 2,000 subscriptions, rising to 5,000 by *brumaire*, while the *Père Duchesne* began with that figure, rising to 12,000 by *vendémiaire*. The Jacobin club newspaper, the *Journal de la montagne*, had 2,000 subscriptions bought up until a quarrel between its editor, Laveaux, and Bouchotte's secretary, Vincent, led to their cancellation in *vendémiaire*, while several other newspapers — including the *Antiféderaliste* and the *Batave* — also profited to a similar level. Even after Bouchotte's dismissal in *germinal* of Year II, the practice was carried on, with Audouin's *Journal universel* and the *Journal des hommes libres* as the chief beneficiaries.[81]

Patronage on this scale was certainly manna from heaven for many struggling editors, but it was just a short step from disbursing money to the more complicated stage of setting up an official newspaper that could provide a totally controlled flow of information and propaganda. In November 1792 the Convention had founded the *Bulletin de la Convention Nationale*, which contained a condensed account of its own proceedings and was distributed widely throughout the country to administrators, schools and *sociétés populaires*.[82] The problem was that it was informational and factual in tone, restricted to Convention proceedings, and little likely to convert the sceptical or rouse the faint hearted. Something more lively was needed, but something too which was not an openly government-sponsored affair, due to the distrust that such newspapers had created under the *ancien régime* and, more recently, as a result of Roland's *Sentinelle*. When the dantonist Committee of Public Safety took the decision to launch the *Feuille de salut public* in June 1793, therefore, it did so secretly and never openly acknowledged its role. The paper was put under the control of the Minister of the Interior, Garat, and its editorship entrusted to a man who enjoyed close links with both Danton and the minister, Alexandre Rousselin. When the membership of the Committee was altered in mid-July, the project was kept on, and Garat took over from Rousselin as editor-in-chief. At the end of the month the paper picked up subscribers to two newspapers that had closed down, the *Chronique de Paris* and the *Thermomètre du jour*, and was allocated a direct subsidy from the Committee which covered all its costs over and above subscription revenue — almost 100,000 *livres* — for the next year. Thus, throughout the terror, the Committee of Public Safety had its own newspaper to present its own case and argue its corner.[83]

Yet official papers sprang up in the provinces too, set up by departmental authorities or representatives on mission in several areas of federalism or counter-revolution, to boost republican morale. The first came in the Vendée and the Loire-Inférieure in April and May 1793, during the early weeks of the rising there, followed by the Sarthe and the Indre-et-Loire in July, and the *Bulletin du département des Côtes-duNord* published in Saint-Brieuc between *brumaire* and *frimaire*. They were, for the most part, produced in wall-poster form so that they could reach the maximum local audience, mixing in official proclamations and military news with short articles of propaganda, and lasting only as long as the local political crisis itself.[84] Further south, in Lyons and Marseilles, the effort was more prolonged. The besieging army at Lyons published a daily *Bulletin de l'armée campée à Limonay* between mid-August and early October, and three of the main political papers that appeared in the city after its reconquest — the *Journal de ville-affranchie*, the *Journal républicain* and the *Père Duchesne* — were all edited by protégés of Fouché, the representative on mission, and subsidised out of official sources.[85] Similarly, in Marseilles representatives on mission — this time Pomme and Charbonnier — were behind the appearance of the *Journal républicain de Marseilles et des départements méridionaux*, which appeared during the winter months of Year II and was even edited by two Parisians, Sébastien Lacroix and Pierre Mittié *fils*.[86] In the Dordogne too, during the following spring, it was the representative on mission, Lakanal, who was behind the appearance of a *Journal d'instruction populaire* in Sarlat, which was aimed at a peasant audience and conveniently provided a glossary of difficult words and phrases for their benefit —

explaining such esoteric terms as *philosophe* or *Pyrénées*.[87] The only department to launch into print on its own initiative was that of the Gers, which first decided to publish its own newspaper in September 1793, then changed its mind and subsidised an existing local paper instead in October, the *Journal du département du Gers*, before returning to its original intention and financing a *Documents de la raison. Feuille antifanatique* between *nivôse* and *thermidor* of Year II. For this it found an editor in an idiosyncratic local literary figure, Pierre-Nicolas Chantreau, who was later also to be an active journalist in the Directory.[88]

Two other important sources of an official press were the army and the Jacobin club network. The growth of newspapers catering for a military readership, which dates from the 1770s, has been carefully traced in a detailed study by Marc Martin.[89] None of the *ancien-régime* titles lasted long, however, and neither did several new papers launched in 1790 and 1791, which attempted to cater for military interest, mainly among the officer class, in the political and administrative changes then taking place. Once war broke out, however, new ground was broken with the publication of newspapers for troops at the front, published from army units themselves and designed to raise troop morale. The first in this new mould was the *Argus de l'armée du Nord*, which, between June 1792 and January 1793, was used by Dumouriez both to reinforce his own authority within the army that he commanded and to control the flow of news from the front back to Paris, rather like a modern news agency, so that it would be presented in the best possible light. It was terminated by the Ministry of War when Dumouriez dissented from the Convention's policy towards the annexation of Belgium, but in April 1793 the concept was revived, in the context of civil war, by Tallien. An experienced radical journalist himself, Tallien arrived in Chinon in April 1793 as representative on mission, charged with organising the defence of the area against the Vendée revolt. In an attempt to revive both civilian and military morale, he organised a *Bulletin de la commission centrale du département d'Indre-et-Loire près l'armée de Chinon*, which appeared as a wall-poster and carried proclamations and official decisions and decrees.[90] It probably lasted only a matter of weeks — for only the first number has survived — but was followed in July by similar papers for two other armies, the army of the *côtes de la Rochelle* and the army of the *côtes de Cherbourg*, in Angers and Cherbourg respectively, set up once again by representatives on mission. The *Courrier de l'armée des côtes de la Rochelle* was launched on 12 July, partly to restore troop morale after a defeat at Châtillon some five days previously, but also to prepare opinion among the troops for the replacement of Biron as commander by Ronsin. The *Journal de l'armée des côtes de Cherbourg*, on the other hand, followed a victory at Pacy-sur-Eure and, edited by an employee of the Ministry of Foreign Affairs, Jean-Jacques Derché, lasted for six months, until 21 *frimaire*.[91]

Late August also saw the beginnings of the *Bulletin de l'armée des côtes de Brest*, different because it was launched by the local army commander himself, Canclaux, in an apparent attempt to immunise his troops from the radical politics contained in newspapers sent by the Ministry of War from Paris. Understandably, Bouchotte took umbrage, Canclaux lost his command, and the paper closed down in late October.[92] With the passing of the immediate crisis of federalism the momentum behind the military press now vanished, with the sole exception of the Spanish border, where the *Avant-Garde de l'armée des Pyrénées-Orientales* appeared in late February 1794. The impetus behind it was, once more, the Commander-in-Chief, Dugommier, who had been appointed in late *nivose* and came fresh from the siege of Toulon. His aim was to restore morale in a badly dispirited army, and in this he enjoyed the support of the two representatives on mission, Milhaud and Soubrany, busy on a parallel political purge. Almost exclusively designed for military consumption, it survived until the following autumn.[93] The one significant military newspaper of the terror that was not produced at the front was the *Soirée du camp*, but it was a special case, launched by Carnot for specifically political purposes in late *messidor*, and edited by two of his own *protégés*. Aristide Valcour and Camille. The text of each number — written in a bluff and vulgar style akin to that of the guillotined *Père Duchesne* — was vetted by him personally before going to press, and once the crisis of 9 *thermidor* was over, he was quick to wind it up. The lessons that he had learnt, however, were to be put to use again in the spring of 1796.[94]

Like military journals, Jacobin club journals also grew from roots laid down earlier in the revolution: by the Grenoble club in December 1789, by clubs in Angers, Versailles, Arras and Aurillac in 1791, and others in Castres, Nancy and Caen during the spring and summer of 1792. All of these were the result of local initiatives, rather than of any centrally organised campaign, and none of them was financially successful, for only the Nancy newspaper was still going in 1793. Yet in early June of 1793, the *Journal de la montagne* was launched by the Paris club, and three affiliated provincial clubs followed before the end of the year: Limoges was the first, with the

Journal du département de la Haute-Vienne in early September; Toulouse followed with the *Journal révolutionnaire* before the end of the month, and the Douai club published two numbers of a short-lived *Feuille décadaire* during *brumaire*. More followed during the spring and summer of 1794: in Rheims, for example, the club took over an existing *Feuille rhémoise* that was in danger of folding up, while in Marseilles, Sedan, Chalons-sur-Marne and Bordeaux, new newspapers were launched from scratch.[95]

By the summer, nine provincial clubs had their own papers and although their precise content varied with local conditions or with the editorial and financial resources available, they were without exception unashamedly propagandist in tone, publicising the activities of their own particular club and preaching the doctrines of Jacobin orthodoxy. The *Journal révolutionnaire de Toulouse*, for example, always devoted its leading article to Toulouse news, exuding a perpetual and unrealistic optimism over the popularity of the revolution in the city which even the most committed of its readers must occasionally have found excessive. 'Whoever takes a calm look at the political situation in this city cannot fail to notice that public opinion is becoming firmer and more determined every day. Reason is also gaining ground in this whole region,' it claimed on 17 *brumaire*. On 9 *nivôse* it proclaimed: 'Toulouse has always been a temple of the arts and of philosophy. Today it has become one of the favoured theatres of the revolution.' It did also carry departmental and national news, as well as reports from the *armée des Pyrenees*, but only occasionally did hints of internal club divisions and conflicts seep out.

The *Journal du vrai Jacobin*, which started in Sedan in *ventôse*, was much more open in its reflection of political divisions, and markedly more anglophobic — no doubt because of closer geographical proximity to the war zone. Published by a smaller club, with more limited resources, it also had a more restricted news coverage, as did the *Journal de la société populaire de Châlons-sur-Marne*, or the *Tribune de la société populaire de Marseille*, the latter of which was little more than a resumé of club debates.[96] Yet all of them were designed to boost the morale of members and neighbouring clubs, in this way compensating for the weakness of the independent Jacobin press: for no major city in any part of France was able to sustain an independent Jacobin paper during the terror for more than a matter of months, because — as one of the longest lived of them, the *Esprit public*, told its readers in Angers when it closed down in the late autumn of 1793 — of '. . . the small number of subscribers'. The only apparent exception to this was in Besançon, where the *Vedette*, launched back in November 1791 by the Lazarist priest, Claude Ignace Dormoy, continued to publish throughout the terror; but even its survival was considerably helped by a decision of the depart-. mental authorities to subscribe to 700 copies, for distribution to local Municipalities and *sociétés populaires*.[97] In reality, therefore, the Jacobin press was an artificial creation, a hot-house plant kept alive by government money, and with no visible means of support once that flow of money ceased.

The flow of money did stop soon after 9 *thermidor* Year II, when Robespierre's arrest heralded the end of the terror. Post-thermidorean politics saw the dismantling of the revolutionary government, the collapse of its censorship and a drastic reduction of the level of the official or semi-official press. Yet just as its impact on the political history of the revolution was substantial — and its interpretation still divides historians in the latter half of the twentieth century, some 200 years after the event — so its effects on the press were also important. In concrete terms, it eliminated several dozen newspapers, guillotined many editors and printers, and imprisoned many more, and spawned a large propaganda press dependent for its survival on public finance. Imprisonment and subsidy were nothing new, for several of these methods of control had already been used under the *ancien régime*; but they had never been justified before in the name of democracy, and never deployed with such thoroughness. For politicians of the Mountain, for members of Jacobin clubs throughout the country, and for militant *sans-culottes*, the survival of the revolution mattered above all else, and justified the temporary suspension of private and public liberties. In this survival the press had an important propaganda role to play, which was well summarised by Payan and Fourcade, reporting for the *commission de l'instruction publique* in the summer of 1794:[98]

Newspapers are like theatres: they have a moral impact. For this reason they must be placed under some kind of control. What shape should this control take? That is an extremely delicate and important question, which relates to the very principles of freedom, and can therefore only be answered within the context of the principles of the revolutionary government, and the supreme law of the safety of the people . . . To publish and comment on legislation is something that is immeasurably influential and dangerous under the regime of a revolutionary government, and where does the power to do such a thing come from? Is it something given to journalists by the nation, or acquired through their own ability? How can public opinion belong to such small men? It is time that the law caught hold of a class of counter-revolutionaries that it has so far left untouched.

They then went on, with due deference, to urge that the Committee of Public Safety be empowered to take such action. They were out of date, for it had already done so, but after *thermidor* its powers lay in ruins and all hopes of moral control melted away.

From now on, until Bonaparte's seizure of power in 1799, the Jacobin press would be fighting, not to mould public morality, but just to survive. The initiative was to pass, for the first time in the revolution, to the right-wing press, buoyed up by a dramatic reversal in public opinion. The difficulty of accommodating to this, and to the threat that it implicitly posed to the survival of the republic, was a problem bequeathed to the post-thermidorean Convention and the Directory.

Notes

1. Fréron and Desmoulins had abandoned the *Orateur du peuple* and *Révolutions de France et de Brabant* respectively after the Champ de Mars massacre. For the failure of the *Tribun*, see Raoul Arnaud, *Journaliste, sansculotte et thermidorien. Le fils de Fréron (1754–1802). D'après des documents inédits* (Paris, 1909), pp. 163–4.

2. *Courrier de Strasbourg, prospectus*. See also copies of 3 January 1792, pp. 6–7; 4 January, pp. 10–11; 9 January, pp. 25–6, etc. The impact of the *Courrier*'s reports on the Parisian press can be seen in the *Patriote Français, Annales patriotiques, Gazette universelle*, and *Logographe* during January and February 1792.

3. X. Maeght, *La presse dans le département du Nord sous la révolution française*, Thèse de troisième cycle (Lille, 1971), pp. 307–24; X. Maeght, 'Deux journaux du département du Nord en 1792', *A.h.r.f.*, no. 216 (1974), pp. 216–34. For the clearest statement of Dumouriez's involvement, see Marc Martin, *Les origines de la presse militaire en France à la fin de l'ancien régime et sous la révolution (1770–1799)* (Paris, 1974), pp. 159–62.

4. B.M. Le Mans, Fonds Maine 2490 and 2491; see also Paul Mautouchet, 'Philippeaux journaliste', *La Révolution Française*, 19ᵉ année, no. 5 (1899), p. 402ff.

5. B.M. Annonay (nos. 10, 11, 14); see also A.N. F19 403, letter of mun. of Annonay, 12 May 1792 and Léon Rostaing, *Les anciennes loges maçonniques d'Annonay et 'les clubs, 1766–1815* (Lyons, 1903), 175–6; M. Kennedy, 'Some journals of the Jacobin club of Marseilles, 1790–1794',

French Historical Studies, VII (1972), pp. 609–11.

6. For the *Journal du département de Loir-et-Cher*, see B.N. 8° Lc¹⁰ 201; for the Tarn, see A.D. Tarn L 1531, and C. Portal, *Le département du Tarn au XIXe siècle. Note de statistique* (Albi, 1912), p. 230; for the sole surviving copy, A.N. AD XXA 390.

7. Copies in A.D. Mayenne L871 and B.M. Laval 30983.

8. *Journal des frontières*, 10 June 1792, p. 1; see copies in B.N. 8° Lc¹¹ 713ter; A. Ronsin, *Les periodiques lorrains antérieurs à 1800* (Nancy, 1964), pp. 78–9. For copies of the *Journal du département de la Corrèze*, A.D. Corrèze 175 T1.

9. *Patriote du département de la Mayenne*, no. 1, 1; *Journal du département de Loir-et-Cher, prospectus*, p. 3.

10. Raymond Manevy, *La révolution et la liberté de la presse* (Paris, 1964), pp. 48–51 A. Söderjhelm, *Le régime de la presse pendant la révolution française*, (Helsingfors and Paris, 1900–1); I, pp. 149–52.

11. Victor Forot, *Le club des Jacobins de Tulle* (Tulle, 1912), p. 186.

12. Herve Pommeret, *L'esprit public dans le département des Côtes-du-Nord pendant la révolution, 1789–1799* (Saint-Brieuc, 1921), pp. 162–4.

13. A.D. Hérault L1080: 'Extrait des registres de la municipalité de la ville de Clermont de l'Herault, le 20 juin 1792':

We have noted that newspapers whose malice was already well known to us arrived free to their recipients, something that we were able to check on inspection of the subscription registers held by the directress of posts. Having looked at these more closely . . . we became convinced that they contained dangerous, unconstitutional and seductive principles, liable to mislead the people and betray the constitution.

14. A.D. Hérault L893:

The merchants of Bédarieux subscribe to Parisian newspapers to keep themselves informed of various events which affect their commercial operations, and to get regular knowledge of exchange rates. In that way they can calculate if they are better off buying their currency in Paris or Marseilles, as their contacts with the latter are daily, while those with Paris are less frequent.

15. A.D. Hérault L1080.

16. A.M. Grenoble LL 2, 16 July 1792; A.N. F¹⁸ Bouches-du-Rhône 29, pièce li.

17. *Encyclopédie départementale des Bouches-du-Rhône*, VI, p. 565; G. Brégail, *La presse périodique dans le Gers pendant la révolution* (Auch, 1922), p. 16.

18. L. Meister, *Un champion de la royauté au début de la révolution. Louis-François Suleau (1758-1792)* (Beauvais, 1921), Chapter 17, *passim*; J. Peltier, *The late picture of Paris, or a faithful narrative of the revolution of the tenth of August*, 2 vols (London, 1792), pp. 209–14.

19. Söderjhelm, *Le régime de la presse*, I, p. 221ff; W.J. Murray, *The right wing press in the French Revolution* (London, 1986), pp. 192–4; for the return of the *Journal de Paris*, see A.N. F⁷ 3445, director of the post to Roland,

1 Oct. 1792, and E. Hatin, *Histoire politique et littéraire de la presse française*, V (Paris, 1859-61), p. 187.

20. H. Wallon, *Histoire du tribunal révolutionnaire de Paris, avec le journal de ses actes* (Paris, 1880), I, pp. 14-18, *Bulletin du tribunal criminel du 17 août*, nos. 2 and 3.

21. Murray, *The right wing press*, pp. 195-201; P. Caron, *Les massacres de septembre* (Paris, 1935), pp. 36, 53, 60, 267, 271; A.N. F⁷ 4694 d.1 pièce 6.

22. B.H.V.P. Ms. 723; B.N., Ms. n.a.f., Charles Nusse, *Histoire de la presse*, 5 vols, IV, p. 111.

23. Ibid., J.D. Popkin, *The right wing press*, pp. 16-24.

24. B.H.V.P. Ms. 725.

25. J.D. Popkin, 'The royalist press in the reign of terror', *Journal of Modern History*, LI (1979), p. 686ff.; B.H.V.P. Ms. 726.

26. B.H.V.P. Ms. 727; M. Tourneux, *Bibliographie de l'histoire de Paris pendant la révolution française* Paris (1900-13), II, p. 654; Nusse, *Histoire de la presse*, IV, p. 108; A. Tuetey, *Répertoire général des sources manuscrites de l'histoire de Paris pendant la révolution française*, 11 vols (Paris, 1890-1914), IX, nos. 548, 1018, 1323; *Les semaines parisiennes*, v, 192-240. For the continued popularity of the *Observateur* later in 1793, see P. Caron, *Paris pendant la terreur. Rapports des agents secrets du Ministre de l'Intérieur*, 6 vols (Paris, 1910-64), I, pp. 67, 115, 130: '. . . they sold so quickly that by 9.15 in the evening there were none left at the Palais Royal'.

27. P. Laborie, *Étude sur le Patriote français. Journal libre, impartial et national* (Diplome d'Études supérieurês, Toulouse, 1959-60), pp. 67-8.

28. Soderjhelm, *Le régime de la presse*, I, pp. 232-4; *Moniteur*, 28 October 1792, p. 312; 1 November 1792, pp. 348-50.

29. See F.-A. Aulard (ed.), *La société des Jacobins*, 6 vols (Paris, 1889-95), IV, pp. 372, 377-8, 410-12, 420-1, 423, 444, 451-2, 463, 495-6, 501, 514, 528. Robert, denouncing Brissot at the club on 30 November, complained:

> So how is it that such a negligible man can do so much harm to the public good? I will tell you: it is because he has a newspaper, and it is because his friends have newspapers . . . indeed Brissot and his friends have at their command all the loudest trumpets, and have momentarily perverted public opinion.

30. H. Gough, 'Les Jacobins et la presse. Le Journal de la Montagne' in *Actes du Colloque Girondins et Montagnards (Sorbonne, dec. 1975)* (Paris, 1980), p. 274ff.

31. Aulard, *Société des Jacobins*, IV, pp. 624, 629, 634-6.; V pp. 33, 427, 449-51.

32. A. Mathiez, 'Les dépenses de la liste civile en 1791 et 1792', *A.h.r.f.*, II, (1925), p. 489; A. Mathiez, 'Le logographe, journal des Lameth', *Annales révolutionnaires*, VI (1913), pp. 102-4.

33. C. Perroud, 'Roland et la presse subventionnée', *La Révolution Française*, LXII (1912), p. 206.

34. Ibid., pp. 207-13, 315-32, 396-419. A.N. AFII 7, reg. 45 pièce 16; B.N. (N.A.F.) 6243, pièces 156 and 158; 9533, pièce 249. See also,

for the *Sentinelle*, Hatin, *Histoire politique*, VI, pp. 240-50.

35. Perroud, 'Roland', p. 319; B.N. (N.A.F.) 6243, pièces 138, 156, 158; N.A.F. 9533 pièce 249; A.N. AFII 7 reg. 45, pièce 16; *Oeuvres de Maximilien Robespierre avec une notice historique, des notes et des commentaires par Laponneraye*, 3 vols (Paris, 1840), III, pp. 372-3.

36. For the *Journal des Hommes Libres*, see Max Fajn, *The Journal des Hommes Libres de tous les pays, 1792-1800* (The Hague-Paris, 1975); for the *Journal de la savonette republicain*, see copies in B.N. 8° Lc² 761.

37. The *Bulletin de amis de la vérité* was edited by the former Cordelier, Nicolas de Bonneville, whose radicalism had waned after the incident of the Champ de Mars: see Philippe Le Harivel, *Nicolas de Bonneville. Préromantique et révolutionnaire, 1760-1828* (Strasbourg, 1923), Chapter 5, and Gary Kates, *The Cercle Social, the Girondins and the French Revolution* (Princeton, 1984), pp. 247-55. For the *Chronique du Mois*, Marcel Dorigny, *La Chronique du Mois ou les Cahiers patriotiques (novembre 1791-juin 1793). Economie et politique dans un périodique girondin* (Mémoire de maîtrise, Sorbonne, 1971-2), Chapter 3, *passim*.

38. *Courrier d'Avignon* 1 Jan. 1793, p. 1; G. Clause, 'Un journal de grande information, au début de la révolution à Reims. "La correspondance générale de L'Europe" rédigée par N.-J.F. Couplet dit Beaucourt', *Mémoires de la société d'agriculture, commerce et arts de la Marne*, XCII (1977), pp. 253-7.

39. E. Forestié, *Histoire de l'imprimerie et de la librairie à Montauban. Bibliographie montalbanaise* (Montauban, 1898), pp. 267-8; M. Vogne, *La presse périodique en Franche-Comte des origines à 1870* (Besançon, 1977-8), I, pp. 76-8.

40. *Courrier de Strasbourg*, 11 and 17 April 1793, 341 and 365; Kennedy, 'Some journals', p. 611.

41. L. Trenard, *Lyon de l'encyclopédie au préromantisme* (Lyons, 1958), I. pp. 348-50.

42. A.D. Somme L3073; for the *Observateur montagnard*, see the only surviving copy, in B.N. 8° Lc² 2580; it was still appearing during the following winter, when Jumel participated in a fraternal delegation from Tulle to Limoges: see A. Fray-Fournier, *Le club des Jacobins de Limoges (1790-1795). D'après ses délibérations, sa corréspondance et ses journaux* (Limoges, 1903), pp. 219, 235. For the *Vérité au peuple*, see B.N. 4° Lc¹⁰ 118ter and Colomb de Batines and Ollivier Jules, *Mélanges biographiques et bibliographiques relatifs à l'histoire du Dauphiné*, 2 vols (Valence and Paris, 1837), I, pp. 63-4 (but note that this erroneously dates the paper as 1797). Many provincial journals deliberately distanced themselves from what were seen as essentially Parisian quarrels: see *Observateur du Midi* (Musée Calvet, 8° 26.632), 15 Nov, 1792:

> Our distance from the centre of argument that is ripping the Convention apart prevents us from passing a judgement. But what does it matter to us whether it be Girondins, Brissotins or Maratists who assure our freedom? The French people want to be free, and they will be. Intriguers will merely destroy themselves and the Republic will remain intact.

43. *Moniteur* 2 Feb. 1793, pp. 330–1; 28 Feb. 1793, p. 568ff.; G. Walter, *Marat* (Paris, 1933), pp. 332–8.

44. *Moniteur*, 10 March 1793, pp. 654–5.

45. Ibid., 11 March 1793, p. 668; A.-M. Boursier, 'L'émeute parisienne du 10 mars 1793', *A.h.r.f.*, 208 (1972), pp. 210–15; A.N. C²⁴⁹ CII 384, pièce 2; L. Guibert, *Un journaliste girondin* (Limoges, 1871), pp. 143–60; Laborie, *Étude sur le Patriote français*, pp. 24–5.

46. *Moniteur*, 11 March 1793, p. 668.

47. *Révolutions de Paris*, 4–11 May 1793, p. 301ff; 18–25 May, pp. 379–86; F.-A. Aulard, *Recueil des actes du comité de salut public*, 27 vols (Paris, 1889–93), IV, p. 318; Soderjhelm, *Le régime de la presse*, I, pp. 249–51.

48. A.N. BB³ 80 d.5, 13 and 14; A. Tuetey, *Répertoire général des sources manuscrites de l'histoire de Paris pendant la révolution française*, 11 vols (Paris, 1890–1914), VIII, pp. 448–65.

49. *L. Prudhomme aux patriotes. Le 13 juin 1793, l'an II de la République française* (Paris, undated); *Portrait en miniature du sieur Prudhomme. En attendant son portrait en grand. Le comité révolutionnaire de la section de l'Unité, au calomniateur Prudhomme* (Paris, undated), pp. 4–5.

50. See A.N. BB³ 81 registre 2; for official reservations on the committee's zeal, see P. Caron, *Paris pendant la terreur. Rapports des agents secret du ministre de l'intérieur*, 6 vols (Paris, 1910–64), I, p. 48.

51. Trenard, *Lyon*, I, pp. 348–50; R. Gerard, *Un journal de province sous la révolution. Le 'Journal de Marseille' de Ferréol de Beaugeard, 1781–1797* (Paris, 1964), pp. 161, 184–7; B.M. Bordeaux D44546; Labadie, *La presse à Bordeaux pendant la révolution* (Bordeaux, 1910), pp. 111–19.

52. D. Stone, 'La révolte fédéraliste à Rennes', *A.h.r.f.*, 205 (1971), pp. 367–87; *Bulletin des autorités constituées réunies à Caen, chef-lieu du département du Calvados (juin-juillet 1793), ré-édité par un bibliophile normand* (Paris-Caen, 1875); Vogne, *La presse périodique*, I, pp. 115–16; A. de la Bouralière, *Bibliographie poitevine* (Poitiers, undated), p. 104; H. Clouzot, *Notes pour servir à l'histoire de l'imprimerie à Niort et dans les Deux-Sèvres* (Niort, 1891), pp. 123–5.

53. Général Herlaut, *La querelle de Bouchotte et de Custine* (Paris, undated), pp. 1–28.

54. A. Soboul, *Les sans-culottes parisiens en l'an II* (Paris, 1958), p. 91ff.

55. Herlaut, *Le colonel Bouchotte. Ministre de la guerre en l'an II*, 2 vols (Paris, 1946), II, p. 83ff.

56. J.-P. Bertaud, *Camille et Lucille Desmoulins. Un couple dans la tourmente* (Paris, 1986), Chapter 8, *passim*; F.-A. Aulard, 'Une gazette militaire en l'an II' in his *Études et leçons sur la révolution française* (Paris, 1893), pp. 212–26.

57. C. Bellanger (ed.), *Histoire générale de la presse française*, Tome I. *Des origines à 1814* (Paris, 1969), I, p. 508.

58. *Moniteur*, 26 vendémiaire II, p. 135.

59. H. Welschinger, *Le journaliste Lebois et 'L'Ami du peuple'* (Paris, undated), pp. 5–6; Caron, *Rapports des agents du Ministre de l'Intérieur*, I xxxix.

60. P. Caron, *Rapports des agents du ministre de l'intérieur dans les départements (1793–an II)* 2 vols (Paris, 1948–51) I, p. xxix; A.N. AFII 66, reg. 484 pièces 14–15, 18, 22, 54. *Papiers inédits trouvés chez Robespierre, Saint-Just, Payan etc. supprimés ou omis par Courtois*, 3 vols (Paris, 1828), II, pp. 13–15; *Rapport fait au nom de la commission chargée de l'examen des papiers trouvés chez Robespierre* (Paris, 1795), p. 180; see also N. Hampson, *The life and times*

of *Maximilien Robespierre* (London, 1977), pp. 227–8.

61. *Archives parlementaires de 1787 à 1860*, 1e série, 94 vols (Paris, 1867–1985), 72, pp. 375–6.

62. *Refléxions politiques sur le gouvernement révolutionnaire, la liberté de la presse et les élections du peuple, dans les circonstances actuelles* (Paris, undated) B.N. · 8° Lb⁴¹ 4321.

63. B.N. Ms. Fr. 7004, pièces 85–97; *l'Esprit public*, xx, pp. 162–3. See also the views of two Jacobin deputies on mission in Alsace and Lorraine during the spring of 1793:

> We have been in a position to realise that, of all the causes of rural unrest, nothing is more dangerous than the variety of newspapers which are distributed everywhere, propagating incorrect opinions, or false and contradictory news . . . In a time of revolution nothing is more dangerous, and we feel bound to say that the Convention must immediately decree a ban on all newspapers, periodicals and journals for the duration of the revolution . . . At the very most it should authorise just one newspaper, which could be controlled by a censorship committee of four commissaires. (*Supplément au rapport des citoyens Couturier et Dentzel, députés-commissaires de la Convention nationale aux départements de la Meurthe, de la Moselle et du Bas-Rhin . . . 3 juin 1793* (undated), pp. 96–7.

64. Laborie, *Étude sur le Patriote français*, pp. 94–9.

65. Guibert, *Un journaliste girondin*, pp. 193–241; S. Gorceix, 'Antoine-Joseph Gorsas. Journaliste et conventionnel', *Information Historique*, 15 (1953), pp. 182–3.

66. A.N. F⁷ 4634, d.1; W292 no. 204. Leon Cahen, *Condorcet et la révolution française* (Slatkine, 1970).

67. A.N. F⁷ 4694 d.1; see also the denunciation in A.N. BB³ 81, d.5 of 8 and 9 *floréal* an II: '. . . this newspaper, distributed lavishly in the frontier departments, seems to be written just to alert our enemies to military operations, reveal the weak spots where they could profitably attack, and frighten the defenders of freedom'.

68. A.N. W⁴¹¹ no. 945; F⁷ 4775(32). Two of Tournon's colleagues on the *Mercure* were more fortunate. The editor, Allard, was arrested on 12 *messidor* on the suspicion of royalism, but successfully denied the charges, while the printer, Jean Cussac, was arrested on 18 *messidor*, accused of having printed unpatriotic newspapers and betrayed the popular cause in electoral assemblies. He too successfully denied the charges and was released before the end of *thermidor*. Both men appear to have been the victims of internal sectional feuds. (A.N. F⁷ 4673 d.3; F⁷ 4658 d.3).

69. A.N. W⁴¹¹ no. 945.

70. E. Fleury, *Camille Desmoulins et Roch Marcandier*, 2 vols (Paris, 1852), II pp. 370–7; Hatin, *Histoire politique*, V, pp. 476–82.

71. Nusse, *Histoire de la presse*, IV, p. 136; A.N. F⁷ 4685 d.5; W307 no. 392.

72. A.N. W³⁰⁸ no. 401.

73. Nusse *Histoire de la presse*, IV, pp. 128–33; Murray, *The right wing press*, pp. 201–6; Olivier Blanc, *La dernière lettre* (Paris, 1984), pp. 218–21.

74. Trenard, *Lyon*, I, p. 350; M. Loche, 'Journaux imprimés à Lyon (1633–1794)', *Vieux Papier*, fasc. 229 (1968), pp. 1–28.

75. A.D. Gironde 14L28, d.Marandon; Labadie, *La presse à Bordeaux*, pp. 58, 74–5, 90.

76. A.N. F⁷ 4774(76) d.3; W⁴⁷⁵ no. 321; L. Hugueney, *Les clubs · dijonnais sous la révolution* (Dijon, 1905), p. 84.

77. A.N. W³⁴³ plaq. 662; E. Muhlenbeck, *Euloge Schneider, 1793* (Strasbourg-Paris, 1896), p. 349ff.

78. Gerard, *Un journal de province*, p. 159ff.; D. Escamez, *La presse périodique à Toulouse de 1789 à 1794*, Mémoire de maîtrise (Toulouse, 1969), pp. 42–4; Maeght, *La presse*, pp. 127–31; R. Pacquet *Bibliographie analytique de l'histoire de Metz pendant la Révolution*, 2 vols (Paris, 1926), I. pp. 686, 940, 946; Robert Vivier and Jean Watelet, *Bibliographie de la presse française 1865–1944, t. 37: Indre-et-Loire* (Paris, 1970), p. 9.

79. P. Caron, 'Les dépenses secrètes du conseil exécutif provisoire', *La Révolution Française* 83 (1930), p. 229; A.N. AFII 10 d.63, pièces 19 and 42.

80. A.N. AFII reg. 484 pièces 6, 12 and 31; F.-A. Aulard, 'La presse officieuse sous la terreur' in his *Études et leçons sur la révolution française*, Iᵉʳ série (Paris, 1890); M. Edelstein, *La Feuille villageoise* (Paris, 1977), p. 330.

81. A.N. AFII 10 d.66 pièces 15, 29–30, 46; Tuetey, *Répertoire général*, X, 500; A. Mathiez, 'La presse subventionée en l'an II', *Annales Révolutionnaires*, 10 (1918), pp. 112–3; Caron, 'Les dépenses secrètes', pp. 234–5; G1. Herlaut, *Le colonel Bouchotte, ministre de la guerre en l'an II*, 2 vols (Paris, 1946), I. p. 83; Marc Martin, 'Journaux d'armées au temps de la Convention', *A.h.r.f.*, 210 (1972), pp. 603–4.

82. M. Bouloiseau, 'Les débats parlementaires pendant la terreur et leur diffusion', *A.h.r.f.* 173 (1963), pp. 337–45; A.N. C²⁴⁹ , CII 384 pièce 9. It was the *comité des petitions* of the Convention which looked after the distribution of the *Bulletin*, through its correspondence bureau, sending four copies to each District for its own retention, four more for the use of the Municipality in which the District sat, one for its school, two for the local courts and one for each cantonal *chef-lieu*. Jacobin clubs also received a copy direct:

> No doubt it would be desirable . . . for the bulletin to be delivered even to the tiniest villages in the country; but this is clearly impracticable because of the immense number of copies, and the impossible task of daily deliveries that it would entail; so all that we can do is to send one, through your good offices, to each canton. (A.D. Bas-Rhin 1L 755).

83. A.N. AFII 66 reg. 484 pièces 2–5, 8–11, 33; F.-A. Aulard, 'La presse officieuse sous la terreur', in his *Études et leçons sur la révolution française*, I (1890), pp. 229–34; *Recueil des actes du comité de salut public*, v, pp. 459, 506; vi, p. 374; P. Caron, 'Les publications officieuses du Ministere de l'Intérieur en 1793 et 1794', *Revue d'histoire moderne et contemporaine*, XIV (1910), pp. 3–20. The *Chronique de Paris*, having lost Condorcet and Delaunay d'Angers as editors after the decree of 10 March 1793, had struggled on until 25 August 1793, before its printer, Fiévée, handed over

subscribers to the *Feuille du salut public*. A wall-poster newspaper, the *Sans-culotte observateur*, was also financed by the Ministry of the Interior to the tune of 27,872 *livres* (ibid., pp. 20–7); and between October 1793 and January 1794, the Committee of Public Safety subsidised the *Antiféderaliste*: Michel Eude, 'La commune robespierriste. L'arrestation de Pache et la nomination de l'agent national Claude Payan', *A.h.r.f.*, 12 (1935), p. 151ff.

84. Bouralière, *Bibliographie poitevine*, p. 104; *Département de la Loire-Inférieure. Bulletin du comité central des trois corps administratifs de la ville de Nantes* (B.N. Fol. Lc[11] 745(26)); *Bulletin du département de la Sarthe* (B.N. Fol. Lc[10] 355(15); *Bulletin du département d'Indre-et-Loire* (B.N. Fol. Lc[10] 184(11)); *Bulletin du département des Côtes-du-Nord* (see scattered copies in A.N. BB3 10).

85. Loche, 'Journaux imprimés', pp. 21–2; Trenard, *Lyons*, I, pp. 351–2; A. Vingtrinier, *Histoire des journaux de Lyon depuis leur origine jusqu' à nos jours* (Lyon, 1852), pp. 41–8, 51–8.

86. M. Kennedy, *The Jacobin Club of Marseilles* 1790–1794 (Ithaca and London, 1973), p. 68; P. Caron, *Rapports des agents du Ministre de l'Intérieur*, II, pp. 279–80; F.-A. Aulard (ed.) *Recueil des actes du comité de salut public*, 30 vols (Paris, 1889–1951), XI, p. 32.

87. *Journal d'instruction populaire. Rédigé par la commission d'instruction sociale établie à Sarlat par le représentant du peuple Lakanal* (B.N. 8° Lc[11] 930bis).

88. G. Brégail, *La presse périodique dans le Gers pendant la révolution* (Auch, 1922), pp. 22–40; G. Brégail 'Un apôtre jacobin. Pierre-Nicolas Chantreau. Professeur, journaliste, agent secret (1741–1808)', *Bulletin de la Société Archéologique du Gers*, 3e and 4e trimestre (1924), pp. 198–213. The departmental administration of the Meuse had also planned to establish a newspaper in May 1793, but after consulting the Ministry of the Interior, called it off because of financial difficulties: see A.N. F[18] Meuse 12, letter of 28 June 1793.

89. Martin, *Les origines de la presse militaire*.

90. Ibid., p. 164; sole surviving copy in B.N. Fol. Lc^2 2575.

91. Ibid., pp. 164–5, 168–70; see also G. Lavalley, 'La presse en Normandie d'après des documents rares ou inedits. Journal de l'armée des côtes de Cherbourg', *Mémoires de l'Académie Nationale des Sciences, Arts et Belles-Lettres de Caen*, 1899, pp. 229–45.

92. Martin, *Les origines de la presse militaire*, p. 164.

93. Jean-François Brousse, *Trois siècles de presse roussillonaise* (Mémoire: Institut Français de Presse, Paris, 1963), pp. 6–7, 17; Martin, *Les origines de la presse militaire*, p. 169; *Recueil des actes du comité de salut public*, x, p. 217; xi, p. 32.

94. Aulard, 'Une gazette militaire', pp. 212–26; Marc Martin, 'Les journaux militaires de Carnot', *A.h.r.f.*, 229 (1977), pp. 407–12; Marc Martin, *Les origines de la presse militaire*, pp. 240–3.

95. Gough, 'The provincial Jacobin club press during the French Revolution' *European History Quarterly*, 16 (1986), pp. 55–72.

96. *Journal révolutionnaire de Toulouse*, 17 brumaire and 9 nivôse II; *Journal du vrai jacobin*, 16 ventôse II, pp. 18–19; 19 ventôse, pp. 1–2; 16 prairial II, p. 33; etc.

97. Vogne, *La presse périodique*, I, p. 82.

98. B.N. Ms. Fr. 7004.

4

Paradise Regained:
Thermidor to *Fructidor*, 1794–1797

The fall of Robespierre on 9 *thermidor* brought a rapid end to the terror and a violent reaction against both its personnel and policies. The structures of the revolutionary government and the powers of the Committee of Public Safety were rapidly diluted, and before the end of the year, the Paris Jacobin club had been forced to close its doors, with several provincial clubs soon following suit. Bands of *jeunesse dorée*, enjoying the open collusion of leading politicians, physically eliminated Jacobin and *sans-culotte* influence from the streets of Paris and of several provincial cities, and in the spring of 1795 two *sans-culotte* risings were crushed in the capital, bringing an end to the street power of popular radicalism. By the summer of 1795 the constitution of 1793 had been replaced by the more moderate constitution of Year III, which restored political predominance to the propertied classes and introduced the novelty of a bicameral legislature, discussed and rejected in September 1789. The Directory was officially inaugurated at the beginning of *brumaire* Year IV, and by then the revolution appeared to have returned to the path of moderate constitutional politics. Yet it was not to be, for the scars of five years of revolution went too deep. Instead, over the next four years, the Directory proved unable to find an adequate political consensus and progressively slid towards arbitrary government. Attacked from the outset by the radical left and counter-revolutionary right, wooed by Jacobins and the moderate left, as well as by constitutional monarchists, buffeted and bankrupted by the effects of the continuing European war, it became increasingly beleaguered.

In September 1797 the *fructidor coup d'état*, engineered by three of the five Directors and carried through with assistance from the army, led to the arrest of several right-wing deputies and a fatal weakening of constitutional government. Two years later, in November 1799, the coup of 18 *brumaire* brought Napoleon to power. This political instability had an inevitable result on the fortunes of the press. In the immediate aftermath of *thermidor*, a substantial degree of press freedom returned, as a reaction against the terror. It benefited the right-wing press most, which rapidly rebuilt itself during the period of the themidorean reaction, and all attempts to control it through new censorship legislation proved ineffective. Amongst the right-wing press in Paris there were many royalist titles, but a left-wing press also survived, although it was numerically much weaker, and it also contained a small handful of titles which supported the revolutionary socialism of Gracchus Babeuf. Neither extreme was as well represented in the provinces, but there was nevertheless a deep ideological divison within the press of most major cities, and the result was once again a press which was able to reflect the full range of political opinion in the country.

The weeks following Robespierre's execution saw demands from several quarters for the return of press freedom. As early as 15 *thermidor* a crypto-royalist newspaper, the *Correspondance politique*, carried a plea for it, written by J.J. Dussault, one of the leading stars of the constitutional monarchist press in the months to come. Two weeks later, on 28 *thermidor*, on the other side of the political divide, the issue was raised at the Jacobin club where Réal, deputy for the Isère, and a future journalist himself in the *Journal de l'Opposition* and *Journal des patriotes de '89*, argued that press freedom was ' . . . the one powerful way to prevent abuse of power'.[1] This initiated a series of debates over the next three weeks which split the club down the middle. Several of the architects of *thermidor*, such as Fréron and Tallien, supported Réal's argument that freedom of expression was an essential consequence of the end of the terror, and found themselves supported by journalists like Jean-Charles Laveaux, a former editor of the club's own newspaper, the *Journal de la montagne*, who had just spent six months in prison for attempting to launch a newspaper at the time of Danton's arrest in the previous spring.

Yet the majority of club members feared, and with good reason, that a complete relaxation of censorship would only give free rein to the rapidly mounting forces of political reaction, encourage the return of the right-wing press, and hasten the end of the revolutionary government. They therefore conceded the need for a modification of censorship, but not its total abolition. As Isoré put it on 19 *fructidor*, in response to Laveaux's speech:[2]

I am not surprised that people want to have it believed that Jacobins do not want press freedom. But it is false. Jacobins only reject unlimited freedom, something that is irreconcilable with revolutionary government. I make the observation in order to refute in advance anyone wanting to denigrate our club.

Similar reservations also prevailed in the Convention, when Tallien brought the argument there on 2 *fructidor*, repeating a speech which had already received a distinctly frosty reception at the Jacobin club the night before. A week later, Fréron's attempt to revive the issue and gain a formal declaration in favour of freedom was vigorously countered by Amar, a member of the Committee of General Security, who argued that its effect would be merely to legalise royalist propaganda. The whole matter was referred to the *comité de législation* for consideration, and it there died a silent death.[3] There seems little doubt that, while most deputies probably favoured some liberalisation of the law, they were unwilling to abandon controls completely at a time when the political situation remained fluid, and the risks involved too great.

Yet public opinion was already beginning to outflank their reluctance. The law of 22 *prairial* was abolished on 14 *thermidor*, and the revolutionary tribunal reorganised nine days later, causing both moderate and right-wing papers and pamphlets to flood back rapidly into circulation. Many of their owners and editors co-ordinated their campaigns at regular meetings in restaurants and cafés, or in the salons that returned to fashion as centres of political debate, and they appear to have enjoyed the tacit support, as well as possible financial assistance, from the Committee of General Security.[4] Among the most influential initially was the *Orateur du peuple*, edited by the former terrorist Stanislas Fréron, which first hit the streets in later *fructidor* — some six weeks after Robespierre's death. Deliberately resurrecting the title that had made his reputation as a leading radical in the summer of 1790, Fréron now used it to invoke the posthumous support of his former friend and colleague, Marat, and with editorial help from Dussault, who moved over from the *Corréspondance politique*, unleashed a constant flow of invective against the terror and its architects in the Jacobin club and sections of Paris, working in close harmony with the more physical exploits of the *jeunesse dorée*. Close to him in both content and style was Tallien, who similarly revived a ghost from the radical past with his *Ami de citoyens* on 23 *fructidor*, aided by his former secretary, the talented pamphleteer Mehee de la Touche, who had been imprisoned as a Dantonist during the summer and now wasted little time in gaining his revenge, both in the *Ami* and in a number of celebrated polemical pamphlets. He effectively took over control of the paper from Tallien during the winter, before closing it down in the following spring to pass on to the editorial chair of the *Journal des patriotes de '89.*

Other titles sharing a similar preoccupation with revenge for the terror included the *Ami de la Convention*, which appeared in *vendémiaire* and *brumaire*, on alternate days to the *Orateur du peuple*, and was particularly concerned to discredit the public prosecutor, Fouquier Tinville; the *Fusée volante* edited by J.-F.-N. Dusaulchoy, and the *Observateur des Jacobins*, which concentrated its fire on the ailing Jacobin club. Alongside them lay a number of right-wing papers that had survived the terror and were now able to vent their resentment and relief — most notably, the *Journal de Paris*, the *Républicain universel* which featured regular editorials from the young Charles Lacretelle, and the *Messager du soir*, which picked up contributions from another influential newcomer to journalism, Isidore Langlois.[5] Most attractive of all, because of the size and renown of its editorial team, was the *Nouvelles politiques*, successor in August 1792 to the *Gazette universelle*, which was half-owned by the veteran of the *ancien-régime* literary establishment, Jean-Baptiste Suard, and attracted regular contributions from attenders of Mme Staël's salon such as the young Guizot and Dupont de Nemours. Several other right-wing papers were royalist, rather than republican, especially the *Bulletin national*, the *Postillon des armées*, the *Journal de Perlet* — which boasted over 20,000 subscribers by the summer of 1795 — and the *Quotidienne*, which dated back to the end of 1792 and now obtained the editorial services of another celebrated thermidorean pamphleteer, Jean-Pierre Gallais. Two of them, the *Eclair* and the *Courrier républicain*, rapidly added to their appeal by organising express delivery to the provinces, gaining a strong hold on public opinion there.[6]

The provincial press also reflected the rapid change in political mood. In Angers and Grenoble two long-running papers, the *Affiches d'Angers* and the *Courrier patriotique*, both of which had kept their heads low during the terror, now became outspokenly anti-Jacobin.[7] In several other towns, newspapers that had been suspended during the terror returned, determined to avenge their fate. In Toulouse, for example, Jean-Baptiste Broulhiet, who had been imprisoned in September 1793, emerged from prison in *fructidor*

Year II and resumed publication of his *Journal universel* during the following spring, under the new and evocative title of *L 'Antiterroriste*. He wasted little time in attacking prominent local Jacobins by name and played an important role in encouraging the thermidorean reaction in the city. Carefully avoiding any open commitment to royalism, he nevertheless championed the same values of social order and hierarchy that it championed, defending ' . . . good citizens, . . . the friend of order . . . who obeys the law to the letter, pays his taxes promptly, fulfils the functions entrusted to him with justice and impartiality, insults no one, is a good son, a good father, good husband and good friend'. Jean-Baptiste-Magloire Robert, a Rouen journalist who had migrated to Paris and published an *Observateur de l'Europe* there during the early months of the terror, returned to Rouen to relaunch it in *pluviôse* of Year III. Five months later Ferréol de Beaugeard, who had fled Marseilles in August 1793 after the collapse of the federalist revolt, resumed publication of his *Journal de Marseille* and soon orchestrated the vengeance of the city's bitter thermidorean reaction.[8]

Elsewhere new titles appeared, dedicated to the same political aim. In Cognac, for example, there were two brief pamphlet journals, *Celui qui vole la République* and the *Pot pourri décadaire*. An *Ami du 10 août* appeared in Vienne, in the Isère, for a few weeks during *ventôse* and *germinal* of Year III, while Vesoul saw the prospectus for a *Vengeur de la patrie* in the following month and Châlons-sur-Saône, a short-lived paper, whose title has not survived.[9] If these were ephemeral, others proved more durable. The *Journal du Midi* and *Thermomètre du Midi*, both in Avignon, lasted for several months in the spring and summer of 1795, while Grenoble saw a new daily paper launched at the beginning of *floréal* Year III, the *Réveil-matin extraordinaire*, which was to last until the following autumn. In Aurillac, where no newspaper had appeared since the demise of the Jacobin *Cantaliste* at the end of 1791, the *Décadaire du Cantal* was published for six months between *ventôse* of Year III and *vendémiaire* of Year IV, virulently pursuing a vendetta against a group of former terrorists, imprisoned and awaiting trial. Local animosities also dominated the columns of the *Neuf thermidor* in Besançon, which likewise spanned the summer of 1795 and was edited by a group of departmental administrators who had been imprisoned during the terror. In Brest the *Ami des principes* was to last 15 months before its owner, Picquenard, transferred it to Paris, while in Rheims the barbed pen of Henri Delloye lay behind the *Feuille rhémoise* which ridiculed local Jacobins — often by name — until mid-August 1796.[10]

Longest lasting of all these post-thermidor creations, however, was the *Journal de Lyon*, founded in early *nivôse* Year III by Alexandre-Michel Pelzin, former spokesman for the Marseilles sections during the federalist revolt. After staying in Paris, where he had gone to plead the Marseilles case during the terror, Pelzin returned to Lyons in *brumaire* of Year III and launched the *Journal de Lyon* shortly afterwards with a prospectus containing a vituperative broadside against the activities of Collot d'Herbois in the city during the previous winter. The polemical tone of the first two numbers prompted the Municipality to order his arrest, but he was released without trial, and survived another spell in prison two months later, to keep the paper going until the *fructidor* coup. Pelzin was always cautious enough to voice formal support for the constitution, but relentlessly pursued political vendettas against former Jacobins, and denounced ' . . . this wretched revolutionary government, established by a handful of tyrants who not only usurped our rights, but also had the audacity to deride us.'[11]

In contrast to this the Jacobin press, both in Paris and the provinces, went into rapid decline. The Committee of Public Safety's own newspaper, the *Feuille du salut public*, was wound up in early *fructidor*, when its subsidy was withdrawn, and the Jacobin club paper, the *Journal de la montagne* followed suit in late *brumaire* when the club was closed down. Meanwhile the withdrawal of government subsidies also weakened the independent Jacobin press, already decimated during the terror. Only the *Journal des hommes libres* and the *Journal universel* commanded anything like a national circulation and there were only two significant additions to them during the winter of 1794–5.[12] The first, the *Ami du peuple*, was launched by a radical printer and former activist in the section Beaurepaire, Rene Lebois, on 29 *fructidor*, in an angry response to Fréron's bogus claim to the legacy of Marat, and for several months featured anonymous contributions from a leading deputy of the Mountain, Chasles. Its epigraph was pugnacious and direct — 'I don't talk about press freedom, I make use of it' — and its early numbers celebrated the transferral of Marat's remains to the Pantheon, as well as replying to Fréron's attacks in the *Orateur du peuple*. The second, the *Journal de la liberté de la presse*, was launched on 17 *fructidor*, with Gracchus Babeuf as editor, initially as a journal of the thermidorean reaction, campaigning for press freedom. However, Babeuf soon realised that complete freedom would only help the right and changing his title to *Tribun du Peuple* on 14 *vendémiaire*, joined Lebois in defending Jacobinism and *sans-culotte* interests against the social and political policies of the Convention.[13] Meanwhile, in the provinces the Jacobin club press built up over the previous year collapsed, with the sole exception of the *Journal du club national* in Bordeaux, which was taken over by its printer, Delormel, and run independently. Several editors of independent newspapers that had also been Jacobin during the terror now either trimmed their sails or, like the *Vedette* in Besançon, closed down altogether.[14]

The alarming speed with which the political balance of the press tilted to the right prompted the Convention to search in the spring of 1795 for legislation to control it. On 12 *floréal* legislation was introduced by Marie-Joseph Chenier, on behalf of the three executive committees (Public Safety, General Security and Legislation), which provided for the authors or editors of pamphlets and journals found guilty of either discrediting the legislature or advocating the return of the monarchy to be sentenced to exile for life. It was passed without difficulty, but was bitterly attacked by the right-wing press as a blow against press freedom, and ultimately proved to be ineffective when juries, because of the severity of the penalties, refused to convict. In the space of 14 days in the first half of *thermidor*, the editors of no less than seven right-wing papers were arrested, only to be released quickly as the charges against them collapsed. An appeal from the committees to the Convention for a more effective substitute was crowded out by the debate on the new constitution, and the law remained effectively powerless.[15] The carrot was therefore substituted for the stick, and subsidies used once again to bolster up the more moderate republican press. On 28 *prairial*, Louvet was asked by the Committee of General Security to revive the *Sentinelle* which he had abandoned in November 1792, and he agreed to do so, resuming publication on 6 *messidor* with a guaranteed subsidy equivalent to the value of 2,000 subscriptions. Over the following weeks other papers also benefited, including the *Journal du bonhomme Richard*, which used a popular vernacular style to defend both Convention and constitution, the more moderate *Journal des patriotes de '89* and the *Messager du soir*. During *fructidor*, on the eve of the crucial referendum on the constituion, funds were also released to help in the launch of the *Ami des lois* and the *Censeur des journaux*.[16]

It seems unlikely that any of these papers did much to influence the result of the referendum on the constituion, but dispute over the results of the accompanying referendum on the two-thirds decree helped spark off the *vendémiaire* uprising in Paris in early October

1795, the last of the great Parisian *journées*. In its aftermath the governing committees used emergency measures to close down several right-wing titles and order the arrest of their owners and editors, while a military commission set up to try the cases of those directly involved in the insurrection condemned Michaud, editor of the *Quotidienne*, to death in his absence, along with the editors of the *Courrier universel*. Michaud went into hiding, however, as did the editors of the *Courrier républicain*, the *Quotidienne* and the *Messager du soir*, to avoid arrest. Worse still, their papers quickly reappeared under different names — the *Courrier universel*, for example, changing into the *Courrier de Seine-et-Marne* between 16 *vendémiaire* and 12 *brumaire*, so rendering the whole exercise futile.[17] The new Directors therefore started their term of office with a strong right-wing press still in existence, and a small but vocal Jacobin press attempting to rival it. Yet it had no effective law with which to control either, and only a weak governmental press to defend its own cause. Moreover, it was bound by a constitution which contained a specific guarantee of press freedom, for article 353 banned the reintroduction of prior censorship on any form of printed material, and asserted the right of authors to publish freely, subject only to the possibility of subsequent prosecution under the terms of the civil or criminal law. Yet the only existing legislation, that of the preceding *floréal*, had already been proven to be inadequate. Another article, 355, allowed for executive censorship to be brought in, in cases of national emergency, but it had be voted through by both Councils for one calendar year at a time, and neither Council was likely to concede that anything like a national emergency existed in the winter of Year IV. The Directory therefore had only two options: either to try prosecutions once more with the Chenier legislation, or use a third article of the constitution, article 145, which empowered it to order the arrest and trial of anyone suspected of plotting to overthrow the republic. Both methods were used against the editors of some 14 newspapers in the winter of 1795-6 — including Lebois' *Ami du peuple* and Charles Duval's *Journal des hommes libres* — but each time without success, as juries refused to convict, either because of the severity of the punishment or because they refused to recognise the existence of a plot.[18]

The alternative to prosecution was to step up surveillance and subsidy. Surveillance was used from an early stage, with the creation within the Ministry of Police of a *bureau des journaux* to monitor press content. The Directors themselves also set up a *bureau d'esprit public* for the same purpose, and from 17 *brumaire* onwards, an official of the Ministry of the Interior covered the same ground. He in turn was helped by a request from the Minister to the *bureau central* of Paris, and departmental *commissaires* throughout the country, for subscriptions to be taken out to every newspaper within their area,. and copies forwarded to his office.[19] The policy of subsidies went hand in hand with this. Shortly after taking power the Directors consulted former members of the outgoing executive committees on the subsidies that had been given to journalists over the previous summer and autumn. Early in *frimaire* it took steps to continue them. The *Sentinelle*, the *Censeur des journaux*, the *Journal du bonhomme Richard*, the *Ami des lois* and the *Journal des patriotes* all had block subscriptions for two or three thousand copies renewed over the winter months, and steps were taken to extend the policy to other friendly titles. A three-month subscription for 3,000 copies of the *Orateur plebéién*, a new paper launched on 21 *brumaire*, was placed on 11 *frimaire*; but it was withdrawn by the end of the month when its editorial content proved to be too Jacobin. Similarly, an order was placed for 2,000 copies of the *Courrier de Paris*, but it too was dropped some weeks later when it was considered to be too conservative. Finally, in the spring of 1796, all subscriptions were withdrawn on the orders of the two Councils, which opposed them as an unwarranted and expensive extension of executive power.[20]

Nevertheless, in the meanwhile, the Directors had taken the process a stage further, following in the footsteps of the monarchy and the Committee of Public Safety, by launching its own newspapers. The initial decision to do this was taken as early as 18 *brumaire* and the first copy of what was initially called the *Bulletin officiel*, a daily paper, came out on 16 *frimaire*. It lost its first editor, Antonelle, after only two numbers when his Jacobin sympathies became too apparent, but his place was quickly taken by Thuau-Grandville, a former editor of the *Moniteur*, and changed its title, on 2 *frimaire*, to the *Rédacteur*. It published government circulars and decisions, but also covered foreign and domestic news along with occasional articles of political comment written by the Directory's own secretary, a former journalist from Lille, Lagarde. Every issue was reviewed by Lagarde or his staff before going into print, and with an initial print run of 20,000 and its distribution throughout the country handled by the offices of the Ministry of Justice, it was clearly intended to convey government policy directly to the voting public. It also had an indirect impact, as it was used by other journalists as a source of news and government policies.[21]

The second paper was the *Journal des défenseurs de la patrie*, which appeared four months later, on 28 *germinal* of Year IV. It was the brainchild of Carnot, who, as the Director most closely involved in military policy, was anxious to counter Babeuf's propaganda amongst the army, where Jacobin sympathies still lingered on, and to raise troop morale and tactical awareness for the impending spring offensive into Germany and northern Italy. Printed on the same presses as the *Rédacteur*, it was also a daily paper and had a print run of some 12,000–15,000 copies. It was edited by a former military doctor, Paul Gabriel Lepreux, who largely confined himself to stitching together news items fed into him by generals, ministers and government agencies. In practice it too, like the *Rédacteur*, served as a primitive news agency for army news and propaganda, publishing articles that were taken up and used by the independent press. In this way Carnot clearly hoped to control the flow of military information to the public.[22]

The impact of all these efforts was disappointingly slight. Government administrators in the provinces were enthusiastic enough, delighted to receive a newspaper free of charge at a time when even basic salaries were hard to come by, and frequently writing in to enthuse on the way in which it helped them to explain government policy to their local population. For many the mere fact of receiving a newspaper free, at government expense, was a valuable symbol of prestige within their local community. Yet the fact that both the *Rédacteur* and the *Journal des défenseurs* were government newspapers — and widely known to be so — induced a healthy scepticism amongst the public at large, and it is significant that neither paper had more than a few hundred voluntary subscribers. Moreover, the independent moderate press fared little better, with most papers suffering badly when governmental subsidies were withdrawn in the spring of 1796. The *Journal du bonhomme Richard* and the *Journal des patriotes de '89* both closed down in the following autumn for financial reasons, while the *Ami des lois* only survived with difficulty. The *Moniteur* could normally be expected to support the government of the day, but it was mainly a journal of information, expensive, densely packed, and unlikely to gain political converts. The *Journal des lois*, which dated back to 1793 and was edited by an impoverished but dedicated anticlerical printer, Galetti, lent its consistent support, as did the *Annales patriotiques*, which, following Carra's execution in 1793, had been taken over by Louis-Sébastien Mercier.[23] Alongside them were several new titles launched in the winter of 1796–7, which also aimed at the middle ground, but few of them appear to have had much influence either. Panckoucke, who had handed over the *Moniteur* to his nephew Agasse in 1795, launched the *Clef du Cabinet des Souverains* in the winter of Year V, similar to the *Moniteur* in its emphasis on news and a' strong editorial team, which included major names such as Garat, Peuchet and. Fontanes.[24] The *Ami de la patrie*, was launched in the spring of 1796 by a group of pro-government deputies, and edited by a veteran Jacobin from Laigle, in the department of the Orne, Coesnon-Pellerin. It had a more readable style, but was always suspected by the government of being too Jacobin, and by the public at large of being in government pay. As a result it fell between two stools, never attracted many subscribers, and survived only because of the considerable financial sacrifices of Coesnon-Pellerin and his backers.[25]

In the provinces, support was even thinner on the ground. The *Feuille politique* in Bordeaux, and the *Papillon* in Rouen appear in the main to have backed Directory policies. So too did the *Vedette normande*, again in Rouen, which was edited by a former priest with a chequered political career, Philibert Guilbert, and had been helped on to its feet in the autumn of 1795 by government subsidies, which ensured its wide distribution throughout the department of the Seine-Inférieure. The *Observateur du département de l'Yonne* in Sens, and the *Journal du département de l'Allier* in Moulins, also lent their support, as did the *Nécéssaire* in Dijon the *Courrier du département du Gers* in Auch, and the *Journal du département d'Ille-et-Vilaine* in Rennes. However, none of them were very dynamic papers and several closed down before the summer of 1797. Taken together, they certainly formed a fragile basis for the moulding of public opinion.[26]

Their fragility is more evident when compared with the comparative strength of the Jacobin and right-wing press. The Jacobin press was certainly thin on the ground in Paris. Babeuf's *Tribun du peuple*, which he resumed after release from the Plessis prison on 20 *vendémiaire* Year IV, and Sébastien Lalande's *Éclaireur du peuple*, both defended the policies of insurrection and social revolution until they were closed down in the spring of 1796, with the uncovering of the Conspiracy of Equals. The *Journal des hommes libres* and René Lebois' *Ami du peuple*, to defend the more traditional ideals of radical Jacobinism, criticising the government's failure to eliminate royalism, and its neglect of the wretched living conditions of the poor. Lebois in particular latched on to the discontent caused by bread shortages in the winter months of 1795–6, using wall-posters to supplement the impact of the *Ami*, and he was a founder member of the Pantheon club, which acted as a focal point for Jacobin agitation. He later gave a great deal of publicity in his paper to Babeuf's trial.[27]

In *brumaire* of Year IV, another Jacobin newspaper appeared, the *Orateur plébéien*, edited by Eve Demaillot and Leuliette. It also featured regular articles from Marc-Antoine Jullien, a journalist who had worked on the *Antifédéraliste* during the terror, had since contributed several articles to the *Journal des hommes libres*, and was also the initial editor of the *Rédacteur* for its first two numbers. He later went on to edit the *Courrier de l'armée d'Italie* for Bonaparte.[28] However, it was not until the spring of 1797, in the aftermath of the massive electoral gains made by the right in the partial elections of *ventôse* and *germinal*, that the Jacobin press in Paris really gained strength. The *Bouche de fer* was launched on 2 *prairial* by Vincent Barbet and Jean-Claude Darcet, changing title to *Echo des cercles patriotiques* a month later, to emphasise its role in the encouragement of the activities of the *cercles patriotiques* in the capital.[29] Then in *thermidor* came the *Défenseur de la vérité*, the *Acquéreur des biens nationaux* — which sprang directly out of the ban imposed on the constitutional circle of the Hôtel de Montmorency — the *Démocrate constitutionnnel* and an *Éclaireur du peuple*, launched by Lebois as a replacement for his *Ami du peuple*.[30]

In the provinces the Jacobin press grew to be much stronger, despite the collapse of the club press during the thermidorean reaction, and to a greater extent than in Paris tended to act as a rallying point around which small groups of Jacobins could structure their activity and disseminate propaganda, at a time when the formation of political clubs was difficult or illegal. The process of recovery began in the summer of 1795 with the launch of the *Observateur républicain* in Toulouse, set up with active encouragement from the representative on mission, Clauzel, who was anxious to check the strength of the thermidorean reaction in the city. Its editors, Dardenne and Dufey, were also members of the city's constitutional circle, and used the paper to campaign openly against the influence of Broulhiet's *Antiterroriste*. They had a shaky start, having to rely on financial help from the Toulouse Municipality in the early stages, but quickly gathered strength, and by the summer of 1796, had succeeded in putting the paper on to a sound financial basis.[31] Other Jacobin papers followed during the summer of 1796 in Châlons-sur-Marne and in Tarbes, and also in Marseilles, where a former member of the city's Jacobin club during the terror, Pierre Peyre-Ferry, launched the *Observateur du*

Midi. Autumn saw the *Ami des principes* in Angers, edited and owned by another former Jacobin, Etienne-René Jahyer, who used his prospectus not only to denounce the influence of the wealthy conservative bourgeoisie in the city, but also to distance himself from accusations of *babouvisme*, devoting the paper to ' . . . law and order, without which the republic cannot exist'.

Meanwhile, the *Chronique de la Sarthe* was launched in Le Mans by René Bazin, another former Jacobin, who had been *agent national* in the city during the terror and had spent over a year in jail since, as a result of the thermidorean reaction. On his release he had helped found a political club, the *Exclusifs*, which combined its activity closely with the paper, and probably also had financial support from the departmental *commissaire*, Jouennault, who sympathised with his aims.[32] The *Observateur du Lot* also started up in Cahors during the autumn, edited by a former constitutional priest and Jacobin, Brunies, who worked as a professor in the *école centrale*. During the following winter a *Bulletin du département de l'Eure* was launched in Evreux, by a young printer, J.B.P. Touquet, who had also been active during the terror, and the spring election campaign of 1797 produced several more. In Grenoble the *Clairvoyant* was launched on 20 *ventôse* Year V, edited by J.-B. David and by Pierre Cadon, the latter of whom had been a former president of the Jacobin club in 1793. It featured regular contributions from former club members, and leading articles from Pierre-Vincent Chalvet, Stendhal's negligent teacher at the city's *école centrale*, who was instrumental in building up a network of constitutional circles in the department over the summer of 1797.[33] That same month Bias Parent l'aîné launched the *Questionnaire* in Nevers, while the summer saw the *Pacifique ou journal de l'Oise* launched in Beauvais by a Jacobin printer, Tubeuf. Tours had a *Journal patriotique*, the work of another radical printer, Norbert Lhéritier, and in the days before the *fructidor* coup, an *Extrait des journaux patriotes* was launched in Nancy. Its editor, Claude Thiébaut, was a *marchand épicier*, originally from Verdun, who had been a departmental administrator and propagandist during the terror, and emerged from a spell of imprisonment during the thermidorean reaction to found the city's constitutional circle.[34]

Not all of these newspapers lasted long, but almost a dozen managed to struggle through until *fructidor* and, linked as they were to groups of local militants and to constitutional circles, played a crucial role in keeping democratic radicalism alive. Thiébaut was probably the odd man out amongst all these, for he was the closest in sympathy to Babeuf. Already, in the spring of 1796, he had published an *Observateur démocrate* in Metz, which had been closed down by the Directory after it had stoutly defended Babeuf's critique of property and urged its readers that ' . . . the fruits of the earth are for everyone, and the land belongs to no one'.[35] The others lay more in the mainstream of democratic Neo-Jacobinism and the basic themes which recur in their pages are the defence of democracy, the need for republicans to unite against a common enemy, the denunciation of the revival of royalism, and condemnation of the social consequences of economic hardship and currency inflation. The *Journal des Hautes-Pyrénées*, for example, vigorously denied that Jacobins remained terrorists at heart, arguing that this was royalist abuse, designed to divide republicans and weaken them: 'They are dividing us, discouraging and terrifying us, trying above all to confuse the word "opinion" with "faction" so that they can pin guilt on us. This has always been the policy of tyrants. . . ' . The *Ami des principes* in Angers did likewise, denouncing the word 'terrorism' as a catch-all phrase used by enemies of the republic, but also arguing that the basic policies of the terror had been essential for national survival. The *Observateur du Midi* in Marseilles also echoed their call for unity: 'Let us be frank and agree that only republicans and royalists now exist . . . all who are in favour of the republic have the same basic motives of spririt and energy, and have the same interest in . . . maintaining the regime.'[36]

Yet the democratic press was heavily outgunned by its right-wing opposition, which had far greater financial backing and public appeal. In Paris, during the course of 1796 and 1797, the titles that had already sprung to prominence during the thermidorean reaction were joined by new ones, covering the whole range of right-wing loyalties, from conservative republicanism to intransigent counter-revolution. In the winter of Year IV, Dupont de Nemours launched the *Historien*, to amplify the criticism of the regime that he voiced in the Council of Elders, and in the following spring a Swiss-born printer, Bridel, launched the *Miroir*, another tacitly royalist paper, edited by two talented publicists, Beaulieu and Souriguières.[37] In the autumn of 1797 the comte de Barruel-Beauvert revived the *Actes des Apôtres*, which appeared at irregular intervals over the next two years in the form of letters written to a *rentier*, and drew on the style of its famous predecessor of 1789–91. At the same time the *Journal général de France* was revived, dormant since its forcible closure in August 1792. The *Grondeur* followed in *frimaire*, owned and printed by Gorsas' widow and rapidly building up for itself a sizeable circulation through a clever mixture of satire, scorn and ridicule, precariously balanced between constitutional royalism and conservative republicanism. A new *Chronique de Paris* appeared in the spring of 1797, and a satirical journal, *le Thé ou Journal des dix-huit* came out shortly afterwards, including among its many articles a list of journalists executed or murdered during the previous eight years. Right-wing successes in the spring elections encouraged more over the summer, including *l'Europe politique et littéraire*, the *Journal du petit gautier* (which picked up the pieces of the *Petit gautier* that had closed down in August 1792), *le Mémorial*, *l'Aurore* and the *Annales universelles*.[38]

The provincial press was not far behind. Cities such as Rouen, Toulouse, Marseilles, Grenoble, Lyons and Angers had already seen right-wing papers resurface during the thermidorean reaction. Over the next two years they too were joined by newcomers. During the spring of 1796 a *Renommée de la Mortagne* was launched in the Orne, and, distributed in great numbers around the rural areas of the department, featured political reports copied from the right-wing press in Paris, and articles which attacked and ridiculed local Jacobin activists by name.[39] Mid-*thermidor* saw the beginnings of an *Annales troyennes* in the Aube, edited by a so-called *société des amis des lettres et des moeurs*, and edited by the president of the departmental administration, while *brumaire* saw the launch of the *Journal du Lot* in Montauban and the *Nouveau journal des journaux* in Bordeaux.[40] Most of these titles were republican rather than royalist, but the spring elections of 1797 changed this. In Montpellier, for example, *le Mois de germinal* was launched in *ventôse*, sporting the motto 'One religion, laws and morality', and conspicuously using the Gregorian calendar. It soon changed title to the *Journal des départements du Midi*, and spawned a clone in the shape of the *Journal du département de l'Herault* owned by a printer, Tournel, who had lost the printing contract for *le Mois de germinal*, and set up in rivalry as an act of revenge. Both titles were eventually closed down over the summer after surviving prosecution attempts for royalism. In Le Mans an *Espion constitutionnnel*, launched in *nivôse*, had been joined shortly before the elections by an openly royalist *Conciliateur*, but both were prosecuted unsuccessfully for royalism during the early summer and, although acquitted, subsequently ceased publication. Royalist papers also appeared in Dijon and Sens, and conservative republican papers in both Chartres and Tarbes.[41]

The dividing line between conservative republicanism and royalism is not always easy to discern, as the legal ban on advocating royalism forced several editors to use ambiguous terms. Moreover, for many conservatives the shape of the regime was less important than its capacity to defend certain basic values. The *Journal du Lot*, for example, was unequivocally republican, and defended the constitution of the Directory as an essential legal bulwark against a reversion to the practices of the terror. Inevitably it was vigorously anti-Jacobin too, linking Jacobins with babouvists and anarchists, and frequently denouncing local former terrorists such as Jeanbon Saint-André. On the other side of the coin, it laid great store by the return of traditional Catholicism as a means of restoring traditional morality and public order to the country, and repeatedly denounced the law of 3 *brumaire* Year IV against non-juror priests, as both unconstitutional and destabilising.[42] Broulhiet's *Anti-terroriste*, on the other hand, was closer to constitutional royalism. It too featured regular attacks on Jacobin 'cannibals' and 'blood drinkers', even providing its readers on 22 April 1796 with a list of local Jacobins who had been particularly prominent during the terror. In the spring of 1797 it returned to the topic during the run-up to elections to the Councils, arguing that a Jacobin had certain set characteristics: '. . . his reason is a dagger, his element blood, his resources pillage, his dearest hope complete anarchy in order to legitimise his theft and murder'. It too regretted the decline of religion, and argued that divorce had broken up families and led to a growth of abandoned children. So peace and order were its slogans: peace in war, once Bonaparte had achieved his victories in north Italy; and order at home once true religion had been restored and freedom of expression guaranteed.[43] Beaugeard's views in the *Journal de Marseille* were almost identical, particularly his preoccupation with order, and with the role of religion in restoring both it and social discipline. The *Observateur de l'Europe* in Rouen was more extreme, however, denouncing the financial chaos of the country, and the effects of currency speculation and fiscal dishonesty. However, its editor, Robert, studiously avoided readers' requests to come clean on its attitude to the monarchy, making his point more subtly by articles calling for the end of religious persecution and an amnesty for the royalist rebels involved in the *vendémiaire* rising.[44]

The provincial right-wing press as a whole may not have posed an open threat to the regime, but it was certainly critical of it, and of the social disorder over which it ruled. Taken with its Parisian counterpart, it reflected the strength of conservative opinion in the country at large in most major towns. In Lyons, Troyes, Alençon,

Chartres, Montauban, Nîmes and Montpellier, the right-wing press dominated the political scene. In Toulouse, Marseilles, Grenoble, Angers, Rouen, Tarbes, Dijon, Sens, Metz and Le Mans, although rivalled by local Jacobin or republican papers, it was the dominant. voice. Only in Châlons-sur-Marne, Evreux, Nevers, Moulins, Rennes, Tours, Beauvais and Nancy did moderate republican or Jacobin papers predominate, and they were hardly major cities. The provincial press, although more equally divided than in Paris, was therefore predominantly right-wing, with a significant minority dedicated to the overthrow of the regime.

Yet it was the Parisian balance that probably worried the Directors most. They held a low view of the morality of most journalists, and of the political value to the country of an independent press: but they also held a correspondingly high view of the press's political influence and, with the failure of the *Rédacteur* to wield it in a way favourable to themselves, began to look towards the Councils for press legislation to enable them to exercise tighter control. As early as mid-*frimaire* of Year IV the Council of Five Hundred, at their request, set up a commission to investigate the need for new legislation. The commission failed to reach agreement, and the question was therefore considered instead in a formal debate which began on 23 *ventôse* Year IV, and lasted for six days. A sharp division of opinion rapidly emerged, with deputies on the left calling for urgent legislation to control the right-wing and royalist press, and those on the right opposing it in the name of press freedom. The result was deadlock until, in the following month, in the aftermath of the uncovering of the Babeuf plot, the Directors again pressed for action. This time both Councils responded positively with a law, passed on 27 *germinal*, which laid down the death penalty (commutable to deportation in certain circumstances) for publications which advocated the overthrow of the regime, the murder of any of its officials, the return of the monarchy or the terror, and the abolition of property.

A second law, on 28 *germinal*, then went on to define the legal responsibility for publication, making it obligatory for all newspapers and posters to carry the name of their editor, and the name and address of their printer; and in cases where these were omitted, the seller was made responsible for content.[45] Yet this legislation, like many of its predecessors, proved a dismal failure because of the very severity of its penalties. On 17 *floréal*, for example, the business manager of the babouvist *Eclaireur du peuple*, Manques, was charged with advocating the abolition of property, but promptly acquitted at his trial. Nine days later it was the turn of René Lebois, of the *Ami du peuple*, then of Rene Vatar of the *Journal des hommes libres*, both of whom were also acquitted. Attention then switched to right-wing papers, with prosecution of Langlois and Porte of the right-wing *Messager du soir*, and of several others subsequently, all of whom also had the cases against them dismissed.[46]

The Directors therefore returned to the Councils in the autumn of 1796, mindful of the fact that the spring elections of 1797 were only six months away, and that the continued growth of the right-wing press could have a direct effect on their results. On 9 *brumaire* they urged deputies to examine once again the need for press legislation, and for the first time suggested recourse to article 355 of the constitution, which would enable the Minister of Police to exercise police powers over it for a year.[47] The Council of Five Hundred rejected this, but instead set up a commission to look at the matter, which reported back on 5 *frimaire* with a package of alternatives, including proposals to tighten up the existing regulations on *colporteurs*, the establishment of another official government journal, and the strengthening of the law of 27 *germinal*. However, right-wing deputies took the lead in opposing all three measures, well aware of the fact that press freedom suited their cause, and the debates on the question became bogged down. Only the proposals on *colporteurs* passed into legislation before the spring, and as a result the growth of the right-wing press during the spring elections and the following summer went largely unchecked.[48]

The result was mounting criticism of the Directors in the press from both royalists and conservatives, couched in increasingly personal and violent terms and reflecting majority opinion in both councils. A constitutional deadlock between executive and legislature developed over the summer months, with the majority of deputies wanting an end to war, the dismantling of legislation against the emigrés and a relaxation of religious restrictions on the Catholic Church. Two of the Directors, Carnot and Barthélemy, sympathised with these demands, but three were firmly opposed, Barras, Reubell and Lépeaux. Relations between them and the Councils became embittered, the press was polarised on either side, and during June Barras made his first contacts with Hoche in search of a military solution to a political problem. On the morning of 4 September, 18 *fructidor*, cannon fire announced the start of a *coup d'état*. Fifty-three deputies were ordered under arrest, ready for deportation, along with Carnot and Barthélemy, and constitutional government had clearly broken down. The consequences for the press were not slow in following.

Notes

1. A. Söderjhelm, *Le régime de la presse pendant la révolution française* (Helsingfors and Paris), II, pp. 3–4; J.D. Popkin, 'The royalist press in the reign of the terror', *Journal of Modern History*, 51 (1979), pp. 697–8; F.-A. Aulard, *Paris pendant la réaction thermidorienne*, 5 vols (Paris, 1898–1902), I, p. 51. See also the arguments in *Instrument révolutionnaire ou la véritable cheville ouvrière. Discours sur la liberté indéfinie de la presse . . . par le républicain Genisset* (Paris, an II).

2. *Courrier républicain*, 314, 24 *fructidor* II, p. 79.

3. Söderjhelm, *Le régime de la presse*, II, pp. 4–23; R. Manevy, *La révolution et la liberté de la presse* (Paris, 1964), pp. 71–4; F.-A. Aulard, *La société des Jacobins*, 6 vols (Paris, 1889–95), VI, pp. 419–21; K. Tönnesson, *La défaite des sans-culottes. Mouvement populaire et réaction bourgeoise en l'an III* (Oslo-Paris, 1959), pp. 65–7.

3. C.F. Beaulieu, *Essais historiques sur les causes et les effets de la révolution en France* (Paris, 1803), VI, pp. 194–6; C. Lacretelle, *Dix années d'épreuves pendant la révolution* (Paris, 1842), pp. 196–7, 206, 243. For the impact of Fréron, see F.-A. Aulard (ed.), *Paris pendant la réaction thermidorienne et sous le Directoire*, 5 vols (Paris, 1898), I, pp. 93, 115, 122, 130.

5. For a contemporary overview, see *La revue des journaux* (Paris, 1797), pp. 5–11, 26.

6. J.D. Popkin, *The right-wing press*, pp. 16–24; Edmond and Jules de Goncourt, *Histoire de la société française pendant le Directoire* (Paris, 1855), Chapter XII, *passim*; J. Godechot, 'Le Journal de Perlet pendant la réaction thermidorienne', *Revue du Nord*, LXVI (1984), pp. 723–32.

7. B. Bois, *La vie scolaire et les créations intellectuelles en Anjou pendant la Révolution (1789–1799)* (Paris, 1929), pp. 470–1; A.D. Isère, L85.

8. M.J. Lescure, *La presse périodique à Toulouse sous la révolution, de 1794 à 1800* Diplôme de maîtrise d'histoire (Toulouse, 1969–70), Chapter 1; M. Schlumberger, 'La réaction thermidorienne à Toulouse', *A.h.r.f.*, 204 (1971), pp. 270–2; T. Lebreton, *Biographie normande* (Rouen, 1850–1), pp. 349–50; A.D. Seine-Maritime L304, pièces 52–3, 82–3; A.N. F^7 4286, no. 30; B.M. Rouen, Norm MM1046(2); R. Gerard, *Un journal de province sous la révolution. Le 'Journal de Marseille' de Ferréol de Beaugeard, 1781–1797* (Paris, 1964), pp. 230–3.

9. Pierre Martin, *L'imprimerie et la presse à Cognac sous la révolution* (Cognac, 1921), pp. 11–12; M. Vogne, *La presse périodique en Franche-Comte des origines à 1870* (Besançon, 1977–8), III, p. 120; A.N. F^{18} Saône-et-Loire 21, pièce 13; A.N. ADXXA, 14; C. de Batines and J. Ollivier, *Mélanges biographiques et bibliographiques relatifs à l'histoire du Dauphine* (Valence-Paris, 1837), p. 64.

10. Musée Calvet 4° 3770(8–9); B.M. Grenoble Jd755; E. Maignien, *Bibliographique historique du Dauphiné pendant la révolution française* (Grenoble, 1891), III, p. 182; Batines and Ollivier, *Mélanges biographiques*, p. 63;

A.D. Cantal L782; Vogne, *La presse périodique*, III, pp. 120-4; C. Brelot, *Besançon révolutionnaire* (Paris, 1966), pp. 151-3; R. Kerviler, *Essai d'une bibliographie des publications périodiques de la Bretagne*, 3ᵉ fasc. (Paris, 1898), p. 4; G. Clause, 'Un journal de la réaction thermidorienne: la Feuille rhémoise', *Études Champenoises*, I (1974), pp. 29-76.

11. *Journal de Lyon*, 68, 25 *frimaire* an IV, p. 557; A.N. F⁷ 3448B, administration centrale du département du Rhône au Ministre de la Police, 23 *frimaire* an IV; L. Trenard, *Lyon de l'encyclopédie au préromantisme* (Lyons, 1958), II, p. 421; Renée Fuoc, *La réaction thermidorienne à Lyon (1795)* (Lyons, 1957), p. 41.

12. A.N. F¹⁸ Seine 21, xliii; H. Gough, 'Les Jacobins et la presse. Le Journal de la montagne (juin 1793 — brumaire an II) in *Actes du Colloque Girondins et Montagnards* (Sorbonne, dec. 1975) (Paris, 1980), pp. 285-7; for the *Journal des hommes libres*, see M. Fajn, *The Journal des hommes libres de tous les pays, 1792-1800* (The Hague-Paris, 1975), Chapter 3, *passim*.

13. C. Pichois and J. Dautry, *Le conventionnel Chasles et ses idées démocratiques* (Gap, 1958), pp. 75-87; R.B. Rose, *Gracchus Babeuf. First revolutionary communist* (London, 1978); *Journal de la liberté de la presse*, i, p. 3; *Tribun du peuple*, xxviii, p. 237.

14. H. Gough, The provincial Jacobin club press during the French Revolution', *European History Quarterly*, 16 (1986), pp. 66-7.

15. *Moniteur*, 15 *floréal* III, pp. 357-60; 16 *floréal*, pp. 361-5; *Rapport et décret sur le prompt jugement des émigrés trouvés sur le territoire de la république . . . et les peines portées contre ceux qui provoqueraient l'avilissement de la représentation nationale, ou le retour à la royauté etc.* (Paris, Year III); Söderjhelm, *Le régime de la presse*, II, pp. 43-4. For criticism of the legislation, see *Pensées libres sur la liberté de la presse, à l'occasion d'un rapport du représentant Chenier* (Paris, undated), and *Opinion sur la liberté de la presse, par Jean-Bon Saint-André, représentant du peuple* (Paris, Year III).

16. A.N. D XLIII pièces 49-50. The *Sentinelle* lasted until 14 *floréal* Year VI; the *Censeur des journaux* was edited by J.-P. Gallais and was to turn against government policies after Gallais was imprisoned in *pluviôse* Year IV for criticism of Merlin de Douai — see A.N. F¹⁸ Seine 21, pièce 1, and F. Gendron, *La jeunesse dorée. Episodes de la révolution française* (Quebec, 1979), p. 272.)

17. Söderjhelm, *Le régime de la presse*, II, pp. 46-7; G. Lefebvre, *Le Directoire* (Paris, 1946), p. 94; A.N. F⁷ 4696 d.2; AFII 52.

18. A.N. F¹⁸ Seine 21, pièce xlvii; A. Debidour, *Recueil des actes du Directoire executif*, 4 vols (Paris, 1910-17), I, pp. 312-18, 439, 493, 533, 515, 806; II, pp. 319 and 707. For Lebois, see H. Welschinger, *Le journaliste Lebois et L'Ami du peuple* (Paris, undated), pp. 14-15.

19. Laurence Stoll, *The "Bureau Politique" and the management of the popular press*, unpublished PhD thesis, University of Wisconsin, 1975, p. 32. The reports for the Ministry of the Interior are in A.N. F⁷ 3448A. For the ambiguous attitude of the Directory towards the press, at once disliking its practitioners but respecting its influence, see Nathalie Lambrichs, *La liberté de la presse en l'an IV. Les journaux républicains* (Paris, 1976), pp. 19-31.

20. Debidour, *Recueil*, I, pp. 45, 213, 299-300, 346, 470, 633, 638, 668; II, pp. 238, 292, 506; III, pp. 137 and 462. A.N. F¹⁸ Seine 21, pièces xlvi, l, liv, lxi, lxxvi.

21. Ibid., I, pp. 43, 151, 164, 204, 212–13; A. Mathiez, *Le Directoire* (Paris, 1934), p. 356ff. The *Rédacteur* was translated into German for the two Rhine departments, as well as for the Moselle and Mont-Terrible: see A.N. F^{18} 10A d.6, pièces 52–3.

22. Debidour, *Recueil*, II, p. 133; M. Martin, *Les origines de la presse militaire en France à la fin de l'ancien régime et sous la révolution (1770–1799)* (Paris, 1974), pp. 265–86; M. Martin, 'Les journaux militaires de Carnot', *A.h.r.f.*, no. 229 (1977), pp. 413–28.

23. M. Tourneux, *Bibliographie de l'histoire de Paris pendant la révolution française* (Paris, 1900–13), II, pp. 671–2.

24. S. Tucoo-Chala, *Charles-Joseph Panckoucke et la librairie française, 1736–1798* (Paris and Pau, 1978), pp. 484–90.

25. For Coesnon-Pellerin, see the dossier in A.N. F^7 3448B and A.N. F^{18} Seine 21, letter of 2 *messidor* IV; A.N. AFIII 45, d.163, pièce 174.

26. For Bordeaux, see A.N. F^{18} (Gironde)16, liv; A.D. Gironde 3L54, 21 *nivôse* IV; A.M. Bordeaux 138, pièces 129–30; for the *Vedette Normande* in Rouen, see A.N. F^{18} (Seine-Maritime)23, pièce xxviii; A.D. Seine-Maritime L304, pièces 68, 95–7, 106, 111, 129, 143, 159; for the *Papillon*, see scattered copies in A.N. F^7 3448A and F^{18} (Seine-Maritime)23, pièce xxix; for Moulins, see A.N. F^7 3448B, analysis of *germinal* IV: 'This paper appears to be controlled by the departmental administration, and judging by the praises it lavishes on it, may even be financed by it.' For Auch, see G. Brégail, *La presse périodique dans le Gers pendant la révolution* (Auch, 1922), pp. 49–60, and G. Brégail 'Un Apôtre jacobin. Pierre-Nicolas Chantreau. Professeur, journaliste, agent secret', *Bulletin de la Société Archeologique du Gers*, 3e and 4e trimestres (1923–5), pp. 53–5; for Rennes: P.-M. Juret, *La presse à Rennes* (ms., Rennes, 1964), pp. 9–10.

27. Welschinger, *Le journaliste Lebois*, p. 14ff.; Lefebvre, *Le Directoire*, p. 103; Pichois and Dautry, *Le conventionnel Chasles*, pp. 75–88.

28. Martin, *Les origines de la presse militaire*, pp. 303–5; M.V. Daline, 'Marc-Antoine Jullien après le 9 *thermidor*', *A.h.r.f.*, avril-juin 1964, avril-juin 1965, juillet-aôut 1966.

29. See no. 1 of 22 *messidor* an V; its first number contained a lengthy panegyric on the role of the circles and subsequent numbers kept up a sustained polemic against royalism — see especially nos. II, 1–5; III, 13–14; IV, 8–10; IX, 4–5, etc. It was never financially healthy and in the spring of 1798 merged with the *Ami des Théophilanthropes* — see ibid., VII, 30 *germ*, VI, p. 56.

30. *Acquéreur*, no. 2, 10 *thermidor* V, pp. 13–14:

Those of us who have bought national lands will without doubt lose a powerful means of support if these circles are closed. For the most part it is us who have organised them, and our interests have been clarified and defended in them.

See also Jean Dautry, 'Les démocrates parisiens avant et après le coup d'état du 18 fructidor an V', *A.h.r.f.*, 118 (1950), pp. 141–51.

31. Lescure, 92ff; A.N. F^{18} Haute-Garonne, 16, Saint-Amans to Minister of the Interior, *frimaire* IV; A.D. Haute-Garonne, L2563, extrait des délibérations de l'administration municipale de Toulouse, 3 *pluviose* IV.

32. G. Clause, 'Un journal républicain de l'époque directoriale à Châlons-sur-Marne, "Le Journal du département de la Marne", 1796–1800', *Mémoires de la société d'agriculture, sciences et arts du département de la Marne*, XC (1975), pp. 275–313; XCI (1976), pp. 319–56; Gerard, *Un journal de province*, pp. 261–9; J.-A. Bernard, 'Les Journaux de Marseille pendant Ịa révolution, de 1790 à 1797', *La Révolution Française*, XXXVIII (1900), pp. 165–6.

33. I. Woloch, *Jacobin legacy. The democratic movement under the Directory* (Princeton, 1970), pp. 188–93; J.-J. Lebon, *La presse montalbanaise des origines au début du dix-neuvième siècle*, Diplôme d'Études Supérieures (Toulouse, 1972), pp. 140–1; Michel Berthier, *Le Clairvoyant. Étude d'un journal révolutionnaire grenoblois (1787–1800)*, TER (Grenoble, 1968); Jacques Solé, 'Le professeur d'histoire de Stendhal: Peirre-Vincent Chalvet (1767–1807)', *Stendhal Club*, Année no. 10. XXXIX (1968), pp. 283–91; G. Thuillier, 'Parent l'aîné et le Journal de la Nièvre en l'an VI', *Mémoires de la Société Académique du Nivernais*, LIV (1967), pp. 55–6.

34. For Beauvais, see A.N. F^7 4286 'Pièces du citoyen Tubeuf, journaliste de l'Oise'; A.N. F^7 3449, Tubeuf to Minister of Police, 13 *pluviôse* VI; for Nancy, A.N. F^7 4286 no. 22; A.N. F^7 3448B; P. Clémendot, *Le département de la Meurthe à l'époque du Directoire* (Paris, 1966), p. 119ff.; Albert Troux, *La vie politique dans le département de la Meurthe, d'août 1792 à octobre 1795*, 2 vols (Nancy, 1936), II, pp. 229–30, 273, 370.

35. *L'Observateur démocrate*, 5–22 *ventôse* IV, p. 6.

36. *Journal des Hautes-Pyrénées*, 24 *germinal* IV, p. 87; *Ami des principes*, 4 *thermidor* V, p. 152; *Observateur du Midi*, 1 *germinal* IV, pp. 2–4.

37. A. Saricks, *Pierre Samuel Du Pont de Nemours* (Lawrence, 1965), pp. 242–51.

38. For details of many of these, see *Revue des journaux rédigés à Paris*, *passim*.

39. A.N. F^7 3450 contains some copies of the *Renommée*; see also ibid., *juge de paix du canton de Mortagne* to Minister of Police, 2 *vendémiaire* VI.

40. Emile Socard, 'Le journalisme à Troyes', *Revue de Champagne et de Brie*, I (1876), pp. 235–41; for the identity of the editors, A.N. F^7 3448B 'Extrait de la lettre du commissaire du Directoire Exécutif près l'administration municipale de Troyes, du 30 fructidor an V'; Lebon, *La presse montalbanaise*, pp. 121–71; E. Labadie, *Le presse à Bordeaux pendant la révolution* (Bordeaux, 1910), p. 98.

41. For Montpellier, see A.D. Hérault L1079, *commissaire près l'Hérault* to Minister of the Interior, 25 *germinal* V; A.D. Hérault, L1080, *commissaire près l'Hérault* to Minister of Police, 24 *vendémiaire* VI and Minister of the Interior to *commissaire près l'Hérault*, 18 *thermidor* V; see also J. Duval-Jouve, *Montpellier pendant la révolution*, 2 vols (Montpellier, 1879–81), II, pp. 337–9. For Le Mans, see A.N. F^{18} 21 Sarthe, pièce XXVI; A.N. BB^{18} 733; M. Reinhard, *Le département de la Sarthe sous le régime directorial* (Saint-Brieuc, 1935), pp. 219–21, 251–2, 253. For Dijon, see C. Brelot, *La vie politique en Côte-d'Or sous la Directoire* (Dijon, 1932), pp. 92–4; for Sens, A.N. F^7 7271 and 7275, nos. 1531–3; for Chartres, see M. Jusselin, *L'administration du département d'Eure-et-Loire pendant la Révolution* (Chartres, 1935), pp. 164, and B.M. Chartres, Fonds Jusselin, 32/5: 'Le répertoire du département d'Eure-et-Loire'.

42. Lebon, *La presse montalbanaise*, pp. 125–60.

43. Lescure, *La presse périodique*, pp. 41–50.

44. *Observateur de l'Europe*, 16 *messidor* IV, p. 3; 24 *messidor* IV, p. 1; *thermidor* IV, pp. 1–2.

45. Söderjhelm, *Le régime de la presse*, II, pp. 65–77; M. Lanfranci, *Le régime de la presse sous la révolution* (Paris, 1908), pp. 97–110; E. Hatin, *Manuel théorique et pratique de la liberté de la presse* (Paris, 1868), II, pp. 54–9.

46. Debidour, *Recueil*, II, pp. 222, 319, 339, 383, 424, 707.

47. Ibid., IV, p. 165.

48. M. Lanfranci, *Le régime de la presse* pp. 111–19. For hesitations over the idea of an official newspaper, see *Discours de J.-B. Noaille, député du Gard, sur le rapport relatif à la répression des délits de la presse. Séance du 13 frimaire an V* (Paris, undated).

5

Paradise Lost: The Scratch of the
Minister's Pen, 1797–1799

On the day of the *fructidor* coup, article 145 of the constitution was used to order the arrest of the printers, owners and editors of some 32 right-wing Parisian newspapers. On the following day the Council of Five Hundred set up a small commission to investigate the possibility of further action, and on the basis of its recommendations, some 42 titles were banned on 22 *fructidor*. In the meantime, on 19 *fructidor*, the Council voted for implementation of article 355 and gave the Directors powers to ban for a calendar year any newspaper that they considered a threat to political stability. In practice these powers were exercised by the Minister of Police who, whenever he decided that a newspaper should be suspended from publication, sent a written report to the Directors stating his reasons. If they agreed — and they usually did — the Minister then issued orders for its presses, subscription registers and offices to be impounded and sealed, and the order was made public.[1] The editors, staff writers, administrators and printers of the paper were not arrested, and as many rapidly discovered, they remained free to launch another paper if they wished. In practice, therefore, it was the printer who was usually hardest hit, losing the use of his presses; or alternatively his landlord, who found his premises sealed up and his tenant unable to pay the rent.

Several other measures, taken over the following weeks and months, tightened this grip still further. On 7 *vendémiaire* Year VI, the Minister of Police asked the postal service for information on subscribers to titles that had been banned in *fructidor*, living in the Nord and the Midi, so that their geographical areas of strength could be checked. Two days later, on 9 *vendémiaire*, a stamp tax of 5 *centimes* per sheet was imposed on all political newspapers — those dealing with the sciences and the arts were exempt — which raised their cost by some 25 per cent and killed off many of those on smaller circulations. It was the first time that stamp duty, commonly used in England as a check on press circulation, had been used in France, and its use was to continue almost unbroken until the Third Republic. On 13 *vendémiaire* the Minister of Police asked all departmental *commissaires* to send a list of the newspapers published in their department, along with a signed declaration of participation from their owners, editors and printers, and to ensure that a copy of each and every edition was sent to Paris so that it could be checked for political content. Nine days later this measure was also extended to the Parisian press.[2] On 8 *brumaire* the power of departmental and municipal *commissaires* was extended to allow them to impose provisional bans on papers that they suspected of royalism, subject to later confirmation from Paris, but this proved too tempting in many local contexts where there were old scores to settle and was withdrawn quickly on 23 *brumaire*. Nevertheless, many local administrators preferred to turn a deaf ear to its repeal and continued to act on their own initiative until well into the following spring.[3] Meanwhile, on 5 *frimaire* the existing regulations on *colportage*, restricting *colporteurs* to calling out just the title of their newspapers, were reiterated, and private delivery systems, heavily used by the right-wing press since 1795 as a convenient way of evading official surveillance, were banned. Finally, on 6 *pluviôse*, departmental *commissaires* were also empowered to stop and search private coaches to ensure that this was being observed.[4]

This battery of measures gave the Directory more control of the press than the Committee of Public Safety had ever enjoyed, and although article 355, which underpinned it all, was only granted initially for one calendar year, it was renewed in the following *fructidor* and remained in practical effect almost until the Napoleonic coup in *brumaire*. Its initial implementation was certainly patchy, for, as the surviving records of the Ministry of Police indicate, there was considerable confusion within the offices of the Ministry over the identity of the editors, printers and owners of the major right-wing titles. As a result, very few of those named in the decrees of 18 and 22 *fructidor* were ever arrested and none was ever deported. Some, like Jean-Baptiste Suard, took refuge abroad, while others went into hiding and continued writing from there. One of the few Parisian journalists to be detained was Lacretelle, political editor of the *Messager du soir*, but although he stayed in prison for the next two years, political influence was brought to bear to ensure that he was never deported.[5]

In the provinces, distance, and the difficulties of establishing responsibility, also ensured that arrests were few and far between. On 18 *vendémiaire* Year VI, for example, a ban was imposed on the *Ami des campagnes*, published in Revel in the Haute-Garonne, and an order given for the arrest of its editor, Marc-Antoine Durand. The order was temporarily reversed twelve days later, however, and Durand was released under surveillance. When a new arrest order then came through on 21 *brumaire*, it was already too late, for he had gone into hiding. Attempts to track him down in Carcassonne and elsewhere over the following weeks proved fruitless, and although he was finally condemned to death in his absence on 22 *messidor* Year VI, he never presented himself for execution and was still at liberty in 1800 when he had both the arrest order and sentence duly reversed.[6] Similarly, in Alençon the *Renommée de la Mortagne* was banned on 18 *vendémiaire*, and its printer, Marre, placed under arrest. However, Marre promptly claimed that he was illiterate, and that although he was the paper's owner, he had merely printed the text supplied to him by its real editor, one of his employees named Fourbet. Fourbet, of course, was nowhere to be found, and five months later, in *ventôse* of Year VI, he wrote from hiding to deny the charges, alleging that Marre had indeed written the newspaper, with collaboration from certain of his friends (whom he obligingly named), and was only offloading the responsibility on to himself because of a quarrel over money that they had had when he had left Marre's employment, shortly before the *fructidor* coup. One of them was lying — possibly both — and local officials were divided over where responsibility lay. Marre was consequently released and the whole affair allowed to drop.[7]

Any ban imposed by the Minister of Police under article 355 could also be avoided by reviving the offending newspaper under another name, and many owners proved to be adept at removing both presses and registers from their premises when a ban was imposed, well before the police arrived, acting on a leak or tip-off. Even when they failed to do this, most kept duplicates of their subscription registers and had little difficulty in finding another printer to take on the paper. As a result, many banned papers resurfaced under new guises. The *Censeur des journaux*, for example, which had begun life in 1795 with government assistance, and then drifted off towards the republican right in the following year, was banned on 18 *fructidor*; but its editor, Gallais, went into hiding and continued publishing it, first as the *Diurnal* and then, when this was banned in *frimaire*, as the *Nécéssaire*. When this too was banned in the summer of Year VI, he finally suspended publication for a year, until the political climate improved. Jean-Baptiste Suard's *Nouvelles politiques*, also banned on 18 *fructidor*, likewise appeared under new titles — first as the *Nouvelliste*; then on 1 *vendémiaire*, after a new ban, as *le Narrateur universel*; then on 27 *frimaire* as *le Narrateur politique*; and on 7 *nivôse* as *le Publiciste*. Under the latter title, with the help of Suard's political contacts, it then remained in existence until 1810. The royalist paper, the *Véridique*, went through five name changes in the same way, between *fructidor* and the following *germinal*, while the *Grondeur* changed names, in the space of a little over twelve months, to *le Rêveur*, *le Fanal* and *le Flambeau*, mixing its metaphors of sleep and light.[8]

This kind of dexterity was also mirrored in the provinces. Five provincial papers were included on the original proscription list of 22 *fructidor*: the *Journal de Lyon*, the *Antiterroriste* in Toulouse, the *Courrier maritime* of Le Havre, the *Observateur de l'Europe* in Rouen, and the *Nouveau journal des journaux* in Bordeaux. In subsequent weeks a number of others, in Rodez, Marseilles, Tarbes, Troyes, Montauban, Chartres and Dijon, avoided the inevitable by closing down, and their editors went into hiding.[9] A months later, on 18 *vendémiaire*, the Directors also ordered the closure of the *Journal de Marseille*, a major organ of right-wing propaganda in the Midi, and of the *Ami des campagnes* in Revel and the *Renommée* in the Orne. In addition, the *Courrier patriotique*, in Grenoble, was finally banned in the following spring, after a prolonged campaign of denunciation from municipal and departmental administrations of Grenoble and the Isère.[10]

Yet not all of them closed down as they should have done. The *Courrier maritime du Havre*, for example, was banned on 20 *fructidor*: yet for some unknown reason, the order never reached the departmental *commissaire* of the Seine-Inférieure, Duval. He eventually wrote to the Minister of Police on 5 *frimaire*, registering his surprise at the fact that the *Courrier* — 'whose continued publication since the *fructidor* coup was a political scandal for republicans' — was still allowed to appear, and asking for orders. In fact the Ministry had detected the error and a new order was on its way to him, which he duly put into effect on 7 *frimaire*, sealing the paper's press and its subscription register. However, its owner, Le Picquier, promptly donated his other press, along with a copy of the subscription register, to a young apprentice who worked in his shop, named Gilbert, and the paper duly reappeared under Gilbert's name, quite legally, as the *Journal du commerce du Havre*. In the meantime, Le

Picquier appealed to the Minister of Police to reverse the ban, arguing that his only concern had been to provide commercial news for the local maritime trade, and a living for himself, his wife and three children, his mother, a mulatto servant, and his workers. Sotin, the Minister of Police, ignored the plea and, on 28 *frimaire*, placed a ban on the *Journal du commerce* as well, after it too had begun to publish right-wing articles. With both his presses gone, Le Picquier reluctantly gave up, and waited for better times.[11]

Others were more tenacious. In Bordeaux, for example, the *Nouveau journal des journaux*, which had begun publication in *brumaire* of Year V, was banned on 22 *fructidor*, and a warrant issued for the arrest of its owner, editor and printer, Pierre Lawalle. When municipal officials arrived to seal the presses and to arrest Lawalle on 3 *vendémiaire*, however, all they found were Lawalle's wife, Francoise Peltier, his brother, a few sticks of furniture and a broken-down press that was no use to anyone. Lawalle himself, they were told, had fled to Spain, while the press used for the *Nouveau journal* had already been sold to other printers, the Crutty brothers. The officials went on to the Crutty brothers' premises, where, despite protests that it had been purchased in good faith, they sealed the offending press. However, Mme Peltier had already moved into action on her own behalf, buying another press and using it to print a replacement for the *Nouveau journal*, first as *le Frelon* and then as *Extrait des journaux ou nouvelles du jour*. There was nothing illegal in this, but on 19 *vendémiaire* the *Extrait* was also banned, and its press sealed, for publishing an article critical of the way in which the press had been treated since the *fructidor* coup. Mme Peltier therefore bought another press, resurrected the paper as the *Gazette bordelaise*, and continued without hindrance until the following *floréal*, when it too was banned for royalism. Again the press was sealed, but six days later Mme Peltier resumed with *le Télégraphe bordelais*, this time employing a nominal editor, Eugène Homberg, and an independent printer, Bernard Coumès. The departmental administration was unimpressed and banned *le Télégraphe* on its own authority within two days, claiming it to be a flagrant reincarnation of the *Gazette*, and impounding Coumès' press. Nevertheless, Mme Peltier promptly retaliated with *le Bordelais*, using another printer and entrusting editorial control to two brothers of Irish descent, André and Edouard Kirwan. The title changed again on 1 *messidor*, probably in response to another ban, but the paper then survived unscathed for another year until *messidor* of Year VII, when Edouard Kirwan was arrested for publishing an article advocating the restoration of

Louis XVIII. André promptly went into hiding to avoid the same fate, but a third brother stepped into the breach and continued the paper as the *Journal de Bordeaux*. Another ban came in *vendémiaire* of Year VIII, and another title change to *le Spectateur*. Yet under this title — its ninth in three years — the paper was able to continue until March of 1801.[12]

Mme Peltier was certainly persistent, but even she pales into insignificance when compared with Jean-Baptiste-Magloire Robert and Angélique Lefebvre in Rouen, joint owners of the *Observateur de l'Europe*, a paper which had originally been published in Paris but was relaunched in Rouen in January 1795. Within weeks of the relaunch the *Observateur* had become noted for its royalism, and in *thermidor* of Year III, its presses had been sealed on the orders of the Committee of General Security. However, Mme Lefebvre successfully appealed against the decision, arguing that she had divorced Robert in 1794 — this appears to have been a tactical move, designed to protect their property in the event of prosecution, for the couple had two children and continued to live together — and pointing out that the presses used for the *Observateur* were hers, and not her husband's. Meanwhile, Robert avoided the ban by using a new title, *l'Éclipse*, and when that too was banned in the winter of Year IV, he evaded an arrest warrant issued against him by going into a safe hiding place in his former wife's house.[13] The case against him was soon dismissed in his absence, and in the meantime, *l'Éclipse* reappeared under its original title of *Observateur de l'Europe*, campaigning against the Directory until the *fructidor* coup.[14] On 22 *fructidor*, the *Observateur* was duly banned and orders given for Robert's arrest. Three days later the paper's two presses were sealed, but Robert himself vanished into his hiding place in the house and could not be found.

Meanwhile, the *Observateur* reappeared as *le Compilateur*, but it too was banned after only seven numbers and Mme Lefebvre's third press, on which it had been printed, was sealed up. She promptly protested, presumably with tongue in cheek, that she was not responsible for either paper's contents, but was merely a poor divorcee attempting to eke out a living for herself and her two children through printing.[15] This was plainly unconvincing, as it was common knowledge that she and Robert worked together and that he was still somewhere in the house; and it can have come as no surprise to anyone when a new paper appeared in *frimaire*, *le Bulletin*, from the presses of another Rouen printer, Jacques Duval. Although nominally edited by Duval, its real editor was Robert, and within two months, it too had earned a ban, partly for using clandestine distribution methods, which were illegal since 6 *nivôse*, and partly for vigorously defending a local *juge de paix*, Quillebeuf, who was about to stand trial in Rouen for alleged victimisation of republicans prior to 18 *fructidor*.[16] Before the ban could be put into effect, however, it underwent a title change to *Courier de l'armée d'Angleterre*, and when the departmental *commissaire* arrived on 7 *ventôse* to seal the press, Duval argued that he had already become suspicious of the political tone of the *Bulletin* some days previously, and had decided to stop printing it, launching the *Courrier* as his own paper instead.[17] The *commissaire* did not believe this, sealing his presses anyway, and Robert and Lefebvre then appear to have returned for a while to their old haunts in Paris, publishing a *Fidèle historien* there, to service their loyal clients in Normandy. However, Paris was risky, there was still an arrest warrant out there for Robert, and he was almost recognised there on a number of occasions.

In *messidor* of Year VI, therefore, the couple returned to Rouen, accompanied by an unemployed actor, Thomas, whom they now employed as their front man. In *thermidor* he launched *l'Observateur français*, to put the old firm back in business. However, the departmental *commissaire* was intrigued to know where he had obtained his press and a search of the Roberts' house on the *rue de l'École* quickly revealed that one of the three presses sealed there ten months previously had been removed through a secret door and was now missing. A visit to Thomas's appartment soon revealed that it was there, with traces of sealing wax still adhering to it, and despite vigorous protests from Thomas and his two workers (one of whom was Robert's brother), who claimed that it had been legitimately purchased, it was duly sealed up again. Thomas wasted little time in finding another printer for the *Observateur*, but on 15 *vendémiaire* the Directory banned it.[18] He bounced back with the apt title of *l'Optimiste*, and this too was banned on 28 *brumaire*; but before any action could be taken, Thomas, who was leaked the news by a contact in Paris, transferred all his equipment to a new location and changed title to *Journal des journaux*. When this too was banned later in the month, the press was spirited away again and used to produce the *Chronique française et étrangère*; and then, when this was also banned, the *Journal politique*. Only when this was banned too, in mid-*nivôse*, was the press finally located and sealed.[19] Thomas and the Roberts now abandoned their efforts, supplying their subscribers instead with the Paris-based *Messager des relations extérieures*, for which Robert wrote a column of local news. However, in *floréal* of Year VII they returned to business with the *Affiches de Rouen*, again using Thomas as their front man, which survived well into the Consulate. Persistence had paid off and, by one means or another, the Roberts had kept their subscribers happy for two years, defying government censorship.[20]

Yet the Roberts had undeniably enjoyed a certain amount of good fortune. That good fortune was not available to everyone and by the spring of 1798 the right-wing press had been reduced to a mere shadow of its former self; and it was to remain that way for over a year. In the meanwhile, however, the Jacobin press had also come to share a similar fate. At first, in the aftermath of the *fructidor* coup, the Directors had been prepared to accept support from the Jacobin left, in their efforts to build up a broad republican front against right-wing opinion. Their efforts were initially concentrated on the partial elections to the Councils due in the spring of 1798; and, acknowledging that the press had a crucial role to play in this, they suggested to the leading republican and neo-Jacobin newspapers that they should concentrate on publishing articles that encouraged loyalty to the constitution and stressed the advantages of representative government.[21] Delighted to be welcomed in from the cold, most Jacobin journalists co-operated enthusiastically, optimistic that they could also pressurise the government into further democratic reforms. Thus, in addition to a rapid spread of the constitutional circles that had started up in the previous summer, the winter of 1797–8 saw a further growth in the Jacobin press.[22] In Paris, although some new titles were launched in *fructidor* and *vendémiaire*, most of them proved short-lived, bankrupted by poor circulation figures, the stamp tax, or a combination of the two.[23]

Instead, it was in the provinces that the press was most dynamic. Here, there were already a dozen Jacobin journals appearing before the coup, and in the following months, the figure rose to almost 20. In Metz, where one newspaper, the *Abeille*, already defended the cause of moderate republicanism, a group of local Jacobins, who had set up a legal advice centre for republicans at odds with their right-wing administrators during the previous spring, launched the *Journal des amis*, a daily paper, on 2 *vendémiaire*. It was edited by Trotebas, a Jacobin veteran from the terror, who had already tried to launch a Jacobin paper in the spring of 1796. With his collaborators on the paper he also helped to found the town's constitutional circle in *pluviôse*.[24] In Marseilles, Pierre Peyre-Ferry revived the

Observateur du Midi which had closed down after the adverse election results of the previous spring, under the new title of *Anti-Royaliste ou le Républicain du Midi*. He was also active throughout the winter in the constitutional circle of Marseilles, as were several of his helpers on the paper.[25] In Nevers, Bias Parent l'Aîné, another Jacobin journalist who had been forced to abandon his paper during the spring of Year V, returned with a *Journal de la Nièvre* which, again, was closely linked to his activity in the constitutional circle at Nevers.

At the other end of the country, in Auch, the *Eveil des républicains* was another revival, launched by the printer Pourquiès-Armagnac and edited by Pierre-Nicolas Chantreau, a former Jacobin who had edited the *Documents de la raison* for the departmental administration during the terror.[26] In Bordeaux a former constitutional priest, Latapy, launched a *Courrier de la Gironde* on 1 *vendémiaire*. He was a leading member of the *Cercle de la Grand'Quille* which met at the *église Saint Michel*, as well as *commissaire près l'administration municipale du sud de Bordeaux*, and used the *Courrier* to spearhead the circle's propaganda, as well as to fight his own political battles with the departmental *commissaire,* Lahary.[27] Close by in the Dordogne, Louis-Jean-Pierre Ballois launched the *Observateur du département de la Dordogne* in early *nivôse*; while in Chartres too, early *ventôse* saw a group of local Jacobins launch the *Chronique d'Eure-et-Loir*, calling for support for the men of 1789 and of 1793:

> Ceux-là enfin sont républicains qui, foulant aux pieds les préjuges de la naissance, le prestige des faveurs de la cour, l'expectative assurée des honneurs & des richesses, ont pris parti dans les rangs populaires & n'ont pas cessé de servir la cause sacrée de la liberté.[28]

Most of these newspapers took up the same themes that had permeated the neo-Jacobin press since 1795. They called for republican unity, urging moderates — the men of 1789 — to trust Jacobins and work with them in their common interest of consolidating the republic. Most of them were quick to denounce signs of royalism in their area, and urged their readers to remain vigilant against their activity. 'As a general rule', warned the *Ami des principes* in Angers, royalists must be marginalised in a republic, especially in its early years.'[29] Many of them publicised the existence and activity of their local constitutional circles, especially in Bordeaux, Marseilles and Périgueux; or, as in Angers, repeatedly lamented the fact that they did not have one. Two other issues were also important. The first was the concern of many editors that the *fructidor* coup had only been a partial success, and that in particular, the purges of local administrators and judges had not gone far enough. The *Journal des Hautes-Pyrénées* was emphatic on this issue, launching repeated attacks on its local departmental administration and courts, and calling for the ban on Jean Barère (the brother of Bertrand, who had been a prominent member of the Committee of Public Safety), which prevented him from sitting in the Council of Five Hundred, to be lifted, The *Bulletin du départment de l'Eure* was similar, with Touquet pursuing a bitter campaign of criticism against the departmental administration of the Eure, and most of the municipal administrators of Evreux too, for their past record of tacit royalism.[30]

The second issue was that of preparation for the spring elections of 1798, which offered a crucial opportunity of returning a solid core of neo-Jacobins to the two legislative Councils. Some of them mentioned names: the *Ami des principes*, for example, suggested to readers that they might vote for the outgoing deputy, Talot, as well as for another local man, Clemençeau. The latter was apparently widely disliked for his heavy drinking, but Jahyer suggested that Mirabeau and Voltaire had also been renowned drinkers, while Robespierre had only drunk water.[31] Most of the others refrained from specific recommendations, just urging their readers to vote, and giving general guidance. The *Journal des Hautes-Pyrénées* therefore asked readers to

> . . . make their choice from men who can be respected because of their misfortunes, their constant loyalty to the republic, and their daily sacrifices to its service; to gentle and honest people who have never acted in their own self-interest and never been degraded by underhand activity; to principled patriots whose careers date back to 1789; generous and without pride, always ready to give their services to others and gentle in their ways.

The *Bulletin du département de l'Eure* voiced the same advice in less lyrical terms: 'No risks. No novelties. Republicans whose honesty and courage are known to you, men devoted to the defence of the republic. These are the kind of people who will finally bring an end to the crises of the revolution.'[32]

Yet the Directors had no intention of letting the Jacobin revival get out of hand: quite the contrary, for as the spring elections of

1798 approached, they began to take action against many of the more radical constitutional circles, and to use their extensive censorship powers against the Jacobin press, just as vigorously as they had already done against their royalist rivals. The first warning shots came on 13 *frimaire* when the *Ami de la patrie* and *Défenseur de la vérité*, both Parisian papers, were banned for alleging that there were still royalist deputies left in the two Councils.[33] It was in *ventôse*, however, with elections drawing near, that decisive action was taken. The initiative came from the provinces, when, on 28 *ventôse*, the Municipality in Nancy closed down the *Patriote de la Meurthe* because its editor, Thiébault, claimed that it had several royalists among its ranks, and had failed to enforce legislation against nonjuring priests. Its action in banning the paper on its own initiative was illegal, but the departmental *commissaire* supported it in a letter to the Minister of Police, alleging that the *Patriote* had consistently pursued '. . . systematic defamation of magistrates and subversion of public order', and the Minister let the ban stand.[34] On 3 *germinal*, action then came from the Minister of Police himself, with a ban on the *Ami des principes* in Angers, long solicited by the departmental *commissaire* who loathed its editor, Jahyer, and denounced it as being '. . . edited in constant spirit of opposition to the measures taken by the government in accordance with the constitution and legislation'.[35] Early *germinal* also saw the end of the road for Bazin's *Chronique de la Sarthe*, banned shortly after Bazin had been elected to the Le Mans Municipality, because, in the Minister's words, it was '. . . edited according to principles contrary to the constitution of Year III'. In Metz the *Journal des amis* was also closed down, just days before the first meetings of the electoral assemblies there. Finally, in Nevers, the *Journal de la Nièvre* was banned on 7 *germinal*, on the highly dubious grounds that its editor, Parent l'aîné, had advocated the use of violence in the town's primary assemblies.[36]

In *floréal*, once the election results were in, and the Directors had duly modified them, three other papers were also closed down: the *Observateur du département de la Dordogne*, the *Bulletin du département de l'Eure* and the *Observateur de l'Yonne*. All of them, significantly enough, had been brought to the minister's attention by their respective departmental *commissaires*, who regarded them as dangerously radical, and a threat to public order. In *messidor* it was the turn of the *Courrier de la Gironde*, sunk under the twin salvos of the departmental *commissaire* and one of the city's deputies to the Council of Five Hundred. Meanwhile, the Pacifique in Beauvais failed because of bankruptcy, and in Paris the *Ami de la patrie* and *Journal des hommes libres* were banned again.[37] Nine provincial journals had therefore vanished during the spring of Year VI, victims of the Directors' determination to stifle Jacobinism as a political force. Like their right-wing counterparts, some attempted to sidestep bans by adopting new titles; but unless they were also prepared to moderate their criticism of the government, they met with little success. In Paris the *Journal des hommes libres*, for example, went through no less than seven title changes, all of them successively closed down, before temporarily abandoning the struggle at the end of the year. In Le Mans René Bazin tried to convert the advertising supplement of his banned *Chronique* into a fully fledged political paper, *l'Indicateur*, and when this was banned, he launched *l'Abeille* in its place, which suffered a similar fate.[38] Those who were willing to moderate their views and support government policies, on the other hand, could survive. In Nancy, Angers, Bordeaux and Sens, editors resumed publication under another title after a government ban, but kept out of further trouble by toeing the Directory's political line. In Châlons-sur-Marne, Grenoble, Auch and Chartres, others evaded a ban in the first place by avoiding controversy as soon as the Directory's attitude became clear.[39] The end-result was the same, and certainly no Jacobin showed the tenacity of the Roberts in Rouen or of Mme Peltier in Bordeaux, possibly because none of them had the requisite financial resources.

In its drive to discipline the press, the Directory also returned to the policy of patronage and subsidy, already used briefly in the winter of 1795–6. Shortly after the *fructidor* coup, it established a small secret agency, which later became known as the *bureau politique*, to organise its propaganda for the spring elections of 1798. Its own secretary-general, Lagarde, was put in charge and a protégé of Merlin de Douai, Nicolas Regnard, became its effective organiser. Both men were experienced journalists — Lagarde in Lille, and Regnard as a former contributor to the *Journal des hommes libres* — and they quickly commissioned pamphlets and employed writers to draw up articles for insertion into newspapers. One of their earliest recruits was Vincent Barbet, an experienced pamphleteer and journalist, who was planted on to the editorial staff of the *Messager du soir*, a right-wing paper which had been allowed to survive the coup, with the express task of influencing its editorial policy and converting its readers into supporters of the republic. The move was a lamentable failure, as the rest of the staff cold-shouldered him, and Barbet gave up after only two months. He continued to work for the *bureau*, however, along with many other writers, and a number of newspapers, including the *Moniteur* and *Rédacteur*, published the articles that he and others supplied.[40] The Directors also resumed the policy of cash subsidies to moderate republican papers, abandoned under pressure from the Councils in the spring of 1796. On 17 *frimaire*, after prolonged lobbying, the Minister of the Interior subscribed to 300 copies of the *Pacificateur*. Two months later the *Journal des campagnes et des armées* was given 2,000 francs per month, and smaller hand-outs followed for the *Journal des théophilanthropes*, the *Conservateur* and the *Indépendant*, the latter edited by the former Jacobin journalist, Aristide Valcour. At best, however, the amounts involved were small and intended only to ensure bare survival. They certainly did little to build up a powerful pro-governmental press.[41]

By the summer of 1798 the political crisis of the previous year was beginning to recede into the distance. The Directors were adamant that the powers given them under article 355 needed to be renewed for a further year, but there were doubts in the Councils over the need to do this, and when it came up for debate in *thermidor* Year VI, it was decided to renew them, but to draw up an adequate press law in the interim which, once passed, could supersede them and return the press to a more normal footing.[42] It was *frimaire* before the Council of Five Hundred eventually came round to discussing the matter, but it ran into immediate difficulty, as the majority of deputies still feared that any relaxation in press control would merely benefit the extremists on both sides. The matter was therefore dropped until the following *prairial*, by which time the annual spring elections of *germinal* had returned a high proportion of Jacobin deputies hostile to censorship, and the whole mood in the Councils had changed. On 28 *prairial* the Council of Five Hundred formally voted through a press law to replace the *fructidor* decrees, but before the Council of Elders had time to consider it, the *coup d'état* of 30 *prairial* had intervened to replace three of the Directors. Censorship effectively collapsed. Article 35 was formally repealed on 14 *thermidor*, and the Councils undertook to replace it with new press legislation.

However, in the meanwhile royalist and Jacobin titles had already resumed publication, an open press war resulted, and the new Directors became alarmed. In mid-*thermidor*, they urged the Councils to pass an adequate press law swiftly, and by the end of the month several deputies in the council of Elders had become so concerned by the resurgence of both Jacobin and royalist titles, and in particular by an outspoken condemnation of Barras and Sieyès in the *Journal des hommes libres*, that they asked the Directory to revive the legislation of *germinal* Year IV to prosecute its editor, Vatar.[43] The Council of Five Hundred refused to back their call, arguing that the detailed implementation of legislation was the concern of the executive rather than the legislature, and the Directors, obviously doubting the effectiveness of the *germinal* legislation, resorted to tougher measures instead. On 16 *fructidor* they cited the legislation of 22 *fructidor* Year V and ordered the immediate arrest and deportation of the 65 editors and publishers originally listed in it. Then, on the following day, they invoked article 145 of the constitution to ban eleven newspapers and order the arrest of their owners and editors. This prompted the Council of Five Hundred to accelerate its consideration of new press legislation, but it was already too late, for the Directors pressed ahead with their use of article 145 during late *fructidor* and early *brumaire* and ordered the postal services not to handle any paper that it had banned, or any attempted resurrection of it using a new title. On 13 *brumaire* they provided the service with a list of papers that it was allowed to deliver, which pointedly excluded those of the extreme left and the extreme right. Executive censorship had returned with a vengeance, and the *fructidor* legislation might just as well never have been repealed.[44]

On his accession to power, Bonaparte was to waste little time in refining the machinery bequeathed to him by his predecessors, and returning the political press to the kind of government control that it had experienced under the *ancien régime*. In this he did not innovate, but merely built on the legacy inherited from the last two years of the Directory, of censorship, police control and complete distrust of editorial freedom. This in turn was an almost inevitable response to the political disintegration of the country since the fall of the monarchy in 1792, and part of a wider contraction of its civil and political liberties, imposed by moderate republicans against their royalist and neo-Jacobin opponents. Yet it also reflected a growing disenchantment with the role of the press: for if, as most observers readily admitted by the end of the decade, newspaper sales were a barometer of public opinion, then public opinion was decidedly conservative for the four years that the regime lasted. But journalists did not only reflect public opinion: by their coverage of news and editorial comment, they also helped to mould it, confirming prejudices and adapting residual beliefs. Because of this there were many moderate republicans who despaired of its ability to do this intelligently and who, like counter-revolutionary propagandists in 1790 or 1791, argued that its trivialisation of political issues made it a hindrance rather than a help to stability and progress. From being an essential bulwark of political liberty in 1789, the press had become a dangerous subversion, and this change in mood helps to explain the ease with which Bonaparte battened down his own authority upon it.[45]

Notes

1. A. Söderjhelm, *Le régime de la presse pendant la révolution française* (Helsingford and Paris, 1900–1), II, pp. 106–14.

2. A.N. F[7] 3448B and F[7] 4286; for the financial problems caused by the stamp tax, see the case of Ballois' *Défenseur de la constitution* in A.N. F[18] Seine 12, viii, and *Réflexions essentielles relatives aux droits de timbre sur les journaux, par J.B. Nougaret*, (Paris, undated), which attacked the measure for its effect on the poor and on the printing industry.

3. A.D. Rhône L459 and A.D. Hérault L1080. In some cases administrators ignored the repeal: the departmental *commissaire* of the Hérault, for example, was reprimanded in *frimaire* for banning the circulation of several legal Parisian newspapers in his department (A.D. Hérault, L1080). See also the problems in Sens, where the Municipality had sealed all the presses belonging to the printer, Tarbé, in late *fructidor*, because some weeks previously, he had printed a royalist paper, the *Journal politique et littéraire*. Tarbé, however, also used one of the presses to publish his own *Affiches de Sens*, which was a non-political advertising journal, and appealed to the Minister of Police to order the seals to be removed. This the Minister did on 11 *vendémiaire*, but the Municipality only removed them on the one press used for the *Affiches*, retaining them on the other presses, quite illegally and despite repeated orders from Paris, until the following summer (A.N. F[7] 3448B).

4. For the use of private transport by the royalist press, see W.R. Fryer, *Republic or restoration in France? 1794–1797* (London, 1965), pp. 196 and 216; and below, Chapter 7.

5. C. Lacretelle, *Dix années d'épreuvres pendant la révolution* (Paris, 1842), pp. 320–6; A.N. F[7] 3448B and F[7] 3450; A.D. Haute-Garonne L2563.

6. A.N. F[7] 3448B; F[7] 3452; A.D. Haute-Garonne L2563.

7. A.N. F[7] 3450.

8. Several such cases are traced in B.H.V.P., Ms. 726 and 727; for the *Grondeur*, see A.N. F[7] 3452.

9. Max Fajn, 'La diffusion de la presse révolutionnaire dans le Lot, le Tarn et 'Aveyron, sous la Convention et la Directoire', *Annales du Midi*, 83 (1971), p. 306; A.N. F[7] 3448B (Extrait de la lettre du commissaire du Directoire exécutif près l'administration municipale de Troyes du 30 fructidor an V); ibid., (Le commissaire du pouvoir exécutif près l'administration municipale du canton de Troyes, le 19 frimaire an VI); ibid., (Le commissaire près l'administration municipale du centre de Marseilles, le

8 fructidor VI); ibid., (Le commissaire près les Hautes-Pyrénées, le 26 vendémiaire VI); ibdi., 'Notes faits sur quelques numéros du Journal du Lot échappés à l'éclipse qui s'en est faite depuis la publication de la loi du 19 fructidor'); Brelot, *La vie politique en Côte-d'Or sous la Directoire* (Dijon, 1932), pp. 92–4, 99ff.

10. A.N. F^7 3448B and F^7 3449.

11. A.N. F^7 3448B; F^7 3450; A.D. Seine-Maritime L304.

12. A.N. F^7 3448B and F^7 3451; A.D. Gironde 3L56; A.M. Bordeaux D156, D177, 138, 136. For the papers involved, see B.M. Bordeaux MF1147.

13. Theodore Lebreton, *Biographie normande*, 3 vols (Rouen, 1861), III, pp. 349–50; *Causes (en partie) inconnues des principaux événements qui ont eu lieu en France depuis 32 ans, et Vie de l'auteur; par J.-B.-M. Robert, ancien avocat au Parlement de Normandie*, 2 vols (Paris, 1817), I, pp. 252–5, 309–10, 491–6.

14. A. Tuetey, *Répertoire générale des sources manuscrites de l'histoire de Paris pendant la révolution française*, 11 vols (Paris, 1890–1914), IX, no. 1323; X, nos. 548, 554, 661, 1018, 1384; A.D. Seine-Maritime L304, pièces 52–3.

15. A.N. F^7 4286 no. 30; A.D. Seine-Inferiéure L304 pièces 82–3; *Ville de Rouen. Analyse des délibérations de l'assemblée municipale et électorale du 16 juillet au 4 mars 1790* (Rouen, 1905), p. 493. Scattered copies for the summer of Year IV are in B.M. Rouen Norm. MM 1046–2.

16. A.N. F^7 4286 no. 30:

. . . the three numbers of *le Compilateur* . . . are only an accurate transcription of the meetings of the two Councils and of the proclamations of the Directory; there is no comment in them, and they contain no articles dealing with anything other than the debates of the Councils and meetings of the Directory.

17. A.N. F^7 3449, *commissaire près la Seine-Inférieure* to Minister of Police, undated; ibid., commissaire de police de la section de l'est au commissaire près l'administration municipale de Rouen, 10 pluviôse VI.

18. Ibid., *commissaire près la Seine-Inférieure* to Minister of Police, 27 *pluviôse* VI:

It is obvious that this new paper is just a continuation of the Bulletin, which the author rightly feared was about to be banned, and which he wanted to keep going by using a new title in order to serve the same crowd of anti-republican subscribers.

The municipal *commissaire* of Rouen was inclined to be more charitable towards Duval: see his letter of 1 and 24 *ventôse* in ibid.

19. A.N. F^7 3451 *commissaire près la Seine-Inférieure* to Minister of Police.

20. A.N. F^7 3450; see also the comments of the *commissaire de la Seine-Inférieure* on the *Affiches de Rouen* in a letter to the Minister of Police of 27 *pluviose* VII in A.N. F^7 3451; and in the same carton, *commissaire près le Calvados* to Minister of Police, 27 *messidor* an VII:

It is the most inflammatory paper that royalism has produced. It has appeared again since 30 *prairial* and is widely distributed

throughout the department under my care, especially in the commune of Caen. It is more prompt than other papers, especially in
its reports of the Councils and in its news from Paris, and is consequently avidly read. It can be found in the hands of all the incorrigible
aristocrats, whose counter-revolutionary hopes it encourages inces-
santl,. As they know very well that anything which flatters them
alarms republicans, they lose no opportunity of spreading the *Affiches
de Rouen* around. They peddle it from house to house to ensure that
it is read; they lend it freely, and ensure that it can be found in public
places so that it is read in cafés. Here is how they have ensured its
presence in cafés. They have proposed to café owners who have
subscriptions to other papers to lend them those papers in the
mornings, and then return them in the afternoon along with a free
copy of the *Affiches*. Most owners have taken the offer up, and as
cafés are usually most crowded in the afternoons the *Affiches de Rouen*,
which is just another name for the *Observateur de l'Europe*, gets publicity
which kills off the remnants of any republican spirit . . .

See also ibid., *commisiaire près la Seine-Inférieure* to Minister of Police, 28
messidor VII and A.N. F⁷ 3452 for the complaints of the *commissaire* of the
Manche.
    21. F.-A. Aulard, *Paris pendant la réaction thermidorienne et sous le Direc-
toire*, 5 vols (Paris, 1898), IV, pp. 534–6; see also the comments of the
Minister of Police in a letter to the *commissaire près le Rhône:*

> It is in the run up to elections that it is crucial to watch over journa-
> lists whose writings could mislead public opinion, or give hope . . .
> to royalism. During this same time patriot journalists must be
> encouraged by republican public officials. (A.D. Rhône L459)

    22. I. Woloch, *Jacobin legacy. The democratic movement under the Directory*
(Princeton, 1970), Chapter 4.
    23. See J.-R. Suratteau, 'Sur quelques journaux fructidoriens
(septembre-octobre 1797)', *A.h.r.f.*, 259 (1985), pp. 76–104.
    24. J.-J. Barbé, *Les journaux de la Moselle, bibliographie et histoire* (Metz,
1928), p. 25; A.D. Puy-de-Dome L6389; Isser Woloch, 'The revival of
Jacobinism in Metz during the Directory', *Journal of Modern History*, 38
(1966), p. 21ff.
    25. Woloch, *Jacobin legacy*, pp. 110–12, 126, 285; for the hostile attitude
of the local *commissaire*, see A.N. F⁷ 3448B.
    26. G. Thuillier, 'Parent l'aîné et le Journal de la Nievre en l'an VI',
Mémoires de la Société Académique du Nivernais, LIV (1967), p. 56; G. Brégail,
La presse périodique dans le Gers pendant la révolution (Auch, 1922), p. 60ff.
    27. Woloch, *Jacobin legacy*, pp. 86–8; for copies of the Courier, see B.M.
Bordeaux H. 12.438.
    28. For the *Observateur*, see two copies in A.N. F⁷ 3448B and scattered
copies in A.N. C 531 and AFIII 517 plaq. 3310; see the comments of the
departmental administration: 'We believe it to be edited in a way favourable
to the government's principles, and we will be careful that it is only used
to ensure the popularity of the law and the Republic.' For Chartres, see

Chronique d'Eure-et-Loir, 6 *ventose* VI, p. 15; for a biographical sketch of Conard, see B.M. Chartres, Fonds Jusselin, R32/1–4, pp. 97–126.

29. *Ami des principes*, 6 *ventôse* VI, pp. 283–4.

30. *Journal des Hautes-Pyrénées*, 5 *brumaire*, VI, p. 339; 8 *pluviôse* VI, p. 426; 10 *nivôse* VI, p. 397; *Bulletin du département de l'Eure*, 15 *vendémiaire* VI, p. 159; 23 *vendémiaire* VI, p. 176; 25 *vendémiaire* VI, p. 177.

31. *Ami des principes*, 22 *germinal* VI, pp. 67–8.

32. *Journal des Hautes-Pyrénées*, 16 *germinal* VI, 68; *Bulletin du département de l'Eure*, 5 *ventôse* VI, pp. 393–6.

33. A.N. F[7] 3450: the *Ami* was later allowed to reappear.

34. A.N. F[7] 4286 no. 22; P. Clémendot, *Le département de la Meurthe à l'époque du Directoire* (Paris, 1966), p. 262; A. Ronsin, *Les périodiques lorrains, antérieurs à 1800* (Nancy, 1964), pp. 81–2.

35. A.D. Maine-et-Loire 1L99, 2 *germinal* VI; A.M. Angers I 143; E. Quéruau-Lamérie, 'Notice sur les journaux d'Angers pendant la révolution', *Révue de l'Anjou*, nouvelle série, 24 (1892), pp. 310–11.

36. A.D. Sarthe L 181, *commissaire près l'administration centrale* to Minister of Police, 10 *germinal* VI; see also ibid., letter from Sarthe to the Minister of Police, undated, which clearly reveals the *commissaire*'s own reluctance:

> Both the Directory's orders and yours have been carried out, and whatever the current public outcry over the decision . . . taken against a citizen who has just been elected to the municipality by the majority of sections in this town, I have had to do as I am told. I have done my duty.

Not surprisingly, he was dismissed shortly afterwards. Woloch, 'The revival of Jacobinism', pp. 21–5, 32; Thuillier, 'Parent l'aîne', pp. 55–61.

37. A.N. F[7] 3449 Minister of Interior to Minister of Police, 22 *germinal* VI; Henri Labroue, *L'esprit public en Dordogne pendant la révolution* (Paris, 1911), pp. 154–5; A.N. F[7] 34489; A.N. F[7] 7144 no. 1615; for the *Courrier de la Gironde*, see A.N. F[7] 3449, *commissaire près l'administration centrale* to Minister of Police (23 *floréal* and 5 *prairial* VI); and *commissaire central* of Bordeaux to Minister of Police, 23 *germinal* VI; see also A.N. F[18] Gironde, 16 lv, pièce 6ff. For the bankruptcy of the *Journal de l'Oise*, see Tubeuf's correspondence in F[7] 3448B and F[7] 3449, and in A.N. F[7] 4286.

38. For Bazin's efforts, see the correspondence in A.N. F[7] 3449 also A.D. Sarthe L167 fol. 186, letter of 1 *prairial* VI; A.D. Sarthe L181, Minister of Police to *commissaire près l'administration centrale*, 17 *messidor* VI; A.D. Sarthe L214, *commissaire près l'administration municipale du Mans* to *commissaire près l'administration centrale*, 22 *messidor* VI; A.M. Le Mans L1027.

39. Ronsin, *Les périodiques lorrains*, pp. 81–2; *Lettre de Jahier le jeune à ses amis. Angers le 24 germinal an VI de la République* (undated); A.D. Maine-et-Loire 1L938, letter of 16 *brumaire* VII. G. Clause, 'Un journal républicain de l'époque directionale à Châlons-sur-Marne, 'Le Journal du département de la Marne', 1796–1800', *Mémoires de la Société d'Agriculture, Sciences et Arts du Département de la Marne*, 91 (1976), pp. 343–5; Berthier, *Le Clairvoyant. Étude d'un journal révolutionnaire grenoblois, 1797–1800* T.E.R. (Grenoble, 1968), Chapters II and III, *passim*.

40. A. Mathiez, *Le Directoire* (Paris, 1934), 358ff; L. Stoll, 'The "Bureau

Politique'' and the management of the popular press', unpublished PhD thesis, University of Wisconsin, 1975.

41. A.N. F⁷ 3448B; AFIII 45 d.162-3; F⁷ 3449.

42. Söderjhelm, *Le régime de la presse*, II, pp. 153–4; *Motion d'ordre de Bertrand (du Calvados), sur les moyens de s'opposer à la dépravation de l'esprit public.* *Séance du 11 thermidor an VI* (Paris, undated).

43. M. Fajn, *The Journal des hommes libres de tous les pays, 1792–1800* (The Hague-Paris, 1975), p. 100.

44. Söderjhelm, *Le régime de la presse*, II, p. 180ff; Georges Bourgin, 'Les journaux à Paris en l'an VII', *Cahiers de la presse*, II, (1939), pp. 137–44; F.-A. Aulard, 'Une statistique des journaux en l'an VIII, à la veille du 18 brumaire', *La Révolution Française*, 26 (1894), pp. 288–98.

45. C. Bellanger (ed.), *Histoire générale de la presse française. Tome I. Des origines à 1814* pp. 549–67; A. Cabanis, *La presse sous le Consulat et l'Empire* (Paris, 1975); Pierre Riberette, 'Un journal officieux sous le Consulat; le Bulletin de Paris', *Revue de l'Institut Napoleon*, III (1969), pp. 121–32.

6

Proprietors, Journalists and Printers: The Making of Newspapers

Much of this book has so far been concerned with the political development of the press, for it was the crisis of 1789 that allowed it to flourish, and continued instability during the 1790s that shaped its existence. Yet there is another aspect of its development which, although inevitably affected by political events, evolved on a much slower time-scale. This is its material life: the patterns of ownership and production, editorial work and reporting, marketing and sales, distribution and profits. All of these had to adapt to a new and much changed environment in the decade after 1789, with increased consumer demand, and growth had to take place without the aid of dramatic innovation, for the technology of reporting, printing and distribution remained firmly rooted in the age of Gutenberg until well into the nineteenth century. What took place, therefore, was largely the adaptation of artisanal production and distribution techniques to a modernised political environment, the development of the old within the new, by means of a series of improvisations. Continuity mingled with innovation to enable the press to play the pivotal political role that it did.

Despite the explosive growth in the press between 1789 and 1799, its main proprietorial structures were little changed from those of the *ancien régime*. Before 1789 most newspapers had been under personal ownership, belonging either to the editor himself, to the printer, or to some third party such as a publisher or investor. This remained common throughout the revolution. Ferréol de Beaugeard, for example, who had launched the *Journal de Marseille* in 1782, was its sole owner, wrote out the text every week in longhand, and took it to a printer to have it run off and distributed. He paid the printer a set fee for his work, and handled the subscription registers and readers' correspondence himself.[1] Alternatively,

160

there were printer-proprietors, such as Mame in Angers or Couret de Villeneuve in Orléans, who controlled the contents of their newspapers themselves, sometimes with part-time editorial help from workers and friends, and supervised both printing and distribution from their own workshops. Then, almost exclusively in Paris, there were large-scale publishers such as Panckoucke who owned their paper, hired the editorial staff, subcontracted the printing out, and employed clerks to look after distribution and sales.

The simplicity of all three kinds of arrangement probably facilitated the rapid growth that took place after 1789, for it made improvisation easily possible. Brissot, for example, when he launched the *Patriote français* in 1789, arranged for a bookseller, Buisson, to handle the advertising and distribution ends, as well as arranging the printing, while he himself just wrote the copy. He parted company with Buisson in September after an acrimonious quarrel caused by complaints from subscribers about non-delivery, but ended up, in the following year, making similar arrangements with a printer, Lepage, on the *place du Théâtre Italien*. He controlled content, while Lepage looked after printing and distribution, taking all the paper's profits and simply paying Brissot a flat salary of 6,000 *livres* per year. Lepage did very well from the deal, but it suited Brissot too, as it absolved him from tedious financial and administrative work, in which his track record was poor. Camille Desmoulins made similar arrangements for the *Révolutions de France et de Brabant* when he first launched it in December 1789, contracting with a bookseller, Garnery, to look after the printing and distribution, in return for a salary of 6,000 *livres* per year. Then, in the spring of 1790 when the contract came up for renewal, he accepted the offer of better terms from another bookseller, Gyrey, who paid him 10,000 *livres* instead. The *Gazette de Paris*, on the opposite side of the spectrum, was owned jointly by its editor, du Rozoi, and a secretary to the prince de Conti, de Rosuel. Du Rozoi wrote the text, the printing was subcontracted out, and the task of collecting the printed sheets from him, folding and collating them, distributing them to *colporteurs* and to the post, was carried out by a Madame Feuchère, who was paid at the rate of 3 *livres* per annual subscription. She in turn employed clerks and handlers to help her.[2]

An example of the flexibility inherent in this kind of arrangement is provided by the records of an unsuccessful attempt to prosecute Stanislas Fréron in the summer of 1790. Fréron had been bound since 1781 by a legal undertaking with his step-mother,

Mme Fréron, owner of the *Année littéraire*, not to write for any newspaper, and in return for this was paid a small annual annuity which helped finance his dissipated lifestyle. When the revolution came, however, he was attracted by the glamour of politics, envied the prominence that journalists acquired, and surreptitiously broke the agreement by writing anonymously for the *Ami des citoyens*. Then, in the spring of 1790, he decided to launch the *Orateur du peuple*, under cover of anonymity, and needed a front-man to act as nominal editor. Walking with his long-time friend, the Marquis de la Poype, in the gardens of the Palais Royal one morning, he came across Marcel Enfantin, a former exchange dealer who had arrived in Paris from Marseilles some two years previously and fallen on hard times. Enfantin was carrying some printer's proofs, and the three men fell into conversation, as a result of which la Poype engaged Enfantin to act as the nominal owner of the *Orateur du peuple*, with the job of carrying Fréron's copy to the printer, and supervising its distribution and finances. La Poype duly found an impecunious bookseller in the *rue de la Bûcherie*. Mme L'Espinasse, to look after packaging and delivery, while Enfantin engaged a printer, Laurens Jr, in the Saint-Jacques. Laurens backed out of the deal when he saw the polemical contents of the first number and La Poype, acting on the advice of Mme L'Espinasse, engaged other printers, Chambon and Delachave in the *rue de la Bièvre*, signing a contract with them which, among other things, stipulated when the copy would be delivered, the time by which printing should be complete, and the details of price. That contract quickly turned sour, as Chambon and Delachave found themselves out of pocket because of the costs of night printing, and La Poype had to return to Laurens Jr, persuading him to print the *Orateur* again by paying a premium for the extra labour costs that night work entailed. Later, after yet another disagreement, he transferred to a cheaper printer, Pellier, in early June. This was not the end of the matter, for the *Orateur* subsequently migrated to other print shops, but what is clear is the ease with which it could do so, and the improvised nature of the entire operation. Everything was done in an *ad hoc* way, and involved the active participation of just a handful of people. Yet it was from just such a basis that most of the major titles of the revolution began.[3]

More complicated contractual arrangements did, however, exist where both owners and printers preferred a more secure basis for work; and the *Miroir*, launched in 1796 and owned by its editor, Jean Michel Souriguières, provides one such example. In the autumn of 1796 Souriguières signed a contract with Georges Bridel, owner of the *Imprimerie de l'Union*, to print the paper, through which he retained full ownership, along with total control over editorial content, provided half the costs of paper and wages, and took two-thirds of the profits. For his part, Bridel provided the press and printshop, heat and light, and half the cost of paper and wages, in return for one-third of the profits. The deal was complicated, and appears to have worked to Bridel's disadvantage, for he sold out in the spring of the following year, and his successor, Talairac, renegotiated the contract to have the costs shared on the same basis as the profits, two-thirds to one-third.[4] On the whole, it was amongst the Parisian press that the more detailed arrangements prevailed, because of the complications of scale. Yet even here personal ownership remained the norm. Panckoucke's *Moniteur*, for example, was a large newspaper by eighteenth-century standards, with a sophisticated subdivision of editorial and administrative labour; yet it was Panckoucke alone who owned and directed it until 1795, financing it initially from the profits that he had made from his pre-revolutionary publishing and journalism.[5] Similarly, Etienne Feuillant's *Journal du soir* claimed to employ some 60 print workers, copyists and office staff, and to provide work for over 200 *colporteurs* in Paris alone, while Prudhomme's *Révolutions de Paris*, as early as 1790, had several presses, a press manager, sales manager, numerous print workers and several hundred part-time workers. Yet both were the personal property of their owners and, in Prudhomme's case at least, the necessary money came from illicit pamphleteering prior to 1789, and the huge profits made by the paper in its early months.[6]

The explanation for the survival of personal ownership probably lies with cost: for although launching and publishing a newspaper was by no means cheap, neither was it inordinately expensive. Large-scale capital was rarely required, particularly during the early months of the revolution, when the market was wide open, and as a result partnerships and shareholding arrangements, even in the rare cases where they did exist, were usually restricted to those directly involved, such as the owner, editor and printer. The *Ami du Roi*, when it was launched at the beginning of June 1790, was owned jointly by five people, two of whom were its distributors, a third its owner, and the fourth its editor.[7] The *Union, ou le journal de la liberté*, a bilingual paper established towards the end of 1789, was floated on capital, half provided by its editors and half by an English-born textile merchant, Marshall, who was attracted by the spectacular commercial success of so many newspapers launched over the summer of 1789. When, after poor initial sales, however, Marshall tried to pressurise the editors into shifting their political bias towards the right, in the hope of exploiting the growing conservative market that the *Gazette de Paris* and *Actes des Apôtres* had just begun to tap, they refused and broke away from him to relaunch the paper under a different name.[8] The *Journal de la société de 1789*, launched by the *société de 1789* in the spring of 1790 with Condorcet as editor, was intended to be financed by shares issued to each of the club members, but too few subscribed for it to be viable, suggesting that the habit was slow to grow.[9] The *Rédacteur*, launched and financed by the Directory in the winter of 1795–6, was more formally structured as a limited company, with seven shares divided out amongst four shareholders, and the printer holding a majority share. There were regular shareholders' meetings, policy decisions and annual accounts. Nevertheless, although several other papers, such as the *Journal de Paris* and the *Nouvelles politiques*, were also co-owned, shareholding arrangements appear to have been quite rare, in sharp contrast with contemporary developments in England. Most newspapers, like Prudhomme's, were launched on personal savings, money borrowed from friends, or the proceeds of subscriptions paid in advance of publication.[10]

If there was little change in managerial structures, there was nevertheless some change in the nature of ownership, for the collapse of the privilege system in the summer of 1789 changed owners overnight from crown tenants-at-will into freeholders. The right to publish without prior censorship, enshrined in article 11 of the Declaration of the Rights of Man in late August 1789, and reiterated in the constitutions of 1791, 1793 and 1795, survived until Napoleon's decree of 27 *nivôse* Year VIII. Anyone could therefore set themselves up as newspaper proprietors in the intervening ten years, without the need to obtain any kind of prior permission; and until the summer of 1796, when the law of 28 *germinal* obliged owners to put their names on their papers, along with the name and address of the printer, there was no obligation for either them or the editor to reveal their identity at all.[11] Yet freedom brought in its wake a number of problems rarely encountered in the strictly policed world of the *ancien régime*, the most recurrent of which revolved around rival ownership claims. When Brissot cancelled his arrangement with Buisson in mid-September of 1789, for example, Buisson promptly claimed that the *Patriote* was as much his as Brissot's, and that as he was owed a substantial amount of money for work already done, he intended to continue it under his own name. An acrimonious dispute developed, which was only resolved after lengthy negotiations conducted, ironically, by the same royal officials who had twice banned the paper earlier in the year. Brissot was allowed to keep the *Patriote*, but Buisson was allowed to use the word 'patriote' in any future paper that he chose to launch, something which he did in creating the *Annales patriotiques* in early October.[12]

Arbitration, this time from the provisional municipality's police committee, was also called in to settle an unpleasant quarrel between Louis Prudhomme and Antoine Tournon over the ownership of the *Révolutions de Paris*. Tournon originally went to Prudhomme with a plan to publish a pamphlet, *Historique des révolutions*, but Prudhomme persuaded him to turn it into a newspaper, and hired other writers to supplement his material. Tournon's stamina quickly faltered after the first number and Prudhomme soon took control of the paper, employing half a dozen of his own editorial writers, including Loustallot, who rapidly dominated it. In late October Tournon therefore left, in protest, to launch his own *Révolutions de Paris*, claiming it to be the authentic continuation of the original. Camille Desmoulins took his side, and the case was taken before the police committee, which finally arrived at an unsatisfactory compromise on 4 November, acknowledging that Prudhomme was the 'chef de l'entreprise', with the right to continue the paper and serve its subscribers, but also conceding that Tournon was the 'inventeur et auteur' of the idea and could also continue with his own paper under the same title. This he did until a lack of subscribers forced him to close down in the following spring.[13]

The royalist *Ami du Roi* was also similarly split by ownership quarrels, shortly after its launch on 1 June 1790, and in its case even the existence of a contract proved to be of no assistance. According to the contract, drawn up in the spring of 1790, the paper was to be the joint property of five people: Mme Fréron, its editor Galart de Montjoye, its printer Crapart, the bookseller Briand, and an unnamed cleric. However the quality of the early numbers disappointed readers, and Mme Fréron therefore turned to her brother, Thomas-Marie Royou, asking him to write the Assembly reports instead, in the hope that he would liven up the paper. This annoyed Montjoye, and in early August Royou and Mme Fréron therefore broke away to set up their own *Ami du Roi*, claiming it to be the legitimate continuation of the original. Matters then became more complicated when, within days, Montjoye quarrelled with Crapart and Briand, and separated from them to launch his own *Ami du Roi*, while Crapart continued with his version. Catholic royalism had its first newspaper trinity, and although the split between Crapart and Montjoye was resolved in early November, their combined rivalry with Royou continued until the latter's death in the summer of 1792.[14]

Yet even the famous had their problems, for in the winter of 1789–90, Mirabeau discovered — after complaints from subscribers that copies of his *Courrier de Provence* were either arriving late or not at all, and a warning from his printer that the contract would lapse unless he was paid for his work — that the paper's profits were being soaked up by his distributors, M. and Mme Lejay. They appear to have been using the money to renovate their bookshop and feather their nest, and when Mirabeau confronted them and angrily threatened to take the business away, Mme Lejay, who was evidently the strong personality in the partnership, coolly replied that she would then continue the paper herself, referring to it as '. . . her own property as much as if it were a landed estate and we her labourers'. Mirabeau therefore had to patch up a compromise and the voracious couple retained the gains that they had made.[15] Indeed, the threat to take over a paper was by no means an empty one, for it was usually the distributor who held the trump card in the form of the subscription lists. Gabriel Feydel, for example, closed down the *Observateur*, a paper that he had launched in August of 1789, in early April of 1790, to allow himself time to concentrate on other work, only to find that his publisher promptly hired other editors to continue it. To protect his reputation, he therefore resumed publication in the following August.[16] Marat too, after his escape to London in January 1790, found that his *Ami du peuple* was being plagiarised, and returned to Paris in May of 1790 to reclaim it as his own, using the courts to silence the clones. A year later, Poncelin de la Roche Tilhac, editor and owner of the *Courrier français*, after a quarrel with his distributor, Gueffier le jeune, found that Gueffier was supplying subscribers with his own version of the paper, renamed the *Courrier des français*, and refusing to hand over the subscription registers. Poncelin had to send free copies of his own version to departmental administrations around the country, asking them to supply it to any of his subscribers that they knew, and take Gueffier to court to regain his title and his subscription registers.[17]

The most audacious case of a stolen title, however, occurred in Lille, where, in the latter weeks of 1789, a local lawyer, Joseph-Jean

Lagarde, advertised for subscribers to a newspaper that he planned to launch early in the new year, *l'Abeille*. In mid-December he was approached by a café owner, Ravel, who also ran a small reading room as an annexe to his café, offering to help him in the venture. Legarde agreed, and on 26 December 1789, the two men arranged that, in return for looking after the administration and the dispatch sides of the business, and giving Lagarde access to all the newspapers stocked in his *cabinet littéraire*, Ravel was to take one-third of the profits. Lagarde, for his part, retained complete editorial control and two-thirds of the profits. However, once he had the list of subscribers, Ravel demanded a 50 per cent share of the profits, and when this was refused, he broke away to supply subscribers with a newspaper of his own, under the almost identical title of *l'Abeille patriote*. Lagarde had no legal means of redress, as the agreement had been verbal, so he had to struggle to keep the *Abeille* going by building up his subscription list all over again. In the end the quarrel proved pointless, as both newspapers were failures. Ravel was barely literate, and finally sold his *Abeille patriote* in early April 1790, while Lagarde also sold out four months later, having scraped together just 55 subscribers.[18]

Another important innovation brought about by the change in the nature of ownership was a rapid growth in the number of journalists: for once censorship collapsed and anyone was free to break into print, many hundreds did so. Martin and Walter's catalogue of the newspaper holdings of the *Bibliothèque Nationale* for the revolution lists just over 700 editors or contributors, and because its coverage is by no means complete, this probably means that the true number was well over a thousand. Some of these were survivors from the *ancien régime*, who adapted without difficulty to the new political freedom of the revolution. Mallet du Pan, for example, who had been writing the political section of the *Mercure* since 1783, became a leading exponent of *monarchien* policies until he decided to emigrate in the summer of 1792.[19] Jean-Baptiste Suard, a former editor of the *Gazette de France* and contributor to the *Journal de Paris* before the revolution, continued to write for the *Journal de Paris* until August 1792, and then bought a half share in the *Nouvelles politiques* to continue his journalism during the Directory. Condorcet, La Harpe, Rivarol, and Garat, who had been regular contributors to the *Mercure*, also went on to write for other papers during the revolution, while Beffroy de Reigny continued his rather eccentric literary journal, *les Lunes du cousin Jacques*, before turning to political journalism in the *Lendemain*, *Défenseur du peuple* and *Consolateur*. Du

Rozoi, editor of the *Gazette de Paris*, had similarly learnt his trade under the *ancien régime*, working on the *Journal helvétique* and two other minor papers during the 1770s. Several provincial journalists also made the transition without difficulty. Broulhiet politicised the *Journal universel* in Toulouse; Ferreol de Beaugeard, the *Journal de Marseille*; Couret de Villeneuve, the *Journal général de l'Orléanais*; and Mame, the *Affiches d'Angers*. In the future department of the Vaucluse, Sabin Tournal made the *Courrier d'Avignon* into the flagship of local Jacobinism, as did Paris de Lespinard in Lille with the *Feuille de Flandres*, which he had launched in 1781.

Nevertheless, the survivors were vastly outnumbered by the hundreds of newcomers, who came from a variety of backgrounds. Many, as Robert Darnton has illustrated, emerged from the underground literary world of pre-revolutionary Paris, from Grub Street where swarms of ambitious writers, frustrated in their ambition of ascending to the literary establishment, found themselves forced to eke out a precarious living by penning pamphlets, ghost writing for political agitators such as Mirabeau, or writing pornographic innuendo against the court. They shared a strong resentment against the literary and scientific establishment which had rejected them, and found camaraderie and friendship in pseudo-scientific activities such as Mesmerism, the analysis of the properties of heat and light, or in political issues such as the anti-slavery campaign.[20] Marat came from this background, as did Carra, Gorsas, Fréron, Brissot, and many others. Contemporaries were quick to argue that their radicalism, and the tenacity with which the hounded personalities and institutions of the *ancien régime*, was largely revenge for years of resentment, and no doubt there is some truth in this. Yet there were others from a similar background who took alternative paths. Charles Théveneau de Morande, for example, had spent almost 20 years in the literary underground in London, publishing pornographic brochures on court intrigue and debauchery in France, and editing the *Courrier de l'Europe*. He was brought back to Paris in the summer of 1791, not to vent his anger in radicalism, but to use his talents for the court against Brissot in the *Argus patriote*, between June 1791 and May 1792. Jacques-Louis Gautier de Syonnet also mixed in the underground literary world prior to the revolution, working as an actor, bookshop clerk and police spy, but used his invective in the cause of royalism, as editor of the *Petit Gautier* from late 1789 onwards.[21]

Moreover, the literary underground was not the only recruiting source, for many perfectly respectable writers were attracted by the prestige and money that journalism could now bring. Sabatier de Castres, editor of the first right-wing paper of the decade, the *Journal politique national*, was a writer with an established reputation for anti-*philosophe* polemics before 1789, while his fellow editor, Rivarol, had come to Paris from Provence in 1777 and made his name with a celebrated prize essay for the Berlin Academy in 1783 on the universality of the French language. He later wrote extensively for the *Actes des Apôtres* before emigrating to London in the summer of 1792.[22] Among other prominent names from the *ancien-régime* literary world were Jean-Baptiste Suard; Louis-Sébastien Mercier, who was nominal editor of the *Annales patriotiques* in the autumn of 1789 and later contributed to the *Chronique de Mois* and the *Bulletin des amis de la vérité*; and Jean-François de la Harpe, who wrote the literary section of the *Mercure* from late 1789 onwards and later co-edited the *Mémorial* in the First Directory.[23] Among the less well-known figures were Louise de Kéralio, biographer of Elizabeth I of England, and compiler of an anthology of feminist writing, who turned her hand to the radical *Mercure national*, working with her husband François Robert in radical politics from their base in the Cordeliers club. Caroline Wuiet was editor of a series of right-wing gossip papers between 1797 and 1799, and had been a child prodigy before 1789, writing both an opera and a play while still in her teens. Several Jacobin journalists also came from a similar background: for example, Thomas Rousseau had published several pamphlets and translations prior to 1789, including a French edition of Thomas More's *Utopia*, and had picked up pensions from both the court and the Parlement of Paris. He launched two papers of his own before becoming editor of the *Journal de la montagne* in the summer of 1794. His predecessor on the paper, Aristide Valcour, had been both author and actor prior to 1789, and had also edited several other papers during the revolution. Nicolas de Bonneville, editor of the *Cercle social* and *Bulletin des amis de la vérité*, had published several respected translations prior to 1789, and developed his mystical masonic views in several publications during the revolution.[24]

Lawyers also readily turned to journalism. Loustallot, the major contributor to the *Révolutions de Paris* before his premature death in September 1790, had worked as an *avocat* in both Bordeaux and Paris in the 1780s, until, possibly as a result of pamphlet work, he attracted Prudhomme's attention over the summer of 1789. Camille Desmoulins had been an unsuccessful lawyer for four years, before his success as a pamphleteer encouraged him to launch the *Révolutions de France et de Brabant*, while François Robert had been an *avocat* in Givet, in the Ardennes, and only arrived in Paris in 1789, while working on a case. Once there, he settled into political life, found work on the *Mercure national* and married Louise de Kéralio. Jean-Joseph Lagarde was a lawyer in Lille on the eve of the revolution, cut his political teeth on the ill-fated *Abeille*, then went on to an administrative career. After a brief interlude as a printer, he profited from the patronage of Merlin de Douai to transfer to Paris, become secretary-general of the Directory, and serve Napoleon, ending up as prefect of the Seine-et-Marne. By then he would have known Hugues-Bernard Maret, who had arrived in Paris from Dijon in 1788, to take up a position as *avocat au conseil du roi*, and then became caught up in the political excitement of 1789, making his name as a parliamentary reporter. He also went on to a successful administrative career in the Napoleonic empire.[25]

Many priests were journalists too, both jurors in the early revolution and secularised priests during the Directory. In Paris, the *abbé* de Fontenai remained chief editor of the *Journal général de France* until 1792, helped by the *abbé* Barruel and the *abbé* Brottier. On the opposite side of the fence, Claude Fauchet, bishop of the Calvados, was editor of the *Bouche de fer* in 1790–1, and of the *Journal des amis* in the spring of 1793. Among his political opponents then was Chasles, who had published a *Correspondant* in Chartres during 1790, before being elected to the Convention, and later worked with René Lebois on the early numbers of the *Ami du peuple* during the thermidorean reaction. Pierre Pontard, constitutional bishop of the Dordogne and deputy for the department to the Legislative Assembly in 1791–2, launched an eccentric *Journal prophétique* in November 1791, published in both Paris and Perigueux, and largely devoted to the mystical and apocalyptic prophecies of a former duchess, Suzette Labrousse.[26] In Strasbourg Jean-Jacques Kaemmerer published the *Religionsbegebenheiten* in 1791–2 to support the ideas behind the civil constitution, while his fellow refugee from the Rhineland, Euloge Schneider, was responsible for the Jacobin *Argos* in 1792–3. In Besançon a Lazarist priest, Claude-Ignace Dormoy, founded the *Vedette* in November 1791, and nursed it through as the mainstay of the Jacobin party in the city during the terror. Laval had three priests, Rabard, Seguéla and Labau, as editors of the *Patriote de la Mayenne* in 1792–3; Lyons had the effervescent *abbé* Laussel as editor of several ephemeral titles between 1790 and 1793; while in the remoteness of Tulle, in the Corrèze, a former Parisian priest, Jumel, published a local version of the *Père Duchesne* during the terror.[27]

Several laicised priests later found teaching positions alongside lay people in the *écoles centrales* of the Directory, forerunners of the Napoleonic *lycées*, and frequently active centres of Jacobinism. The lightness of the teaching load appears to have been a considerable help. Bias Parent l'aîné, editor of the *Questioneur* and the *Journal de la Nièvre* in Nevers, had left the priesthood during the terror, been *agent national* in Clamecy and a fervent dechristianiser. Imprisoned after *thermidor*, he moved to Nevers after his release, became a member of the departmental administration, and professor of history in the *école centrale*. In Rheims the editorial team of the *Journal du département de la Marne* contained two professors, both of them former priests then Jacobin activists during the terror, Etienne-Memmie Mathieu and Claude-Etienne Leger. The main contributors to the *Affiches d'Angers* between 1795 and 1797 likewise taught in the *école centrale*, while in Grenoble Pierre-Vincent Chalvet, Stendhal's negligent history teacher, was the driving force behind the neo-Jacobin *Clairvoyant* in 1797–8. In Auch, Pierre-Nicolas Chantreau, a former Parisian and government agent, who had settled in the region in 1792 and appears to have emulated Chalvet's idleness once appointed to the *école centrale*, edited most of the political journals to appear in the town during the Directory.[28]

Printers also remained active in journalism, particularly in the provinces, where they had been heavily involved during the *ancien régime*, often combining a strong political commitment with a keen commercial sense. In Toulouse, while Broulhiet owned the *Journal universel*, his fellow printer, Auguste Gand, produced the rival *Nouvelliste national*. In Orléans, Couret de Villeneuve's *Journal général* had a rival in Jacob l'aîné's *Annales orléanaises*, while in Le Mans, Monnoyer owned and edited the *Affiches du Maine*, and his son produced the more political *Journal général*. In Beauvais the young Jacobin printer, Tubeuf, launched the *Pacifique* in 1797, and in Tours, Norbert Lhéritier adapted the *Affiches de la généralité de Touraine* to politics in 1789, later launching the neo-Jacobin *Journal général du département d'Indre-et-Loire* in the summer of 1797. In Rennes the press was dominated by three printers, René Vatar, Nicolas Audran and Michel Chauseblanche; in Nantes by Brun l'aîné, Augustin-Jean Malassis and P.F. Hérault; in Montauban by Vincent Teulières, Fontanel and Charles Crosilhes; and in Angers by Jahyer, Mame and Pavie. In Agen the only newspaper of the entire decade, the *Journal patriotique de l'Agenais*, was produced by the town's only printer, Raymond Noubel, while in Auch it was Pourquiès-Armagnac who owned and directed all the papers that Chantreau edited. The same kind of dominance was also true in Montpellier, Alençon and Strasbourg.

The political importance of the press also helps to explain the involvement of politicians, for it was too powerful a weapon for them to neglect, and a valuable asset in a political career. Mirabeau's *États-Generaux* supplemented his voice between 1789 and 1791. Barère wrote the highly successful *Point du jour*; Barnave, Duport and Lameth used the *Logographe* from the spring of 1791 to support their campaign to moderate the force of radicalism; while Robespierre used the *Défenseur de la constitution* and *Lettres à ses commettants* to defend his position after the outbreak of war, and in the opening months of the National Convention. Many deputies, from Brissot to Marat, Carra to Phillipeaux, owed their seats to the fame that journalism had brought them, and the same is true of local politicians such as Barbaroux, who began his political career as co-editor of the *Observateur marseillais* in the summer of 1790, or the irrepressible François Robert in Fécamp and Rouen. At the very local level, Pierre Conard, for example, was a cabinet maker in Chartres in 1789, and an enthusiastic supporter of the revolution. He joined the *société révolutionnaire des sans-culottes* in 1793, and was concierge of the former church of Sainte-Hilaire where it met. After it closed down in 1795 he tried to make a living by handling subscriptions for newspapers. That in turn developed into a second-hand bookshop, finally leading to the launch of the *Chronique du département d'Eure-et-Loire* in February 1797, which provided a focal point for the city's few Jacobin activists.[29]

Not far away, in the town of Laigle in the Orne, the career of Coesnon-Pellerin went further. Originally intended for the priesthood, he had been set up in business instead by friends of the family, when orphaned by the death of his parents. He must have done well, for in 1789 he was elected to the Municipality of Laigle, and later bought his own press to launch a newspaper to support the revolution. This led naturally to membership of the local Jacobin club, a place on the *comité de surveillance* during the terror, and inevitable arrest in *ventôse* of Year III during the thermidorean reaction. Once released in the autumn of 1795, however, he responded to an appeal from a local deputy to the Council of Five Hundred, Colombel, to move to Paris and publish a newspaper there. He sold all his possessions in Laigle for 18,000 *livres*, and moved to Paris to edit the *Ami de la patrie*, but it struggled along until the spring of 1798, leaving him bankrupt and broken. The last trace of him in the archives is a letter begging for a minor government administrative post.[30]

Growth in the numbers of journalists was accompanied by an increase in their status. By the late 1780s journalism had largely shaken off the stigma attached to it since the late seventeenth century, when it was seen as a servile occupation, subject to government control and to censorship. Instead there was a growing acceptance of the utility of the press, and of the role of the journalist in providing readers with carefully compiled accounts of political events, from which they could form their own opinions and assessment.[31] Acceptance of this role survived well beyond 1789 in the many new informational papers which sprang up to report Assembly debates, or to cover governmental and administrative news, such as the *Journal des débats* or the *Journal du soir*. Yet complete neutrality in the face of the revolution was impossible, and during the course of 1789 a second quite different role, that of the journalist as political commentator and crusader, had been proclaimed by Brissot, Desmoulins and Marat. Mediating between politicians and people, the journalist changed from historian to participant. He was now a political educator, explaining ideology and legislation to a newly enfranchised electorate, and a primitive opinion pollster who funnelled their demands and perceptions back up to legislators. He was a local patriot, encouraging communal solidarity in the new administrative units created by the revolution, and a vigilant watchdog of local authorities, denouncing laxity and corruption in the name of the people. He was an arbiter of political disputes, spokesman for local clubs, literary critic, economic analyst and political sage. One deputy, Décombérousse, during a debate on the press held in the council of Elders during the course of Year VII, even urged that the annual festival of the republic should be marked by a public award to the journalist who '. . . has done most to encourage love of the republic and of its laws in his newspaper'.[32]

This new role thrust many journalists into an active political career, in a way which would have been inconceivable under the *ancien régime*; yet it was not accepted by everyone. From a very early stage, many right-wing critics argued that the sheer speed of journalism meant that it was inevitably superficial, and that the scale of its financial rewards attracted hordes of unscrupulous writers, anxious to sell their pen and opinion to the highest bidder. This hostility was shared by governments throughout the decade, and not least by the Committee of Public Safety and the Directory, both of which tended to equate opposition with sedition.[33] Yet despite frequent condemnation, several arrests and the occasional execution, journalism retained relative freedom until the *fructidor* coup, and was able to establish a role for the press in parliamen-. tary government which the liberal opposition of the Restoration was later to articulate and expand. Moreover, along with this new-found influence went money. Already, under the *ancien régime*, the editors of the major Parisian papers had been well paid. Fréron, for example, had probably made 20,000 *livres* per year out of the *Année littéraire* during its better years in the 1760s, which was almost ten times the amount paid to Rousseau for the first edition of his *Nouvelle Héloise*. Suard earned a similar amount from the *Journal de Paris* in the late 1780s, and Linguet earned 10,000 *livres* for his work on the *Journal de Bruxelles* between 1773 and 1776.[34] Panckoucke, who was generous with his editors during the *ancien régime*, and anxious to attract writers of high calibre, paid la Harpe 6,000 *livres* in 1776 for editing the *Mercure*, and, seven years later, he paid Mallet du Pan 7,700 *livres* for working on the *Journal de Bruxelles*.[35]

The provincial press, operating on a shoe-string, had only one newspaper that could match this — the *Courrier d'Avignon*, which had an unusually high circulation in the Midi. Its editor from 1784 onwards, Sabin Tournal, was provided with a heated and furnished office, all the journals and pamphlets necessary for his work (which remained his after use), and a 12,000 *livres* indemnity in the event of his contract being terminated before its three-year term. His salary was linked to circulation, ranging from 2,000 *livres* per annum if there were only 1,000 subscribers, to 10,000 *livres* when there were 4,000. In addition he received a written guarantee that his nephew could succeed him if he chose to retire early, and an undertaking that if the owners decided to launch another paper, it would not be marketed in the *Courrier*'s own stalking ground of the Midi.[36]

After the outbreak of the revolution, these kinds of salaries and ancillary arrangements became more widespread. Mallet du Pan's basic salary was lifted to 12,000 *livres* per year at the end of 1789, with additional incentive payments linked to circulation. Within a year this was revised to 2,000 *livres* per thousand subscribers, which probably lifted his earnings to over 20,000 *livres* per year. Tournal's average salary on the *Courrier d'Avignon* was also almost doubled, to 7,000 *livres*; while Desmoulins was able to secure 10,000 *livres* per year for the *Révolutions de France et de Brabant*, and Loustalot, 25,000 *livres* for his year's work as political columnist on the *Révolutions de Paris*.[37] Moreover, the few editorial contracts that have survived show that Tournal's kind of pre-revolutionary arrangement, with incentives tied to circulation and side benefits, became more widespread, and was extended to provide guarantees against the political risks brought by the revolution. Mallet's new contract in November 1789, for example, included an allowance for secretarial costs, a guaranteed income of 3,000 *livres* per annum if he were forced to retire early because of illness, and a retirement annuity of 3,000 *livres* per annum if he completed 15 years' service. Isidore Langlois, political editor of the right-wing *Messager du soir* in 1795, had a salary equivalent to 90 annual subscriptions, to provide a hedge against inflation, along with a bonus of 1 per cent of the value of all subscriptions over 4,000. He was also provided with a heated office, all the books and pamphlets that he required, a month's sick leave entitlement per year, and a promise of half pay if imprisoned or forced into hiding to avoid arrest.[38] Overall the financial rewards of journalists therefore appear to have risen as a result of the revolution, partly because of increased production rates and partly because of the intense competition generated by political interest. This was almost entirely restricted to Paris, however, for apart from the exceptional case of the *Courrier d'Avignon*, and the odd anomaly — such as the *Courrier de Strasbourg*, which in 1792–3 was able to employ a full-time editor because of the interest generated by war — most provincial papers had only sufficient resources for part-time work.

The increased status and rewards that journalists enjoyed did not, however, bring about any changes in the day-to-day working practices. Certainly the work was faster, as the pace of political life and the volume of news increased. At the beginning of 1789, for example, Paris had only two daily newspapers; but by the end of the year it had 23, and several dozen more that had three or four editions per week. The importance of the daily press continued for the rest of the decade and must have imposed new demands on journalists' work habits. Yet the basic techniques of news gathering and reporting changed very little indeed, and continued to be carried out in much the same way as it had been since the early news sheets of the sixteenth century. A primary source of news for all eighteenth-century journalists came from other newspapers. Provincial journalists had always taken items from the Parisian press, and had been legally obliged so to do for their political coverage before 1789. This continued during the revolution, even when no longer legally binding, largely because Paris was at the centre of the political stage. Indeed, many provincial journals quickly introduced special

175

columns of extracts from the Parisian press, in order to keep readers up to date with events in the capital and Versailles. The *Corréspondance de Bretagne* did so in July 1789, the *Affiches de Dauphiné* shortly afterwards, the *Journal universel* in Toulouse in January 1790, and the *Journal de Marseille* in the following August. At the height of the terror the *Journal de Ville-Affranchie* in Lyons boasted: 'This is not a new journal that we are offering to the inhabitants of Ville-Affranchie, but a distillation of all the best existing patriotic newspapers.'[39] Such was the importance that many provincial journals attached to the Parisian press that several of them altered their publication days to fit in with their arrival on the mail coach. In Grenoble the *Affiches de Dauphiné* did this on three separate occasions in 1789; in Toulouse the *Antiterroriste* and *Observateur républicain* both did so in 1795; while Henri Delloye changed his *Feuille rhémoise* from a daily paper into one which appeared every other day in the winter of 1795–6 because of a corresponding cut in the postal service from Paris. The aptly named *Extrait des journaux patriotes*, which was launched in Nancy in *vendémiaire* of Year VI, lived up to its title by announcing that it would appear every day, just four hours after the Parisian mail coach had arrived.[40]

Provincial editors argued that their cannibalisation of the Parisian press enabled them to provide news drawn from a wider range of newspapers than any one individual could afford to buy, and an analysis of that news which exposed contradictions and inconsistencies in a way that only a professional editor could do.[41] Yet the flow of information did not run exclusively from Paris to the provinces, for provincial journalists used each other quite frequently, especially in the early years of the revolution, when the novelty of setting up departmental and municipal administrations and political clubs prompted comparison with experiences elsewhere. Counter-revolutionary activity prompted many to use newspapers from the Midi, and once war had broken out, interest spread to the frontier areas of the north and east. For their part Parisian journalists frequently used the provincial press for the same reason, providing their readers with nationally based news, including the latest information from trouble spots of federalism or counter-revolution, and using papers which reflected their own views and prejudices. The royalist *Rocambole des journaux*, for example, drew its news from the Midi exclusively from right-wing provincial papers such as the *Journal d'Arles* or the *Révolutions d'Avignon*; while the *Gazette de Paris* used the *Journal général de France*, the *Ami du Roi* and the *Journal de Paris*. In Toulouse, during the Directory the conservative *Antiterroriste* drew heavily on the *Courrier français* for its Parisian news and Beaugeard's *Journal de Marseille* for its reports on the Midi, while its rival *Observateur républicain* used the Jacobin *Journal des hommes libres*, along with the Directory's own *Rédacteur*.

Many papers made it quite clear in their titles that they were basically compilations. The title of the *Extrait des journaux patriotes* speaks for itself, as does that of the *Bulletin et journal des journaux*, launched in Paris in October 1790 by Mme Beaumont. Yet whether it formed a part or the whole of their work, contemporaries agreed that editors' skill lay in the careful selection and presentation of the stories that were used. News had to be fresh, the most authentic reports selected, false information weeded out, and contradictions or gaps revealed. As Henri Delloye of the *Feuille rhémoise* told his readers:[42]

> Copy other newspapers? That is both beyond my talents and below my dignity, even discounting the difficulty in getting paper and the cost of printing. My function is to extract news from other journals, abridge items which are useful and readable, and draw conclusions which they have missed. That is all I try to do.

The importance of selectivity and discrimination was stressed in titles such as the *Abeille*, which used the metaphor of the bee extracting pollen, or the *Glaneuse*, with its image of the separation of wheat from chaff. Yet most editors readily admitted that there was an element of hit and miss in the whole process, for news frequently arrived in a fragmented or garbled form, and even the most scrupulous editor could make mistakes. All that could be done, therefore, was to use common sense to sort out the probable from the improbable, placing trust in newspapers which had a good track record, informing readers when conflicting reports were impossible to resolve, and being prepared to adjust a story as and when more news came in. Many editors in fact asked their readers to report inaccuracies, and were usually more than ready to print revised reports as more information became available.[43]

All this involved a great deal of hard work, scouring newspapers, checking and cross checking stories, and hurriedly drafting a report in time to meet the printer's deadline. The larger papers employed clerks to do the spadework for them, but in the majority of cases it was the editor himself who did the work. In Marseilles Beaugeard complained that it took him two hours every day to work through the 30 or so titles that he received, and he admitted that he often ended up more confused than when he had started. Camille Desmoulins replied rather testily to a reader, who urged him to publish the *Révolutions de France et de Brabant* more frequently, that. the reading of newspapers, along with readers' letters, took up three-quarters of his time and left him with little option but to restrict himself to weekly production.[44]

The potential cost of getting a wide enough spread of papers would have also been a problem, had there not been a number of ways around it. Many journalists were members of reading clubs or Jacobin clubs, which often had a reading room attached. Those who were printers or booksellers often handled subscriptions to other papers for their clientele and could surreptitiously scan them for news before delivering them to customers. Stendhal later recalled how, in his childhood, the postmaster in Grenoble would call into his parents' house for coffee in the mornings, before delivering the papers, so giving his father the chance to read the papers he was delivering.[45] The most common expedient, however, was a continuation of the *ancien-régime* practice of exchanges with other journalists. Beaugeard received 33 *Affiches* in this way, in exchange for his *Journal de Marseille* in 1789, and four years later had expanded to exchange with an extra six. During the Directory the *Journal du département de la Marne* appears to have reached similar arrangements with no less than 41 Parisian journals, five provincial and ten foreign. A *Bulletin*, launched in Bordeaux in the spring of 1790, made the unlikely claim of having access to all the Parisian press, and the *Courrier du département du Pui-de-Dôme*, the more plausible claim of having made arrangements with 25 other papers in the spring of 1792. Most other newspapers did similarly, and there are occasional references in documentation to the arrangements being made.[46] Du Boullay, editor of the drab weekly *Affiches de Tours*, for example, was so embarrassed by the offer of an exchange from Marat in December 1789 that he volunteered to pay at least the cost of a half subscription to the *Ami du peuple* to make up the difference in value. More aggressive and self-confident was the attitude of Caillot, owner of the *Courrier extraordinaire* during the Directory, who, during the course of a promotional trip to the north-east in Year V, made arrangements with a bookseller in Ghent for the exchange of 15 titles — mostly Belgian and Italian — and urged his workshop foreman in Paris to make similar arrangements with the *bureau des gazettes* in Bale:

Write to him immediately. Send him one of our papers so that he will know what it is like. Ask him to get as many others as possible to do exchanges with us, or else to tell us which are the essential ones to take out subscriptions to.[47]

Yet if other newspapers were an essential source, so too were personal correspondents, for they provided editors with news that they could claim to be exclusive. Consequently, many editors boasted of the extent and range of their network.[48] News items were often prefaced with phrases such as 'Extract from a letter from . . .', 'Our correspondent writes to us from . . .', or 'We have received a letter from . . .'. Yet it is not always easy to tell which of these were genuine letters, and which were passed off as such by the editor, to dress up news received through other channels or copied from other papers. The task is not made easier by the habit of some journalists of compressing several genuine letters into one false one, in order to save space or make a report more concise. Marat unashamedly did this, arguing that it enabled him to save space. There is nevertheless ample evidence that editors did work hard to create correspondence networks, and used them extensively when they did. Louis Bablot, for example, tried to get correspondents throughout the Marne for his *Observateur de la Marne* in 1790, while the *Journal de Seine-et-Marne* appealed to National Guard units and local administrators throughout the Seine-et-Marne to send news in to it. François-Louis Bayard, editor of the *Journal de la municipalité et des districts de Paris*, wrote round to the municipal authorities of all major cities during the course of 1790, asking them to forward information and news and the *Journal du département de la Meurthe* did the same for its neighbouring departments, dangling out the incentive of a subscription discount for all those who co-operated. The *Journal des 86 départements* did the same in 1793. Similarly, during the Directory Panckoucke offered departmental and municipal administrators a discount on the *Clef du Cabinet* if they sent in regular reports, and in the spring of Year VI the *Journal du soir* offered free copies to departmental *commissaires*, who provided speedy news of election results, adding the phrase: 'Would it be in order to ask you to drop me a short note every day on anything important that crops up locally?'[49]

Quite often there was no need for a financial incentive, as political loyalty operated instead. The *Journal du département de la Marne*, for example, was helped out during the Directory by a number of municipal *commissaires* sympathetic to its neo-Jacobin politics, who kept it in touch with events around the department. Elected deputies could do the same for provincial papers, providing them with news from Paris. Poncet-Delpech wrote reports on the proceedings in the National Assembly for the *Journal national* in Montauban in 1789–90, . as did Rouzet for the *Journal universel* in Toulouse during the winter of 1792–3, and Gay-Vernon for the *Journal du département de la Haute-Vienne* in the terror. After the outbreak of war soldiers could also be useful, sending back reports on events at the front.[50] Exactly how many papers went beyond this, and established networks of paid correspondents, is difficult to say. Panckoucke had one in the 1780s for the *Journal de Bruxelles*, and no doubt continued it during the revolution for use in the *Mercure* and *Moniteur*. The *Courrier d'Avignon* spent 3,200 *livres* on correspondents in 1786, in Rome, London, Paris and major European cities, and no doubt kept this up after 1789. Du Rozoi had correspondents in Coblentz for the *Gazette de Paris*, and during the summer of 1792 had a secret informant in the high command of the *armée du Nord*, and another in London who was paid ten *livres* per month. Paul Capon, editor of the *Courrier de Villeneuve-les-Avignon*, claimed in December 1789 to have a well advanced plan for correspondents in Poland, Denmark, England, Italy, Spain and most European courts, although there may have been an element of sales talk in this, and the Paris-based *Spectateur national* also had an extensive network. Seven years later, during the Directory, the *Annales universelles* was paying for regular reports from a certain Edward Thompson in Dover, and the *Courrier extraordinaire* 30 *livres* per month to a correspondent in Brussels. No doubt there were many such deals, involving former *nouvellistes à la main* who had been put out of work by the growth of the press, underpaid government officials, booksellers, impoverished writers and translators. Many were still active during the Consulate and Empire.[51]

The sources of local news were much less complicated. Editors, or their friends, could usually cover local events, interviewing the participants or quoting from the accounts of eye witnesses. They themselves were often the witness and Couret de Villeneuve, in Orléans, suggested that local administrators could help journalists by providing a special box where they could take note on public ceremonies without being disturbed by the noise and jostle of the crowd.[52] Many attended meetings of their local Municipality or Department in person, or had friends who were members and could report on decisions. Others were members of their local Jacobin club, and were able to cover its debates as well as use its correspondence and circulars. Several urged their readers to keep them abreast of local events, and at least one, the *Feuille hebdomadaire* in Lorient, had a wooden box outside the editor's house, into which subscribers could drop notes and reports. The more unscrupulous ones also had informants. The *Postillon des armées*, a right-wing paper banned in *fructidor* of Year V, gained some of its political news from an informer in the finance section of the Ministry of Police, while another editor offered bribes to the printing workers on a rival newspaper to steal news from it as it went to press.[53]

All these were essentially variations on well established *ancien-régime* practices, and real breakthroughs in reporting speed would have to await the development of the telegraph in the early 1820s and the first news agencies later in the same decade. One meagre area of innovation did, however, emerge in the reporting of legislative debates, an activity new to France in 1789, and still in its infancy in England where reporters had only been allowed access to the House of Commons since 1771. During the summer of 1789 reporters travelled out from Paris to Versailles at dawn, sat amongst the noise and bustle of the public gallery in the *salle des menus plaisirs* to take their notes on debates, and returned to the capital in the evening with a manuscript for the printer to run off overnight. It was tiring work, made worse by the noise and chaos in the public gallery, the difficulty in hearing speakers and the problems of establishing their identity. Mirabeau's editors on the *Courrier de Provence* complained of the impossibility of putting a shape on to '. . . the most irregular and poorly conducted debates ever to have existed . . .', while the *Bulletin de l'Assemblée nationale* asked its readers to remember that its reports were '. . . written in the middle of the Assembly, amidst the noise of debates and discussion . . .', and could therefore not always be clear-cut and logical.[54] Some of these problems were overcome with time. Familiarity with names and faces made identification easier, while many deputies fell into the practice of having their speeches printed beforehand and distributed to journalists in advance. Most reasonably sized papers also employed notetakers to provide the raw material for their political editor, and found no shortage of recruits, glad of the work and flattered by its glamour and prestige.[55] Substantial improvements then came with the move to the *salle du Manège*, however, for journalists were now closer to their publishing base and had the luxury of small lodges, specially constructed for them around the edge of the hall, and allocated to the major papers by the *comité des inspecteurs de la salle*. Not every journalist managed to get a lodge, and there were occasional quarrels and unseemly incidents, as outsiders wheedled themselves into a lodge for an important debate, only to change the lock on the door and barricade the original owner out as soon as they had the opportunity. Nevertheless, by and large the system worked and was retained when the Convention moved in the spring of 1793.[56]

The style of reporting varied greatly. Many newspapers continued the traditional factual style of eighteenth-century journalism, while others chose instead a commented version which put speakers and speeches into context and attempted a critical assessment of the shape of the debate. The latter style had already been well developed in England by William Woodfall, in reporting the debates of the House of Commons for the *Morning Chronicle*. Woodfall possessed extraordinary stamina, sometimes writing in the public gallery for up to twelve hours at a stretch, pausing only to crack open an egg in his hat; and although his French counterparts might not have shared his gastronomic tastes, they also showed similar powers of endurance.[57] Maret displayed a similar talent for conveying the atmosphere of debates in the *Moniteur*, while Garat, writing for the *Journal de Paris* between the spring of 1789 and autumn of 1791, treated his readers '. . . to a kind of drama rather than a meeting of legislators'.[58]

Some went further, inventing rapid note-taking methods in order to improve their speed and accuracy. The most innovative was that of the *société logographique*, a small company which, in June 1790, was allocated a special lodge in the *salle du manège* and spent the next six months perfecting a method that was used to provide Assembly reports to the *Journal des États-généraux* from January 1791 onwards, and to the *Logographe* from the following April. The method required twelve or more note-takers, each equipped with notepaper divided into numbered vertical columns. As debates began the first note-taker went to work, writing in his first column until the flow of words outpaced him, when he would signal to the second note-taker, who did likewise, and so on, around the group. When the turn came back to the first note-taker, he resumed writing in his second column, as did those who followed him, and when the sheets of paper were full they were collected up and given to a *logographe en chef* who co-ordinated them into a final version, which was then carried off to the printer. The system provided a most detailed account of debates, but the manpower involved made it costly and, by the summer of 1791, Le Hodey de Saultchevreuil was paying the *société* 2650 *livres* per month for the right to carry reports in the

Journal des États-généraux. Nevertheless it must have been worth his while, for the *société* remained in business until 10 August 1792, when the *Logographe* was closed down for its royalism. It was subsequently given permission to retain its lodge, absolved of all responsibility for the *Logographe*'s bias, but never returned to action, and an effort to resume the system by an eccentric charlatan from Bordeaux, François Guirault, proved abortive in the following spring.[59]

If traditional methods remained the norm for reporting, the same overall pattern of continuity also holds true for the production side, for printing techniques remained firmly rooted in the age of Gutenberg.[60] Presses were still hand-operated, made of wood, and required the labour of a minimum of two workers. They had two horizontal surfaces, the *marbre* and *platine*, which were squeezed together with the paper in between, to make the impression. Type was set by a compositor, using pre-cast individual letters which he transferred from the letter case to the composing stick, from there into the galley, and from the galley into an iron chase which held the completed page — or form — ready for the printing process. The form was placed into the press on a plate, called the coffin, to be inked, and a sheet of paper placed into the frisket, which was folded over on to the form, so that the two could be winched under the *platine* and squeezed together by a hand-operated screw lever. It was time-consuming and laborious, and although a new Didot press had been introduced in 1771 which simplified the process somewhat, few of them were in operation during the 1790s. The average printing rate was therefore 300 sheets per hour, printed on one side only; printed on both sides the rate was 150 per hour, which resulted in approximately 1,500 sheets per ten-hour day. Since the average newspaper consisted of four pages *in-quarto*, or eight pages *in-octavo*, two copies could be printed on each sheet and a production rate of 300 copies per hour per press was possible, using only one press, once the typesetting had been completed. Typesetting, however, was time-consuming and it was therefore common practice for journalists to hand in their copy to the printer in stages during the course of the day, so that typesetting could be staggered, and ready to print off overnight. Sabin Tournal, on the *Courrier d'Avignon*, for example, had to hand in the bulk of his copy by 8 a.m., following up with the rest before the late afternoon, so that printing could start in the late evening. The contract for the *Orateur du peuple* in the summer of 1790 similarly stipulated that the first part of the manuscript should be handed in between 4 p.m.

and 5 p.m., and the remainder four hours later, so that the first batch of a thousand copies could come off the presses at 4 a.m. on the following morning, and the third and final thousand some seven hours later.[61]

The revolution saw no changes in this cumbersome procedure, but it did nevertheless stimulate rapid expansion in the printing trade. Since the reign of Louis XIV printing had been closely controlled by the government for the purpose of censorship, and during the course of the eighteenth century the number of print-shops in Paris had been progressively reduced from 51 in 1701 to 36 in 1789. Those 36 employed just under 1,000 workers, deployed on almost 300 presses, and enjoyed a cosy and profitable monopoly. One cynical observer compared them with the '. . . gardener's dog, who wanted nobody to come near the pile of hay on which he slept'. In the provinces a similar development had taken place for the 360 print-shops of 1701 reduced to 254 by 1777, with the major reductions taking place in large towns such as Lyons, which saw its numbers reduced from 30 to 12, and Rouen which was reduced from 23 to 10. Altogether, by 1777, some 149 towns had at least one printer, but many of them had only one. The size of individual enterprises was small, and the total work-force slightly less than that of Paris, at around 900.[62]

Once the monopoly was breached in the summer of 1789, many newcomers set themselves up in business overnight, renting out attics or cellars and often sharing presses. Many of the early entrepreneurs were journeymen and apprentices, traditionally independent and troublesome, and long resentful of the restrictions which prevented them from setting up their own business.[63] René Lebois, for example, owner of the neo-Jacobin *Ami du peuple* during the Directory, had been a journeyman printer before 1789, then moved from one print-shop to another between 1789 and 1792, and finally set up on his own during the summer of 1793. Others were booksellers and publishers who, like Panckoucke, were eager to expand their businesses into printing, while some were complete outsiders, with a keen eye for the economic potential, who hired experienced print-workers as the nucleus of their work-force, or profited from the collapse of the apprenticeship requirements by training their own personnel on the job. Experienced print-workers were at a premium during the early years and were able to demand the high wages they had been denied under the *ancien régime*. Many editors complained of the difficulty that this caused them in meeting schedules, as workers walked out in the middle of a job to move to better pay.[64]

The overwhelming majority of new print-shops were small, set up with a minimal amount of capital and operating off one or two presses at the most, largely because the costs involved were not prohibitive. A new printing press, during the latter decades of the *ancien régime*, could be picked up for 400 *livres*, while a second-hand one, in good working order, cost 300 *livres* or less — the equivalent of four months wages for a journeyman printer. A print-shop needed more than just a press, but an estimate of 1791 nevertheless put the total cost of equipping a shop for the comparatively straight-forward requirements of newspaper production — which did not require a large volume or variety of typeface — at 2,146 *livres*. This was certainly well within the reach of any modest entrepreneur, using his own savings, or borrowing from friends and business associates. The press and equipment of the *Antifédéraliste* for example, was sold in January 1794 for 2,400 *livres*, while that same month saw the value of a well equipped print-shop in Montpellier, with five presses and a wide range of type and ancillary equipment, put at 9,887 *livres*. One in Paris, similarly equipped, with only four presses but including extensive furnishings, four months of the lease on its premises and a newspaper printing contract, was valued at 12,000 *livres* in 1797.[65] At the top end of the market the capital value was markedly higher. Panckoucke's print-shop, for example, acquired in the summer of 1790 and comprising some 27 presses by the summer of 1794, was valued at 58,515 *livres*; but its main custom was the printing of books and it was therefore more lavishly equipped than was necessary for newspapers alone.[66]

The scale of the expansion in the printing trade was dramatic, for the 36 print-shops in Paris in 1789 increased to almost 200 by the spring of 1791 and to over 400 by the spring of 1796. Even as late as 1800, when Bonaparte imposed controls, there were still some 220 printing establishments in operation.[67] A similar growth also took place in the provinces, where printers now reversed the con-traction of the eighteenth century. Strasbourg increased its print-shops from six to 23 during the decade, Bordeaux from eight to 30, Auxerre from two to nine, and Amiens from three to seven. Dozens of small provincial towns now also had their first press, often set up to cater for the new administrative needs brought about by the creation of departmental and municipal authorities, but fre-quently diversifying into newspaper printing and ownership too, in order to maximise their business. By 1797, according to one pam-phlet estimate, 100,000 people in the country as a whole — a figure which included families and dependants — owed their living to journalism, most of them because of their involvement with the printing end of the enterprise.[68]

One consequence of this expansion was a marked decline in quality and reliability, as print-shops opened up and closed down. overnight, print-workers moved unpredictably from one shop to another, and the meticulous training of the *ancien régime* vanished with the collapse of the guilds. A second consequence, directly related to this, was that it now became easy for journalists or entrepreneurs to find a printer for their paper, as the ease with which the *Orateur du peuple* moved from one to another during the summer of 1790 proved. A third was that competition kept prices down. Printing costs are difficult to analyse with any accuracy, because of the lack of adequate archival records. They were also often affected by short-term factors such as the price of paper, which rose sharply when drought immobilised paper mills in the summer of 1789, for example, and almost doubled within a year of the outbreak of war in 1792, because of inflation, transport and labour problems.[69] The currency inflation of 1795–6 also caused severe difficulties, and at least one paper quoted its subscription rates in terms of grain, in a vain attempt to retain the real value of its revenue. Nevertheless, printers proved adept at resorting to cost-cutting techniques to counteract such problems, using low-quality paper, reducing the size of their margins, or printing in smaller type.

During the last decades of the *ancien régime*, the standard cost for printing a four-page newspaper *in-quarto* format was about 40 *livres* for the first 1,000 copies, and close to half that price for each succeeding thousand, as typesetting costs were traditionally offset against the first 1,000 copies.[70] Prices appear to have dipped sharply with the outbreak of the revolution. In May 1790, for example, the first thousand copies of the *Orateur du peuple* (eight pages, *in-octavo*) cost 28 *livres*, and each succeeding thousand only 7 *livres* 15 *sols*. This gives an average cost, on a print run of 3,000, of 14 *livres* 10 *sols* per thousand. According to Jean-Paul Bertaud, during 1791 and the first half of 1792, the *Ami du Roi* cost slightly more, at around 17 *livres* per thousand on a circulation of little over 3,000, while the *Gazette de Paris* in the spring of 1792 worked out at 21 *livres* 12 *sous*.[71] War then caused costs to rise, for the *Père Duchesne* (eight pages, *in-octavo*), cost 52 *livres* for the first thousand in the winter of 1793–4, and an average of 28.8 *livres* per thousand overall during the terror; while in the summer of 1794 the *Soirée du camp* averaged out at 14.4 *livres* per thousand on a half-size format (four pages, *in-octavo*).[72]

Costs in the provinces appear to have been consistently higher, because competition was less intense. Even prior to 1789 the *Courrier d'Avignon*, on the basis of two sets of figures in the 1780s, cost between 32 and 38 *livres* per thousand, on a print run of 3,000 copies. Prices also remained high after 1789, for Babeuf paid 96 *livres* for just 500 copies of his *Correspondant picard* in 1790, while 200 copies of the *Feuille hebdomadaire de Lorient* cost the equivalent of 96 *livres* per thousand in the same year. Euloge Schneider paid 20 *livres* for 200 copies of his *Argos* in Strasbourg during 1792 and 1793, while the Jacobin club paper in Chalons-sur-Marne during the terror cost 33 *livres* 4 *sous* for 300 copies — or over 100 *livres* per thousand. Yet even these prices lay well within the bounds of the possible, and the growth of the provincial press after 1789 suggests that they were far from prohibitive to anyone willing to venture into print.[73]

Overall, therefore, the production side of the newspaper press expanded rapidly during the revolution, but largely within its existing structures. The number of titles increased, the public was offered a wider choice, political comment became free, and journalism emerged as a respectable and sizeable profession. Yet news was gathered and written up in much the same way as it had been over the previous 200 years, and copies were run off on presses that Gutenberg's ghost would easily have recognised. What changed was the whole scale of the operation and the raw material that it had to handle. Yet the scale of the operation was largely determined by the increased market that the press had to cater for, and the problems of marketing and sales are the subject of the next chapter.

Notes

1. R. Gerard, *Un journal de province sous la révolution. Le 'Journal de Marseille' de Ferréol de Beaugeard, 1781–1797* (Paris, 1961), p. 37ff.

2. J.-P. Bertaud, *Camille et Lucille Desmoulins. Un couple dans la tourmente* (Paris, 1986), pp. 89–90.

3. A.N. Y10508B.

4. A.N. F[7] 3448B.

5. S. Tucoo-Chala, *Charles-Joseph Panckoucke et la librairie française, 1736–1798* (Paris and Pau, 1978), p. 475ff.

6. G. Villacèque, *Les Révolutions de Paris, journal patriote 1789–1790*, Diplôme d'Études Supérieures, (Toulouse, 1961), pp. 57–8. See also L. Prudhomme, *Aux patriotes* (Paris, 1793), pp. 1–2.

7. *L'Ami du Roi des Français, prospectus* (undated).

8. Gustave Rouanet, 'Robespierre et le journal l'Union', *Annales Révolutionnaires*, IX (1917), pp. 145–65.

9. Leon Cahen, *Condorcet et la révolution française* (Paris, 1912), pp. 238–41.

10. *Mémoire à consulter, et consultation, pour les citoyens Gratiot et Périès, propriétaires en partie du Journal intitulé des Défenseurs de la Patrie, 9 prairial an VIII, 29 mai 1800* (Paris, undated), pp. 2–3; P.-L. Roederer, *Oeuvres du comte P.-L. Roederer*, 8 vols (Paris, 1853–9), VII, p. 288; A. Suard, *Essai de mémoire de M. Suard* (Paris, 1881), pp. 198, 217–18, 248. For share-holding arrangements in England, see Michael Harris, 'The management of the London newspaper press during the eighteenth century', *Publishing History*, IV (1978), pp. 95–112; I.R. Christie, 'British newspapers in the later Georgian age', in I.R. Christie, *Myth and reality in late eighteenth century British politics* (London, 1970), p. 315. For the emergence of shareholding and outside capital in France after 1815, see Bertrand Gille, *La Banque et le crédit en France de 1815 à 1848* (Paris, 1959), pp. 196–7, 283–4.

11. E. Hatin, *Manuel théorique et pratique de la liberté de la presse* (Paris, 1868), pp. 54–5.

12. A.N. V^1 553; P. Laborie, *Étude sur le Patriote français. Journal libre, impartial et national* (Diplôme d'Études Supérieures, Toulouse, 1959–60), pp. 27–31; M. Kennedy, 'L'"Oracle des Jacobins des départements": Jean-Louis Carra et ses "Annales patriotiques" ' in A. Soboul (ed.), *Actes du Colloque Girondins et Montagnards* (Paris, 1980), p. 249ff.

13. Villacèque, *Les Révolutions de Paris*, pp. 58–60; *Révolutions de Paris. Réponse au sieur Prudhomme, propriétaire et éditeur des Révolutions de Paris* (Paris, undated).

14. *Ami du Roi*, lxxxvii, 26 August 1790, supplément; xciii, 1 September 1790, p. 381; J.P. Bertaud, *Étude des journaux: l'Ami du Roi de Royou, l'Ami du Roi de Montjoye, le Courrier extraordinaire de Duplain* (D.E.S., Paris, 1958–9), pp. 5–6.

15. J. Bénétruy, *L'Atelier de Mirabeau* (Paris, 1961), pp. 260–1: 'They have made over thirty thousand *livres*, and not given us a penny of it.' See also E. Dumont, *The great Frenchman and the Little Genevese* (trans.) (London, 1904), pp. 69–73.

16. A.D. Haute-Vienne, L394.

17. G. Walter, *Marat* (Paris, 1933), pp. 162–7; for Poncelin, see *Messieurs* (A.D. Haute-Vienne, L394):

> As he had been working on this act of piracy for a long time, he was careful enough to collect all the subscriptions which were in the post, and to pretend that we were just entering a new subscription period. When I asked him to return the subscription registers to me, he never even replied.

18. *Prospectus de l'Abeille, par le Sr. Lagarde cadet* (undated); Maeght, *La presse dans le departement du Nord sous la révolution française*, Thèse de troisième cycle (Lille, 1971), pp. 164–97.

19. For the political evolution of Mallet du Pan, see F. Acomb, *Mallet du Pan (1749–1800). A career in political journalism* (Durham, NC, 1973), Chapter VI, *passim*.

20. Robert Darnton, 'The high enlightenment and the low life of literature in pre-revolutionary France', *Past and Present*, LI (1971), pp.

81-115; see also Robert Darnton, 'J.-P. Brissot, police spy', *Journal of Modern History*, 1968, p. 324. Contemporaries aired similar opinions: see *Le Disciple des Apôtres, prospectus* (Paris, 1790); *Dénonciation des inquisiteurs de la pensée. Par M.J. de Chénier* (Paris, 1789), pp. 42-6; Mallet du Pan, *Mémoires et correspondance*, I (Paris, 1851), p. 130; B.M. Orléans, Lenoir ms. 1421-3. · For an article which attempts to portray Carra in this mould, see Michael Kennedy, 'The development of a political radical. Jean-Louis Carra, 1742-1787', *Proceedings of the Third Annual Meeting of the Western Society for French History* (Texas, 1976), pp. 147-50.

21. Armand Lods, 'Un journaliste de la révolution. Le Petit gautier', *La Révolution Française*, 63 (1912), pp. 506-12; P. Robiquet, *Théveneau de Morande. Étude sur le XVIIIe siècle* (Paris, 1882).

22. M. de Lescure, *Rivarol et la société française pendant la révolution et l'émigration (1752-1801)* (Paris, 1883); W.J. Murray, *The right wing press in the French Revolution* (London, 1986), pp. 56-8.

23. Christopher Todd, *Voltaire's disciple: Jean-François de la Harpe* (London, 1972); Alexander Jovicevich, *Jean-François de la Harpe, adepte et rénégat des lumières (New Jersey, 1973)*, Chapters IV and V: 'Financial reasons, a talent for journalism, and the chance to influence events and public opinion, prompted him to edit a newspaper again.'

24. Chantal Vincelet, *Recherches sur Mademoiselle de Kéralio et François Robert* (D.E.S., Paris, 1967); Emile Souvestre, *Les drames parisiens* (Paris, 1859), pp. 1-104; C. Lacretelle, *Dix années d'épreuves pendant la révolution* (Paris, 1842), *passim*; J.D. Popkin, *The right-wing press* pp. 42-8; H. Gough, 'Les Jacobins et la presse. *Le Journal de la montagne* (juin 1793-*brumaire* an II) in *Actes du Colloque Girondins et Montagnards* (Sorbonne, 14 décembre 1975) (Paris, 1980), p. 278ff.

25. L. Antheunis, *Le conventionnel belge François Robert (1763-1826) et sa femme Louise de Kéralio (1758-1802)* (Wetteren, 1956); Marcellin Pellet, *Elysée Loustallot et les Révolutons de Paris (juillet 1789-septembre 1790)* (Paris, 1872), pp. 5-7; B.M. Bordeaux, Ms. 713, xlvi, pp. 95-6; F.-A. Aulard, *La société des Jacobins*, 6 vols (Paris, 1889-95), pp. 288-97; Maeght, *La presse*, pp. 132-9; J. Balteau, M. Barroux and M. Prevost (eds), *Dictionnaire de biographie française* (Paris, 1933-), XXXIII, pp. 535-9.

26. R. Darnton, *Mesmerism and the end of the Enlightenment in France* (Harvard, 1968), I, pp. 128-9; A.N. F^id II, P10; C. Pichois and J. Dautry, *Le conventionnel Chasles et ses idées démocratiques* (Gap, 1958), Chapters 1 and 2; Jules Charrier, *Claude Fauchet: Évêque constitutionnel du Calvados*, 2 vols (Paris, 1909).

27. E. Barth, 'Notes biographiques', *Revue d'Alsace*, 1880, pp. 270-2. For Laussel, see *abbé* Laussel, *L'honnête criminel* (Paris, 1793); Bill Edmonds, 'A Jacobin débâcle: the losing of Lyons in spring 1793', *History*, LXIX (1984), pp. 2-3; and P. Caron, *La première terreur. Les missions du conseil exécutif provisoire et de la commune de Paris* (Paris, 1950), pp. 69, 74, 76, 184, 197. For Dormoy, see C. Brelot, *Besançon révolutionnaire* (Paris, 1966), pp. 92-3; M. Vogne, *La presse périodique en Franche-Comte des origines à 1870* (Besançon, 1977-8), I, pp. 64-94, 144-59. For Jumel, see F. Braesch, *Le Père Duchesne d'Hébert. Réimpression avec notes* (Paris, 1922-38), p. 57; V. Forot, *Le Club des Jacobins de Tulle* (Tulle, 1912), pp. 282 and 300.

28. G. Thuillier, 'Parent l'aîné et le Journal de la Nievre en l'an VI',

Mémoirs de la Société Académique du Nivernais, LIV (1967), *passim*; G. Clause, 'Un journal républicain de l'époque directoriale à Châlons-sur-Marne, "Le Journal du département de la Marne", 1796–1800', *Mémoires de la Société d'Agriculture, Sciences et Arts du Département de la Marne*, XC (1975), pp. 277–83. E. Quéruau-Lamérie, 'Notice sur les journaux d'Angers pendant la révolution', *Revue de l'Anjou*, nouvelle série, 24 (1892), pp. 307–8; Jacques Solé, 'Le Professeur d'histoire de Stendhal: Pierre-Vincent Chalvet (1767–1807)', *Stendhal Club*, année 10 (1939), pp. 283–91.

29. *Chroniques, légendes, curiosités et biographies beauceronnes. Grandeur et décadence d'un patriote chartrain (1756–1832)* (B.M. Chartres, Fonds Juselin, R32, 1–4).

30. A.N. F^7 3448B; A.N. AFIII, d.163, pièce 174; *La Renommée, ou Journal de la Mortagne*, xliv, 10 *ventose* V, pp. 4–5; I. Woloch, *Jacobin legacy. The democratic movement under the Directory* (Princeton, 1970), pp. 291–2.

31. S. Tucoo-Chala, 'Presse et vérité sous l'ancien régime', *Revue du Nord*, LXVI (1984), pp. 713–21.

32. *Opinion de Decomberousse, sur la résolution concernant la repression des délits de la presse* (Paris, an VIII), p. 9.

33. Even Marat had reservations: see his comments in *Ami du peuple*, 382 (25 February 1791):

The journalist profession is a fairly casual thing these days. Any simple person who has scribbled a stupid poem, or sent in a silly article to a newspaper, is now trying to make his fortune by launching a newspaper . . . With an empty brain, lacking information, ideas and views, he slopes off to a café to pick up the latest rumours, slander against patriots, or the lamentations of those who have lost by the revolution; he then returns home with his head full of the rubbish, puts it on paper and carries it to his printer, so that on the following morning anyone idiotic enough to buy it can read it. This is a true picture of 95 per cent of these gentlemen.

34. A. Suard, *Essai de mémoires de M. Suard*, pp. 178–9.

35. Tucoo-Chala, *Panckoucke*, p. 203; Acomb, *Mallet*, pp. 155–6, 189.

36. Musée Calvet, Fonds Chobaut, Ms. 5989, pièces 381–9.

37. Acomb, *Mallet*, p. 225ff; Bertaud, *Camille et Lucille Desmoulins*, p. 90.

38. Popkin, *The right-wing press*, pp. 45–6.

39. M. Loche, 'Journaux imprimés à Lyon 1633–1794', *Bulletin de la Société Archéologique, Historique et Artistique. Le Vieux Papier*, fasc. 229 (1968), pp. 22–3. See also Beaugeard's comments in the *Journal de Marseille* (quoted in Gérard, *Un journal de province*, p. 50); 'Editors use each other's material with pleasure, and this means that the number of readers of any one article is almost incalculable.'

40. *Affiches de Dauphiné*, 30 July 1789, p. 71; 28 November 1789, p. 142; *Feuille rhémoise*, 121, 25 *nivose* IV, p. 33; *Extrait des journaux patriotes*, 1 *vendémiaire* VI, p. 8.

41. See, for example, the prospectus of the *Journal patriotique de l'Agenais*: 'He takes articles from the best newspapers, sometimes using the most ingenious description of important events, and at other times articles which provide a convincing analysis of the characters of the participants.'

(R. Marquant, 'Aux origines de la presse agenaise: Le 'Journal patriotique de l'Agenais' 1789–1793, *Revue de l'Agenais*, 1945–7, p. 14).

42. *Feuille rhémoise*, 25 nivôse IV, p. 33.

43. See, for example, *Courrier de Strasbourg*, 6 February 1792, p. 123; 5 April 1792, p. 328.

44. *Révolutions de France et de Brabant*, xi (undated), p. 512; Gérard, *Un journal de province*, p. 49.

45. Stendhal, *Vie de Henri Brulard* (Paris, 1958), p. 154.

46. Gérard, *Un journal de province*, p. 49; Clause, 'Journal du département de la Marne', p. 311; A.N. F^{18}, Marne 18, xxxviii(2); E. Labadie, *La presse à Bordeaux pendant la révolution* (Bordeaux, 1910), pp. 63–4; *Courrier du département du Pui-de-Dôme, prospectus*.

47. A.N. BB(30)162, d.3; A.N. F^7 3446.

48. See the claims of the *Annales orléanaises*: 'Three writers, an editor and 28 co-operators in different provinces, are the solid bases on which we are founding the success of our work.' (31 December 1789, p. 81)

49. G. Clause, 'Le journalisme à Châlons-sur-Marne en 1790 et 1791', *Mémoires de la Société d'Agriculture, Commerce, Sciences et Arts du Département de la Marne*, 89 (1974), p. 311; *Journal de Seine-et-Marne, prospectus*, p. 3; A.M. Bordeaux, I, 38, pièces 4, 13, 21; A.D. Haute-Vienne L873; A. Dietrich lxiii, Lamort to Dietrich, 26 June 1790.

50. Daniel Ligou, *La première année de la révolution vue par un témoin (1789–1790). Les 'Bulletins' de Poncet-Delpech, député du Quercy aux États-Généraux de 1789* (Paris, 1961), pp. 7–11; D. Escamez, *La presse périodique à Toulouse de 1789 à 1794*, Mémoire de maîtrise (Toulouse, 1969), pp. 28–9; *Journal du département de la Haute-Vienne*, 10 September 1793, pp. 13–15. Friends also played a role: Bablot, editor of *le Caducée* in the Marne, had a friend in Paris who provided him with news relevant to the Marne; Delloye, of the *Feuille rhémoise*, a correspondent in Bordeaux where he had previously worked as an actor (G. Clause, 'Le journalisme à Châlons-sur-Marne en 1790 et 1791' *Mémoires de la Société d'Agriculture, Commerce, Sciences et Arts du Département de la Marne*, 89 (1974), pp. 297; G. Clause 'Un journal de la réaction thermidorienne: la Feuille rhémoise', *Études Champenoises*, I (1974), pp. 29–76).

51. Tucoo-Chala, *Panckoucke*, p. 202; *Spectateur National, prospectus* (1790); J. de Beylié, 'Contribution à l'histoire de la presse sous la révolution (Le Logographe)', *Bulletin de la Société de Statistique, des Sciences Naturelles et des Arts Industriels du Département de L'Isère*, 4e Série, XI (1910), p. 52; A.N. F^7 3445; A.N. F^7 3446, Caillot to Denis, 9 *pluviôse* V; A.N. F^7 3448B, Rebmann to Reubell, 23 *fructidor* V. See also *Journal de la Municipalité et des districts de Paris, prospectus* (1789), where Bayard claims that his printer, Lottin, who is also official printer to the Municipality, is able to supply him with news.

52. *Journal général de l'orléanais*, 203 (1790), p. 827.

53. *Feuille hebdomadaire*, 12 August 1790, p. 366; A.N. F^7 3448^B, Rebmann to Reubell; F^7 3446, Caillot to Denis, 9 *pluviôse*, V.

54. Benetruy, *L'Atelier de Mirabeau*, *p. 187; Courrier de Versailles. Avis aux Lecteurs* (1789); *Bulletin de l'Assemblée nationale*, 7 July 1789, p. 1. See also Dumont, *The great Frenchman and the little Genevese*, p. 73.

55. Lacretelle, *Dix années d'épreuves*, pp. 30–1; Anon., *Livre du centenaire*, pp. 9–10; Acomb, *Mallet du Pan*, pp. 210–11.

56. A.N. AA[40] d.1228.

57. A. Aspinall, 'The reporting and publishing of the House of Commons' debates, 1771-1834' in Richard Pares and A.J.P. Taylor (eds), *Essays presented to Sir Lewis Namier* (London, 1956), pp. 227-57.

58. E. Hatin, *Histoire politique et littéraire de la presse française* (Paris, 1859-61), V, p. 60. For an example of claimed impartiality, see *Courrier National, prospectus*, August 1789; for the defence of an interpretative approach, see Rivarol in *Journal national*, 2e abonnement, no. 7.

59. de Beylie, 'Contribution', p. 47; M. Tourneux, *Bibliographie de l'histoire de Paris pendant la révolution française* (Paris, 1900-13), II, pp. 413-16; A.N. AA[40] d. 1228; A.N. F[7] 4737, d. 1; *Le Logotachigraphe, prospectus*; J.F. Reichardt, *Un prussien en France en 1792*, (Paris, 1892), pp. 226-8; F.-E. Guiraut, *Guiraut au calomniateur Chéry, membre du comité de surveillance* (Paris, 1793), pp. 2-4.

60. Couret de Villeneuve, *Bareme typographique, suivi d'un précis théorique et pratique sur l'art de l'imprimerie* (Paris, 1797); M.S. Boulard, *Le Manuel de l'Imprimeur* (Paris, 1791); C. Bellanger (ed.), *Histoire générale de la presse française. Tome I. Des origines à 1814* (Paris, 1969), pp. 10-18; Jacques Rychner, *Genève et ses typographes vus de Neuchâtel 1770-1780* (Geneva, 1984), pp. 159-80; R. Darnton, *The business of enlightenment. A publishing history of the encyclopedia, 1775-1800* (Cambridge and London, 1979), pp. 227-45.

61. Boulard, *Le Manuel*, p. 23; J. Rychner, 'À l'ombre des lumières: coup d'oeil sur la main d'oeuvre de quelques imprimeries du XVIIIe siècle', *Revue française d'histoire du livre*, 1977, p. 629; Musée Calvet ms. 5989, pièces 331-9; A.N. Y10508B ('Convention faite entre MM. Chambon et de la Chave pour l'impression du journal intitulé l'Orateur avec M. Martel').

62. Boulard, *Le Manuel, p. 2; Catalogue chronologique des libraires et des libraires-imprimeurs de Paris* (Paris, 1789), p. 231ff; Haim Burstin, *Le faubourg Saint-Marcel à l'époque révolutionnaire. Structure économique et composition sociale* (Paris, 1983), p. 239ff. See also R. Chartier, 'L'imprimerie en France à la fin de l'ancien régime: l'état général des imprimeurs de 1777', *Revue Française de l'Histoire du Livre*, 3 (1973), pp. 253-79; Henri-Jean Martin, 'La librarie française en 1777-1778', *Dix-huitième Siècle*, 11 (1979), pp. 95-6; Jean Quéniart, 'L'anémie provinciale' in H.-J. Martin and R. Chartier (eds), *Histoire de l'édition française. II, Le livre conquérant* (Paris, 1984), pp. 282-93.

63. Resentment also surfaced in the form of a *Corps typographique et philanthropique*, which was founded in the spring of 1790 by *compagnon imprimeurs*. It had an elected committee, weekly meetings, a small library and meeting place on the *rue Huchette*, welfare provisions, and an arbitration service to settle disputes between *compagnons* and employers: see Paul Chauvet, *Les ouvriers du livre en France. De 1789 à la constitution de la fédération du livre* (Paris, 1956), pp. 6-26.

64. For the havoc that this caused, see A.N. V[1] 551, letter of the syndic of the *Chambre syndicale* of Bordeaux, 14 March 1789; *Le Modérateur*, xxiv (24 October 1789); *Nouvelles lunes du cousin Jacques*, xx (16 May 1791): '. . . it is hopeless to try to keep workers; they ask for ridiculous wages, even more than the profit margins on publications; and this will continue until

we get some controls back on the printing trade.' See also R. Darnton, L'imprimerie de Panckoucke en l'an II', *Revue Française d'Histoire du Livre*, 23 (1979), pp. 361-2; and for the background of most printers, B. Vouillot, 'L'imprimerie et la librairie à Paris sous le Consulat et l'Empire (1799-1814)', *École Nationale des Chartes. Position des thèses* (Paris, 1979), p. 134; and Popkin, *The right-wing press*, p. 56. For the role of speculators, see *Réponse de l'Agence de l'envoi des lois aux mémoires . . . adressées à la Convention nationale, par plusieurs imprimeurs de Paris* (Paris, 1795), p. 6: 'This trade has become open to any speculator who is dazzled by the few cases of rapid success, and who thinks that all he has to do to start up business is buy some presses and a few characters . . ..

65. Frédéric Barbier, 'L'imprimerie strasbourgeois au siècle des lumières (1681-1789)', *Revue d'Histoire Moderne et Contemporaine*, XXIV (1977), p. 171. For the cost of print-shops, Couret de Villeneuve, *Barême typographique, suivi d'un précis théorique et pratique sur l'art de l'imprimerie* (Paris, 1797), p. 66ff.; A.N. T^{528} pièce 14; A.D. Hérault, L1079; A.N. F^7 3448B.

66. Darnton, *The business of enlightenment*, p. 181.

67. *Club typographique et philanthropique. Feuille hebdomadaire dédiée à MM. les Contribuables*, nos. I-XXIX, *passim*; *Réponse de l'Agence de l'Envoi des Lois*, p. 6; *Observations présentées au Conseil des Anciens, sur la résolution du 13 brumaire, qui fixe à un taux excessif le port des journaux* (undated), pp. 2-3; Vouillot, 'L'imprimerie et la librairie', p. 134.

68. F.C. Heitz, *Catalogue des principaux ouvrages et des cartes imprimées sur le département du Bas-Rhin* (Strasbourg, 1858), p. 22; *Histoire d'une imprimerie bordelaise 1600-1900. Les imprimeries G. Gounouilhon, la Gironde, la petite Gironde* (Bordeaux, 1901), pp. 198-9; Ferdinand Pouy, *Recherches historiques sur l'imprimerie et la librairie à Amiens* (Amiens, 1861), p. 19; H. Ribière, *Essai sur l'histoire de l'imprimerie dans le département de l'Yonne* (Auxerre, 1858), p. 71; G. Peignot, *Tableau général des imprimeries en France depuis 1704. Essai historique sur la liberté d'écrire* (Paris, 1832), pp. 127-40. See also the case of the printer Didot, who was arrested in April in 1790 and asked why he printed the *Actes des Apôtres*:

I noted to him that it was astonishing that he, coming from a family whose reputation was so well known in the artistic world, and having enrolled in the National Guard, should print works such as the *Actes des Apôtres* . . . he replied that it was because of the lack of other work . . . (H. Maspéro-Clerc, 'Vicissitudes des "Actes des Apôtres" ', *A.h.r.f.*, 190 (1967), p. 483.

69. J.-P. Bertaud, *Amis du Roi. Journaux et journalistes royalistes en France de 1789 à 1792* (Paris, 1984), p. 52; *Journal général du Loiret*, 10 October 1792; de Villeneuve, *Barême typographique*, p. 44;

. . . the costs of paper . . . because of the scarcity of rags, whose export was banned, probably too late, on 6 April 1793, the recruitment of most printing workers, the domestic revolts which have held up transport in the departments of what were formerly Normandy and the Auvergne, are mounting at an alarming rate every day.

70 Ibid., (*Barême*) pp. 53, 91–3; Darnton, 'L'imprimerie, pp. 362–3; Gilles Feyel, *La 'Gazette' en province à travers ses réimpressions, 1631–1752* (Amsterdam and Maarssen, 1982), p. 102.

71. A.N. Y10508B; Bertaud, *Amis du roi*, p. 53ff.

72. M. Martin, *Les origines de la presse militaire en France à la fin de l'ancien régime et sous la révolution (1770–1799)* (Paris, 1974), pp. 236–8.

73. R. Moulinas, *L'imprimerie, la librairie et la presse à Avignon au XVIIIe siècle* (Grenoble, 1974), p. 357; V.M. Daline, *Gracchus Babeuf à la veille et pendant la grande révolution française (1785–1794)* (Moscow, 1976), pp. 258–9; *Feuille hebdomadaire*, 1 April 1790, p. 58; R. Jaquel, 'Euloge Schneider en Alsace', *A.h.r.f.*, 9 (1932), p. 25; G. Clause, 'La société populaire de Châlons-sur-Marne vue à travers son journal (floréal an II-vendémiaire an III, avril-septembre 1794), *Mémoires de la Société d'Agriculture, Commerce, Sciences et Arts du Département de la Marne*, 84 (1969), p. 136.

7

Selling the Finished Product

An essential precondition to press marketing and sales was the availability of a sizeable literate market, and the groundwork here had been set by over a century of continuous growth in literacy rates. Based on the evidence of signatures at marriage, the literacy rate for men between 1686–90 and 1786–90 rose from 29 to 47 per cent; and that for women, over the same period, from 14 to 27 per cent. Men therefore outnumbered women by almost two to one, although that gap was progressively closing. There were also marked regional variations, with the well known Saint-Malo to Geneva line dividing off a relatively literate north and east of the country from a retarded south and south-west. Urban populations were also more literate than their rural counterparts, so that some 90 per cent of men and 80 per cent of women in Paris were able to sign their names on the eve of 1789. Taken as a whole, the national figures suggest that over six million adults could read during the revolution, and although many of these may have had a marginal grasp of the language used in a political newspaper, they nevertheless represented a sizeable potential market.[1]

For most people politics was the major area of interest, and the majority of Parisian and provincial newspapers carried reports of legislative debates, along with political news from Paris and around the country. Some of them, most notably the *Moniteur*, the *Journal des débats* and the *Logographe*, specialised in legislative reporting, while several provincial papers, including the *Nouvelliste national* in Toulouse or the *Journal pour département de l'Orne* in Alençon, did so too, lifting reports almost verbatim from the Parisian press. Other papers in Paris, such as the *Chronique de Paris* or the *Journal de Paris*, mixed politics in with articles of more general interest, such as miscellaneous Parisian news, theatrical reviews, literature and the like, attempting to provide their readers with varied fare, much along the lines of the *Morning Chronicle* in England. Most departmental papers also tried to provide variety, giving a short summary of news from the capital, but concentrating mainly on the activities of local municipal and departmental administrations, political events or festivals, the activities of Jacobin clubs, and correspondence from readers. In this way they continued the tradition of the *ancien-régime Affiches*, tapping the roots of local patriotism and pride.

Nevertheless there were papers which deliberately narrowed their appeal to specific groups. The *Journal des débats*, launched in October 1789, pitched its appeal to deputies, both by providing a full coverage of the debates of the National Assembly and by offering them a substantial discount on the subscription price. The *Corréspondance patriotique*, launched by Dupont de Nemours in October 1791, sought its readership amongst former members who were ineligible for election to the Legislative Assembly and had returned to their constituencies, encouraging them to send in news so that the links built up over two years of legislative endeavour could be maintained.[2] The *Journal de la municipalité et des districts de Paris*, on the other hand, launched in October 1789 by François-Louis Bayard, specialised in reporting the activities of the Paris Municipality and Districts, hoping to attract subscribers from both Parisian and provincial administrators who needed to follow the decisions and precedents being set in the capital. Departmental and municipal authorities were also a target for the *Journal des décrets de l'Assemblée nationale*, which in the spring of 1790 claimed an improbable 7,500 of them among its subscribers, and for Tallien's wall-poster version of the radical *Ami des citoyens* which, in the autumn of 1791, circulated Municipalities in the hope that they would take out a subscription. 'This paper', advised Tallien, 'placed at the door of a village church, can educate all the inhabitants and, as its price is very low, every village should be able to afford one.'[3]

In October 1790 the *Correspondant fédératif* came up with a slight variant, offering to handle complaints and petitions on behalf of district, departmental and municipal authorities with the appropriate ministerial office or sub-committee of the National Assembly.[4] In the provinces too, several newspapers looked for custom from administrators, including the *Journal des districts* in Béziers, the *Courrier de la révolution* in Tours, the *Courrier de Strasbourg*, and the *Feuille politique* in Bordeaux. The *Courrier de Strasbourg* was unsuccessful, as departmental administrators had little trust in its owner, but the *Feuille politique* had better luck in the winter of Year

IV, gaining official endorsement from the departmental administration of the Gironde, which advised municipal authorities throughout the department to subscribe to it in order to keep abreast of news and administrative decrees.[5]

Political clubs provided another possible market, and none more so than the Jacobin network which, as early as the summer of 1791, numbered almost a thousand clubs. Most of them subscribed to at least one Parisian paper, and usually to their own local departmental papers as well, while the larger clubs subscribed to several, for use in meetings or for members to read. In Beauvais, for example, the club subscribed to no less than nine Parisian journals in the spring of 1790, costing some 20 per cent of its annual budget; when the time for renewals came up their relative merits were discussed and those which were unoriginal or too conservative were dropped in favour of another. During the first three years of the revolution, the club in Montpellier took out subscriptions to 27, Strasbourg to 22 and Castres 21.[6] At the other end of the scale the tiny village club in Artonne subscribed to the *Moniteur* as early as July 1790, each member chipping in 36 *sols* to cover the cost for three months, and by September had set up a small reading-room where it could be consulted, together with other pamphlets and brochures. In the following month it added the *Feuille villageoise*, renewing the subscription to both in the following autumn and having the back copies bound. In January 1793 it added the *Mercure universel*, and during the terror a fourth title, the *Journal de la montagne*, was also made available.[7]

It is understandable, therefore, that several newspapers deliberately pitched their appeal to clubs, hoping to cash in on what was potentially a very lucrative market. The *Journal des clubs ou sociétés patriotiques* was launched in October 1790 to provide a central record of club activities, but was rapidly eclipsed by Choderlos de Laclos' *Journal des amis de la constitution*, which was specifically authorised by the Paris club to print its correspondence. A weekly paper, it devoted around a half of its 48 pages to résumés of letters sent in by various clubs, and its initial success was such that several of them, looking for a way to cut down on the large postal bills incurred by the numerous circulars and correspondence that they received, suggested that it be adopted as the sole source of mutual communication. This would have given Laclos immense influence. Many clubs promptly opposed the proposal as a threat to their independence, and it quickly collapsed. The Paris club did, however, authorise the *Journal des débats de la société des amis de la constitution* to publish extracts from its correspondence from the end of May 1791 onwards, and periodically advised affiliated clubs on which papers to buy — including, from the summer of 1793, its own *Journal de la montagne*.[8] Overall, however, the *Annales patriotiques* was the most popular with clubs, partly because it offered a lot of news for the price, and partly because it provided a blend of political radicalism and social moderation. It had some 1,200 clubs on its lists by the spring of 1793. Closely behind came the *Feuille villageoise*, the *Journal des amis de la constitution* and the *Moniteur*, with several other titles, including some provincial ones, bringing up the rear.[9] With the closure of Jacobin clubs during the thermidorean reaction, however, the market that they represented disintegrated, and because of the ban on political co-ordination between clubs under the Directory, the constitutional circles never effectively offered the same market opportunity.

The armed forces were also an attractive target. Several newspapers in 1790–1 claimed to cater for the interests of the National Guard, while the navy was wooed by Picquenard's *Ami des principes* in 1795 and the *Marin français* in Year VII. Military newspapers catering for the army dated back to the early 1770s, but tended during the *ancien régime* to be aimed at the officer corps. So too was the first new title of the revolution, the *Journal militaire*, launched in 1790. Yet the outbreak of war in 1792 saw the appearance of the *Argus de l'armée du Nord*, produced within the *armée du Nord* itself, under Dumouriez's watchful eye, aiming more directly at the rank and file, and during the terror the practice spread to both generals and representatives on mission, as they sought to raise morale and strengthen propaganda. It was a tradition followed by Carnot during the First Directory, and by Bonaparte on his Italian and Egyptian campaigns, with the *Courrier de l'armée de l'Italie* and the *Courrier de l'Egypte*.[10]

Social groups were also catered for. The *Chronique du mois*, for example, was aimed at active citizens, with a specific focus on bankers, financiers and merchants, ' . . . who need to know both the domestic and foreign situation, in order to be able to conclude commercial agreements which will be financially beneficial both to the nation and themselves'. Its appeal was to the elite, ' . . . to a readership that is sufficiently well off to be able to buy it without having to save on the essentials of daily life, but also to a well educated readership, capable of reading articles of forty to sixty pages, austerely laid out and written in complex prose'.[11] The *Journal du commerce de Rouen*, launched in 1791, concentrated on a similar clientele, and there can be little doubt that a market for financial and commercial news existed on a national scale. The merchants of Bédarieux, for example, protested in the summer of 1792 against a decision of their departmental administration to ban the circulation of the right-wing Parisian press in the Hérault, on the grounds that only it provided the regular information on commodity prices and exchange rates from Paris and Marseilles that was essential for their business.[12] The *Moniteur hypothécaire*, on the other hand, catered only for purchasers of *biens nationaux*, publishing details of all land sales in the country so that creditors could check that the security for their loans was not being quietly disposed of — a concern which ' . . . deserves mainly the attention of traders, large scale merchants, large landowners, capitalists, those living off investments, men in public life, and anyone else in business'. Lawyers too had their special press, amongst others the *Proclamateur et corréspondant encyclopédique*, launched in *germinal* of Year V, while there was even a multipurpose newspaper launched in Paris in 1791, the *Journal des sept classes*, which appeared daily and concentrated on a different speciality for each day of the week: constitutional and political affairs on Saturdays, trade on Sundays, legal affairs on Mondays, and so on.[13]

Many provincial papers tried to attract rural subscribers from the local peasantry, partly no doubt to boost their circulation figures, but also from a genuine concern to preach the benefits of the new order to the peasantry. The *Journal patriotique* in Grenoble, the *Journal de Versailles* and the *Journal patriotique de département de la Dordogne* are just three among many which published articles on rural economy, agricultural improvement and the benefits of the abolition of feudalism.[14] The *Patriote du département de la Mayenne*, in the spring of 1792, carried a special column entitled 'Instructions aux Habitants des Campagnes' in which a fictitious patriotic priest explained the principles of the revolution, and the advantages that it had brought, to a simple peasant audience, while the *Courrier du Midi* in Avignon did similarly in a special weekly supplement.[15] Paris, not to be outdone, produced no less than 18 peasant newspapers over the decade as a whole. The *Feuille du cultivateur* leaned towards the practical issues of farming, the *Journal des laboureurs* more towards political issues, as befitted its editor, Lequinio, who was deputy to the Legislative Assembly and Convention for the Morbihan. The most successful and durable of them all, however, was the *Feuille villageoise*, which blended the practical and ideological into what its historian has called ' . . . the first relatively successful newspaper for peasants in French history'.[16]

Most peasant papers aimed in practice either at the upper end of rural society, or at rural notables, government officials or priests who, it was hoped, would read out the contents to parishioners after Sunday mass or at village meetings.[17] Yet public reading sessions were a feature of urban life too, organised by clubs, administrative authorities or proselytising individuals for the benefit of the unlettered and poor. Claude Dansard, a schoolmaster from the Mathurins district of Paris, founded the *Société fraternelle des deux sexes* in this way in February 1790, and it inspired the growth of *sociétées populaires* throughout the capital by the summer of 1791, which were to remain influential until the end of the terror.[18] In addition, although literacy was certainly a limiting factor, there were several newspapers which tried to sell directly to the artisans and poor, often selling copies by the number, instead of the usual method of subscription, to bring the cost down. Much of the early radical press, rooted in the Cordeliers District, catered for just such a readership, as did Hébert in the *Père Duchesne* and the *Sans-culotte observateur*, a wall-poster of the autumn of 1793. The *Journal des départements méridionaux* in Marseilles, during the spring of 1792, hoped to find an echo among ' . . . hard working and honest artisans, worthy farmers, committed workers . . . ', while the *Patriote de la Meurthe*, a neo-Jacobin newspaper that appeared in Nancy during the winter of Year VI, sold ' . . . at the most reasonable price possible in order to offer poor republicans the means of educating themselves and regaining their courage'.[19] The poster version of Tallien's *Ami des citoyens* was pitched at the same market, and offered reductions for bulk purchases from provincial Jacobin clubs which might want to distribute them to their poorer members. The *Journal de la société populaire de Lyon* made the fatal mistake of offering a 60 per cent discount on its subscription rates to such people, only to find that almost all its readers promptly classified themselves as such and bankrupted it within weeks.[20]

Appealing to the poor in many areas meant using pâtois or minority languages. All but two of the newspapers to appear in Alsace during the entire revolution were in German, as no one except the upper bourgeoisie and outsiders spoke French. Toulouse saw a brief *l'Homé franc, journal noubel en patois fait exprès per Toulouse* in 1791, which promised to ' . . . explicarei de moun milieu co que le pople souben non pot pas coumprene, parco que l'y pardon pas soun lengatge', while Dunkirk had a paper in Flemish during 1792, largely aimed at port workers and sailors. Malines and Brussels also had Flemish papers in 1799 — the latter raising the hackles of local government officials who suspected that it was being deliberately used to spread counter-revolutionary ideas.[21]

Although their literacy rates were lower than those of men, women were another possible market. Some subscribed to ordinary political newspapers: 4 per cent of the subscribers to the *Journal de la montagne*, for example, were women. Several papers also featured articles which advocated a political role for them, notably the *Journal de la société de 1789*, in which Condorcet argued the case for the extension of the suffrage, or the *Bouche de fer*, in which Etta Palm D'Aelder's speeches to the *Cercle social* found a ready home. Yet newspapers aimed specifically at women date back to 1710, and between then and 1789 no less than 21 different titles had appeared, featuring articles on literature, news, fashion, morality and aesthetic taste, for middle class and aristocratic taste. Only one, the *Magasin des modes*, was still in existence when the revolution broke out, but some 23 new titles appeared over the next ten years, beginning with the *Étrennes national des dames* in December 1789, and the *Événements du jour* and *Feuille du jour* in January 1790, the latter of which was directly political and claimed to be edited by 'une société de femmes de lettres'. All three were short-lived, and most of the rest tended to cater instead for the hardy perennials of education, love, marriage and personal problems, within the new social context of the revolution. They also had difficulty surviving, and only the *Journal des modes* had any real success, lasting from 1797 until mid-way through the July Monarchy in 1839.[22]

Once a suitable market had been identified, a successful launch was important, both to get a foot in the market and to bring in the initial subscription money needed to cover printing and administrative costs. As one owner stated in a letter to the Minister of Police in 1797:[23]

> In the early stages of a new enterprise one normally has little capital; it is therefore common, in such circumstances, to advertise the paper aggressively to the public in order to encourage sales and to get the initial subscriptions in, without which costs just cannot be met.

Many of the techniques used during the revolution were inherited from the *ancien régime*. Posters and prospectuses, for example, were distributed through the postal network and the book trade, with postmasters and booksellers usually allowed 10 per cent of the value of the subscriptions that they handled. The *Journal des dames*, for example, sent 60,000 prospectuses around Europe in 1787 to boost its sales; in 1789 Couret de Villeneuve sent off 6,000, announcing a political supplement for his *Journal général*; the *Courrier d'Avignon* distributed 20,000 in December 1789 when it was changing into a daily paper; Babeuf, some 10,000 for his abortive *Corréspondant Picard* in 1790; and Pelzin's *Journal de Lyon*, 200 large posters and 1,000 prospectuses at the end of 1794. Prospectuses were cheap to produce and distribute, but their success rate was usually low: according to Roederer, part owner of the *Journal de Paris* during the Directory, it took a thousand prospectuses, on average, to attract one subscriber.[24]

A more economical alternative was to place an advertisement in national or local newspapers. Many provincial newspapers appear to have provided this service free to Parisian journalists in the early part of the revolution, probably flattered by the request and attracted by the prospect of their 10 per cent commission. Some also provided their readers with a short analysis and appraisal of the paper's contents: the *Journal général de l'orleánais*, for example, did this for the *Point du jour*, the *Journal de la ville*, the *Lettres à Monsieur le comte de B **** and several others during the latter half of 1789, and by the end of the year boasted of handling subscriptions for almost 50 newspapers nation-wide.[25] Freelance subscription agents were an extension of this, acting for individual titles in their local area. The *Annales universelles* had a person in Bayonne in 1797, Julien, who tried to rustle up subscribers in south-western France and northern Spain, feeding back valuable information on reader reaction to the paper's content; while the *Archives nationales* had a bundle of correspondence from Romain Caillot, owner of the *Courrier extraordinaire*, chronicling his attempts to recruit similar agents in the north-east during the summer of the same year.[26] Other newspapers tried to enlist the co-operation of administrative bodies or government officials: François Robert offered municipal authorities 10 per cent of the value of each subscription that they obtained for him, which would be donated to the charity of their choice — ' . . . and in this way the municipality will become a kind of philanthropic organisation'. Panckoucke, for his part, circulated departmental *commissaires* during the Directory, on behalf of his *Clef du Cabinet*, offering 4 francs per annual subscription, which was no doubt an attractive bait to poorly paid government officials. Similar tactics were used by the *Courrier historique et politique*, the *Indépendant* the *Journal patriotique du département de la Dordogne*, and the *Journal des amis* in Metz.[27]

Another method was to distribute sample numbers free to selected people for short periods of a week or ten days, in the hope that they would be interested enough to take out their own subscription. Bayard did this for the *Journal de la municipalité* in 1790, sending free copies to all the Parisian Districts, while Robert did the same for the *Mercure national* during the spring of 1791, providing a week's free copies to selected Municipalities, followed by a letter urging them to subscribe.[28] It was a system still being used by the *Corréspondance politique, littéraire et commerciale* in 1797, and by the end of the decade had become a sophisticated art, with large papers sending as many as 6,000 free copies to a target list of potential subscribers, and changing the list every ten days so that, over a three-month period, they could reach up to 54,000 potential customers. According to Roederer, a thouand of these might end up as subscribers, but it was a great deal of work for a quite meagre return. Pierre-Louis Waudin, a lawyer from the district Saint-Severin in Paris, found this out in the autumn of 1789, when he launched a *Censeur patriote* by distributing free copies of the first six numbers to some 1,200 people. His reward was a meagre 15 subscriptions, along with 40 requests to continue the free gift.[29] Of course, if all failed, there was always the possibility of continuing Panckoucke's practice of the 1770s, of buying up smaller titles in order to take over their subscription list and subscribers. This was how the *Journal de Genève* and *Mercure* had consolidated themselves before the revolution, and was used in 1800 by the Bertin brothers for the *Journal des débats*, buying up subscription lists from right-wing papers such as the *Éclair* and *Quotidienne*, that had been closed down by the Ministry of Police.[30]

Colporteurs could be successful sales agents too, not so much in rural areas, where sales were low and confined to more traditional wares, as in towns and major cities. Several papers, and particularly the small ones, tended to test the market through *colporteurs* in the initial stages, selling on the streets to test consumer reaction and their own stamina, and to build up their finances. This was the way that Mirabeau's *Lettres à ses commettants* had started in May 1789, and it had the additional advantage of enabling papers to sell without having to print a subscription address, so making it difficult for the police to take repressive action against them.[31] Some, such as the *Petit Gautier* or the *Lendemain*, were even published in separate *colporteur* editions, featuring prominent headings that *colporteurs* shouted out to attract custom, and this was something that worried politicians and administrators who feared that sensational headlines would cause disorder. As early as 1 September 1789 they were banned in Paris from calling out anything other than the titles of their newspapers, and before the end of the year their numbers were limited to 300, each of them having to wear a badge and carry a permit. However, the enforcement of these measures proved difficult and were consistently ignored over the following years. As late as the winter of 1797–8, attempts were still being made to enforce them.[32]

Nevertheless, in marked contrast to contemporary English practice, street sales probably accounted for no more than 10 per cent of total newspaper turnover, the great bulk instead being sold by subscription, paid in advance for three-month, six-month or annual periods. Customers either paid directly to the newspaper subscription office through the post, or used their local bookseller or printer, both of which were established practice under the *ancien régime*, and were to remain so until well into the nineteenth century. Proprietors liked subscription sales because they encouraged customer loyalty and provided adequate capital in advance of publication, and of additional assistance was the low postal tariff for newspapers, inherited from the *ancien régime* and raised only once during the revolution.[33]

Yet subscriptions entailed delivery, either direct to the subscriber or to his bookseller, and this involved a good deal of organisation. Local subscribers were therefore usually offered discounts if they collected their copies directly from the print-shop, which appear to have been equivalent to the savings made by the paper on packaging and delivery costs. The *Citoyen surveillant* in Riom, for example, offered a 10 per cent discount, as did the *Affiches du Maine*.[34] Others organised their own local delivery service, using *colporteurs* or casual labour: de Pussy's *Courrier national* had one in Paris as early as July 1789, which promised delivery before 9 a.m. in even ' . . . the most distant quarters of Paris'; the *Journal de la ville, Nouvelles éphémérides. Journal des débats* and *Courrier français* all quickly followed suit within weeks, and by the summer of 1791, the *Journal général* of Smits and Lebrun was able to pledge that all its deliveries were completed by 6 a.m. The *Folies du matin*, in more picturesque terms, promised delivery ' . . . at the same time as the cries of chimney sweeps and of old clothes merchants can be heard in the streets'.[35] In the provinces the *Journal général de l'orléanais* employed two men to carry out town deliveries, as did other papers in Lorient, Chalons-sur-Marne and Toulouse. In Lille, Paris de Lespinard, editor of the *Feuille de Flandre*, had run a profitable local postal service since February 1784, which he also used to distribute his paper.[36]

Deliveries further afield required careful use of the postal service, and this in turn placed severe constraints on production schedules, for papers had to be off the press by specific times in order to catch the post. Moreover, although Paris and most large cities had a daily service on major routes, many of the smaller and more remote towns had one that operated only on certain days of the week. Thus, for example, when the *Affiches de Dauphiné*, which was published in Grenoble, decided to increase its output to twice weekly in August 1789 to profit from the news as it came in on the latest mail, readers in the Haute-Dauphiné were warned that the Thursday morning edition would only be able to leave Grenoble on the Saturday morning, leaving them well behind with the news. The *Citoyen surveillant* in Rioms changed its publication day from Saturdays to Thursdays in 1791, after only five editions, ' . . . since it is our only opportunity of dispatching the paper on the same day to the entire department, and to all the neighbouring departments as well'. Similarly, in the spring of 1793 the *Courrier d'Avignon* was able to increase its output from six to seven times weekly because the postal service on the main route to Marseilles, Lyons and Toulon had been increased to cover the extra day.[37] Efficient planning was therefore vital: editors frequently assured their customers that they took every possible care over dispatch procedcures, and on some occasions changed their schedules to suit client preference. The *Journal patriotique du département de la Dordogne*, for example, changed its publication day from Wednesdays to Sundays in January 1791 in response to readers requests: 'the reason they gave was that, as the Sunday post was always less interesting, they would have more time to devote on that day to our paper.'[38]

Nevertheless, performance frequently fell short of promise, and there were frequent complaints from subscribers over newspapers arriving late or not at all. Editors usually blamed this either on the inefficiency of the post — the *Journal révolutionnaire de Toulouse*, for example, apologised to its readers for 'accidental mistakes on the part of postal workers' — or else on deliberate sabotage: the *Défenseur de la vérité* in Le Mans denouncing their 'culpable errors'.[39] Most problems were probably due to straightforward inefficiency, an inevitable result of the dramatic increase in the volume of material handled by the service after 1789, and generated both by the mushrooming of the revolutionary bureaucracy and by the explosion in the newspaper press. Manpower was not increased to compensate, and from the summer of 1792 onwards the requisitioning of men and horses by the army, combined with the damage caused to roads by troop movements and neglect, brought the service close to collapse. To make things worse, some 200 postmasters, or 15 per cent of the total, resigned between 1789 and 1793, many of them because they had lost their exemption from *taille* with the abolition of privilege in 1789. Nevertheless, there are enough complaints of deliberate sabotage to suggest that it was a contributory factor too.

As early as December 1789 Poncelin de la Roche Tilhac complained that he delivered his papers promptly to the post at 9 a.m. each morning, only to have them held up by the service which '. . . uses underhand methods and perverse tricks, to take away from us the credit for our punctuality'. Paul Capon moved his *Courrier du Midi* to Avignon in 1791 because the postmaster in Orange — 'and all the refractory priestly rabble which holds secret meetings with him' — were not only holding up copies in the post, but also writing their own insulting comments in the margins of individual copies and confiscating subscribers' letters.[40] Similar complaints came from the *Défenseur de la Vérité* in Le Mans in 1793, while Parent l'aîné in Nevers complained in the winter of Year VI that his local postmaster was not only holding up the distribution of the neo-Jacobin *Journal de la Nièvre*, but even spattering copies with blood to provide a primitive colour supplement. Neither were such problems confined to the Jacobin press, for the *Antiterroriste* in Toulouse was one of several right-wing papers in the Directory also to complain of the same problem.[41]

On the other hand, postal mistakes and deliberate sabotage were not the only causes of delivery problems: good old-fashioned inefficiency on the part of newspaper proprietors was often a factor too. A bundle of letters conserved in the Archives Nationales, in a dossier dealing with the bungled attempt to arrest Marat in January 1790, contains complaints from subscribers as far apart as Chartres and Montpellier, Belvès and Avallon, venting their frustrations at inefficient delivery of the *Ami du peuple*. A surgeon from Chartres complained that he had waited for up to three weeks without receiving anything, only to have all the back numbers arrive one day in a single bundle ' . . . and, to make things worse, you also get the same paper twice: gradually you begin to get exasperated, and then totally discouraged at being so badly served for having paid in advance'. All this came at a time when Marat was dodging arrest, in Versailles and Paris, and his preoccupations lay elsewhere; but letters to Brissot contained in the same dossier contain similar complaints about the *Patriote* at the time of his break with Buisson.[42]

Delivery problems prompted some proprietors to organise their own alternative delivery system instead. There were also additional reasons for this, however, not least that of attracting more subscribers by arriving first with the news, and the wish, especially during the Directory, to avoid surveillance and postal control. The first private system was organised by Joseph Duplain in the spring of 1790, for the *Courrier extraordinaire ou le premier arrivé*. He contracted with a private coach firm to deliver copies of the paper to major provincial cities, starting with Lyon in July 1790 and spreading subsequently to Lille, Calais, Rouen, Dunkirk and Orléans. Because the coaches were light, and copies were taken from the front end of the print run, they were able to leave Paris at 3 a.m. and have papers in Lyons, for example, within 56 hours, some 40 hours ahead of their orthodox rivals. They were also able to carry two passengers and provide a free parcel delivery service for subscribers.[43] The system had its teething troubles and Duplain cancelled the contract with his initial coach contractor after disputes over costs and delivery times. Moreover it was expensive, with subscribers paying twice the rate that those opting for normal postal delivery had to pay. Nevertheless, after a slow start, the paper became well established and lasted until August 1792, when Duplain was arrested on suspicion of royalism. Released a month later, after the September massacres, he resumed publication in October, rebuilding his delivery system and concentrating his attention on the north-eastern departments and Belgium. A special edition was printed at 4 p.m. which covered the early part of the Convention's debates, and rushed from Paris to Ecouen by horseback, then to Amiens by postillion, where it was put into the normal post and delivered to subscribers a full 24 hours ahead of its rivals.[44]

Duplain was executed during the summer of 1794 on suspicion of counter-revolution, but the *Courrier* was continued by his former subscription manager, Husson, along with two former collaborators, Poujade de Ladevèze and Duval. Its focus now swung exclusively to the Midi, concentrating on Lyons, and the departments of the Rhône valley, while for security reasons no copies were available in Paris at all. Every evening at 11 p.m. dispatch riders left with bundles of copies, bound for Nogent-sur-Vernisson: and there, having gained a day on the post, they handed in their bundles to the local postmaster who, for a fee, divided them up into separate packets which were then dispatched, in the normal post, to Clermont-Ferrand (for Montpellier and the Midi) and Moulins (for Lyon, the Rhône valley and Switzerland).[45] The *Courrier* had its presses sealed after the *vendémiaire* rising and Ladevèze was con-. demned to death; but he had gone into hiding, and Husson, who was himself arrested briefly in *nivôse*, continued the *Courrier* with him and Duval under a different title. This did not last long, however, for Ladevèze broke away in the spring of 1796 to launch the *Véridique* and Duval followed suit with the *Précurseur*. All three of them used express delivery systems, the *Précurseur* innovating still further by having its text written in Paris, the copies printed in Briare (in the Loiret) and then rushed by private coach to Lyons and the Midi, helped by royalist money.[46]

Another newspaper to use express delivery was the right-wing *Éclair*, which, during Year III and the early Directory, used coaches to deliver to the north-eastern departments and Belgium. It was banned after the *fructidor* coup and changed its name to the *Annales politiques et littéraires*, using its old distribution network to deliver copies to Arras, Amiens and Lille, then from Lille, through another independent distributor, to Ghent, Dunkirk, Courtrai, Bruges, Tournai, Menin, Tourcoing and Brussels. According to the departmental *commissaire* of the Oise,

> It is snapped up and devoured in both the urban and rural areas of most of the department. There it holds a monopoly of opinion which has had grave effects on political views; what is worse is that, to its great advantage, it is distributed by private vehicles.[47]

A printer named Roman Caillot also published an express edition of his *Courrier des départements* in the spring of Year V, attempting unsuccessfully to rival the *Éclair* in the same region, only to find that his carriage contractor was falling down on the job because he was secretly providing a similar service for another paper, the *Tableau de Paris*. The *Ami de l'ordre*, on the other hand, presents a slight variant, as it was written in Grenoble, printed in Paris and distributed exclusively and clandestinely in the Midi by specially recruited *colporteurs*.[48]

All of these were right-wing papers, and it is little surprise that after the *fructidor* coup in 1797 the practice was finally banned by the Minister of Police, Sotin, in a circular of 2 *nivôse* Year VI. He was partly concerned to eliminate evasion of the stamp tax and to boost the revenue of the ailing postal service, but his overriding motive was political, that of crushing the clandestine right-wing press. Their very clandestinity made that difficult, and Sotin weakened his own case by allowing an exception in favour of the republican *Echo de la république française*, until protests from rivals forced him to withdraw it in the winter of Year VII. By then all clandestine distribution, for newspapers at least, appears to have stopped.[49]

The whole purpose of distribution was to sell, and to set the revolutionary press in its proper context, some idea of sales and profit figures is important. Yet the evidence for both is fragmentary, since the collapse of government controls in 1789 has meant that the revolution has left less archival residue than the more highly censored and controlled press of the Empire.[50] We are instead dependent on evidence provided at the time by newspapers themselves, on papers seized during police raids, and on the occasional references of private correspondence. The result is patchy at best, and no reliable circulation figures for any one newspaper exist over the decade as a whole. Nevertheless, an approximate idea of the figures involved is possible. Eighteenth-century readership was obviously low by twentieth-century standards, because of low literacy and depressed living standards. During the 30 years before the revolution, for example, most provincial *Affiches* had a few hundred subscribers at most: the *Annonces et avis divers pour les Pays-Bas français*, for example, published from Lille by Panckoucke in 1761-2, began with some 600 subscribers, but tailed off rapidly. The *Affiches d'Angers*, some 14 years later, had a mere 200 and the *Journal de Marseille*, during its early years between 1781 and 1784, survived on a mere 300.[51] The only significant exception to this pattern, the *Courrier d'Avignon* which had some 3,000 subscribers during the 1780s, was outside French jurisdiction and enjoyed its high circulation because of the relative freedom from censorship that this gave it.

Once press freedom came in 1789 the total circulation of the provincial press certainly rose sharply, but the rise was spread out over many more titles, with the result that the sales of individual newspapers increased only marginally. Only four provincial titles in the whole decade appear to have attracted more than a thousand subscribers: the *Courrier d'Avignon* (which doubled its subscriptions to 6,000 by the end of 1789), the *Journal général de l'orléanais* (which boasted 1,200 subscribers in 1791), the *Feuille de Flandre* (with around 1,000 at the end of the same year), and the *Courrier de Strasbourg* with over 12,000 in the spring of 1792.[52] Elsewhere, circulations were lower. The *Journal de Marseille* increased from 300 subscribers in 1789, to 400 by the summer of 1793, when it embraced the cause of the federalist rebellion, then to marginally over 500 when it returned in the summer of 1795 as an organ of the thermidorean reaction. Similar figures have also been suggested for two other right-wing papers of the First Directory, the *Antiterroriste* in Toulouse, the *Gazette bordelaise*, and the *Clairvoyant* in Grenoble. During the summer of 1794, the Jacobin club newspaper in Bordeaux the *Journal du club national*, peaked at around the same level, with just under 500 subscribers.[53]

All of these were major provincial titles, however, and many others had circulations which were closer to, or even below, the levels of the *ancien régime*. The *Journal patriotique*, operating in virgin territory in Agen between 1790 and 1792, oscillated between 250 and 400, and the *Ami des Campagnes* in the Haute-Garonne, and the *Journal de la Nièvre*, both appearing during the Directory, had some 300 each. A surprising number survived on even smaller figures, usually thanks to considerable financial sacrifice on the part of the owners: the *Journal du département du Maine-et-Loire* in Angers with 129 subscribers, the *Feuille hebdomadaire* in Lorient with little over 100, and the *Argos* in Strasbourg with perhaps as few as 80. Indirect evidence, such as complaints from editors over mounting losses, or the decision of many to take up part-time employment, suggests that many more struggled to survive with sales at a similar level.[54]

The sales of the Parisian press were on average higher, helped by the larger market available in Paris itself, and by the considerable provincial sales that most of them were able to attract because of their position at the centre of political life. During the 1780s the sales of Panckoucke's *Mercure* had oscillated violently between 2,800 and 23,500, depending on the interest generated by political events, such as the American War of Independence, while those of the *Gazette* similarly varied between 6,000 and 12,260. Most other titles had circulations in the low thousands.[55] The political crisis of 1789 had the predictable effect of boosting sales: those of the *Mercure*, which had declined rapidly from their high point of 20,000 in 1783, at the height of the American War of Independence to about 11,000 by the end of 1788, rose rapidly again during the course of 1789 to around 15,000, before declining steadily to a little over 8,000 by the early months of 1793. The first two copies of Mirabeau's *États-Généraux*, in the spring of 1789, sold 12,000 copies within a matter of days, to what must have been largely a Parisian audience, through *colporteurs*, and Hatin suggests a figure of 20,000 for its successor, the *Courrier de Provence*, although this was probably a peak, rapidly eroded by competition and the paper's own internal problems. Four months later Duplain's *Lettres à M. le Comte de B**** claimed sales of 11,000; the *Journal des décrets de l'Assemblée nationale pour les habitants des campagnes* had close to 8,000 in the spring of 1790, the *Journal du soir* some 10,000 by January 1792, and the *Moniteur* just over 8,000 later in the same year.[56]

Figures for the right-wing and radical press were slightly lower. The *Révolutions de Paris*, when it first appeared in 1789, had a short period of phenomenal success, with sales of 200,000 claimed for its early numbers; yet this figure probably included the many reprints that these early editions went through and its real circulation was probably nearer to 10,000. Marat had about 4,000 subscribers for the *Ami du peuple* in January 1791, although his sales fluctuated wildly, in tune with his periods of seclusion and hiding and variations in the political temperature. The *Orateur du peuple* began in the summer of 1790 with sales of less than 3,000, although one source claims 15,000 subscribers in the following spring, while Camille Desmoulins attracted around 3,000 readers within a month of launching the *Révolutions de France et de Brabant* in the winter of 1789–90. The *Feuille villageoise* had some 15,000, in 1790, dropping to 11,000 in the following year, while a maximum figure of 10,000 has been suggested for the *Patriote français*.[57] As for the right-wing press, the *Gazette universelle* had around 7,000 subscribers early in 1792, the *Actes des Apôtres*, with its distinctly esoteric appeal, about 4,500 during the course of 1790, and Royou's *Ami du Roi* 5,700 at its peak, in April 1791. The *Gazette de Paris* reached its maximum of 5,000 in the summer of 1790, declining to little over 2,000, two years later.[58]

Figures of this level remained standard for the rest of the decade. The *Annales patriotiques*, for example, had 12,000 subscribers during the spring of 1793, while the Paris Jacobin club's *Journal de la montagne* attracted a little over 5,000 at the height of the terror. During the thermidorean raction the right-wing press gained its revenge, with the *Nouvelles politiques* attracting 10,000 in the latter months of 1794, the *Orateur du peuple*, 15,000 in the following spring, and the *Journal de Perlet*, 21,000 in the summer of 1795.[59] Only in exceptional cases, such as the lavish government purchases that pushed the *Père Duchesne*'s print run to several hundred thousand during the terror, could any paper expect to do markedly better, and during more normal times — earlier in 1793 — the sales of the *Père Duchesne* had been around 9,000. As a result no single newspaper dominated the market, and even the most popular titles never exceeded the sales of the *Mercure*, at the height of its popularity in the early 1780s. Instead a great many more papers achieved comparable figures, and the natural result of this was an expanded overall market.

A reasonable estimate of the weekly circulation figures of the Parisian press in the 1780s, on the eve of the revolution, would be close to 100,000. What happened to that figure during the early years of the revolution we do not know, but by the winter of 1793, the postal administration was complaining that the number of papers leaving Paris had risen to 80,000 per day, or some 560,000 per week.[60] The ratio of Parisian to provincial sales varied a great deal between titles, but many Parisian papers sold over half of their copies to the provinces, and if we take a figure of 60 per cent as an average, the total output of the Parisian press must have been over 130,000 per day — and quite probably more — or over 800,000 per week. It could be argued that the 1793 figure was inflated by the bulk purchases being made by the Committee of Public Safety and Ministry of War, but the effect of this was probably more than outweighed by the effects of censorship and newspaper closures, which certainly reduced the number of titles on sale during the same period. The effects of this were evident after *thermidor*, for by the winter of 1795–6, numbers had risen again, with 95,000 papers leaving the capital daily, and two estimates in 1797 put the entire Parisian daily output at 150,000. Even at the time of the *brumaire* coup, after two years of growing disillusion and draconian censorship, the daily output had only fallen to 100,000 — some six or seven times larger than the output of the dying years of the *ancien régime*. Napoleon quickly administered the kiss of death, however, reducing the figure to 36,000 per week within four years, of which some 25,000 were sold outside Paris.[61]

Rather like the evidence for total sales figures, that for their geographical and social distribution is fragmented because of the lack of sources. In the few cases in which subscription registers have survived, they usually give adequate details on a subscriber's geographical location, because an address was essential information for delivery purposes, but they only occasionally mention the subscriber's trade or profession. Even where they do, the information is open to question as it was based on the subscriber's own description of himself, and because eighteenth-century terminology was often vague and imprecise. Because the surviving registers are so few, attempts have been made to supplement them by analysing the occasional bundles of letters contained in the archives, as a result of police raids and arrests, or by analysing the letters that newspapers published from their subscribers, on the assumption that they will reveal a reasonable cross section of the readership. There are problems in the former method, as letters seized may not be representative, and in the latter because letters published were presumably chosen for their news value, not for their social or geographical spread. Consequently, areas of intense political activity tend to be over-represented, and at least one of the studies, which breaks this analysis down on an annual basis, reveals striking fluctuations from year to year, as the focus of attention shifted. Yet in the lack of any other hard evidence, letters can provide at least a general picture.[62]

From a combination of subscription lists and readers' letters, the royalist press of the early revolution, such as the *Gazette de Paris*, appears to have attracted many of their subscribers from the provincial nobility, army officers, the upper ranks of the clergy and the *haute bourgeoisie*, such as bankers and farmers general. Some of the great noble families, such as the Ségurs and the Praslins, feature on the lists of the *Gazette de Paris*, while the royal family was reputed to read the *Ami du Roi* avidly, and several bishops subscribed to other papers. If subscribers from the Third Estate were in a minority, there were nevertheless enough of them, including professors, doctors, lawyers and landowners, to show that conservatism had a distinct appeal to those of them alarmed by the pace and extent of reform. The right-wing press of the Directory had far less noble support, because of the impact of the terror and émigré legislation, and correspondingly more from the ranks of the bourgeoisie, which had been equally alarmed by the radicalism of the terror. Subscription lists show a greater predominance of wealthier peasantry, and of the urban bourgeoisie of government, trade and the professions.[63] In this respect, they differ little from the clientele attracted by the moderate and radical press for much of the decade. Letters to the *Révolutions de Paris*, for example, came from lawyers, administrators, merchants, manufacturers, doctors and teachers, during the course of its first year of production. The only peasantry tended to be the wealthier *laboureurs*, and the only artisans or domestic servants came from Paris. The *Patriote français* also attracted few noble subscribers and few of the very poor, but appealed instead to lawyers, teachers, administrators, merchants and priests. The *Feuille villageoise* attracted a lot of the latter, and was partly intended for them to read out to parishioners; but it too was widely read by wealthier peasantry, lawyers, merchants, manufacturers and members of the liberal professions.

Only with the more radical Jacobin press, during and after the terror, is there any sign of greater involvement of the artisan and labouring classes, and even then this may be partly a reflection of the current fashion of understating one's occupation in order to conform to the popular and democratic ethos. The *Journal de la montagne*, for example, had a larger proportion of Parisian subscribers from the ranks of shop assistants and shopkeepers, artisans and small-time traders; yet its provincial readership, which made up over half the total, was heavily weighted towards the professions, trade and industry, and wealthy farmers. Lebois' *Ami du peuple* during the thermidorean reaction had a more recognisably *sans-culotte* clientele, as the liberal professions, industrialists and traders account for less than 30 per cent of subscribers, while office workers and administrators — reflecting the surviving strength of Jacobin presence in administration — and artisans and shopkeepers, make up the bulk of the rest. This tendency is also marked amongst subscribers to Babeuf's *Tribun du peuple*, where artisans, small traders and shopkeepers account for a massive 72.3 per cent of subscribers, although once more the provincial readership had more involvement from the bourgeoisie.[64]

All this suggests the rather banal conclusion that newspapers were purchased by the same kinds of people who were politically active during the revolution, and although readership was much wider than subscription lists suggest, it seems reasonable to assume that, like the leadership of the revolution, it was predominantly urban and overwhelmingly bourgeois. As for the geographical spread, again only an impressionistic picture is possible. During the period 1790–92 the *Ami du Roi* sold one-fifth of its copies in Paris, and particularly in the wealthier districts of the Marais and the faubourgs Saint-Honoré and Saint-Germain. The remainder went either abroad, where a small number was sold to *émigrés* who appreciated its political slant and wanted to keep up with French news, or to the provinces, where Britanny, the Vendée, the Nord and the Gironde predominate. Subscribers to the *Gazette de Paris* were also prominent in Paris, the Nord and Pas-de-Calais and the Gironde; but it also had sizeable pockets of readership in the Rhône-et-Loire and the Bouches-du-Rhône, both noted areas of counter-revolutionary presence. The *Actes des Apôtres* had most of its clientele in Paris, but the *Rocambole des journaux*, which took over its satirical tradition, analysed on the basis of readers' letters, had its main readership in the west and the Midi. The *Journal général de France*, using the same source, was strong in these two areas also, but also had readers in Britanny and, to a lesser degree, in the central departments of the Puy-de-Dome and Allier. The more moderate message of the *Gazette universelle*, on the other hand, was less popular in the west and centre, but stronger in Lyons, the Isère, the Midi and the eastern departments of the Meurthe, Moselle and Bas-Rhin.[65]

Under the Directory the areas of right-wing strength are less clear cut, partly because of the intense commercial competition which encouraged some owners to concentrate on specific regions, where they were able to set up rapid delivery systems, and partly also because of the greater popularity of right-wing views. The *Éclair*, for example, was strong in the north-east, while the *Véridique* and *Précurseur* concentrated on the Rhône valley and the Midi.[66] The *Courrier extraordinaire* also competed in the north-east, but also had readers in the Vendée, Vienne and Charente-Maritime, as well as in the Doubs, and to a lesser extent in Finistère, the Basses-Pyrénées, the Côte-d'Or, the Rhône and the Bas-Rhin. During the summer of 1797 the *Gazette française* was stronger in the more traditional areas around the Gironde (including the Dordogne, Lot-et-Garonne and Haute-Garonne), the north-east, Normandy and the Rhône valley; but it had little support in the other traditional area of the Midi.[67]

As for the patriot press, letters to the *Révolutions de Paris* suggest that it was very much a northern newspaper in its first year, with strong support around Paris, in Normandy and the north-east, and readers too in the Gironde, the Rhône-et-Loire and some of the less populated departments of the centre, such as the Indre-et-Loire, the Cher, the Puy-de-Dôme, the Vienne and the Saône-et-Loire. Areas such as Britanny, the south-west, the Midi and the Rhône valley, on the other hand, are almost entirely absent. The *Patriote français*, again from readers' letters, made up for it somewhat in the Rhône valley, and was also strong in the Isère, the Pas-de-Calais and the Bas-Rhin, where military correspondents were active in all three cases. It also had readers in the Gironde, the Gard, the Vaucluse and the Bouches-du-Rhône, but almost none in the centre and west. The *Feuille villageoise* did, however, have readers in the centre, as well as in the Rhône valley, in the Gard and the Hérault, and also in Normandy; but it was weak in Alsace and Lorraine — where many priests would have spoken German anyway — and in Provence, where the survival of patois might have limited its appeal to the peasantry.[68]

The radical press of the terror and the Directory reveals just as varied a pattern. The *Journal de la montagne* sold 40 per cent of its copies in the Paris region, and 2 per cent to the armies and abroad. The remainder were mainly concentrated in a broad band running. from Normandy down to Burgundy, in the Rhône, the Isère and the Puy-de-Dome, in the northern and eastern frontier areas, and in the areas of defeated federalist revolt such as Bordeaux, Lyons, Toulon and Marseilles. Britanny was under-represented, for obvious political reasons, as was much of the west and south-west, along with Alsace. Lebois' *Ami du Peuple* shared most of these areas of strength, except for Normandy where it had few readers, and also had few subscribers in the west and the south-west, the centre, the north-east and Alsace. Babeuf's *Tribun du peuple*, on the other hand, had 60 per cent of its subscribers in Paris, and its fewer provincial subscribers concentrated in the scattered areas of the Nord and Pas-de-Calais, and Provence; and there were also some in the Saône-et-Loire, the Rhône, Mont Blanc, the Moselle, the Morbihan, the Dordogne, and the Seine-et-Marne. Readers' letters to the *Journal des hommes libres*, stretching over the period 1792–9, also shows strong support in the Nord and Pas-de-Calais, as well as in the Gironde, the Bouches-du-Rhône, the Var and the Drôme.[69]

Given the fragile nature of the evidence, it would be unwise to read too much into these analyses. The weight of urbanisation and literacy ensures that Paris, Lyons, Bordeaux, Marseilles and the north-east figure prominently, and that the Massif Central and much of the west are weak. Yet some conclusions can be drawn. Firstly, Parisian newspapers were read on a national scale, and were able to find a readership in distant and remote areas of the country. Secondly, the west and Britanny showed a marked preference for right-wing and royalist papers, particularly in the early phase of the revolution. Finally, many areas of the country show no marked preference for any particular political message: if Babeuf had many subscribers in the north-east, so too did many right-wing papers during the Directory. If the *Journal de la montagne* sold well in the Midi, so too did the *Gazette universelle* and the *Précurseur*. In areas of reasonable literacy there were sufficient people on the ground to ensure a readership for most shades of political opinion.

Sales figures in themselves are only rough guides to readership, for in the eighteenth century, even more so than today, one copy of a newspaper might pass through several hands as a result of group subscriptions, and the availability of newspapers in cafés, reading-rooms, or literary clubs. Throughout the eighteenth century, reading clubs, or *cabinets littéraires*, had become widespread in urban France, often organised by a bookseller, printer or café owner as a supplement to their major business. For a small monthly or annual subscription clients would have access to a small room, often heated, where books and journals would be available for consultation or borrowing. Nicolas Gerlache, for example, who patched together a precarious living in Metz in the 1770s from bookbinding, peddling and smuggling, ran a *cabinet littéraire* for journals and books which cost 3 *livres* per month and attracted a great deal of support from the officers in the city's garrison.[70] The bookseller Falcon in Grenoble, whose premises were to be the focal point of Jacobinism in the city once the revolution came, also ran one in the 1780s which cost the same as Gerlache's, but offered a reduced rate to readers who only wanted to consult newspapers of 4 *sols* per entry or 18 *livres* for the whole year. Falcon also allowed subscribers to borrow newspapers once the next issue had arrived.[71]

With the revolution Falcon's club, and many others, catered for the new political press, extending their range of publications. New reading-rooms also opened up. In Vannes, for example, the bookseller Bizette ran one which stocked all the major journals and brochures, with his daughter-in-law, Jeanne Mahé, in charge. During the terror interest was such such that crowds would gather in Bizette's shop as the time for the mail-coach drew near, and only those wearing the bonnet of liberty were allowed in.[72] In Chartres there were several premises, catering for some 200 clientele overall, including one in the Directory run by a local Jacobin journalist, Pierre Conard, which stocked over 20 Parisian papers in the autumn of 1799.[73]

Political clubs also had reading facilities, and particularly the Jacobin clubs, many of which relied heavily on newspapers for their news and opinion. Many of them arranged their meeting days to coincide with the arrival of the mail, and almost all of them had a part of their meetings set aside for the reading out of news and feature articles. Indeed, in the case of the smaller clubs, these sessions were often the only business done. Several larger clubs also had rooms in which the latest issues could be consulted in comfort, although theft was a recurrent problem, forcing many of them to stamp the papers that they received or, in some cases, chain them to wooden planks on tables. Several women's clubs, attached to provincial Jacobin clubs, also used newspapers heavily: one in Blois in the spring of 1792 specified newspaper sessions as one of its major purposes.[74] Many clubs also organised popular reading sessions for the poor, as did municipalities or individual activists, reading out extracts and explaining them in simple language. In Paris especially there were *colporteurs* and activists who read out papers on street corners, on bridges or in the Palais Royal, perched on stools or, in one case, equipped with a mobile rostrum.[75] In rural areas such sessions were more often organised by the juror priest, often after mass, or during the Directory by the local *commissaire* hopeful of gaining support for an unpopular regime.[76]

There were also less structured methods of diffusion. The young Stendhal's father, for example, was brought half a dozen papers every morning by the local postmaster, to read before they were delivered to subscribers. The grandfather, who suspected that the postmaster's generosity was prompted by the free food and drink that he always received, nevertheless took the opportunity to read out bits from them at the kitchen table to the rest of the family. Alternatively there are many instances of friends clubbing together to put up the cost of a single subscription, taken out in the name of one of them, then passing the paper around to each other when it arrived.[77]

Contemporary assessments of the impact of all this vary, but most suggest that there were around ten readers to every subscriber, which suggests that, at the height of the terror, over a million people read a newspaper every day. This was little consolation to journalists, who frequently complained that the practice of group subscriptions robbed them of sales. Some, such as the editor of the *Journal général de l'orléanais*, urged readers seriously to consider the inconvenience of the practice:

> The fact that a co-subscriber may live far away, or may forget to hand on the paper at the agreed time; the daily routine of having to pass it on, and the sheer annoyance that such a repetitive task can cause; the lack of interest in news which can be read only days after the event — all these problems disappear if you take out a personal subscription, and you can then read at your leisure, and share the enjoyment of it with the entire household at minimal cost.

The editor of a newspaper in Nîmes in Year V was, one suspects, more honest with himself and his readers when he bluntly asked them to desist from the practice: 'I would ask those whom it is my pleasure and duty to serve to please not lend their copies too much, so as not to reduce the number of my subscribers.'[78]

218

Nevertheless, despite these fears, there is ample evidence that the better-run papers were able to make handsome profits, although they are difficult to calculate because of the gaps in the records. Printing, editorial and administrative costs formed the main items of expenditure for any newspaper. Printing costs, as we have already seen, varied during the decade, but were certainly cheap in the early years. Editorial costs again varied between papers, depending on size and on the prestige of the editor. As for administrative costs, they were usually minimal on the smaller papers, where family or friends helped out with the task of folding and dispatching, but on larger papers could amount to some 5 or 10 per cent of total outlay.[79] On the revenue side, income came almost exclusively from subscriptions, paid on three-monthly, six-monthly or annual rates, and incorporating an extra charge to cover postal costs in the case of distant subscribers. The cost of a four-page daily newspaper between 1789 and 1792 was around 36 *livres* per year, although this rose slightly from the autumn of 1792 onwards, with costs. The only additional revenue came from advertising, but in contrast with the contemporary English press, French newspapers paid little attention to it. The provincial press of the *ancien régime* had justified its existence on its advertising role, and several papers gained a significant proportion of their revenue from it. The *Journal de Marseille*, for example, probably made 1,700 *livres* per year out of advertisements between 1789 and 1791, which represented some 18 per cent of its total income.[80]

Yet the principal revenue still came from subscriptions, and the tendency during the early years of the revolution was for many *Affiches* to reduce their advertising content as they switched to political news, and to rely increasingly on the new subscriptions generated by that switch. The *Journal universel* in Toulouse, for example, reduced its advertisement space after the summer of 1789, as did the *Journal général* in Orléans; while others, like the *Affiches du Maine*, published an advertising supplement to compensate for the space lost to politics, or like the *Journal de Lyon* and *Journal de Versailles*, an extra weekly copy. On the other hand, some never sacrificed commercial to political considerations, and others quickly reverted to a non-political role once politics became contentious. In all cases, however, the bulk of their money came from subscriptions rather than advertisements. Within the Parisian press, there were some that developed an advertising column or published separate advertising supplements. Yet the revenue that it generated was rarely anything other than icing on the cake, and many of the best-known papers, such as the *Patriote français* or the *Journal général de la cour et de la ville,* carried almost nothing except book announcements for their own publishers and friends. They existed for politics, and anything which used up the space that it required was unwelcome.

Even those newspapers which took advertisements tended to keep their rates comparatively low. The *Moniteur* was expensive, at 20 *sols* per line for the first ten lines, then 15 *sous* thereafter, but provincial papers usually charged about 2 *sous* per line, and many inserted advertisements free for worthy causes such as wet nurses, or domestic servants in search of employment. The *Annales Orléanaises, Journal du département de Loir et Cher* and *Corréspondance d'Indre-et-Loire* inserted all advertisements for subscribers free of charge.[81] As a result, contrary to English practice, advertisements were either peripheral to the paper's main purpose, or something designed to encourage sales rather than reduce price. Only one attempt was made during the whole decade to launch a paper that would be almost wholly dependent for its finance on advertising revenue, and — typically — it was done by Panckoucke in the winter of 1792–3 with the *Aviseur national.* It failed within months, however, because there was insufficient advertising to make it viable.[82] It was to be the July Monarchy before advertisements became revenue generators for the French press, and the reasons for this sharp difference with English practice appear to be related to both economic and political factors. France was economically less prosperous than England, and it was also less compact. Trade on a national scale had not developed to the same extent, and even under the Empire, advertisements in the Paris press were intended only for a Parisian audience. In the provinces, most papers had markedly lower circulations than their British counterparts, and so covered a smaller potential market. The economic instability of the revolution, with the collapse of colonial trade and the severe damage inflicted on the domestic market by emigration and war, aggravated these weaknesses.[83]

Yet it was still possible for a good newspaper to make a substantial profit. Amongst the provincial press, several sources suggest that the break-even figure for a paper, when a profit began to be possible, was about 300. Several papers struggled along for months and even years with circulations even lower than this, but usually at the cost of considerable personal sacrifice on the part of the owners, who sometimes even had a part-time job to help make ends meet. Clément, editor of the *Journal du département de l'Oise* during the terror, made ends meet by working as a lawyer's clerk, scribe, shopkeeper and stationer, while Alexandre, owner and printer of the Jacobin *Observateur de l'Yonne* during the Directory, claimed to make no profit at all.[84] Once the figure of 300 was exceeded, however, profits increased rapidly. The *Journal patriotique de l'Agenais*, a weekly paper whose sales in the three years between 1789 and 1792 peaked at 400, was able to return an annual profit of 1,000 *livres*, or 11 per cent of its annual income. The *Journal de Marseille*, on a similar circulation, probably did slightly better, with profits of around 2,500 *livres* per year, while the *Courrier de Strasbourg*, on a substantially larger circulation of 1,200 during the course of 1792, made a profit of around 15,000 *livres*, or 33 per cent of income. This suggests the advantages of scale, and matches the profits made by the *Courrier d'Avignon* in the dying years of the *ancien régime* which, on a circulation of just under 3,000, amounted to 18,880 *livres*, or 38.5 per cent of income.[85]

Obviously higher circulation figures brought in increased profits, and this benefited the Parisian press in particular. Calculations made by Laborie for the *Patriote français*, for example, suggest that, even assuming a somewhat low circulation of around 5,000 for it in 1790 and 1791, it probably made profits of over 100,000 *livres* per annum. On the opposite side of the spectrum, the *Gazette de Paris* made a profit of almost 25,000 *livres* per annum, or 23 per cent of its revenue, on the basis of 2,300 subscribers; and the *Ami du Roi* made some 88,000 *livres* each year on a circulation of just under 5,000. Calculations made for the *Feuille villageoise* give it annual profits of 24,800 *livres*, or 23 per cent of revenue, on a circulation of 10,000.[86] Camille Desmoulins, in the spring of 1790, noted that the *Révolutions de France et de Brabant* made 30,000 *livres* profit per year on a circulation of 3,000, while Gorsas' widow, after his death, claimed that her late husband had made an annual profit of 50,000 *livres* on his *Courrier*. Even allowing for exaggeration — for she was looking for compensation for the destruction of his presses in 1793 — this is in line with the figures given above for other papers, and suggests a comfortable margin.[87] Evidently the press could be a profitable affair, if well managed — a factor which adds a financial dimension to its growth during these years of success.

Selling the Finished Product

Notes

1. F. Furet and J. Ozouf, *Lire et écrire. L'alphabétisation des Français de Calvin à Jules Ferry* (Paris, 1977), Chapter 1.

2. *Corréspondance patriotique entre les citoyens qui ont été membres de l'Assemblée nationale ronstituants*. B.N. 8° Lc² 643)

3. *Journal de la municipalité, prospectus*; A.N. F⁷ 4589, plaq. 8, d. Bayard; *Moniteur*, 8 January 1792, pp. 55–6; A.N. AA⁴⁰, d. 1228: 'Mémoire pour M. Guillotin, 12 juin 1790'.

4. A.M. Bordeaux I 38, pièce 13.

5. M. Martin, *Les origines de la presse militaire en France à la fin de l'ancien régime et sous la révolution (1770–1799)* (Paris, 1974), pp. 111–12; A.D. Bas-Rhin L63; A.N. F¹⁸ 16, Gironde liv; A.D. Gironde 3L54, 21 *nivôse* V.

6. M. Kennedy, *The Jacobin clubs in the French Revolution* (Princeton, 1984), p. 56; M. Dommanget, 'Le symbolisme et proselytisme révolutionnaires à Beauvais et dans l'Oise. Les journaux patriotes', *A.h.r.f.*, VII (1930), pp. 46–7, 51.

7. F. Martin, *La révolution en province. Les jacobins au village* (Clermont-Ferrand, 1903), pp. 8, 12–13, 55, 59.

8. *Journal des amis de la constitution, prospectus*; *Journal des débats de la société des amis de la constitution*, no. 7, p. 4; Kennedy, *The Jacobin clubs*, pp. 67–72; H. Gough, 'Les Jacobins et la presse'. Le Journal de la Montagne (juin 1793–brumaire an II) in *Actes du Colloque Girondins et Montagnards (Sorbonne, 14 décembre 1975)* (Paris, 1980), pp. 270–1.

9. Kennedy, *The Jacobin clubs*, pp. 364–70; M. Kennedy, 'L''oracle des Jacobins des départements'': Jean-Louis Carra et ses ''Annales patriotiques'' ' in A. Soboul (ed.), *Actes du Colloque Girondins et Montagnards* (Paris, 1980), pp. 253–4.

10. Martin, *Les origines de la presse militaire*, Chapters IV, VII–IX; M. Martin, 'Journaux d'armées au temps de la Convention', *A.h.r.f.*, 210 (1972), pp. 592–605.

11. Marcel Dorigny, *Le Chronique du Mois ou les cahiers patriotiques (novembre 1791–juin 1793). Economie et politique dans un journal girondin* (Mémoire de maîtrise, Paris, 1972), p. 7.

12. *Moniteur*, 13 December 1791, p. 616; A.D. Hérault L893, 'Mémoire concernant les motifs qui engagent les négociants de Bedarieux à faire venir de Paris les papiers publics'.

13. A.N. C¹⁴⁵, C(1) 191, pièce 1; A.D. Puy-de-Dôme L6389; A.D. Seine-Maritime L304, pièce 40; *Moniteur*, x, 18 October 1791, p. 40.

14. *Journal patriotique*, 4 March 1790; *Journal de Versailles, Nouveau prospectus* (1790); *Journal patriotique du département de la Dordogne*, 22 May 1791, pp. 18–19; *Journal d'instruction populaire* (Sarlat). See also the aims of Louis Bablot for the *Observateur de la Marne* in 1790–1, cited in G. Clause, 'Le journalisme à Châlons-sur-Marne en 1790 et 1791', *Mémoires de la Société d'Agriculture, Commerce, Sciences et Arts du Département de la Marne*, 89 (1974), *passim*.

15. *Patriote du département de la Mayenne*, May 1792, pp. 8–11; 9 June 1792, pp. 91–4; 14 July 1792, pp. 171–7; 21 July 1792, pp. 188–92, etc. See also *Courrier du Midi*, xliii, 1 May 1792 and *Observateur du Midi*,

prospectus (1792): 'Juror priests in rural areas will find in it a way of converting their parishioners to a love of the revolution.'

16. Melvin Allen Edelstein, *La Feuille villageoise. Communication et modernisation dans les régions rurales pendant la révolution* (Paris, 1972). The restrictions of the rural market are plaintively outlined by an ailing depart-mental journal in the spring of 1792:

> It is only people in towns who read, and the reason is simple. Most newspapers are either too erudite or too dear for rural dwellers, who on the whole are less well off than those in towns, and until now have not had the chance of education. (*Journal du département du Loir et Cher*, vi, 20 April 1792, p. 42).

17. See Edelstein, *La Feuille villageoise*, pp. 31-4, 63-6.
18. R.B. Rose, *The making of the sans-culottes* (Manchester, 1983), pp. 97-116. For an example of reading sessions in provincial towns, designed to provide popular political education, see J.F. Reichardt, *Un Prussien en France en 1792* (Paris, 1892), pp. 114-16.
19. A.N. F^7 3448B, Thiébaut to Minister of Police, 4 *vendémiaire* VI; *Encyclopédie départementale des Bouches-du-Rhône* (Marseilles, 1914), VI, p. 564. See also a denunciation in January 1797 of the neo-Jacobin *Observateur du Midi* by its rival the *Journal de Marseille*: 'It is regrettable that this paper is widely read in taverns, where it is distributed free in order to influence public opinion.' (René Gérard, *Un journal de province sous la révolution. Le 'Journal de Marseille' de Ferréol de Beaugeard, 1781-1797* (Paris, 1964), p. 269). R. Monnier also notes the case of many former *sans-culotte* militants among subscribers to Babeuf's *Tribun du peuple*, including Jean Martin Valcret, of the section de Montreuil, who, when arrested in the winter of Year IV, had a collection of old papers in his apartment including Marat's *Ami du peuple*, Robespierre's *Défenseur* and Hébert's *Père Duchesne*: R. Monnier, 'De l'an III à l'an IX, les derniers sans-culottes', *A.h.r.f.*, 257 (1984), p. 395.
20. *Ami des citoyens*, 2 December 1791:

> . . . we are retaining the poster format as we think it to be the most useful, enabling the paper to be read by a very large number of people. This poster, placed at the gate of a village church can educate all its inhabitants, and as its price is so reasonable, every village can subscribe to one. (*Journal de la société populaire des amis de la constitution établie à Lyon*, 6 March 1791, p. 248).

21. D. Escamez, *La presse périodique à Toulouse de 1789 à 1794*, Mémoire de Maîtrise (Toulouse, 1969), pp. 13-14; A. Ronsin, *Les périodiques lorrains antérieurs à 1800* (Nancy, 1964), pp. 71-2; X. Maeght, *La presse dans le département du Nord sous la révolution française*, Thèse de troisième cycle (Lille, 1971), pp. 356-60.
22. E. Sullérot, *Histoire de la presse feminine en France des origines à 1848* (Paris, 1966), *passim*; Caroline Rimbault, 'La presse féminine de langue française au XVIIIe siècle. Production et diffusion' in *Centre d'études du XVIIIe siècle de l'Université de Lyon. Le Journalisme de l'Ancien Régime. Table Rode, Lyon, 1981)* Lyons, 1982), pp. 199-216.

23. A.N. F^7 3448B, Van Nuffel to Minister of Police, 6 *brumaire* VI. Later, during the Restoration, Roederer estimated starting costs at almost 100,000 *livres* over the initial three months, but this was for a substantial national paper, in the more difficult atmosphere of post-Napoleonic France: P.-L. Roederer, *Oeuvres du comte P.-L. Roederer*, 8 vols (Paris, 1853–9), VIII, pp. 302ff., 317.

24. A.N. V^1 552; *Journal général de l'orléanais*, 3 July 1789, p. 121; 17 July, p. 129; Musée Calvet Ms. 5207, pièce 109; M. Albert, *La Gazette de Paris et du Rozoi*, Diplôme d'Études Supérieurs (Paris, 1959), p. 27; A. Vingtrinier, *Histoire des journaux de Lyon depuis leur origine jusqu'à nos jours* (Lyons, 1852), pp. 58–75; V.M. Daline, *Gracchus Babeuf à la veille et pendant la Révolution, 1785–1794* (Moscow, 1976), p. 58. Roederer was pessimistic on the value of prospectuses: 'Newspaper proprietors just will not listen when you tell them that 25,000 copies of a prospectus will get less than 25 subscribers . . .' (Roederer, *Oeuvres du comte*, VII, p. 315); yet, for the occasional customer, a prospectus could be decisive: see a letter written to Lebois, editor of the *Ami du peuple*, in 1795: 'A prospectus has just fallen into my hands, and because of its spirit and excellent views . . . I am sending you 15 *livres* for three months subscription.' (A.N. F^7 4286).

25. See, for example, *Journal du département de la Haute-Vienne*, ix, 10 *brumaire* II, p. 76; or a letter from a bookseller in Montreuil-sur-Mer to the editor of the *Courrier extraordinaire* in August 1797: 'One of my friends was giving up the *Gazette des Campagnes* and asked my advice on what to take instead. I remembered your journal, which I saw recently, and advised him to take it.' For the range of publications that a provincial bookseller could handle, see *Journal général de l'orléanais*, 1 January 1790.

26. A.N. F^7 3445 (Jullien to Frasans, 1 *thermidor* V); A.N. F^7 3446 (correspondence of *pluviôse* and *ventôse* V).

27. A.M. Bordeaux I 38, pièce 22; *Journal patriotique du département de la Dordogne*, 16 January 1791, p. 32; A.D. Puy-de-Dôme, L6389; A.D. Hérault, L1083; A.D. Seine-Maritime L304, pièces 23–4, 33–5.

28. A.N. F^7 4589 plaq. 8; A.N. AA^{42}, plaq. 5, d. 1325; A.N. AA^{44}, plaq. 5, d. 1342. See also the case of Paul Claude, arrested on 3 September 1789 for the contents of a Bulletin that he had published, in A.N. Y 10001.

29. Roederer, *Oeuvres du comte*, VII, pp. 318–9; A.N. F^7 3448B, Rebmann to Minister of Police, 28 *frimaire* VI. M. Tourneux, *Bibliographie de l'histoire de Paris pendant la révolution française*, 5 vols (Paris, 1900–13), II, p. 528; see also the case of Renaud, printer of the *Corréspondance politique, littéraire et commerciale*, who, in *vendémiaire* VI sent free copies to 150 selected people, in an unsuccessful attempt to build up the paper's clientele (A.N. F^7 3448B, Renaud to Minister of Police, 28 *frimaire* VI).

30. A. Cabanis, *La presse sous le Consulat et l'Empire* (Paris, 1975), p. 129.

31. *Éclaireur du peuple* iii, 2 *germinal* IV, p. 8; E. Fleury, *Camille Desmoulins et Roch Marcandier*, 2 vols (Paris, 1952), II, pp. 337, 346. The street prices of papers varied according to size and length. The *Père Duchesne* sold for 8 *sols*, the *Ami du peuple* for 3 *sols*, the *Journal patriotique de l'Agenais* for 3 *sols*, and the *Feuille rhémoise* in 1795 for 2 *sols*.

32. For the impact of *colporteurs* in ruining public reputations, see Jean-Sylvain Bailly, *Mémoires d'un témoin de la révolution* (Slatkine Reprints: Geneva, 1975), II, p. 239; see also the complaints of Guillaume Louis Lefèvre against

Momoro's *Moniteur patriote* in December 1789: 'The publicity spread with such malice . . . by this newspaper, which was proclaimed and sold yesterday on the streets of Paris, prevented the plaintiff from leaving his own home, because he learnt that he was threatened with a public hanging.' (A.N. Y10870). For details of the legislation restricting *colporteurs*, see E. Hatin., *Manuel théorique et pratique de la liberté de la presse* (Paris, 1868), pp. 39–41 and for their importance for sales, *Le Rôdeur français*, 5, (undated): 'And, as hawkers alone can make a newspaper successful, and they demand a summary of contents at the top of each paper, we have had to cede to their demands . . . and copy the example of other Parisian journalists.'

33. See Roederer, *Oeuvres du comte*, VII, p. 317 for subscriber fidelity. It is doubtful, however, that such fidelity existed in the early stage of the revolution, for Mirabeau lost 1,500 subscribers to the *Courrier de Provence* rapidly, in the winter of 1789–90, because of distribution problems (J. Bénétruy, *L'Atelier de Mirabeau* (Paris, 1961), p. 273).

34. *le Citoyen surveillant*, 5, 10 February 1791, p. 80; *Affiches du Maine*, 27 September 1790, p. 4.

35. *Folies du matin*, 12 November 1790; *Moniteur*, 1 August 1791, p. 276; *Courrier national*, 15 July 1789, p. 1.

36. Maeght, *La presse*, pp. 122–31; Louis Lenain, *La poste de l'ancien France, des origines à 1791* (Arles, 1965), p. 413; *Journal général de l'orléanais*, 25 December 1789, 225. Delivery charges were usually small: see G. Clause, 'La société populaire de Châlons-sur-Marne vue à travers son journal (floréal an II–vendémiaire an III, avril–septembre 1794), *Mémoires de la Société d'Agriculture, Commerce, Sciences et Arts du Département de la Marne*, 84 (1969), p. 137; Albert, *La Gazette de Paris*, p. 27.

37. *Affiches de Dauphiné*, 13 August 1789; *le Citoyen surveillant*, 5, 20 February 1791, 80; *Courrier d'Avignon*, 24 March 1793, p. 281.

38. *Journal patriotique du département de la Dordogne*, 16 January 1791, p. 1.

39. See *Journal révolutionnaire de Toulouse*, xlix, 23 *ventôse* II, p. 196.

40. *Courier française. Annonce importante* (December 1789); *Courrier du Midi*, 1 May 1792, p. 373.

41. *Défenseur de la vérité*, 9 February, 1793, p. 104; G. Thuillier, 'Parent l'aîné et le Journal de la Nièvre en l'an VI', *Mémoires de la Société Académique du Nivernais*, LIV (1967), p. 55; M. Lescure, *La presse périodique à Toulouse sous la révolution, de 1794 à 1800*, Diplôme de maîtrise d'histoire (Toulouse, 1969–70), pp. 80–1. See also complaints about the *Nouvelles politiques et Annales universelles* in A.N. F^7 3445, and of the *Gazette française* in A.N. F^7 6239A.

42. A.N. BB^{30} 162, d. 3.

43. A. Fribourg, 'Le club des Jacobins en 1790. D'après de nouveaux documents', *La Révolution Française*, LVIII, p. 514–8 *Courrier extraordinaire*, 8 May 1790, p. 8, and 25 June 1790, p. 8.

44. A.N. F^7 4696 d. 1, pièces 8–10; P. Caron, 'Une organisation de journal en l'an II', *La Révolution Française*, 85 (1932), pp. 80–2.

45. A. Debidour, *Recueil des actes du Directoire exécutif*, 4 vols I, pp. 313–4; A.N. F^{18} 21 Seine, liii, liv, lvi, lix.

46. B.H.V.P. Ms. 728; A.N. F^7 3448B, *administration municipale* of Clermont-Ferrand to Minister of Police, 18 *vendémiaire* VI; *administration centrale* of the Hérault to Minister of Police, 8 *nivose* VI; *commissaire près*

l'Isère to Minister of Police, 8 *frimaire* VI.

47. L.Say, 'Bertin l'ainé et Bertin de Vaux', *Le livre du centenaire du Journal des débats, 1787–1799*, (Paris, 1889), pp. 19–27; A.N. F⁷ 3448B (letter of *commissaire près l'Oise*, 23 *vendémiaire* VI).

48. A.N. F⁷ 3446; A.N. F⁷ 3449, *commissaire près l'administration municipalę de Grenoble* to Minister of Police, 1 *germinal* VI.

49. A.N. F⁷ 3449: 'Rapport au Directoire exécutif' (undated):

> The decision was aimed not only at increasing the profits of the postal service, but also at taking away from *chouan* journals the advantage which they had over other papers in arriving early. For this in itself attracted people who wanted the most recent news and increased their readership at the expense of sensible public opinion.

See also the similar comments of Bailleul to La Revellière Lépeaux, on 2 *nivose* VII, in A.N. F⁷ 3450.

50. A. Cabanis, *La presse*, 147, 320–2. Pierre Albert, Gilles Feyel and Jean-François Picard, *Documents pour l'histoire de la presse nationale aux XIXe et XXe siècles* (Paris, undated), pp. 6–9.

51. C. Bellanger (ed.), *Histoire générale de la presse française. Tome I. Des origines à 1814* (Paris, 1969), pp. 334–7; Gérard, *Un journal de province*, p. 64.

52. *Journal général de l'orléanais*, 203 (1791), p. 827; A.D. Bas-Rhin, 50L 10; Maeght, 248. For the more doubtful claim of the *Ami des principes* in Angers, see E. Quéruau-Lamérie, 'Notice sur les journaux d'Angers pendant la révolution', *Revue de l'Anjou*, nouvelle série, 24 (1892), p. 314.

53. Gérard, *Un journal de province*, pp. 64, 67, 195; A.N. F⁷ 3449; Lescure, *La presse périodique*, p. 84; M. Berthier, *Le Clairvoyant. Étude d'un journal révolutionnaire grenoblois, 1797–1800*, T.E.R. (Grenoble, 1968), p 20; A.D. Gironde 14L 23, 'Affaire Lacombe'.

54. R. Marquant, 'Aux origines de la presse agenaise: le "Journal patriotique de l'Agenais", 1789–1793', *Revue de l'Agenais*, 1945–7, p. 41; A.N. F⁷ 3448B, Durand to Directory, 5 *frimaire* VI; Thuillier, 'Parent l'aîné', p. 55; *Journal du département de Maine-et-Loire*, 3ᵉ trimestre, no. 2, pp. 47–8; *Feuille hebdomadaire de la ville de l'Orient*, 1 April 1790, p. 58, and 27 May, p. 176; R. Jaquel, 'Euloge Schneider en Alsace', *A.h.r.f.*, 9 (1932), p. 23.

55. S. Tucoo-Chala, *Charles-Joseph Panckoucke et la librairie française, 1736–1798* (Paris and Pan, 1978) p. 220 ff.

56. A. Tuetey, *Répertoire général des sources manuscrites de l'histoire de Paris pendant la révolution française*, 11 vols (Paris, 1890–1914), II, pp. 502–3; E. Hatin, *Histoire politique et littéraire de la presse française*, 8 vols (Paris, 1859–61), IV, p. 456; *Journal général de l'orléanais*, 40, 2 October 1789, pp. 175–6; Tucoo-Chala, *Charles-Joseph Panckoucke*, pp. 220–3; A.N. AA⁴⁰ d. 1228, letter of Saint-Martin, 12 July 1790, and of Étienne Feuillant, 12 January 1792; *Journal de la ville de Paris*, prospectus (undated).

57. G. Villacèque, *Les révolutions de Paris. Journal patriote 1789–1790*, D.E.S. (Toulouse, 1961), p 28; *Histoire générale de la presse française*, i, p. 452; Anon., *Correspondance inédite de Camille de Desmoulins, député à la Convention nationale* (Paris, 1836), pp. 49–51; G. Walter, *Marat* (Paris, 1933), p. 199; J.P. Gallais, *Catastrophe du club infernal et sa dénonciation par l'universel d'Audouin* (undated), p. 18; Edelstein, *Le Feuille villageoise*, p. 68.

58. A. Laurens, *Les Actes des Apôtres. Journal contre-révolutionnaire, 1789-1790*, Diplôme des Études Supérieures (Toulouse, 1963), p. 142; J.-P. Bertaud, *Étude des journaux: l'Ami du Roi de Royou, l'Ami du Roi de Montjoye*, D.E.S. (Paris, 1958-9), p. 45; Tuetey, *Répertoire général*, II, p. 63; Albert, *La Gazette de Paris*, pp. 8-9.

59. A.N. W²⁹² no. 204, 3ᵉ partie, pièce 19; Gough, 'Les Jacobins et la presse', p. 288; F. Gendron, *La jeunesse dorée. Episodes de la révolution française* (Quebec, 1979), p. 272; P. Laborie, *Étude sur le Patriote français. Journal libre, impartial et national*, Diplôme d'études supérieures (Toulouse, 1959-60), p. 20.

60. A.N. F¹⁸ 10A plaq. 1 d. 4.

61. *Moniteur*, xxvii, 2 nivôse IV, p. 13; xxxiii, 8 nivôse IV, p. 59; J.D. Popkin, *The right-wing press*, pp. 195-6; Cabanis, *La presse*, pp. 145-6.

62. J. Godechot, 'The origins of mass communication media. The coverage of the French press during the French Revolution', *Gazette. International Journal of the Science of the Press*, no. 2 (1962), pp. 81-9; for examples of analyses based on readers' letters, see Laborie, *Étude sur la Patriote français*, pp. 49-66; and Villacèque, *Les révolutions de Paris*, pp. 184-99.

63. Albert, *La Gazette de Paris*; Bertaud, *Amis du Roi*, pp. 57-8; Popkin, *The right-wing press*, pp. 75-7.

64. Villacèque, *Les révolutions de Paris*, pp. 196-200; Laborie, *Étude sur le Patriote français*, pp. 63-5; Edelstein, *Feuille villageoise*, pp. 47-56; Gough, 'Les Jacobins et la presse', pp. 291-5; M. Fajn, 'The circulation of the French press during the French Revolution: the Case of R.F. Lebois' L'Ami du peuple and the royalist *Gazette française*', *English Historical Review*, lxxxvii (1972), pp. 100-2; A. Soboul, 'Personnel sectionnaire et personnel babouviste' in *Paysans, sans-culottes et Jacobins* (Paris, 1966), pp. 287-93.

65. Bertaud, *Étude des Journaux*, pp. 46-50; Albert, *Le Gazette de Paris*, pp. 10-11; P. Bouju, *Un journal contre-révolutionnaire en 1791-1792. La Rocambole des Journaux* (Diplôme d'Études, Paris, 1945), p. 28; Popkin, *The right-wing press*, pp. 68-72, 78.

66. See above, pp. 207-9.

67. Popkin, *The right-wing press*, pp. 78-9.

68. Villacèque, *Les révolutions de Paris*, pp. 182-96; Laborie, *Étude sur le Patriote français*, pp. 50-61; Edelstein, *La Feuille villageoise*, pp. 70-1.

69. Gough, 'Les Jacobins et la presse', pp. 289-90; Soboul, 'Personnel sectionnaire', pp. 284-5; Fajn, 'The circulation of the French press', pp. 103-4; M. Fajn *The Journal des hommes libres de tous les pays, 1792-1800* (The Hague-Paris, 1975), pp. 160-7.

70. R. Darnton, 'Underground booksellers in the ancien régime' in E. Hinrichs, E. Schmitt and R. Vierhaus (eds), *Vom Ancien Regime zur Franzosischen Revolution* (Gottingen, 1978), pp. 442-51.

71. *Cabinet politique et littéraire ou Catalogue des Journaux et autres ouvrages périodiques qui se donnent à lire par abonnement* (Grenoble, 1789): B.M. Grenoble V7746.

72. J.-L. Debauve, 'Deux aspects du commerce à Vannes à la fin du XVIIIe siècle', *Bulletin de la Société Polymathique de Morbihan*, 1957-8, pp. 70-1.

73. M. Jusselin, 'Chambres de lecture à Chartres pendant la révolution', *Bulletin de la société Archéologique d'Eure-et-Loire*, 1963, pp. 221-8;

B.M. Chartres, R 32/5.

74. M. Kennedy, *The Jacobin clubs*, pp. 55-6; Dommanget, 'Le symbolisme', p. 41ff.

75. J.F. Reichardt, *Un Prussien en France en 1792* (Paris, 1892), pp. 114-16; C. Brelot, *Besançon révolutionnaire* (Paris, 1966), p. 126; Tuetey, *Répertoire générale*, II, nos. 1420, 1662, 1867, 1909, 2316, 2628.

76. A.N. F^{18} Oise, 19, lxiv; F^{18} Yonne, 23, clxxxvi; F^{18} Eure, 15, lxxxvi; Edelstein, *La Feuille villageoise*, pp. 63-6.

77. Stendhal, *Vie de Henri Brulard* (Paris, 1954), pp. 110-11, 183-4.

78. *Journal général de l'orléanais. Second Avis* (1790); *Journal des Moeure*, 12 nivose V.

79. There is a great variation in figures: the total costs of the *Gazette de France* in 1793 were 57,343 *livres*, of which printing alone accounted for 44,454 *livres* (A.N. F^{10} d. 66); the budget of the *Courrier d'Avignon* in 1787, on the other hand, shows printing costs to have been 11,100 *livres* out of a total budget of 42, 200 *livres*; the *Ami du Roi*, in 1791, spent close to 25,000 *livres* on printing out of 55,000 *livres* total expenditure (R. Moulinas, *L'imprimerie, la librairie et la presse à Avignon au xviiie siècle* (Grenoble, 1974), pp. 357-8; J.-P. Bertaud, *Les Amis du Roi. Journaux et journalistes royalistes en France de 1789. à 1792* (Paris, 1984), pp. 49-50.

80. Gérard, *Un journal de province*, p. 69; see also *Feuille hebdomadaire*, 3 January 1781, pp. 3-4: 'Les Affiches de la généralité de Limoges doivent, ainsi que les Affiches des autres provinces, leur existence à la nécéssité des Avis divers pour l'utilité commune'.

81. Gérard, *Un journal de province*, p. 69. The *Journal patriotique de Grenoble* charged a flat rate of 12 *sous* for house and property sales, 9 *sous* for property rentals and the sale of vehicles of horses, 6 *sous* for small objects. The *Journal du département de la Haute-Vienne* charged only 4 *sous* for any advertisement, but was subsidised by its *société populaire*. For free advertising, see *Annales orléanaises*, 4 March 1790, p. 323; *Journal du département de Loir et Cher, prospectus*, p. 4; *Corréspondance d'Indre et Loire*, 19 January 1791, p. 28.

82. Tucoo-Chala, *Charles-Joseph Panckoucke*, pp. 473-5.

83. Cabanis, *La presse*, pp. 148-9; for the role of advertising in the contemporary English press, see Ivon Asquith, 'Advertising and the press in the late eighteenth and early nineteenth centuries: James Perry and the Morning Chronicle 1790-1821', *Historical Journal*, XVIII (1975), pp. 703-24.

84. Dommanget, 'Le symbolisme', pp. 46-7, 51; A.N. F^7 3448B, letter of 27 *floréal* VI.

85. Marquant, 'Aux origines de la presse agenaise', p. 43; Gérard, *Un journal de province*, p. 193; A.D. Bas-Rhin, 50L 10; Moulinas, *L'imprimerie*, pp. 357-9.

86. Laborie, *Étude sur le Patriote français*, pp. 35-6; Albert, *La Gazette de Paris*, pp. 38-9; Bertaud, *Les Ami du Roi*, p. 55; Edelstein, *La Feuille villageoise*, pp. 327-9. See also the suggestion that Barère made 3,000 *livres* profit per month on his *Point du jour* in 1790-1, cited in Leo Gershov, *Bertrand Barère. A reluctant terrorist* (Princeton, 1962), p. 71.

87. J.-P. Bertaud, *Camille et Lucille Desmoulins. Un couple dans la tourmente* (Paris, 1986), p. 90; A. Soboul, 'La Fortune de Gorsas', *A.h.r.f.*, XXIII (1951), pp. 183-5.

Conclusion

Napoleon Bonaparte's attitude towards the press was evident from
his career as an army commander, and reflected his authoritarian
views on military and political discipline. He feared its power and
independence, was determined to use it to reinforce his own authority, and quickly brought it under strict governmental control.[1]
On 1 *frimaire* Year VIII the Ministry of Police stopped all co-
operation with editors, so cutting off a major source of minor and
non-political news stories that filled the 'Nouvelles et faits divers'
columns of many papers, and the new constitution of Year VIII
differed pointedly from its predecessors of 1791, 1793 and 1795 in
making no mention of press freedom. Most significant of all was
the decree of 27 *nivôse* Year VIII, which took 60 named Parisian
papers off the market, forbade any of them to reappear under a
different title, and obliged the remaining 13 to register their details
of ownership with the Ministry of Police. Several of them were in
turn closed down over the next three years, while from 1805 onwards
a number of government-enforced mergers reduced numbers still
further. In 1805 too prior censorship returned, with the appointment
of a censor to the *Journal des débats*, and it was extended to the
remainder of the Parisian and provincial press by the end of 1807.
Finally, in 1811, the political press in Paris was reduced to four
titles, and the property in them taken over by the government, to
be distributed amongst its loyal supporters as patronage.

Meanwhile, the provincial press was also brought under control, for although the decree of 27 *nivôse* enforced no closures on
it, several titles were shut down over the following three years for
articles which offended the susceptibilities of their local Prefect or
the Minister of Police. This did not, however, reduce its overall
numbers in the same way as in Paris, partly because several prefects
launched their own news-sheets, to provide administrative news to
their local populations in the early years of the Consulate, and partly
because the new Code of Civil Procedure of 1807, which required
certain judgements and decisions to be published in the local press,
encouraged the launch of informational and advertising newspapers,
similar to the *Affiches* of the *ancien régime*. By 1814, as a result, there
were almost as many provincial newspapers as there had been in
1799, but the crucial difference was that prior censorship ensured
that their political independence was a thing of the past, and that

the political articles that they did publish could only be taken from the columns of the *Moniteur* which, since 1800, was an official government newspaper.[2]

Napoleon therefore squeezed all capacity for independent criticism out of the press and compressed it back into its dessicated *ancien-régime* shape. No title could appear without prior permission, and no article without prior approval by the censor. Political journalism, as the revolution had known it, vanished. Yet Napoleon's fall from power brought no immediate relief. The Charter granted by Louis XVIII on his initial return in 1814 contained an article guaranteeing press freedom, and when Bonaparte made his brief Hundred Day return in the spring of 1815, he made no attempt to revive controls. However, censorship did return with the Second Restoration after the Battle of Waterloo, when, despite the Charter, the need for permission prior to publication was reintroduced, along with financial restraints such as stamp tax and caution money. Censorship rapidly became one of the bones of contention between successive ministers and both liberal and ultra opposition, and adjustments to it a stock government response to political unrest. Nevertheless, it stayed in effect until the regime fell in 1830.

The July Monarchy promptly abolished prior censorship, but retained financial controls and progressively restricted editorial freedom through legislation punishing criticism of the monarchy. This culminated in the law of 9 September 1835 which increased the caution money required, and defined a whole range of press offences which included offensive comment on the monarchy, criticism of the Charter or use of the word 'republican'. Nevertheless, a political press did develop which played an important part in political life for much of the remainder of the century. The revolution of 1830 began from the offices of the *National*, while the list of ministers in the provisional government of February 1848 was drawn up in the offices of the *National* and the *Réforme*, and contained the chief editors of two of the leading republican newspapers, Armand Marrast and Ferdinand Flocon. Napoleon III then quickly brought the curtain down again in 1851, but censorship was progressively relaxed in the 1860s, and the fall of the regime in 1870 restored a degree of freedom that was finally to be enshrined in the press law of 1881.[3] As a result, politicians of all shades became accustomed once more to using the press as a medium for political debate. Guizot, Royer-Collard and Victor Cousin worked together on the *Archives philosophiques*, Benjamin Constant wrote in the *Minerve*, and Châteaubriand aired ultra criticism of liberals and ministers alike in the *Conservateur*. Charles de Rémusat, Saint-Marc Girardin and Charles Nodier brought intellectual style to the profession, and Adolphe Thiers launched his long political career in the columns of the *Constitutionnel*. As Balzac noted in 1840: 'Public opinion is manufactured in Paris; it is made with ink and paper.'[4]

As the political consequences of the revolution confirmed the central role of the press in politics, so economic change began to transform its conditions of production. The Koenig steam press, imported from England during the 1820s, increased printing speeds to 2,000 sheets per hour, and 40 years later, in the 1860s, new rotary presses boosted the hourly figure to over 16,000. By the end of the century, that figure had increased still further, helped by innovations in typesetting and the spread of electrical power, and the circulation levels of the major Parisian dailies began to exceed the one million mark. Meanwhile, the spread of the telegraph in the 1820s, the establishment of the Havas news agency in the 1830s, and the building of the railways during the July Monarchy and Second Empire, accelerated the gathering of news and the distribution of papers. In addition, the beginnings of industrialisation and steady economic growth from the 1830s onwards opened the way to large-scale advertising and commercial exploitation of the press's potential, initiated by Emile Girardin. The extension of the franchise also brought more people into the political net and extended the potential readership to almost the entire adult population by the end of the century. The old wooden hand-operated press, the days of distribution by horse and carriage, and role of lone editor writing out the contents of an entire newspaper by hand, had almost vanished into the mists of time.[5]

From the perspective of the nineteenth century, therefore, the contribution of the revolution to the development of the newspaper press in France was political rather than technical. It brought journalism in from the cold that it had endured under the *ancien régime* and introduced it to the warmer political world that dawned with the Declaration of the Rights of Man. For the first time the press was made a part of everyday political life and, as a result, had a direct impact on the revolution. It opened up political careers, for example, on both the national and local stage to men whose lives might otherwise have been lived out in comparative obscurity. The rise of Brissot or Desmoulins, Carra or Gorsas, Fréron or Marat, owed everything to their talent as journalists, and was matched by many other careers at the lower level of municipal or departmental politics. Journalism became one of several recruiting grounds for the new political élite, enabling literate and ambitious men to 'hold the tablets', in Desmoulin's classical phrase, and acquire a political reputation overnight.

Visitors to France had remarked on the influence and esteem of writers and *philosophes* before the revolution; both these attributes now passed to journalists, whose role in politics now mirrored the role of criticism that they had fulfilled in more literary and academic pursuits. Lacretelle, referring in his memoirs to his period as political editor of the *Nouvelles politiques* in 1796–8, noted that it was a time when he ' . . . enjoyed a certain consideration . . . and . . . a greater reputation than I had ever acquired by more important, more literary works'.[6] Journalism, in other words, had become a profession, which employed many hundreds of people and had become an integral part of political life. As such it had carved out for itself an influence unmatched across the Channel, where the longer habit of open political debate had left the press less room for influence. This was something that was to remain during the nineteenth century, as the careers of men such as Guizot or Thiers suggest, and which was to be remarked on by Walter Bagehot during a visit to France in 1852. Noting the comparative lack of influence of journalists in England, he noted:[7]

> Here a man who begins his life by writing in the newspapers has an appreciable chance of coming to be Minister of Foreign Affairs. The class of public writers is the class from which the equivalent of Lord Aberdeen, Lord Palmerston or Lord Grenville will most likely be chosen.

The second aspect of press influence was a consequence of this — namely, the role of the press in providing news and comment on political affairs. Newspapers provided this in a more extensive, direct and continuous way than any other propaganda medium ever could: extensive because the larger Parisian dailies had a national circulation, and the more successful local papers a regional one; direct because, as we have seen, the vast majority of newspapers were sent directly to subscribers, from whom they passed into the hands of friends and colleagues; and continuous because their regular publication enabled them to publish a constant flow of news and comment, dealing with events as and when they unfolded. This was something that pamphlets, broadsheets and engravings could never do; and neither could songs, music, the theatre, or even political clubs. Moreover, it was something that contemporaries noted. Brissot, for example, claimed in the spring of 1789 that a newspaper was ' . . . instantaneous in its effect, and is read everywhere; it is even read by the less well off. One hundred thousand people may read a newspaper, while scarcely a hundred will look at a brochure.' Charles Lacretelle was also certain of its influence during the thermidorean reaction, noting that ' . . . people may argue that I am placing too much stress on the influence of the periodical press, but I do not believe that it ever made itself so powerfully felt as in this period . . . '[8] La Harpe, at the same time, argued that ' . . . newspapers have become a daily necessity and, when their editors are honest and enlightened, a force for freedom, as well as a source of history.' In addition, as late as 1799, a deputy in the Council of Five Hundred noted, with some exaggeration, that ' . . . some twenty Parisian journalists speak every day to three million of their fellow Frenchmen'.[9] The readiness of successive governments to subsidise newspapers and publish their own, and the way in which Jacobin clubs and constitutional circles, army generals and civilian administrators, all did the same, suggests that journalists were not alone in their estimate of their own importance. The press had acquired a role in information and the formation of opinion which, despite the emergence of new media in our own century, it still retains.

It is nevertheless difficult to isolate the influence of the press from that of other forces at work in the revolution, such as hunger, habit, speeches, pamphlets, friendship or sheer accident. No single event in the revolution was caused exclusively by the newspaper press, but a great many of them were influenced by it in some way. It played virtually no role, for example, in the immediate events that led to the fall of the Bastille in July 1789, but the emergence of radical newspapers in the following weeks, with titles such as the *Révolutions de Paris*, the *Patriote français* and the *Ami du peuple*, helped to encourage and co-ordinate the emergence of a democratic movement in many of the Parisian districts. Certainly, the march to Versailles on 5 October had been preceded by a long campaign in the radical press against the royal veto and in favour of the transfer of the court to Paris. The events at the banquet of the royal bodyguard on 2 October, when the national cocade was trampled underfoot and the Queen received with lyrical enthusiasm, were reported by Gorsas in his *Courrier* on the following day, soon spread to other papers, and prompted the demand of immediate action. Thus, the most detailed analysis of the march of the market women from Paris to Versailles, to fetch the royal family back to Paris reaches the conclusion that ' . . . the press not only prepared the disturbances and made them possible, but also gave them their shape and purpose.'[10]

The influence of the radical press remained strong in Paris in the following two years, although not in the provinces where its tone proved too polemical for most readers, and played an important part in spreading the democratic propaganda of the Cordeliers club. Many of its editors were active in the emerging *sociétés populaires*, encouraged artisans and journeymen in their political apprenticeship, and played a leading role in the debate over republicanism at the time of the flight to Varennes.[11] Nor was the radical press alone, for the right-wing press reflected the various strands within royalism from the spring of 1790 onwards and, by its threats of revenge and ominous rumblings of the consequences of counter-revolution, gave comfort to conservatives as well as reinforcing radical fears of the omnipresence of plots and betrayal.[12] Simultaneously, at a more humble level, departmental papers helped to encourage the ideals of moderate revolution and to foster some sense of local identity in a radically restructured country.

As the revolutionary consensus crumbled from the autumn of 1791 onwards, the press continued to be a sounding board of political opinion. The crucial question of war, for example, was argued out on the floor of the Jacobin club and the Legislative Assembly, where Louis XVI came on 20 April to announce his fateful assent. Yet it was also popularised by a powerful press campaign in papers such as the *Patriote français* and *Annales patriotiques*, which carried the argument throughout the country.[13] Once war was declared the growing hostility towards the monarchy amongst Jacobins and *sans-culottes* was reflected in both the Parisian and provincial press, contributing to the mood that primed the *journée* of 10 August and the storming of the Tuileries. Newspapers also played a major role in the bitter struggle between Girondins and Montagnards in the National Convention during the following winter, and the undoubted influence of the Girondin press contributed to Jacobin fears of their influence in the country at large. This lay behind the attacks on Gorsas' and Condorcet's presses in early March of 1793, and finally led to the closure of the major Girondin newspapers after the *journée* of 2 June had forced their editors and owners out of political life. The shadow of suspicion soon spread to other papers, and indeed to all independent political comment, but for several months the press continued to play an important role in the factional struggles within Jacobinism. It was used by the *Enragés* over the summer of 1793 to press home their demands for more terror and economic reform, by Hébert in his campaigns for a new revolutionary government and for dechristianisation during the autumn of 1793, and by the *Indulgents* in their attempt during the winter months of Year II to regain the political initiative.[13]

After Robespierre's death the rapidity and extent of the thermidorean reaction was to some extent helped by the collapse of press censorship, which left pamphlets and newspapers free to hammer home the themes of revenge, anti-Jacobinism and the need for social and political order. The growth of a healthy right-wing press contributed to the consolidation of a new republican right which, in an ambiguous alliance with crypto-royalists, formed the political majority in the country for much of the Directory. Yet in the early years of the Directory the press reflected the wide range of the political spectrum, from the babouvist and Jacobin left to the royalist right, and there is ample evidence to show that readers chose their paper according to their political preference. Indeed, one recent study of the right-wing press during the period suggests that it had by now lost its ability to influence political events, largely because readers fitted their reading to their beliefs, and served instead largely to further the careers of its editors or provide readers with details on specific events. It probably reinforced views rather than creating them. Nevertheless, the conviction of contemporaries on all sides that newspapers could still have an effect on the uncommitted and influence the result of elections suggests that many floating voters could still be swayed one way or the other.[14] However, once the *fructidor* coup had obliterated both press and electoral freedom, its powers to do even this were strictly limited.

If the press was rarely the major factor in political or social upheaval, it nevertheless always had an influence of some kind, and at times such as the autumn of 1789, the summer of 1793 or the winter of 1794–5, it could be very influential indeed. Moreover, throughout the decade it was one of the more important channels through which fact, opinion and information flowed to a national audience. Used predominantly by the literate, it nevertheless also had an impact amongst the politically motivated illiterate, through public reading sessions and personal contact, and provided them with the rudiments of a political education. It therefore reflected the diverse strands of public opinion and, at the same time, helped to form them. It had made its entry into political life and, once some semblance of political liberty returned to the country with the Restoration of 1815, neither press nor politics would ever be the same again.

Notes

1. M. Martin, *Les origines de la presse militaire en France à la fin de l'ancien régime et sous la révolution (1770–1799)* (Paris, 1974), Chapters VIII and IX.

2. A. Cabanis, *La presse sous le Consulat et l'Empire* (Paris, 1975); R.B. Holtman, *Napoleonic propaganda* (Baton Rouge, 1950), pp. 44–75; C. Bellanger (ed.), *Histoire générale de la presse française. Tome I. Des origines à 1814* (Paris, 1969), 3e partie, *passim*.

3. I. Collins, *The government and the newspaper press in France, 1814–1881* (Oxford, 1959); I. Collins, 'The government and the press in France during the reign of Louis-Philippe', *English Historical Review*, April 1954, pp. 262–82; Charles Ledré, *La presse à l'assaut de la monarchie, 1815–1848* (Paris, 1960). For the role of the press in the revolution of 1830, Daniel L. Rader, *The journalists and the July revolution in France. The role of the political press in the overthrow of the Bourbon Restoration, 1827–1830* (The Hague, 1973).

4. Charles de Rémusat, *Mémoires de ma vie*, 2 vols (Paris, 1858), I, xvi–xvii; Saint-Marc Girardin, *Souvenirs et refléxions d'un journaliste* (Paris, 1859), pp. 55, 76.

5. For Girardin, see Pierre Albert, 'Le Journal des connaisances utiles de Girardin (1831–1836) ou la première réussite de la presse à bon marché,' *Revue du Nord*, LXVI (avril–septembre 1984), pp. 733–44.

6. J.D. Popkin, *The right-wing press*, p. 39.

7. John Moore, *A view of society and manners in France, Switzerland and Germany: with anecdotes relating to some eminent characters*, 2 vols (London, 1779), I, pp. 26–7; Popkin, *The right-wing press*, p. 39; Mrs Russell Barrington (ed.), *The works and life of Walter Bagehot*, 9 vols (London, 1915), I, p. 126.

8. J.P. Brissot, *Mémoire aux États-Généraux. Sur la nécessité de rendre, dès ce moment, la presse libre, et surtout pour les journaux politiques* (Paris, 1789), p. 21; C. Lacretelle, *Dix années d'épreuves pendant la révolution* (Paris, 1842), p. 208.

9. E. Hatin, *Histoire politique et littéraire de la presse française* (Paris, 1859–61), VIII, p. 281; *Opinion de Français sur la liberté de la presse. Séance du 23 prairial an VII* (Paris, 1799), pp. 3–4; see also the assessment of the changing image of journalism in Lenor O'Boyle, 'The image of the journalist in France, Germany and England, 1815–1848', *Comparative Studies in Society and History*, X (1967–8), pp. 290–302.

10. A. Mathiez, 'Les journées des 5 et 6 octobre 1789', *Revue Historique*, LXVII (1898), pp. 41–3; G. Rudé, *The crowd in the French Revolution* (Oxford, 1958), p. 22.

11. *Mercure National*, xxiv (10 May 1791), p. 376; 'Newspapers were no longer enough for them, but had left them with the wish to educate themselves.' See also Rudé, *The crowd*, pp. 212–13; J.R. Censer, *Prelude to power. The Parisian radical press 1789–1791* (Baltimore and London, 1976), Chapters 3 and 5, *passim*.

12. J.-P. Bertaud, *Les Amis du Roi. Journaux et journalistes royalistes en France de 1789 à 1792* (Paris, 1984), pp. 252–3.

13. T.C.W. Blanning, *The origins of the French revolutionary wars* (Oxford,

1986), pp. 99–119; G. Michon, *Robespierre et la guerre révolutionnaire* (Paris, 1938), 31–2.

14. A. Soboul, *Les sans-culottes parisens en l'an II* (Paris, 1958), Chapters II–III; J.-P. Bertaud, *Camille et Lucille Desmoulins. Un couple dans la tourmente* (Paris, 1986), pp. 230–44.

15. Popkin, *The right-wing press*, p. 99.

Bibliography

Archives Nationales

The *Archives Nationales* contains useful manuscript and printed material, detailed references to which are contained in the footnotes. The most relevant series is F^7 (*Police générale*), which contains the papers of the *comité de sureté générale* on suspects and victims of the terror (F^7 4576–4775 (53)), and records from both the Ministry of Interior and the Ministry of Police during the Directory, on police surveillance (F^7 3445–3452). Of the remainder, series V (*Grand Chancellerie*) has interesting material on the decline of the central government's control in 1788–9 (VI 549–553); series Y some cases involving prosecutions for press offences in 1789 and 1790 (including the Fréron case), and series W some trials of the revolutionary tribunal during the terror. Series T (*Séquestre*) contains papers from the *Ami du Roi* (T546) and *Journal de la montagne* (T1495A and B). Sereies AD XXA (*Gazettes, Journaux et Placards*) contains a small but useful collection of newspapers, some of them unobtainable elsewhere.

Minuterie Centrale

This source remains largely untapped for press history. See, however, information on François Robert (Étude Gobin X 786 and X 788), on Loustallot (Étude Dufouleur XVI 889) and Carra (Étude Sully IX 834).

Paris libraries

The *Bibliothèque Nationale* is the main source for the revolutionary press, and the most convenient guide to its holdings is André Martin and Gérard Walter, *Catalogue de l'histoire de la Révolution française. Tome V: Écrits de la période révolutionnaire. Journaux et almanachs* (Paris, 1943). An alternative, which also covers other Parisian libraries, but confines itself to the Parisian press, is M. Tourneux, *Bibliographie de l'histoire de Paris pendant la révolution française*, II (Paris, 1904), while the *Catalogue collectif des périodiques conservés dans les*

238

bibliothèques de Paris et les bibliothèques universitaires, 4 vols (Paris, 1967–77), extends the net still further, and A. Monglond, *La France révolutionnaire et impériale. Annales de bibliographie méthodique et descriptive*, 9 vols (Grenoble, 1930–63) is also valuable.

The *Bibliothèque Nationale* also has useful material in its manuscript department, notably Roland's papers (N.A.F. 6241), which contain a 'Dossier relatif à Champagneux, détenu à la Force en 1793'; Charles Nusse, 'Histoire de la presse' (N.A.F. 23, 114); a 'Rapport sur les Journaux par la Commission de l'Instruction Publique' (Ms. fr. 7004, pièces 85–97); and Couret de Villeneuve, 'Barême typographique' (N.A.F. 4664).

The *Bibliothèque Historique de la Ville de Paris* also has copies of several papers not contained in the *Bibliothèque Nationale*, and an invaluable ms. source, Ms. 722–728 ('Journaux, Bibliographie'), which traces several of the major newspapers of the period.

Provincial sources

I have concentrated on a limited number of departments, listed below alphabetically, giving details of newspaper collections not to be found in Paris.

Corrèze: An almost complete collection of the *Journal du département de la Corrèze* can be found in A.D. 175T1, and LSup. 1148 (*Société des amis de la constitution*) contains useful supplementary material.

Dordogne: Copies of the *Journal patriotique du département de la Dordogne* for 1791, and of the *Affiches de Périgueux* for 1789, are in the B.M. Périgueux (unclassified); there is some material also in A.D. 1L396 (*Surveillance de la presse et du courrier, 1793–an VIII*).

Eure-et-Loire: The B.M. of Chartres has collections of the *Annonces, Affiches et Avis divers de Chartres* (Fonds Jusselin R32/5 and D4169), and the *Journal des indications utiles* (Fonds Jusselin R31/3), neither of which are in the B.N. It also has a good collection of the *Chronique d'Eure et Loir* (Fonds Jusselin R32/1–4) to supplement the single copy in the B.N., and an almost complete run of the *Corréspondant* (Fonds Jusselin R31/1).

Gard: The B.M. at Nîmes has the *Journal de Nismes* from 1786–9 (B.M. 33.640), and a copy of the *Courrier de Nismes* (34.754); the only copy that I have seen of the *Journal des Moeurs* (for 12 *nivôse* V), is in A.N. F^{18} Gard, 16 d. II.

Gironde: The B.M. at Bordeaux has the *Courier de la Gironde* (H12,438); *Bulletin de la commission populaire de salut public* (D44.546); *Journal du club national de Bordeaux* (H12,435); and *Frélon ou Extrait des Journaux* (MF1147). It also has a manuscript history of the local press, the *Fonds Bernadau* (Ms. 713) with useful information. I also used scattered copies of the *Tableau de Bordeaux* in A.N. F^7 3449. Several dossiers in the A.D. were also useful, notably 3L 54–56 (minutes of the departmental administration for Years IV–VI); 3L 138 and 139 (correspondence of the departmental *commissaire* for Year V); 12L 23 (material on the *Club National*: 14L 23 ('Affaire Lacombe') and 14L 28 ('Dossier Marandon'). The A.M. of Bordeaux also has valuable material: see in particular D156 (Register of decisions of the *bureau central* for Year V); D160 (Register of decisions for Year VIII); D177 (Correspondance of the commissaire près le Bureau central); I36 (Police des étrangers, 1791) and I38 (Imprimerie 1789–an VIII).

Garonne (Haute-): There is some material in A.D. L2563 and LSup. 45; but I relied mostly on the research carried out by Escamez and Lescure (see below in the main bibliography), under the direction of Professor Godechot.

Hérault: Several dossiers in the A.D. proved useful, notably L893 (Pétition des habitants de Bédarieux), L1079 and L1080 (Librairie, imprimerie), L1081 (scattered copies of local papers), and L1083 which contained prospectuses and circulars from several Parisian papers.

Isère: The B.M. has several papers to supplement the holdings of the B.N., notably the *Journal des États-Généraux* (013785); the *Réveil-Matin extraordinaire* (Jd755); and the *Vedette des Alpes, Journal patriotique* and *Courrier patriotique* (Jd 35). There is useful material in the A.D. L^{85} (minutes of the departmental administration, Year IV), and in the A.M. of Grenoble: see especially LL2, LL3 and LL9 (Decisions of the municipality for 1790–1798); LL 25 (Municipal correspondence, 1790); LL 23 (Mun. corr., Years VI–VII); LL 57 (*Société populaire*, 1790–an II); LL 62–74 (correspondence of the *société populaire*, 1790–1); I27 (*Surveillance de la presse*). ·

Loiret: The holdings of the A.D. suffered from bombing in 1940, but the B.M. has holdings of the *Annales orléanaises* and *Journal général* to supplement those of the B.N., and also houses the valuable papers of Lenoir, police chief of Paris from 1776–85 (Ms. 1421–3).

Maine-et-Loire: There is useful ms. material in the A.D. 1L 99 (p.v. du Directoire du département, an VI); 1L 394 (Police administrative, 1791–an VII); 1L 938 (Imprimerie, 1791–an VII). The A.M. of Angers was also useful for the minutes of the Municipality (D1 3) and the unclassified register of municipal meetings from Years IV–VI; see also dossier 11–43, which contained useful information on Jahyer. The B.M. has an important letter of Jahyer (Ms. 1585 (40)) and a prospectus for his *Ami des principes* (H5496).

Mayenne: Copies of the *Patriote du Département de la Mayenne* and *Sans-Culotte du département de la Mayenne* are in B.M. Laval 30983 and A.D. L871-2.

Puy-de-Dôme: A.D. L6389 and 6390 contain scattered copies of the *Affiches du département du Pui-de-Dôme* for 1792; *le Citoyen surveillant* for 1790–1; the *Courrier du département du Pui-de-Dôme* (*sic*) for 1791; and a prospectus for a *Courrier du Puy-de-Dôme*, 1791.

Rhone: The A.M. of Lyons contained the following dossiers: L459 (Imprimerie et presse) and L130 (Correspondence of the *commissaire* of Lyons during the Directory).

Sarthe: The A.D. has relevant material in several cartons: L159 and L160 (Correspondence of the administration centrale, Year V); L167 (Correspondence of the departmental *commissaire*, Year VI–Year VIII.); L181 (Correspondence of the *commissaire* with the Minister of Police). The A.M. of Le Mans also has material in 1006 (Register of the société des amis de la constitution, 1790–2) and 1207 (*Surveillance de la presse*). The B.M. then holds several newspapers absent from the collections of the B.N.: *Journal général du département de la Sarthe*, 1791–2 (Fonds Maine 2506); *Courrier patriote du département de la Sarthe*, 1792–3 (Fonds Maine, 2490); *le Préservatif de l'Anarchie*, 1797 (Fonds Maine 2527–8); *Courrier du département de la Sarthe*, 1798 (Fonds Maine 2487). Copies of the *Conciliateur, ou Annales des assemblées primaires* are in A.N. BB[18], 733.

Bibliography

Seine-Maritime: Copies of many of the Rouen papers are in the B.N., but see the B.M. of Rouen for the *Abeille politique*, 1790, (B.M. Norm. M718), and for a full collection of the *Nonciateur* (Norm M904). The A.D. also has valuable information in the following: L304 (Presse); 4MP 4693 and 4MP 4699 (Préfecture: corréspondance); L5699 and L5670 (*Société populaire*: registre des séances 17 pluviôse — 10 germinal an II).

Somme: Copies of the *Journal général de la république française* (1793), and of the *Décade du Département de la Somme* (1797–1800) are in A.D. L3073-5. Copies of the latter are also in the B.M. Amiens, as are copies òf the *Affiches de Picardie* for 1789–90 (HIS 3593).

Vaucluse: The Musée Calvet is a rich source of both printed and manuscript material. Municipal decisions are covered in 1D2 and 1D3, and its orders in 2D7; see also the correspondence in 3D28, some of which relates to the *Courrier d'Avignon*. Most of the newspapers for the period are here too, including the following: *Courrier du Pont du Gard* (4° 3770 no. 3); *le Nouvelliste impartial* (4° 3770 no. 4); *Journal patriotique de France* (4° 3770 no. 5); *L'Ami de Tous* (ibid., no. 6); *Courrier du Midi* (ibid., no. 7); *Journal du Midi* (ibid., no. 8); *Thermomètre du Midi* (ibid., no. 9); *États-Généraux* (8.26624). Its collection of the *Courrier d'Avignon* (4853, 1–4) is also more complete than that of the B.N., covering the period of the terror. (4.4852, no. 10). There is also useful material in Ms. 5989 (Fonds Chobaut).

Vienne (Haute-): The B.M. at Limoges has a complete run of the *Journal du département de la Haute-Vienne* (B.M. 58148); two cartons in the A.D. (L826 and L830 also contain many circulars and prospectuses from the Parisian and provincial press.

Document collections

The most useful major documents collections are: F.-A. Aulard, *Paris pendant la réaction thermidorienne et sous le Directoire*, 5 vols (Paris, 1898–1902); F.-A. Aulard, *Recueil des actes du comité de salut public*, 27 vols (Paris, 1889–1933); F.-A. Aulard, *La Société des Jacobins*, 6 vols (Paris, 1889–1897); A. Debidour, *Recueil des actes du Directoire exécutif*, 4 vols. (Paris, 1910–17); S. Lacroix, *Actes de la Commune de Paris pendant la Révolution*, 15 vols (Paris, 1894–1914); P. Caron, *Paris pendant la terreur. Rapports des agents secrets du Ministre de l'Intérieur*, 6 vols (Paris, 1910–64); M. Tourneux, *Bibliographie de l'histoire de Paris pendant la révolution française*, 5 vols (Paris, 1890–1913); A. Tuetey, *Répertoire général des sources manuscrits de l'histoire de Paris pendant la révolution française*, 11 vols (Paris, 1890–1914).

Selected Bibliography — Books

Acomb, Frances (1973) *Mallet du Pan (1749–1800). A career in political journalism*, Durham, NC

Albert, Madeleine (1959) *La Gazette de Paris et du Rozoi*, Diplôme d'Études Supérieures, Paris

Andrieu, Jules (1886) *Histoire de l'imprimerie en Agenais depuis l'origine jusqu' à nos jours*, Paris-Agen

Angot, A. (1900–10) *Dictionnaire historique, topographique et biographique de la Mayenne*, 4 vols, Laval

Anon. (1901) *Histoire d'une imprimerie bordelaise 1600-1900. Les imprimeries G. Gounouilhon, la Gironde, la Petite Gironde*, Bordeaux

Antheunis, L. (1952) *Le conventionnel belge François Robert (1763–1826) et sa femme Louise de Kéralio (1758–1802)*, Wetteren

Arnard, R. (1909) *Journaliste, sans-culotte et thermidorien. Le fils de Fréron (1754–1802). D'après des documents inédits*, Paris

Audiat, L. (1879) *Essai sur l'imprimerie en Saintonge et en Aunis*, Pons

Barbé, Jean-Julien (1928) *Les journaux de la Moselle, bibliographie et histoire*, Metz

Barjavel, C.-F.-H. (1841) *Dictionnaire historique, biographique et bibliographique du département du Vaucluse*, 2 vols, Carpentras

Batines, C. de, and Ollivier, J. (1837) *Mélanges biographiques et bibliographiques relatifs à l'histoire du Dauphiné*, 2 vols, Valence-Paris

Bellanger, C. (ed.) (1969) *Histoire générale de la presse française. Tome I. Des origines à 1814*, Paris

Bénétruy, J. (1961) *L'atelier de Mirabeau*, Paris

Bertaud, J.-P. (1984) *Les amis du roi. Journaux et journalistes royalistes en France de 1789 à 1792*, Paris

—— (1986) *Camille et Lucille Desmoulins. Un couple dans la tourmente*, Paris

Blanc, Olivier (1984) *La dernière lettre*, Paris

Blanc-Rouquette, M.-T. (1969) *La presse et l'information à Toulouse des origines à 1789*, Toulouse

Blin, P. (1932) *Département de la Sarthe. États alphabétiques et chronologiques des bulletins et journaux du Maine et de la Sarthe, en dépôt dans les bibliothèques du chief-lieu*, Le Mans

Bois, Benjamin (1929) *La vie scolaire et les créations intellectuelles en Anjou pendant la révolution (1789–1799)* Paris

Bonnet, Emile (1898) *L'imprimerie à Béziers au XVIIe et au XVIIIe siècle*, Béziers

Bouju, P. (1945) *Un journal contre-révolutionnaire en 1791–1792. La Rocambole des journaux*, Diplôme d'Études Supérieures, Paris

Bouralière, A. de la (undated) *Bibliographie poitevine*, Poitiers

Braesch, F. (1922–38) *Le Père Duchesne d'Hébert. Réimpression avec notes*, 7 fascs, Paris

Brégail, G. (1922) *La presse périodique dans le Gers pendant la révolution*, Auch

Brousse, J.-F. (1963) *Trois siècles de presse roussillonaise*, Mémoire: Institut Français de Presse, Paris

Cabanis, A. (1975) *La presse sous le consulat et l'empire*, Paris

Caron, P. (1935) *Les massacres de septembre*, Paris

Censer, J.R. (1976) *Prelude to power. The Parisian radical press 1789–1791*, Baltimore and London

Chartier, R. (ed.) *Histoire de l'édition française. Tome I. Le livre conquérant. Du moyen age au milieu du XVIIe siècle*, Paris

Clémendot, P. (1966) *Le département de la Meurthe à l'époque du Directoire*, Paris

Clouzot, H. (1891) *Notes pour servir à l'histoire de l'imprimerie à Niort et dans les Deux-Sèvres*, Niort

Collins, I. (1959) *The government and the newspaper press in France, 1814–1888*, Oxford

Cranfield, G. (1962) *The development of the provincial newspaper, 1700–1760*, Oxford

Darnton, R. (1979) *The business of the Enlightenment. A publishing history of the Encyclopedia, 1775–1800*, London

Debien, G. (1953) *Les colons de Saint-Dominique et la révolution. Essai sur le club Massiac (août 1789–août 1792)*, Paris

Dorigny, Marcel (1971–2) *La Chronique du mois ou les Cahiers patriotiques (novembre 1791–juin 1793)*, Mémoire de maîtrise, Paris

Dumont, Etienne (1904) *The Great Frenchman and the Little Genevese* (trans.), London

Dupeux, G. (1940) *Le journal politique national*, Diplôme des Études Supérieures, Paris

Edelstein, M.A. (1977) *la Feuille villageoise. Communication et modernisation dans les régions rurales pendant la révolution*, Paris

Escamez, Diane (1969) *La presse périodique à Toulouse de 1789 à 1794*, Mémoire de maîtrise, Toulouse

Fajn, Max (1975) *The Journal des hommes libres de tous les pays, 1792–1800*, The Hague-Paris

Feyel, G. (1982) *La 'Gazette' en province à travers ses réimpressions, 1631–1752*, Amsterdam and Maarssen

Forestié, E. (1838) *Histoire de l'imprimerie et de la librairie à Montauban. Bibliographie montalbanaise*, Montauban

Forot, Victor (1912) *Le club des jacobins de Tulle*, Tulle

Fray-Fournier, A. (1903) *Le club des Jacobins de Limoges (1790–1795). D'après ses délibérations, sa corréspondance et ses journaux*, Limoges

Gallois, L. (1845) *Histoire des journaux et journalistes de la révolution*, 2 vols, Paris

Garonne, A. Galante (1971) *Gilbert Romme: histoire d'un révolutionnaire 1750–1795*, Paris

Gaultier, Jean (1959) *Un grand témoin de la révolution et de l'Empire, Volney*, Paris

Gérard, Réné (1964) *Un journal de province sous la révolution. Le 'Journal de*

Marseille' de Ferréol de Beaugeard, 1781–1797, Paris

Grosclaude, Pierre (1961) *Malesherbes, témoin et interprète de son temps*, Paris

Guibert, L. (1871) *Un journaliste girondin*, Limoges

Hatin, Eugene (1859–61) *Histoire politique et littéraire de la presse française*, 8 vols, Paris

—— (1865) *Les Gazettes de Hollande et la presse clandestine aux XVIIe et XVIIIe siècles*, Paris

—— (1868) *Manuel théorique et pratique de la liberté de la presse*, Paris

Heitz, F.C. (1858) *Catalogue des principaux ouvrages et des cartes imprimées sur le département du Bas-Rhin*, Strasbourg

Herlaut, (1e général) (1946) *Le colonel Bouchotte. Ministre de la guerre en l'an II*, 2 vols, Paris

Herluison, H. (1868) *Recherches sur les imprimeurs et libraires d'Orléans*, Orleans

Hugueney, Louis (1905) *Les clubs dijonnais sous la révolution*, Dijon

Jacob, L. (1960) *Hébert. Le Père Duchesne. Chef des sans-culottes*, Paris

Jaillet, C. (1932) *Les Origines de la presse à Vienne (Isère)*, Vienne

Jovicevich, A. (1973) *Jean-François de la Harpe, adepte et rénégat des lumières*, New Jersey

Juret, P.-M. (1964) *La presse à Rennes*, ms. Rennes

Kates, Gary (1984) *The Cercle social, the Girondins and the French Revolution*, Princeton

Kennedy, M. (1984) *The Jacobin clubs in the French Revolution*, Princeton

Kerviler, Réné (1898) *Essai d'une bibliographie des publications périodiques de la Bretagne. 4e fasc.: Loire-Inférieure*, Paris

Labadie, E. (1910) *La presse à Bordeaux pendant la révolution*, Bordeaux

Laborie, P. (1959–60) *Étude sur le Patriote française. Journal libre, impartial et national*, Diplôme d'Études Supérieures, Toulouse

Labroue, Henri (1911) *L'Ésprit public en Dordogne pendant la révolution*, Paris

Lambrichs, N. (1976) *La liberté de la presse en l'an IV. Les journaux républicains*, Paris

Lanfranci, M. (1908) *Le régime de la presse sous la révolution*, Paris

Laurens, A. (1963) *Les Actes des Apôtres. Journal contre-révolutionnaire, 1789–1790*, Diplôme des Études Supérieures, Toulouse

Lebon, J.-J. (1972) *La presse montalbanaise des origines au début du dix-neuvième siècle*, Diplôme d'Études Supérieures, Toulouse

Le Gallo, Y. (1973) *Bibliographie de la presse française. 29. Finistère*, Paris

Le Harivel, Philippe (1923) *Nicolas de Bonneville. Pré-romantique et révolutionnaire, 1760–1828*, Strasbourg

Lescure, M. (1969–70) *La presse périodique à Toulouse sous la révolution, de 1794 à 1800*, Diplôme de maîtrise d'histoire, Toulouse

Levron, Jacques (1931) *La presse creusoise au XIXe siècle*, Limoges

Lhéritier, Michel (1942) *La révolution à Bordeaux dans l'histoire de la révolution française. La fin de l'ancien régime et la préparation des États-Généraux, 1787–1789*, Paris

Ligou, Daniel (1961) *La première année de la révolution vue par un témoin (1789–1790). Les 'Bulletins' de Poncet-Delpech, député du Quercy aux États-Généraux de 1789*, Paris

Luc, J.L. (1964) *Les périodiques publiés dans le Gard. Journaux et revues 1753–1953 conservés à la bibliothèque municipale de Nîmes*, ms., Nîmes

Maeght, Xavier (1971) *La presse dans le département du Nord sous la révolution française*, Thèse de troisième cycle, Lille

Maignien, E. (1891) *Bibliographie historique du Dauphiné pendant la révolution française*, 3 vols, Grenoble

Manévy, R. (1964) *La révolution et la liberté de la presse*, Paris

Marquant, Robert (undated) *Aux origines de la presse agenaise: le 'journal patriotique de l'Agenais' 1789–1792*, Agen

Martin, F. (1902) *La révolution en province. Les jacobins au village. Documents publiés et annotés*, Clermont-Ferrand

Martin, H.J. and Chartier, R. (1984) *Histoire de l'édition française. vol. II. Le livre triomphant, 1660–1830*, Paris

Martin, Marc (1974) *Les origines de la presse militaire en France à la fin de l'ancien régime et sous la révolution (1770–1799)*, Paris

Martin, P. (1921) *L'imprimerie et la presse à Cognac sous la révolution*, Cognac

Maspéro-Clerc, H. (1973) *Un journaliste contre-révolutionnaire. Jean-Gabriel Peltier (1760–1825)*, Paris

Mathiez, A. (1934) *Le Directoire*, Paris

Meister, L. (1921) *Un champion de la royauté au début de la révolution. Louis-François Suleau (1758–1792)*, Beauvais

Milsand, P. (1885) *Bibliographie bourguignonne ou catalogue méthodique d'ouvrages relatifs à la Bourgogne*, Dijon

Moulinas, R. (1974) *L'imprimerie, la libraire et la presse à Avignon au xviii siècle*, Grenoble

Murray, W.J. (1986) *The right wing press in the French revolution*, London

Pasquier, E. and Dauphin, V. (1932) *Imprimeurs et libraires de l'Anjou*, Angers

Peignot, G. (1832) *Tableau général des imprimeries en France depuis 1704. Essai historique sur la liberté d'écrire*, Paris

Pellet, Marcellin (1872) *Elysée Loustallot et les Révolutions de Paris, juillet 1789–septembre 1790*, Paris

——— (1873) *Un journal royaliste, les 'Actes des Apôtres' 1789–1791*, Paris

Perlat, Réné (1838) *Le journalisme poitevin. Coup d'oeil historique*, Poitiers

Pichois, C. and Dautry, J. (1958) *Le conventionnel Chasles et ses idées démocratiques*, Gap

Pommeret, Hervé (1921) *L'esprit public dans le département des Côtes-du-Nord pendant la révolution, 1789–1799*, Saint-Brieuc

Popkin, J.D. (1980) *The Right-Wing Press in France 1792–1800*, Chapel Hill

Port, Céléstin (1876) *Dictionnaire historique, géographique et biographique de Maine-et-Loire*, 3 vols, Paris

Portal, C. (1912) *Le département du Tarn au XIXe siècle. Note de statistique*, Albi

Pouy, F. (1861) *Recherches historiques sur l'imprimerie et la librairie à Amiens*, Amiens

Reboul, R.-M. (1869) *Louis-François Jauffret. Sa vie et ses oeuvres*, Paris-Marseilles-Aix

Requien, E. (1837) *Bibliographie des journaux publiés à Avignon, et dans le département de la Vaucluse*, Avignon

Ribière, H. (1858) *Essai sur l'histoire de l'imprimerie dans le département de l'Yonne, et spécialement Auxerre, suivi du catalogue des livres, brochures et pièces imprimées dans cette ville, de 1580 à 1857*, Auxerre

Ronsin, A. (1964) *Les périodiques lorrains antérieurs à 1800*, Nancy

Rose, R.B. (1978) *Gracchus Babeuf. First revolutionary communist*, London

Rostaing, Leon (1903) *Les anciennes loges maçonniques d'Annonay et les clubs, 1766–1815*, Lyons

Rouchon, Ulysse (1925) *Un fondateur du Journal des débats. Jean-Baptiste Grenier*, Paris

Roumejoux, Anatole de (1971) *Bibliographie générale du Périgord*, 2 vols, Slatkine reprint, Geneva

Rousset, Henri (1900) *La presse à Grenoble. Histoire et physionomie, 1700–1900*, Grenoble

Rouvière, F. (1891) *Lundis révolutionnaires. Études sur l'histoire de la révolution dans le Gard*, Nîmes

Roux, M. de (1910) *La révolution à Poitiers et dans la Vienne*, Paris

Rychner, Jacques (1984) *Genève et ses typographes vus de Neuchâtel, 1770–1780*, Geneva

Seguin, J.-P. (1961) *L'information en France de Louis XII à Henri II*, Geneva

—— (1965) *L'information en France avant le périodique. 517 canards imprimés entre 1529 et 1631*, Paris

Smith, Anthony (1979) *The newspaper. An international history*, London

Söderjhelm, A. (1900–1) *Le régime de la presse pendant la révolution française*, 2 vols, Helsingfors and Paris

Stein, H. (1857) *La presse locale à Montargis au XVIIIᵉ siècle*, Orléans

Stoll, Laurence (1975) 'The 'Bureau Politique' and the management of the popular press', unpublished PhD thesis, University of Wisconsin

Sullerot, E. (1966) *Histoire de la presse féminine en France des origines à 1848*, Paris

Thoumin, F. (1959) *Bibliographie de la presse quotidienne et périodique de la Charente-Maritime des origines à 1944*, Mémoire de maîtrise, Paris

Todd, Christopher (1972) *Voltaire's disciple: Jean-François de la Harpe*, London

Trenard, Louis (1958) *Lyon de l'encyclopédie au préromantisme*, 2 vols, Lyons

Troux, Albert (1936) *La Vie politique dans le département de la Meurthe, d'août 1792 à octobre 1795*, 2 vols, Nancy

Tucoo-Chala, Suzanne (1978) *Charles-Joseph Panckoucke et la librairie française, 1736–1798*, Paris and Pau

Vincelet, Chantal (1967) *Recherches sur mademoiselle de Kéralio et François Robert*, D.E.S., Paris

Vingtrinier, A. (1852) *histoire des journaux de Lyon, depuis leur origine jusqu'à nos jours*, Lyons

Vivie, M.A. (1877) *Histoire de la terreur à Bordeaux*, Bordeaux

Vivier, R. and Watelet, J. (1970) *Bibliographie de la presse française 1865–1944, tome 37: Indre-et-Loire*, Paris

Vogne, Marcel (1977–8) *La presse périodique en Franche-Comté des origines à 1870*, 3 vols, Besançon

Wahl, M. (1894) *Les premières années de la révolution à Lyon*, Paris

Walter, G. (1933) *Marat*, Paris

—— (1948) *La révolution vue par ses journaux*, Paris

Weill, G. (1934) *Le journal. Origines, évolution et rôle de la presse périodique*, Paris

Welschinger, H. (undated) *Le journaliste Lebois et 'L'Ami du Peuple'*, Paris

Westercamp, C. (1932) *Beffroy de Reigny, dit le cousin Jacques, 1757–1811. Sa vie et ses oeuvres*, Laon

Woloch, Isser (1970) *Jacobin legacy. The democratic movement under the Directory*, Princeton

Selected Bibliography — Articles

Alary, M.L.J. 'Histoire politique et littéraire de la presse périodique dans le Bourbonnais et dans le département de l'Allier, de 1782 à 1864', *Bulletin de la Société d'émulation du département de l'Allier (sciences, arts et belles-lettres)* IX, pp. 69–85

Albert, P. (1984) 'Le Journal des connaisances utiles de Girardin (1831–1836), ou la première réussite de la presse à bon marché, *Revue du Nord,* LXV, pp. 733–44

Andréani, R. (1982) 'Un chef-lieu d'arrondissement et ses journaux: Béziers de 1790 à 1858', *Bulletin de la Société Languedocienne de Géographie*, 16, pp. 265–79

Anon. (1967) 'Inventaire de la presse régionale', *Revue d'Auvergne*, 81, pp. 126–32

Asquith, I. (1975) 'Advertising and the press in the late eighteenth and early nineteenth centuries: James Perry and the *Morning Chronicle*, 1790–1821, *Historical Journal*, XVIII, pp. 703–24

Aubert, G. (1937) La société populaire de Douai', *A.h.r.f.,* XIV, pp. 419–20

Aulard, F.-A. (1890) 'La presse officieuse sous la terreur', *Études et Leçons sur la Révolution française*, I, pp. 227–40

—— (1893) 'Une gazette militaire en l'an II', *Études et Leçons sur la Révolution Française*, I, pp. 212–26

—— (1929) 'Babeuf et son imprimeur Guffroy', *La Révolution Française*, 82, pp. 5–24

Azam, D.A. (1938) 'Le Ministère des affaires étrangères et la presse à la fin de l'ancien régime', *Cahiers de la Presse*, 3, pp. 428–38

Beylié, J. de (1910) 'Contribution à l'histoire de la presse sous la révolution (le Logographe)', *Bulletin de la Société de Statistique, des Sciences Naturelles et des Arts Industriels du Département de l'Isère*, 4 série, XI, pp. 45–55

Birn, R. (1983) 'Le Journal encyclopédique et l'ancien régime', *Colloque Voltaire*, Geneva

Bougard, P. and Bellart, G. (1960–5) 'La presse arrageoise des origines à 1870', *Mémoires de l'académie des Sciences, Lettres et Arts d'Arras*, 5e série, iv, pp. 67–71

Bouloiseau, M. (1963) 'Les débats parlementaires pendant la terreur et leur diffusion', *A.h.r.f.,* 173, pp. 337–45

Bourgin, G. (1939) 'Les journaux à Paris en l'an VII', *Cahiers de la Presse*, II, pp. 137–44

Boursier, A.-M. L'émeute parisienne du 10 mars 1793', *A.h.r.f.,* 208, pp. 204–30

Brégail, G. (1913) 'La presse politique dans la généralité d'Auch, à la veille des élections aux États-Généraux de 1789', *Bulletin de la Société Archéologique du Gers*, pp. 159–67

—— (1923–5) 'Un apôtre jacobin. Pierre-Nicolas Chantreau. Professeur, journaliste, agent secret', *Bulletin de la Société Archéologique du Gers*. 3e trimestre (1923), pp. 213–34; 4e trimestre (1923), pp. 332–56; 1e trimestre (1924), pp. 29–57; 2e trimestre (1924), pp. 141–61; 3e et 4e trimestres (1924), pp: 197–235; 1e trimestre (1925), pp. 49–106.

Brouillard, R. (1914) 'Un journal bordelais patronné par Ysabeau', *Revue*

Historique de la Révolution Française et de l'Empire, 5, pp. 343–5

Caron, P. (1910) 'Les publications officieuses du ministre de l'intérieur en 1793 et 1794', *Revue d'Histoire Moderne et Contemporaine*, XIV, pp. 5–43

—— (1930) 'Les dépenses secrètes du conseil exécutif provisoire', *La Révolution française*, 83, pp. 223–54, 326–43

—— (1932) 'Une organisation de journal en l'an II', *La Révolution française*, 85, pp. 80–2

Chartier, R. (1973) 'L'imprimerie en France à la fin de l'ancien régime: l'État général des imprimeurs de 1777', *Revue Française de l'Histoire du Livre*, 3, pp. 253–79

Chuquet, A. (1909) 'Les journaux de Paris en 1789', *Feuilles d'Histoire du XVII au XX Siècle*, I, pp. 219–27

Clause, G. (1969) 'La société populaire de Châlons-sur-Marne vue à travers son journal (*floréal an II–vendémiaire an III, avril–septembre 1794*)', *Mémoires de la Société d'Agriculture, Commerce, Sciences et Arts du Département de la Marne*, 84, pp. 119–37

—— (1970) 'Les journaux jacobins de Reims (mars 1793–mai 1794), *Mémoires de la Société d'Agriculture, Sciences et Arts du Département de la Marne*, 85, pp. 255–86

—— (1973) 'Le premier journal champenois, le Journal de Reims de Havé au cours de la révolution française', *Mémoires de la Société d'Agriculture, Commerce, Sciences et Arts du Département de la Marne*, 88, pp. 183–219.

—— (1974) 'Le journalisme à Châlons-sur-Marne en 1790 et 1791', *Mémoires de la Société d'Agriculture, Commerce, Sciences et Arts du Département de la Marne*, 89, pp. 291–332

—— (1975 and 1976) 'Un journal républicain de l'époque directoriale à Châlons-sur-Marne, "Le Journal du département de la Marne", 1796–1800', *Mémoires de la Société d'Agriculture, Sciences et Arts du Département de la Marne*, 90 and 91, pp. 275–313, 319–56

Darnton, R. (1970) 'The memoirs of Lenoir, lieutenant of police of Paris, 1774–1785', *English Historical Review*, LXXV, pp. 532–59

—— (1971) 'The high Enlightenment and the low life of literature in prerevolutionary France', *Past and Present*, 51, pp. 81–115

d'Aussy, Denys (1888) 'Elisée Loustallot', *Revue de la Révolution*, II, pp. 113–42

Debauve, J.L. (1957–8) 'Deux aspects du commerce à Vannes à la fin du XVIIIᵉ siècle', *Bulletin de la Société Polymathique du Morbihan*, pp. 65–79

d'Estrée, P. 'Farmin du Rozoi', *Revue d'Histoire Littéraire de la France*, 25ᵉ and 29ᵉ année, pp. 221–42 and 409–32

Diné, H. (1965) 'Le journal des Etats-Généraux du Camusat de Belombe, député du tiers de la ville de Troyes (6 mai–8 août 1789)', *A.h.r.f.*, 37, pp. 257–69

Dommanget, M. (1930) 'Le symbolisme et le proselytisme révolutionnaires à Beauvais et dans l'Oise', *A.h.r.f.*, 7, pp. 41–53

Dubled, H. (1962) 'L'activité littéraire en Alsace au XVIIIᵉ siècle' in P. Imbs, A. Kern and C. Claus (eds), *Les lettres en Alsace*, Strasbourg, pp. 209–228

Du Boys, A. (1853) 'Calendriers, annuaires, journaux, revues et recueils périodiques du Limousin', *Annuaire de la Haute-Vienne*, pp. 308–21

Dubuc, A. (1967) 'Le Journal de Normandie avant et durant les Etats-

Généraux', *Actes du 89ᵉ Congrès des sociétés savantes*, tome I, Lyon, pp. 385–404

Ducourtieux, P. (1904 and 1905) 'Contribution à l'histoire des périodiques limousins', *Le Bibliophile Limousin*, 2ᵉ série, 19ᵉ-20ᵉ années, 1-3, 49-51, 89-93, 129-133; 1-3, 29-34, 61-66

Epinal, Jean-Pierre (1975-6) 'L'imprimerie et la librairie au Mans au XVIIIᵉ siècle', *Bulletin de la Société d'Agriculture, Sciences et Arts de la Sarthe. Mémoires*, 4ᵉ série, X, pp. 143-285

Eude, M. (1935) 'La commune robespierriste. L'arrestation de Pache et la nomination de l'agent national Claude Payan', *A.h.r.f.*, 12, pp. 132-61

Fajn, M. (1971) 'La diffusion de la presse révolutionnaire dans le Lot, le Tarn et l'Aveyron, sous la Convention et le Directoire', *Annales du Midi*, 83, pp. 299-314

—— (1972) 'The circulation of the French press during the French Revolution: the case of R.F. Lebois' *L'Ami du Peuple* and the royalist *Gazette de France*', *English Historical Review*, LXXXVII, pp. 100-5

Feyel, G. (1984) 'La presse provinciale au XVIIIᵉ siècle: géographie d'un réseau', *Revue Historique*, CCLXXII, pp. 353-62

Fribourg, A. (1910) 'Le club des Jacobins en 1790. D'après de nouveaux documents', *La Révolution Française*, LVIII, pp. 509-31

Galland, M.A. (1902) 'Les sociétés populaires de Laval et de Mayenne (1791-1795)', *Bulletin de la Commission Historique et Archéologique de la Mayenne*, 2 série, 18, pp. 15-40

Gasc, M. (1978) 'La naissance de la presse périodique locale à Lyon. Les Affiches de Lyon, annonces et avis divers', *Études sur la Presse au XVIIIᵉ Siècle*, 3, pp. 61-80

Godechot, J. (1962) 'The origins of mass communication media. The coverage of the French press during the French Revolution', *Gazette. International Journal of the Science of the Press*, 2, pp. 79-86

—— (1984) 'Le *Journal de Perlet* pendant la réaction thermidorienne', *Revue du Nord*, LXVI, pp. 723-32

Gorceix, S. (1953) 'Antoine-Joseph Gorsas. Journaliste et conventionnel', *Information Historique*, 15, pp. 179-83

Gough, H. (1980) 'Les jacobins et la presse. Le Journal de la Montagne (juin 1793-*brumaire an II)*' in A. Souboul (ed.), *Actes du Coloque Girondins et Montagnards (Sorbonne, 14 décembre 1975)* Paris, pp. 269-96

—— (1986) 'The provincial Jacobin club press during the French Revolution', *European History Quarterly*, 16, pp. 55-72

Grain, N. (1972) 'Les Affiches de Picardie (1787-1793)', *Revue du Nord*, LIV, pp. 19-23

Gralle, J. (1961-2) 'Certains aspects du journalisme à Caen pendant la révolution', *Bulletin de la Société des Antiquaires de Normandie*, 56, pp. 807-10

Greenlaw, R. (1957) 'Pamphlet literature in France during the period of the Aristocratic Revolt (1787-1788)', *Journal of Modern History*, 29, pp. 349-54

Greppo, Fr. (1900) 'Un lyonnais imprimeur et journaliste: le journal des Révolutions de Paris, *Revue Lyonnais*, 5ᵉ série, XIX, pp. 42-59

Jaquel, R. (1932, 1933 and 1935) 'Euloge Schneider en Alsace', *A.h.r.f.*, 9, 10 and 12, 1-27, 103-15, 336-42; 61-73; 118-48

Jenny, J. and Ribault J.-Y. 'Essai d'inventaire chronologique et mèthodique de la presse d'information et d'opinion du département du Cher (1782–1870)', *Cahiers d'Archéologie et d'histoire du Berry*, 3, pp. 25–37

Jouanne, R. (1926) 'La presse alençonnaise de la révolution au Second Empire', *Société Historique et Archéologique de l'Orne*, XLV, pp. 353–81

Jusselin, M. (1963) 'Chambres de lecture à Chartres sous la Révolution', *Bulletin de la Société Archéologique d'Eure-et-Loire*, 11, pp. 221–8

Kennedy, M. (1972) 'Some journals of the Jacobin club of Marseilles, 1790–1794', *French Historical Studies*, VII, pp. 607–12

—— (1976) 'The development of a political radical. Jean-Louis Carra 1742–1787' *Proceedings of the Third Annual Meeting of the Western Society for French History*, pp. 147–50

Kulstein, D. (1966) 'The ideas of Charles-Joseph Panckoucke, publisher, of the Moniteur Universel, on the French Revolution', *French Historical Studies*, IV, pp. 305–19

Lamouzèle, E. (1922) 'Le premier procès de presse à Toulouse sous la Révolution, *Revue des Hautes-Pyrénées*, XVII, pp. 41–53

Lannette-Claverie, C. (1972) 'La Librairie française en 1700', *Revue Française de l'Histoire du Livre*, 3, pp. 3–31

Lavalley, G. (1899) 'La presse en Normandie d'après des documents rares ou inédits. Journal de l'armée des côtes de Cherbourg', *Mémoires de l'Académie Nationale des Sciences, Arts et Belles-Lettres de Caen*, pp. 229–45

Lebrun, F. (1962) 'Une source d'histoire sociale: la presse provinciale à la fin de l'ancien régime. Les Affiches d'Angers (1773–1789)', *Le Mouvement Social*, 40, pp. 56–73

Lecler, A. (1913) 'L'abbé Pierre-Montet Lambertie', *Bulletin de la Société Archéologique et Historique du Limousin*, LXIII, pp. 282–358

Lemaire, L. (1921) 'Joseph Paris de Lespinard, journaliste à Lille sous la terreur', *Bulletin du Comité Flamand de France*, 2e fasc., pp. 299–330

L'Huillier, F. 'Remarques sur les journaux strasbourgeois de la première moitié du XVIIIe siècle (1715–1760)', *Revue d'Alsace*, pp. 129–44

Loche, M. (1968) 'Journaux imprimés à Lyon 1633–1794', *Bulletin de la Société Archéologique, Historique et Artistique. Le Vieux Papier*, fasc. 229, pp. 3–28

Lods, A. (1912) 'Un journaliste de la révolution. Le Petit Gautier', *La Révolution Française*, 63, pp. 506–12

Maeght, X. (1974) 'Deux journaux du département du Nord en 1792', *A.h.r.f.*, 216, pp. 216–34

Maignien, E. (1909) 'Un journaliste dauphinois pendant la révolution. Sabin Tournal', *Petite Revue des Bibliophiles Dauphinois*, II, pp. 106–16

Marc, M. (1977) 'Les journaux militaires de Carnot', *A.h.r.f.*, 229, pp. 405–28

de Maricourt (1862–3) 'Le journalisme à Senlis à la fin du XVIIIe siècle', *Comité Archéologique de Senlis. Comptes-Rendus et Mémoires*, pp. 41–58

Marquant, R. (1945–7) 'Aux origines de la presse agenaise: le "Journal patriotique de l'Agenais" 1789–1793', *Revue de l'Agenais*, pp. 5–43

Martin, M. (1972) 'Journaux d'armées au temps de la Convention', *A.h.r.f.*, 210, pp. 567–605

Mathiez, A. (1918) 'La presse subventionnée en l'an II', *Annales Révolutionnaires*, X, pp. 112–13

—— (1925) 'Les dépenses de la liste civile en 1791 et 1792', *A.h.r.f.*, 2, p. 489

Millot, H. (1925) 'Le comité permanent de Dijon (juillet 1789–février 1790)', *La révolution en Côte-d'or*, nouvelle série, I, pp. 145–56

Mondot, J. (1982) 'Rôle et fonctions du journaliste et de la presse chez W.L. Wekhrlin' in P. Grappin (ed.), *L'Allemagne des lumières. Périodiques, correspondances, témoignages*, Paris

Monnie, R. (1986) 'L'évolution du personnel politique de la section de Marat et la rupture de germinal an II', *A.h.r.f.*, 263, pp. 50–73

Monrayssé, L. (1911) 'Le Journal général de la cour et de la ville et la polémique anti-révolutionnaire, 16 septembre 1789–10 août 1792', *La Révolution française*, 61, pp. 385–427

Moulinas, R. (1977) 'Du rôle de la poste royale comme moyen de contrôle financier sur la diffusion des gazettes en France au XVIIIᵉ siècle in *Modèles et moyens de la réflexion politique au XVIIIᵉ siècle*, Colloque à Lille, 1973, vol. 1, Paris, pp. 383–95

Palmer, R.R. (1952) 'A revolutionary republican: M.A.B. Mangourit', *William and Mary Quarterly*, IX, pp. 483–96

Perroud, C. (1912) 'Roland et la presse subventionnée', *La Révolution Française*, 62, 206–13, 315–32, 396–419

Popkin, J.D. (1979) 'The royalist press in the reign of the terror', *Journal of Modern History*, 51, pp. 685–700

—— (1984a) 'Conservatism under Napoleon: the political writings of Joseph Fiévée', *History of European Ideas*, vol. 5, no. 4, pp. 385–400

—— (1984b) 'Les journaux républicains, 1795–1799', *Revue d'Histoire Moderne et Contemporaine*, pp. 143–57

Quéruau-Lamérie, E. (1982) 'Notice sur les journaux d'Angers pendant la révolution', *Revue de l'Anjou*, nouvelle série, 24, pp. 135–56, 298–332

Quesnot, A. (1938) 'Les Dieppois et la presse périodique à la fin du XVIIIᵉ siècle, *A.h.r.f.*, 15, pp. 54–66

Raphael, P. (1913) 'Panckoucke et son programme de journal officiel en 1789', *La Révolution Française*, 64

Ronsin, A. (1959 and 1960) 'La presse à Dijon de l'origine à 1789', *Pays de Bourgogne*, 26, pp. 11–12, 27–8; 79–80

Rouanet, G. (1918) 'La correspondance ce Bretagne', *Annales Révolutionnaires*, X, pp. 542–9

Sgard, J. (1953) 'La presse provinciale et les lumières' in J. Sgard (ed.), *La presse provinciale au XVIIIᵉ siècle*, Paris

Soboul, A. (1951) 'La fortune de Gorsas', *A.h.r.f.*, XXIII, pp. 183–5

Socard, E. (1876) 'Le journalisme à Troyes', *Revue de Champagne et de Brie*, I, pp. 235–41

Solé, J. (1939) 'Le professeur d'histoire de Stendhal: Pierre-Vincent Chalvet (1786–1807), *Stendhal Club*, Année 10, pp. 283–91

Stone, D. (1971) 'La révolte fédéraliste à Rennes', *A.h.r.f.*, 205, pp. 367–87

Thuillier, G. (1966) 'La presse nivernaise au XIXᵉ siècle', *Annales de Bourgogne*, XXXVIII, pp. 5–41

—— (1967) 'Parent l'aîné et le Journal de la Nièvre en l'an VI', *Mémoires de la Société Académique du Nivernais*, LIV, pp. 55–61

Trenard, L. (1962-8) 'Histoire et presse au XVIIIᵉ siècle', *Bulletin de la Société de l'Académie du Bas-Rhin*, pp. 8–33

—— (1969 and 1970) 'La presse périodique en Flandre au XVIIIᵉ siècle', *Dix-Huitième Siècle*, 1 and 2, pp. 89–105, 77–101

Tucoo-Chala, S. (1984) 'Presse et vérité sous l'ancien régime', *Revue du Nord*, LXVI, pp. 713–21

Uzureau, Chanoine (1930) 'Suppression d'un journal angevin (l'Ami des principes) sous le Directoire (1798)', *l'Anjou Historique*, pp. 182–9

Vaillandet, P. (1926) 'Les débuts de la société des amis de la liberté de la presse', *A.h.r.f.*, VI, pp. 83–4

Vanderschueren, B. (1961) 'Les premières années du 'Journal général de l'Europe'', *La Vie Wallonne*, XXXIV, pp. 245–87

Woloch, I. (1966) 'The revival of jacobinism in Metz during the Directory', *Journal of Modern History*, XXXVIII, pp. 12–37

Index

All newspapers cited were published in Paris, except those whose titles clearly indicate otherwise, and those with the place of publication indicated in brackets.

254